"Indispensable book."

—*Publishers Weekly*

"Excellent . . . wealth of valuable information."

—*CBA Reaction*

"Should be on the reading list for all new parents and those who counsel them."

—Deanna Sollid, R.N., *Birth and Family Journal*

". . . is to the postpartum experience what Lamaze preparation is to the birth experience."

—Ruth Pleva, *ASPO Conceptions*

"Must reading."

—Bookmarks, *Expecting Magazine*

". . . deserves to be a classic."

—*Clarion Ledger*

Living With Your New Baby

A Postpartum Guide for Mothers and Fathers

Newly Revised, Expanded, and Updated

ELLY RAKOWITZ & GLORIA S. RUBIN

Foreword by Elisabeth Bing

B

BERKLEY BOOKS, NEW YORK

Grateful acknowledgment is made to *Consumer Reports* for permission to quote from the article "Car Safety Restraints for Children," Vol. 42 (June 1977), p. 314.

LIVING WITH YOUR NEW BABY

A Berkley Book/published by arrangement with
the authors

PRINTING HISTORY
Franklin Watts, Inc., edition published 1978
Berkley edition/January 1980
Berkley revised trade paperback edition/June 1986
Berkley revised mass market edition/December 1987

ISBN: 0-425-10875-9

10 9 8 7 6 5 4 3 2 1

To Kenneth, Lisa, Mark and Rebecca
in the hope that your generation
will reap the results of the seeds
we have sown in this book . . .

and to the memory of
Jack Bloom,   Charles Frank
and Sol Rakowitz

CONTENTS

3. PRACTICAL PROBLEMS AND SOLUTIONS

4. HAVING A SECOND CHILD

ACKNOWLEDGMENTS

TO REVISED EDITION

Many wonderful people have given freely of their valuable time and expertise during the preparation of this revised edition. Simply acknowledging them is not enough. We wish to thank *wholeheartedly:* Alfred Tanz, M.D., F.A.C.O.G., Clinical Professor of Obstetrics and Gynecology, New York Medical College; Attending Obstetrician/Gynecologist at Lenox Hill Hospital, New York City; pioneer in Lamaze childbirth preparation, co-founder and past president of the American Society for Psychoprophylaxis in Obstetrics, Inc. (ASPO/Lamaze) for his valued comments, recommendations and thorough review of a major portion of the medical information in this book, and for his infinite patience; E. Hakim Elahi, M.D., F.A.C.O.G., Medical Director, Planned Parenthood of New York City; Medical Director, Margaret Sanger Center, New York City; Clinical Assistant Professor of Obstetrics and Gynecology, Cornell University Medical College, N.Y.C.; Attending Obstetrician/Gynecologist at New York Hospital for his invaluable assistance in updating the information on contraception and his constant support of our efforts; Ivan R. Koota, M.D., F.A.A.P., Assistant Professor of Clinical Pediatrics at SUNY Stony Brook Medical School; Attending Pediatrician at L.I.J. Medical Center/Schneider Children's Hospital for his insights into the parenting process and infant behavioral responses, his willingness to share information and act as a sounding board for ideas, and his constant encouragement, all of which were invaluable to the completion of this revision.

We are also eternally grateful to the following individuals who answered our many questions and/or read sections of the manuscript and shared their suggestions with us. We appreciate their wisdom: Fedor A. Kuritzkes, M.D., F.A.A.P., Assistant Professor of Clinical Pediatrics at SUNY Stony Brook

Medical School, Attending Pediatrician at L.I.J. Medical Center/Schneider Children's Hospital; Jacob M. Grijnsztein, M.D., F.A.A.P., Assistant Professor of Clinical Pediatrics at SUNY Stony Brook Medical School, Attending Pediatrician at L.I.J. Medical Center/Schneider Children's Hospital; Marvin Resmovits, M.D., F.A.A.P., Attending Pediatrician at L.I.J. Medical Center/Schneider Children's Hospital; Solly M. Scheiner, M.D., F.A.C.O.G., Clinical Instructor of Obstetrics and Gynecology at New York University Medical School, New York City, Assistant Attending Obstetrician/Gynecologist at Long Island Jewish Medical Center, N.Y.C., Director of Gynecological Education at Parkway Hospital, Forest Hills, N.Y.; Gary Guarnaccia, M.D., F.A.C.O.G., Clinical Assistant Professor at Bellevue Hospital, New York City, Attending Obstetrician/Gynecologist at Long Island Jewish Hospital, New York, Chairman of the Department of Gynecology at Parkway Hospital, Forest Hills, N.Y.; Theodore B. Leibman, M.D., F.A.C.O.G., Instructor of Obstetrics and Gynecology at Einstein Medical College, N.Y.C., Attending Obstetrician and Gynecologist at Englewood Hospital, Englewood, New Jersey; Stephen H. Jaffe, M.D., F.A.C.O.G., Clinical Instructor of Obstetrics and Gynecology at Einstein Medical College, N.Y.C., Attending Obstetrician and Gynecologist at Englewood Hospital, Englewood, New Jersey; Gregory White, M.D., Medical Advisor, La Leche League, International; Elisabeth Bing, a co-founder of ASPO/Lamaze and author of many books in the childbirth field; Norma Shulman, co-director of C/SEC; Nancy Wainer Cohen, founder of C/SEC and currently Education Committee Chairperson of National Cesarean Prevention Movement; Terry Vila, R.N.; Patricia Schlett, R.N.; Jean Colantuano, R.N., C.P.N.P.; Agnes Collins, R.N.C.; Judith Adler, R.N., Director, Weight Control Center at Holy Name Hospital, Teaneck, N.J.; Clemens A. Loew, Ph.D., Director of Psychological Services, Weight Control Center at Holy Name Hospital, Teaneck, N.J., Co-Founder and Board Director, National Institute for the Psychotherapies, N.Y.C., Psychologist in Private Practice in New York City and Ft. Lee, N.J.; Sanford A. Schwartz, Ph.D., N.Y.S. Licensed Psychologist in Private Practice in Flushing, N.Y.; Ruth Pleva, M.S.W., A.C.C.E., Margot Mann, La Leche League Asst. Area Professional Liason for New York City, Member of the N.Y.C. Dept. of

Health Steering Committee for the Promotion of Breastfeeding; Jane Sullivan, International Board Certified Lactation Consultant; Julie Stock, La Leche League International; Maria Cotty, R.N., A.C.C.E.; Ellen Bodner, M.A., P.T., A.C.C.E.; Susan Pack, R.N., A.C.C.E.; David Rubin, Esq.; Janet Jaarsma, Administrator, Young World Day School, Mahwah, N.J.; James Roelofs, Environmental Protection Agency; the reference librarians at the Oakland, N.J. public library; and Gareth Esersky, our editor at Berkley Books, for her patience, support, helpfulness and unique way of making us feel special and important. She has been a pleasure to work with!

We'd also like to thank the countless expectant and new parents who've shared their experiences, thoughts, concerns and suggestions with us through the years.

Gloria would like to say a special thank you to: my husband Marty who takes 100% interest in everything I do and shares equally in the work that results; my children, Kenny and Becky, who have taught me more about parenting than any book, lecture or workshop; my sister and brother-in-law, Lisa and Andy Scher, who are not only family but also valued supportive friends; my dear friend Sheila Shields, whose constant love, interest and support is an invaluable aspect of my life. Every woman who works outside the home has a support network of individuals who listen to and comment on her ideas, help car-pool and/or care for her children, etc., etc., etc. This book could not have been written without the support, encouragement, and assistance of the following individuals: Evelyn Bennett, Mimi Mathiesen, Kathy Rosenberg, Susan Mandel, Patricia Schlett, Jane Sullivan, Sharon Isaacs, Patricia Hoppe, Laura Forbes, Susan Kane, Harriet Halem; Mary Schlendorf; Janet Jaarsma, Robyn Davis, Terry Loughran and the staff of Young World Day School; my parents, Shirley and Martin Rechtman; Marty's parents, Sophie and David Rubin; my brother and sister-in-law, Steve and Ellen Frank.

Elly would like to say a special thank you to: my wonderful children, Mark and Lisa, and daughter-in-law Cindy, my mother, Ethel Bloom, and all my superb friends whose love, encouragement and faith in my abilities will be remembered forever.

ACKNOWLEDGMENTS

TO FIRST EDITION

We would like to express our heartfelt thanks and appreciation to the following individuals who so freely gave of their time to help us make this book a reality: Alfred Tanz, M.D., F.A.C.O.G., Assistant Clinical Professor of Obstetrics and Gynecology at New York Medical College, pioneer in Lamaze childbirth preparation and past president of the American Society for Psychoprophylaxis in Obstetrics, Inc. (ASPO) for his valued comments, recommendations, and thorough review of "Physiological Changes," "Procedures Involving the Mother," "Procedures Involving the Baby," "After a Cesarean Delivery," "The Cesarean Baby," and portions of the sections dealing with bottlefeeding and breastfeeding; Ivan R. Koota, M.D., F.A.A.P., Assistant Clinical Professor of Pediatrics at New York University, for his comments on a major portion of the manuscript and thorough review of "Characteristics of the Newborn"; E. Hakim Elahi, M.D., F.A.C.O.G., Assistant Clinical Professor at Cornell University, for reviewing in detail the section on contraception; Elisabeth Bing, co-founder of ASPO and author of several books in the childbirth field, who gave of her valuable time to read the manuscript and share her thoughts with us; Nancy Lee Krauter, founder and president of the Cesarean Birth Association (CBA) and Ann Costa, La Leche League Leader of Elmhurst/Rego Park, new York, for their review of the portions of the manuscript dealing with their respective fields; Laura Keating, R.N., B.S., Obstetrical Nurse Specialist, for sharing her knowledge and expertise and for assistance in preparing the section on bottlefeeding; Dabid Rubin and Lester W. Rubin for their assistance in preparing the sections dealing with legalities; Solly M. Scheiner, M.D., F.A.C.O.G., Clinical Instructor at New York University and member of ASPO/NY Board of Directors, for his encouragement of our efforts to create this book and answering our many questions; Sue Krasnove, Marjie and Michael Stanko, Carol Binen, and Evelyn Bennett, young parents who read the manuscript and gave us their reactions, insights, and suggestions. Our thanks also to Melba Gandy, executive director of ASPO National; M. Jay Wexler, M.D., F.A.C.O.G., Physicians Division Chairman, Mid-Hudson Chapter of ASPO; Louise Schwartz, Programs Coordinator of the Mothers' Center of Queens, N.Y.; Peggy Haines, R.N., and Gordon Haines, for their review of portions of the manuscript; Stephen A. Senreich, M.D., F.A.C.O.G., Clinical Instructor, Department of Obstetrics and Gynecology, State University of New York at Stony Brook; Rieckie Ehrlich, R.N., B.S., Professional Division Chairperson of Long Island ASPO; Rose Brown, R.N., past president of ASPO/New York; and Barbara Cumbo, R.N., for sharing their technical knowledge; Davika Hubbard, education director of Tremont-Crotona Day Care Center; Judith Lang, assistant director of the Jewish Board of Family and Children's Services; Edward McLaughlin, assistant to the director of the Family Service Association of America; and Lenore Champness, Elizabeth Grey, and Mary Ann Maikish for their assistance.

We also thank the following obstetricians and groups for their interest, cooperation, and participation in making our postpartum questionnaires available for parents interested in sharing their feelings with us: Solly M. Scheiner, M.D., Stephen A. Senreich, M.D., Daniel M. Divack, M.D., Jerome L. Luskin, M.D., Warner C. Hall, M.D., the Mothers' Center of Queens, Woodhaven Child Study Association, and La Leche League of Elmhurst/Rego Park, N.Y. Our special thanks go to all the parents who have shared with us their feelings, some of which have been quoted in the book. We would like to express our warm appreciation to our editor, Carolyn Trager, for recognizing the need for this book, for quietly convincing us we could finish it in half the time we thought it would take, and for her sensitive editing of the manuscript.

Gloria would like to say a special thank you to: my husband Marty for his loving understanding, support, and cooperation during the tumultuous period from the conception to the birth of this book; my son Kenneth, whose smiles and antics are an unending source of fulfillment and pleasure; my parents, Shirley and Martin Rechtman for their encouragement and belief in me; my husband's parents, Sophie and David Rubin, for their encouragement and willingness to help care for Kenneth; my rap group friends Carol Binen, Evelyn Bennett, JoAnne Buchalter, Fran Bluestone, Linda Detweiler, Ann Haddad, Sally Hill, and Fern Nash; Evelyn and Michael Bennett, our good friends and buddies through new parenthood; my dear friend Sheila Shields; Leora Nogah, Kenneth's babysitter and friend, without whose help this book could not have been written.

Elly would like to say a special thank you to: my son Mark and my daughter Lisa for their enthusiasm, interest, encouragement and loving understanding of my almost total involvement with "the book"; my mother Ethel Bloom for her unfailing love; my dear friends and colleagues, Ruth Pleva, A.C.C.E., and Cecilia Worth, A.C.C.E. (a co-founder of ASPO) for sharing their knowledge, expertise, and teaching techniques throughout the years; my dear friends Rose Carasso, Nancy Fagen, Sylvia Rose, and Tery Grant for their constant support and belief in me; all my ASPO instructor-colleagues who have shared their insights and observations and all my Lamaze couples who have shared with me one of the most personal periods of their lives and from whom I have gleaned enormous insights into the feelings and problems encountered during the postpartum period. I am forever grateful.

FOREWORD

I feel this is one of the most important books new parents can have to guide them toward and through the early stages of parenthood.

The family, or the creation of the family, has always been considered one of life's crises. Many of us can still recall the days of extended families, when three or even four generations of one family lived in close proximity, giving support and cooperation to one another. Often there were several members in such a group who could be relied upon not only to act as midwives or babysitters, but also to share their knowledge, wisdom, and experiences of childbirth and parenting with the younger people in the family. Undoubtedly they passed on their prejudices and anxieties as well, mixing the good and the bad, but their presence afforded everyone a feeling of security.

How different it is today for young couples! Frequently, the older generation lives far away, or may visit only occasionally to give a helping hand and advice. There is less emphasis on the traditional family structure that made rigid distinctions between the husband's and wife's duties. Even the distinctions between male and female roles in parenting are beginning to blur.

While these changes offer both men and women greater flexibility, they also impose greater responsibilities. Having options may not always seem like freedom of choice, or an advantage. In the final analysis, however, these changes seem to strengthen the family, because they force young families to find their own values. Modern couples are not entirely without traditions or help from their immediate families, but today's mobile, nuclear patterns of living frequently result in severely limited contact with grandparents, aunts, uncles, and cousins. For many young families this means developing independence and relying on their own practical and emotional resources.

Having been a childbirth educator for many years, I am well aware that an important part of the support the extended family used to give must now come from people in the field of childbirth education. The authors of this book offer their experience and knowledge as guidelines to help new parents. In thorough detail and clear language, they cover virtually every aspect of establishing a sound base for family life.

This practical book gives wonderfully sensible advice on, among many other things, what arrangements to make even before the baby is born, how to find and what to look for in a good pediatrician, how to establish a sensible and healthy diet for both mother and child, how best to use time, how to manage travel with an infant, why and how much to exercise, and how to adjust to one's changing body image. The authors also discuss sexuality and describe the varied emotions, the fears and joys common to the postpartum period. They are reassuring and affirmative, practical and sensitive in their advice.

This book is a *must* for every new parent. It contains invaluable guidance for everyone who is about to live with a new baby.

Having worked with the authors for many years, I know that this book has been written with love and empathy, with great skill, and with infinite care and understanding. There is an old saying that *"to become* a parent is not difficult; to *be* a parent is very difficult." But it is a task which has been made immeasurably more enjoyable and easier by this book.

ELISABETH BING

INTRODUCTION

TO REVISED EDITION

Why a revised edition of *Living With Your New Baby*? Many things have changed in the almost nine years since the book was first written.

There has been a dramatic increase in the number of parent support groups in many sections of our country. Parents in many communities can choose among programs sponsored by local Ys, Mothers' Centers, physicians and private groups. For those participating in parenting groups, we hope this book will serve as a supplement to the support and information being received from those groups, perhaps a stimulus for discussion and an aid to private thought and problem solving. Unfortunately, parenting programs are still not universally available. Also, some parents don't have the time or desire to get involved with groups. Our original purpose—of providing support and information so that individuals and couples don't feel alone while going through the changes in life-style that accompany new parenthood—is still fulfilled in this new edition.

New information is forever forthcoming in the medical sphere. Changes in obstetrical practice, cesarean procedures, contraception, etc., have been included in this edition.

We have changed as well. Our continuing work with parents, our reading, the workshops and conferences we have given and attended over the years since the book was written have increased our awareness of issues, problems and concerns, as well as our repertoire of suggestions for how to facilitate the adjustment process. The birth of Gloria's daughter Rebecca in 1981 gave us the opportunity to retest many of our theories and beliefs in the laboratory of Gloria's home. (Yes, Gloria did experience some postpartum blues!)

New sections have been added that reflect what we've learned: "Winter Survival Strategies," "Early Infant Behavior," "Couple Communications," "Should Both Parents Work Outside the Home," "Sleeping Arrangements," "Repeat Cesarean Deliveries vs. Vaginal Birth After a Cesarean." Most other sections have been expanded.

Many of the parents who read the first edition of our book are going on to have second children. Our expanded section for parents expecting a second or subsequent child was written to meet the needs of these individuals.

The most gratifying result of having written the book has been the opportunity to meet countless expectant and new parents who have shared their experiences with us in the workshops and parenting sessions we have offered. Many of their thoughts and quotes are included in this new edition. Gloria has also especially enjoyed her work with the pediatric practice of Drs. Fedor A. Kuritzkes, Ivan R. Koota, Jacob M. Grijnsztein and Marvin Resmovits in Lefrak City and Great Neck, N.Y., who recognized the need for parent support and information services eight years ago. Ivan Koota and Gloria combined efforts and abilities to create a parents' program that serves the needs of their patients.

We also enjoyed and are grateful for the many letters we received from parents who took the time to share the results of applying the suggestions we made in the original book.

Our lives have been enriched immeasurably by the opportunity to share experiences and ideas with the very special people we've met because of *Living With Your New Baby.*

ELLY RAKOWITZ
GLORIA S. RUBIN
February 1986

INTRODUCTION

TO FIRST EDITION

As a Lamaze childbirth educator and a co-founder of the American Society for Psychoprophylaxis in Obstetrics, Inc. (ASPO/Lamaze), I have always been concerned with ensuring that the labor and delivery experience will be a happy one. Growing numbers of women are finding childbirth a pleasurable, fulfilling experience. I believe the reason for this is directly related to the rise in the number and popularity of childbirth preparation courses available throughout the United States. The classroom environment—offering information, practical techniques and emotional support—encourages expectant mothers to approach the coming event with confidence so they can better deal with almost any labor-delivery situation. They learn how they can make childbirth less painful and more meaningful as a shared life experience with the new father, from whom they can receive physical and emotional support.

However, it has disturbed me that after giving couples the techniques and information with which they can make the labor and delivery experience better, they are abandoned at another crucial moment of their lives—virtually as soon as the baby is born—to fend for themselves when the new family unit begins *its* precarious life.

One of the most trying times in a couple's life together is the postpartum period. To wish them through it nonchalantly, to ignore the hazardous realities forced upon them, is to invite hostility, frustration, hurt, and despair at a time when the relationship is particularly vulnerable and needs all the help it can get in order to flourish.

I believe that just as preparation-for-childbirth classes are a form of insurance for a better birth experience for mother, baby and father, so do preparation-for-postpartum and follow-up postpartum rap/support sessions permit a better adjustment period following delivery.

Having a baby can be a marvelous experience, and there are many joys and benefits to the new parents in the early weeks and months as the baby grows and changes. As with all joyous events and experiences, however, there are some rough spots to be gotten over. If the new parents can manage them by themselves, fine. If they can get a little help from other people, including their physician or nurse/midwife, terrific. If they can get some more from our book, its purpose will have been served. Further, if our book points up the need for more attention to the postpartum period from the medical profession, all the better.

ELLY RAKOWITZ

On July 22, 1976, 6 lb. 8 oz. Kenneth Joshua Rubin was born. I had prepared for labor and delivery by attending a series of classes my obstetrician conducts, by reading everything I could find about pregnancy, labor and childbirth, and finally, during the last eight weeks, by taking the Lamaze course given by Elly Rakowitz. I felt confident. I knew everything that would happen in the hospital. With the help of this preparation and the loving support of my husband, Kenneth's birth was one of the most exciting, gratifying experiences of my life and our marriage. The euphoria I felt that day was gradually replaced by a growing sense of unrest and the question: Did Kenneth's birth signal the end of my independent creative life?

During my pregnancy, everyone—including the supermarket cashier—had wanted to know every detail of how I was feeling. But after the birth I gradually realized that how *I* was feeling mattered only to me, my husband, my obstetrician and a few close friends and relatives. The emphasis was on Kenny: *his* habits, *his* needs and how well I was meeting them. Being thrust suddenly out of the limelight was a shock.

On the day of my last postpartum check-up, six weeks after delivery, my obstetrician shook my hand and said, "Congratulations. Now you're on your own." I wanted to punch him in the mouth. Why did his support end arbitrarily at six weeks?

Jealously, I eyed some of the women in his office who were still pregnant, preparing and pampered.

My feeling of being left out gradually increased. My pediatrician's nurse greeted me with, "Oh, you're Kenneth's mother!" Every telephone conversation seemed to begin with "How's Kenneth?" instead of "How are you?" Even my husband seemed to rush to the baby's crib in the evening before greeting me. I began to feel stifled and hostile.

I resented my mother's assistance during my first week at home, although I desperately needed the help. I wondered why I couldn't manage my own household, even as I realized I couldn't. And as the days, then weeks, went by, the questions flew thick and fast. Why was I always so tired? Why couldn't I get things done around the house? Why didn't I want to have sex? Would there ever be a break in the endless series of things to be done? Would dinner ever be a sane time again? Would I ever get a full night's sleep? Who was this tyrant ruling the house, anyway?

In all fairness, I must admit that I had been warned about these feelings. Elly had talked about the blue feelings I might experience a few days after giving birth, the sudden shifting of attention to the new baby, and the jealousy and other possible emotional rections that might result. My obstetrician had alluded to the fact that there was a big adjustment to be made and talked about something called postpartum depression. I had been warned about these feelings but had not prepared for them.

I was lucky. I knew how to reach out for help. A psychiatrist I consulted assured me that the feelings I was having were absolutely normal and part of the adjustment process. I called Elly. She was sympathetic at a time I needed someone who understood what was happening. She also helped me set up a rap group for new mothers. Knowing that I was not alone in my feelings was important. My husband and I began to discuss exactly what our feelings were and I realized that he was going through a difficult adjustment period, too. I began realistically to search for and find things that made me feel better. I began to get out more and find creative outlets at home. As my own positive sense of self gradually returned and I made the adjustments to new motherhood, I began to feel a strong anger. I had been prepared for pregnancy and childbirth; why hadn't I been more fully prepared for this adjustment period?

Why was I on my own after six weeks? Where was the support that should have been present without my having to seek it out? And what about others in a similar situation? Not everyone reaches out for help and not everyone who reaches out finds help. Why does information about childbirth virtually end with what happens in the recovery room?

It is my hope that this book will help others by providing them with the material I so deeply needed—that those of you who are reading it while going through this difficult adjustment period will realize that you are not alone and that you will glean some help from these pages. We do not claim to provide all of the answers, but at least this is a beginning.

GLORIA S. RUBIN

THE PURPOSE OF THIS BOOK

FOR EXPECTANT PARENTS: To inform them of the possible difficulties to be encountered during the postpartum period and thereby minimize the element of shock which otherwise might negate previous good feelings about parenthood.

FOR NEW PARENTS: To give encouragement and support by acknowledging the existence of trouble spots not readily acknowledged elsewhere and to serve as a handbook/reference guide with suggested options for parents during the postpartum period.

FOR BOTH: To ease them through this very trying time with information, understanding and advice.

This book is about the changes having a baby brings to your life—physically and sociologically—how they affect you, and what you can do about them. This book is also about the feelings that are a result of these changes. We believe it helps to know that others have been or are at the very same place.

While the term "postpartum period" traditionally refers to the first six weeks after having a baby, we recognize the fact that while the majority of physical changes are completed by that time, the emotional and sociological adjustments may not be. Therefore, the period of time covered by this book spans the first three months or so after giving birth.

Although there has been increasing interest and use of alternative birth centers with certified nurse midwives in attendance, the vast majority of babies in this country continue to be born in hospital settings. Therefore, our coverage of the first few days after birth was written with the hospital environment in mind.

1. Preparing for Postpartum

EXPECTATIONS

For most people, the addition of a new baby to the family is an occasion for great joy and excitement. The birth of a child is looked forward to with anticipation. There is every intention to give the baby love and care. But, as with all good things in life, there come some difficulties which, if anticipated and kept in tow, need not overshadow the happiness.

After having a baby enormous changes take place within the new mother, and in the family environment which directly affect the feelings of both parents during the weeks and months to follow. These changes in turn affect your life and your relationship with your mate, your baby, your other children and the other people around you. If you are aware that these exist and greatly affect you both physically and emotionally, you will be better able to deal with the problems and situations occurring during this period. If you are not aware that these changes are normal, they might not seem even remotely related to childbirth and might therefore be overwhelming.

Some factors influencing what your reactions will be are connected to the physiological process that occurs as the new mother's body returns to its pre-pregnant state. Other factors are related to the new role and responsibilities you now have. Because so many of these changes occur in such a relatively brief time span after the delivery, this period brings, in addition to excitement and happiness, the potential for disharmony and misunderstanding. If not recognized and dealt with for what it is—a period of adjustment spiked with hormonal and sociological jolts beyond your control—the relationships between new mother and father and new mother and baby can flounder perilously. A wall built of hurts, jealousies, and resentment from all sides can grow and reach frightening heights.

3

Preparing for postpartum can help you and your mate face the realities of this period so that stress, frustration, guilt, worry and resentment can be reduced.

Start now to make sure all lines of communication are wide open between you and your mate. Discussing your feelings about pregnancy, delivery and postpartum *now* sets the stage for open discussions after you have the baby. Together, try to envision the changes the baby will cause. How will you handle getting up in the middle of the night? Having less time for each other? Giving up a certain percent of your social life? What problems can you foresee and what arrangements can you make now to solve these problems? Read the sections "Changes: In Mothers' Feelings, Life-style, Roles, Relationships" and "Fathers' Feelings." Discuss your reactions. Also, read "Couple Communications."

Do not expect your labor and delivery experience to go *exactly* as you would like or are planning. Know that there is a wide range of emotions you may experience after the baby arrives. Know that there are hormonal changes which may cause some degree of depression during the first weeks after having the baby. Don't expect to fit into your tight jeans or other non-maternity clothes for weeks after delivery. Your sex life might not be what it used to be for a while.

Do not fool yourself into expecting your life to return to "normal" eventually. Once you take the step into parenthood your life has permanently changed and will never again be the same as it was before. Once you accept this fact you'll be better able to cope with the changes in your life after the baby's arrival. The birth of your baby does not mean you must give up all your previous interests and haunts, however. It just means you'll have to plan a bit differently to include meeting the baby's needs as well as your own.

Expect life with your mate to be more difficult after a child is added to your family unit. The situation demands more effort from both of you to maintain a loving relationship in spite of the inevitable added strains.

How you view each other as individuals will change somewhat. The way you evaluate your mate will no longer be in terms of how he or she stacks up against your expectations as a lover, friend and life's companion, and the way he or she compares with the mates of your friends, but also how he or she rates as a parent. How does he compare to your father?

She to your mother? How close do you each come to the other's concept of the ideal mother and father? These are questions that occur to many couples. You will no longer be just lovers and friends; you'll be somebody's parents. Do not be surprised if the weight of that responsibility causes you to reevaluate your roles in the new relationship formed by the addition of a child.

Before the baby is born and/or in the early weeks, it is wise to talk about which one of you will handle what aspects of the baby's care. While mothers of the previous generation did most of the housework and childcare themselves, most of today's mothers expect help from their mates. A new grandfather may announce with pride that he never changed a diaper, as he watches his son up to the elbows in ointment and powder. He fails to realize that a dirty diaper is as much his son's responsibility as his son's mate's. Problems can develop when the new father sees himself only in one role, perhaps uninvolved like his father, while his mate expects him to participate in changing, bathing, etc. On the other hand, if the new mother expects to follow in her mother's footsteps and make all the childcare decisions herself but is faced with a mate who wants to share these tasks, a conflict situation can develop. Will one of you stay home from work to rear the child, or will you seek childcare? A generation ago there was very little need to discuss this; child-rearing was mostly left to the woman. Today's woman may want to continue her career full-time, and today's man can no longer assume that his mate will be the caretaker parent. Many new fathers take on the caretaker role, or childcare options may have to be considered, the sooner the better. Talking these things over early to clarify how you see your roles as individuals and as parents can help avoid later misunderstandings.

In addition, knowing how to bathe, diaper, burp and otherwise care for the baby will give both of you a greater feeling of confidence in handling your child. Consider enrolling in a basic childcare class if one is available. Contact the American Red Cross, your hospital, local department stores, your childbirth educator, your pediatrician and your obstetrician to locate these classes.

Now is the time to begin to think about and to discuss how you and your mate will raise your child. You may come from very different backgrounds and have widely varying views on many issues, such as religion, schooling, bedtimes and how permissive to be. How will you resolve any disagreements? By all means share your feelings and tell your mate about all the things you promised yourself as a child you would not do with your children. Tell each other what you believe the beautiful things were in your childhood, but remember that parenthood is a partnership and at times each of you will have to look for compromises.

Expect also to be tired. Caring for a new baby will take more of your energy than you might think. Expect to be frustrated at not being able to handle every little thing that you'd like to handle perfectly and by yourself. Expect to be disappointed by the realization that the long-awaited baby is not all joy and love; you might feel some resentment toward the new person who changes your life so drastically. And know that some degree of "baby blues" is common to the postpartum period.

AVOIDING ISOLATION AND EXHAUSTION

As we see it, three of the prime non-physiological causes of postpartum blues or depression in women are exhaustion, isolation and feeling out of control of one's life and environment. There are things you can do while still pregnant that will help. The more planning you do now, the easier the situation will be later.

●It is imperative that you arrange now for someone to take care of household tasks during the first week or two you're home from the hospital, or that you resolve to ignore them temporarily. The more rest you get in the early weeks, the faster you will regain strength and the less likely you will be to feel depressed. You might want to hire a high school girl or boy as a helper to do the chores each day or several days a week. Perhaps a professional homemaker or a housecleaning service once each week for the first few weeks would be best for your needs. If you receive offers of help from the baby's grandparents, think about your relationship with your parents and in-laws before accepting. Will you both feel comfortable with their assistance or will their presence be a source of tension to one or both of you? Will they respect your need to feel in control of things and help increase your feelings of competence as parents, or will there be conflict over who makes the decisions about the baby's care and method of feeding? Whoever you "hire," make it clear that the help you want involves laundry, cleaning, cooking and marketing, and that you want to care for the baby and rest. Feeding, diapering and bathing the baby while other responsibilities are removed from you will help you both get to know your baby. If your obstetrician and pediatrician agree that the physical condition of mother and baby are satisfactory, consider leaving the hospital a day early. The money you save might cover the cost of a baby nurse for a week or pay for someone to clean the house once a week for several weeks.

If you are considering hiring a baby nurse for the first week or two, you might be confused by conflicting advice varying from how horrible they are because they take over your baby, your home and your life, to how marvelous they are because they get new parents over the rough spots and into a routine.

A good nurse will see to it that you get your rest. She will recommend that she defer and space phone calls and visits according to how rested you feel. She will teach both parents infant-care techniques and even urge you to try them out under her guidance, thereby easing you into the care of your baby so that when she leaves, you will not feel abandoned and unable to fend for yourselves. Some nurses will also do light housekeeping (dusting, sweeping, washing dishes, etc.) and prepare and serve meals in addition to seeing to the infant's laundry, bathing and feeding needs (if you are not breastfeeding). Most baby nurses, however, will not do your laundry, family shopping or the majority of household tasks. Don't hire a nurse if you can foresee yourself doing the cleaning and other chores while she takes care of the baby. You must rest. If you are planning to breastfeed, you can benefit from a nurse provided that she is supportive of your desire to breastfeed and will give you practical suggestions and encouragement. Some nurses will not even take the job if you plan to breastfeed because they think there is nothing left for them to do if you remove the feeding responsibility from them. (Many breastfeeding mothers disagree.) It's important to clarify this in advance.

If you decide you want a nurse, and they are by no means a necessity, it is best to begin your search with personal recommendations from other new parents. You can also ask your childbirth instructor, obstetrician or the office nurse for recommendations. If none of these yields a name, you can contact a specialized agency and state exactly what your needs are. If at all possible, interview several individuals before hiring. Also, be sure to specify what you expect from a nurse and hear what the nurse expects to give before hiring her.

Whatever arrangements you make—housekeeper, baby nurse, grandparent, etc.—if you are not pleased with the services provided, or your personalities clash, do not suffer through the week or weeks. It is important for you to feel in control of your household. If the services being provided don't meet your expectations, speak up, and if the situation doesn't improve, consider your options. You might be better off making other arrangements.

●Consider setting aside money each week during pregnancy toward a postpartum entertainment fund. How much you save will depend on your current financial situation, but anything you save will be invaluable. Expenses seem to multiply after the baby is born and this may be felt more keenly if the expectant mother worked outside the home and the family now has to adjust to living on one income. Even if the new mother is returning to work, babies are expensive. Childcare, diapers, etc., all add up. Make a pact that no matter how tight finances become, this fund will not be touched, except to hire an occasional babysitter to allow you to go to a movie or restaurant, or be otherwise entertained during your postpartum period.

●Before the baby arrives, locate a babysitter in whom you feel confident. Then, after the baby comes, you will not have to worry about finding someone competent on short notice if you decide you want to go out. Although relatives may volunteer and grandparents are an especially wonderful source of babysitting help, it's good to have someone you can hire. Some couples feel more in control with a paid sitter than with a grandparent. (See "Babysitters." Also, for information on making childcare arrangements when both parents will work outside the home, see "The Working Mother" and "Should Both Parents Work Outside the Home.")

●Try to find friends who are having babies near the time yours is due. Having a buddy to call and talk things over with is a great help. Consider locating or organizing a rap group that can meet during late pregnancy to discuss current feelings, joys and fears, and plan to continue meeting soon after delivery to talk about the changes everyone is going through. Experience-sharing with other new parents will help you realize you are not alone. Also, you will be able to exchange babysitting services if you so desire. (See "Postpartum Support Groups.")

●Fill whatever freezer space you have available with precooked meals. During pregnancy, whenever you prepare a family favorite, double the recipe and freeze half in a ready-for-the-oven dish. Later, on hectic days when you have absolutely no time for cooking, you can heat something quickly. Also, stock up on canned goods for quick casseroles and locate fast-food places that deliver. Prepare at least a two-week's supply of paper plates, cups and plastic utensils so that you will not be concerned with washing dishes (or loading and unloading a dishwasher) while you recuperate and adjust to your new responsibilities.

●Evaluate your home. Are things placed as conveniently as possible? If you live in a multilevel house or apartment, set aside an area on each level for changing the baby. Try to arrange things so you'll avoid running up and down steps. Have duplicates of frequently used items on each level. Consider buying the type of port-a-crib that converts to a playpen, such as one that adjusts so the mattress is about chest level or mid-thigh level. The legs are also adjustable and can be raised or lowered. In the raised position (mattress and legs), this provides a convenient changing/sleeping area on one level of your home, and when the baby is ready for a playpen you will have one available. It also solves the problem of where your baby will sleep when you take him or her for an overnight visit to friends or relatives. No matter what your living arrangements, try to arrange things so you will avoid bending, which in itself is tiring. Rearrange your kitchen now, if necessary, so that things are more conveniently placed and within easy reach.

For a convenient diaper changing area, consider buying a waist-high chest of drawers (or using an old one) instead of an actual changing table. Place a carriage mattress on top and hang a shelf above for diaper changing supplies. A changing table would have no further use when the baby is grown, while a chest can become a permanent fixture in the baby's room and therefore well worth the additional expense. You might get one that is part of a set that can be purchased in matching pieces as your budget allows. If the baby will share your room, a carriage mattress placed on your dresser can serve as a changing table, or place a plastic or rubber sheet on the bed and sit while you change the baby—do not stand and bend. Avoid port-a-cribs and bassinets that aren't adjustable and that force you to bend to lift the baby. These are not good for your back.

Seriously consider breastfeeding your baby. Besides the many other advantages nursing has for mother and child, it is less work than bottlefeeding—no formula to prepare, no bottles to wash and/or sterilize and take along with you when you go out. At 2 a.m. you will not have to stagger to the kitchen half asleep to warm a bottle. Also, nursing forces you to sit down, put your feet up, and relax. If you bottlefeed, you might be tempted to prop a bottle—which is dangerous because the baby may gag and choke—and go about your chores. This defeats your efforts to relax. You can't prop a breast. As you nurse, a hormone is released that will give you a warm, relaxed feeling, conducive to sleeping. Take advantage of this feeling and go to sleep when the baby dozes off at the end of the meal, night or day.

•Resolve now to sleep whenever the baby does—especially during the early weeks. It is unwise to use the baby's sleeping time for chores. If the baby is awake at night, chances are he or she will sleep during the day. Eventually the baby's schedule will conform to most of humanity's, but until it does, get your sleep while the baby sleeps.

•Do not tell anyone what you are planning to name the baby until after the baby is born. This way you are presenting people with the name as an accomplished fact that is not subject to discussion.

•Politely inform everyone that you do not want visitors for the first few weeks after the baby is born. If you wish to spare any hurt feelings, say your doctor gave you those instructions and remember to reiterate them when people call to ask if they may see the new baby. Whatever you do, don't entertain. Without guests you'll feel more relaxed about letting the housework go for a while. You can always invite company as you feel up to it; adhering to the general "no company" rule speeds your recovery. If you do find yourself entertaining, remember the "nightgown trick." If your guests arrive to find you dressed and made-up, they will expect you to make them coffee. If you are in a nightgown and robe, they will assume you are still recuperating and offer to make you coffee.

●Have everything ready in advance for the baby's arrival: furniture, layette, drugstore supplies, etc. It is traditional among some religious groups not to have any baby furniture, clothing, toys, or whatever in the house before the baby is born. If this custom applies to you, perhaps your furniture dealer or baby clothing store will hold your purchases for you until after the birth. While you're in the hospital, furniture can be delivered and a friend or relative can pick up all the other supplies.

●Resolve now to get involved with other-than-baby activities. You will need to keep up old friendships and interests as well as develop new ones. It is important to be your own person in addition to someone's mate and mother. Locate book discussion groups, library programs and lecture or film series that you might be interested in. Investigate courses offered in the adult education center of your local school. Consider purchasing a subscription to the ballet, local theater group, or whatever cultural activities are available in your community, and go! This is especially true if both mother and father are working outside the home in addition to caring for a new baby. Working parents need outlets in addition to family and career.

●Get as much rest as possible while you are pregnant. Going into labor in a state of exhaustion is not wise. You will need your energy for the experience of childbirth. After delivery you'll need additional rest. You might not be able to sleep very well in the hospital and you will most likely lose a night's sleep the day the baby is born. Building up an energy reserve now is helpful.

●In deciding on a hospital, consider not only the quality of its medical facilities but also whether or not it has family-centered maternity care policies such as special visiting-feeding hours for fathers, sibling visiting hours, rooming-in. Check to see whether fathers are welcome in labor and delivery rooms and whether the nursing and medical staff are geared to encourage family bonding at this time. A supportive environment during the first hours and days after delivery can help set the tone for a pleasant postpartum.

●Address and put postage stamps on your birth announcements in advance. If you are ordering specially printed ones, ask the supplier to give you the envelops before you give birth. If you select the pre-printed, fill-in type, you can have the envelopes now. Prepare them so that all you'll have to do is complete the cards, preferably while you're in the hospital, and have them mailed.

●If a car is available to you but you don't yet have your driver's license, take lessons now and try to get your license before the baby comes. It will be more difficult to arrange for lessons and practice time after the baby is born. Being able to drive will give you a much needed mobility that will help you avoid feelings of isolation and depression.

●If a move to another location is anticipated, if at all possible move well in advance of your anticipated due date. You will need time to get settled in your new home—even if you remain in the same community. If you are relocating to another area entirely, you will need time to make new friends, and also locate stores, medical and religious facilities, health care professionals, etc.

Note: Parents expecting the birth of a second child should also read the suggestions in the section "Having a Second Child."

WHAT TO BRING TO THE HOSPITAL

●3 nightgowns (if breastfeeding, either special nursing gowns or nightgowns that button down the front to below the breasts.)

●6 pairs of panties (preferably cotton), and safety pins

●2 sanitary napkin belts (or check if hospital provides self-adhering sanitary napkins)

●bathrobe and slippers

●2 or 3 bras (if breastfeeding, nursing bras or front-opening bras)

●toilet articles (toothbrush, toothpaste, comb, brush, shampoo, mouthwash, make-up, etc.)

●miscellaneous: bed jacket, baby announcements, reading material, telephone number list, diary, pad and pen (to list questions for the obstetrician, pediatrician; to record instructions); travel alarm clock, wash cloth, breast pads

●to bring the baby home: diaper, undershirt, nightgown or stretch suit, hat, outer garment and blanket

●baby's car seat (required by law in some states—see "Traveling With an Infant")

●this book

WHAT TO HAVE IN THE HOUSE FOR THE BABY

Clothing:

●6 cotton undershirts (6 mo. size)

●3 cotton nightgowns

●6 terry-cloth stretch suits

●1 dozen cloth diapers (if using disposables)

●4 dozen cloth diapers (if using cloth diapers)

●6 pairs plastic or vinyl pants (if using cloth diapers)

Other Articles:

●2 or 3 cotton blankets

●3 sheets for crib mattress

●wash cloths, bibs, towels

●safety pins (if using cloth diapers)

●gauze squares

●cotton-tipped flexible sticks

- cotton balls
- soft hair brush
- diaper pail (if using cloth diapers)
- rectal thermometer
- bulb syringe for removing nasal mucus
- petroleum jelly
- alcohol
- mild soap (e.g., Dove)
- antibiotic ointment
- feeding supplies (see "Breastfeeding" and "Bottlefeeding")
- baby nail scissors

These lists represent the items we feel are necessary. Add to these as your situation, desires, and budget allow.

ESSENTIAL PHONE NUMBERS

Prepare a list of important phone numbers for easy access if you need help fast. Be sure your mate knows where to find it. Most probably you will not need the services of all individuals and organizations listed, but you will welcome not having to hunt for those you do.

- Hospital emergency room for immediate medical advice
- Police department
- Fire department
- Poison control center
- Car service (in an emergency you may not be able to drive yourself or your baby to the doctor/hospital)
- Ambulance service
- Obstetrician or certified nurse midwife
- Pediatrician or pediatric nurse practitioner
- General practitioner
- Childbirth educator
- Pharmacy (open twenty-four hours and delivers)
- La Leche League (for questions, information, and advice about breastfeeding)

●American Society for Psychoprophylaxis in Obstetrics (ASPO/Lamaze) or International Childbirth Education Association (ICEA) for new parent information, lectures, rap sessions, etc. (See also "Postpartum Support Groups.")

●Cesarean/Support education concern (C/Sec) or other cesarean support group—to talk about your feelings, to join a special support group or for any cesarean-related help, information or advice

●Parents Anonymous or other such self-help groups—for aid in accepting frustration, anger and hostility, to prevent taking it out on the baby. (All conversations confidential)

SHOULD BOTH PARENTS WORK OUTSIDE THE HOME: HOW TO DECIDE

While some men consider leaving the work force to stay home with their babies, more frequently it is the expectant or new mother who has to decide, with her mate, whether or not she will go back to work after the baby is born. Many couples today find themselves in a bind. The women's movement has brought about increased educational and career opportunities for women, but society has not yet caught up to the extent of providing support for couples who by choice or financial necessity work outside the home after the birth of their babies. A father who wishes to take time off from work to care for a sick child may be frowned on as being "unmasculine" or not a "team player." Many women (and men) fear that taking time off when the baby is sick, they are exhausted, or the sitter doesn't come, will decrease their chances for advancement or even continued employment. (This issue is of even greater concern to single parents!) And some find their relatives are openly hostile to the idea of the baby's being "raised by strangers." Neighbors and friends who have chosen to stay home may be resentful if called upon to help in a pinch. "I'm sacrificing luxuries and a career to do the 'best' for my chil-

dren. Why should I help *them*?" And what are the effects on
the baby? One of the most important factors in how the baby
will fare emotionally is the availability of consistent, high
quality childcare; this is often difficult to find—especially for
infants. (See "The Working Mothers" for a discussion of options.)

If you have the luxury of choosing whether or not to return
to the workforce, how then, should you make the decision?
First, consider the following:

•We suggest that you wait at least three months after you
give birth to decide whether you want to work outside the
home. The early weeks are not typical of what motherhood is
all about and do not afford the proper perspective from which
to make your decision. However, if you must go to work,
because you need the money, because you don't want to lose
your job and it won't be held for you unless you return sooner,
or because you have found that staying home is absolutely not
for you under any circumstances, we strongly suggest you
wait at least six weeks to allow yourself to recuperate from the
childbirth process.

•Realize that children in day care centers or day care
homes have statistically higher rates of upper respiratory infections and other illnesses for the first six months they are in
day care than do their counterparts of the same age who are
individually cared for (either by a parent or a sitter). There are
positives and negatives to this. At some point, most children
get these illnesses. Children who are not in day care will
usually contract them during their first years of nursery or
elementary school. However, conclusive information on the
long-term health effects of having these illnesses at an earlier
age is not yet available. On a more practical side, day care
centers and homes usually have no provision to care for a sick
child, forcing parents to make other arrangements for the duration of an illness. (Centers should be able to care for a child
who becomes ill during the day, at least until someone arrives
to take him or her home.) This raises an important question:
What will you do when your child is ill? Will one of you stay
home from work? Is there a relative available to help?

•Juggling time and balancing everyone's needs are other
issues that will become more real and easier to envision once
the baby is born. Babies take up an incredible amount of time.
Unless you can afford to hire full-time help who will take over

all tasks, caring for the baby and the home and working full-time outside the home will leave you very little free time for socializing, being together with your mate or even having some time alone. "There's always something to do," one mother complained. "And never enough time to do it in." Ideally, you will both pitch in and share the housework and baby care equally, but even where both parents feel an equal commitment to completing these tasks, it takes work and juggling of priorities to make time for everyone's needs. "I know I need time alone with my husband, but how can I leave my baby and go out for the evening? I'm away from her all week. Isn't she being cheated?" one mother asked. Our feeling is that your needs as individuals and as a couple must also be met. Even if you each get a sense of personal satisfaction from your work both inside and outside the home, few people find work satisfies all their needs. An occasional night out together or even alone is also a necessary component of maintaining your sense of self and your relationship as a couple. The baby can only benefit from parents who take their own needs into account. On the other hand, our children have a real need for our undivided attention and it may not be possible to get away as often as we'd like.

•Another issue that may be important to you is the question of whether or not there is a true financial advantage to working outside the home. Add up not only the actual cost of childcare (including fees, food consumed by a sitter, travel expenses to and from a day care home) but also the actual expenses of working (including any special clothing, transportation, lunches). Subtract that from your income after taxes. Does it pay to work?

•Think about how effective you are on the job when you're tired. Do you work with dangerous machinery? Are you responsible for making critical decisions? While many babies will sleep through the night sometime between six weeks and three months, many others will not. In older babies there is also night waking to contend with due to teething and separation anxiety. While many couples who work outside the home solve this problem by taking turns tending to the baby at night, both are usually pretty tired by a week's end.

None of the issues need be insurmountable and we feel a special sensitivity toward those who have no choice and those who face these problems and are stuck in a job they dislike out of a need to earn money and a lack of options on how to earn it. Many mothers who work outside the home tell us that, once they get past any initial feelings of guilt they are able to juggle work, baby and home and evolve a new life-style that includes meeting everyone's needs—at least some of the time. They feel a tremendous sense of satisfaction in their work and an increased enjoyment of their baby because they're not with the baby 100% of the time. "The time together becomes more precious because I'm not always there," said one mother. For others it's more difficult; "I found the constant pressure to be more than I could handle. I was able to work out a part-time arrangement with my supervisor that's really worked well."

In the final analysis, the *right* answer to the question of whether or not both parents should work outside the home should be based on a consideration of: financial need; your ability to locate quality child care; how you define yourselves as individuals and as a couple. (See also sections "Babysitters," "The Working Mother," and "The Single Mother.")

SLEEPING ARRANGEMENTS

In addition to considerations of space when deciding on where the baby should sleep, we suggest you think about the following:

Babies are noisy sleepers. They frequently gurgle and grunt in their sleep. They also have irregular breathing patterns. If you and/or your mate tend to be light sleepers, it might be wise from the very beginning to put the baby in his or her own room or a corner of another room. On the other hand, having the baby in the same room for the first weeks can facilitate middle of the night feedings—especially if you plan on nursing. It also provides the comfort of easily being able to check on the baby in the middle of the night without the fear of waking your infant if he or she is a light sleeper!

Whatever your immediate plans, if your long-term plans

include his or her own room, it's a good idea to get the baby used to sleeping there for at least some part of the day from the beginning and to plan on switching over completely by about three months.

While some parents enthusiastically support the idea of sleeping in the room with the baby, the vast majority prefer that at some point parents and children have their own sleeping quarters. If these are your plans but your current living arrangements make this impossible, it's wise to begin considering your alternatives now. If moving to a larger house or apartment is not feasible, consider building a wall or hanging curtains to partition a room, building a loft area or even using a loft bed to create additional space, or giving the baby your room and using a sofa bed in the living room for yourselves.

Even parents who plan on having their baby share their room for an extended period of time sometimes find that they become uncomfortable with the arrangement. Perhaps at six to nine months the baby, waking frequently, sees the parents, and decides it's time to play. Or the baby turns out to be such a light sleeper the parents find themselves making love in the bathroom! On the other hand, sometimes parents who swear they will never let their baby sleep in their bed find that it's the only way they all get some sleep.

Think about your preferences now, but regardless of what you plan, resolve to be flexible and to react to the situation as it presents itself.

BREAST VS. BOTTLE: HOW TO DECIDE

Perhaps you've already received advice from various friends and relatives on how to feed your baby, or maybe you've been spared this barrage because people have made assumptions about how you are going to manage this important aspect of childcare. Although many expectant grandparents are perplexed at the current trend toward breastfeeding, which they view as old-fashioned, they do not necessarily take any overt stand on the subject. However, some openly express their distaste for the practice. They did not breastfeed and feel compelled to recount all the reasons why they did not: Auntie Rosie had "milk fever" and cousin Dorothy "went dry" and Grandma Natalie "lost her figure" and Mrs. Winston "lost her husband's interest."

If you are considering breastfeeding, someone at some time during your pregnancy might ask: "Why on earth do you want to do that? What are you, a cow?" Or: "You're too nervous to breastfeed." "Your breasts are too small—you won't have enough milk." "Why bother, when you can give the kid a bottle of formula?" And so on. Friends and relatives of any age who have never been exposed to breastfeeding may tell you it's messy, that you'll be too tied down, or that you'll put on a lot of weight. Or, perhaps you will find that you are bombarded with reasons *to* breastfeed and you might be made to feel a little guilty for even considering bottlefeeding. Friends may go on and on about the "special relationship" between mother and nursing baby. Articles in newspapers and magazines stress the breastfeeding advantages to mother and baby, implying that you're doing a great disservice to your baby by bottlefeeding.

Before going into the *real* arguments for and against breastfeeding and bottlefeeding, let us go over the *unreal* arguments—the old wives' tales.

Old Wives' Tales about Breastfeeding

MYTH: *You must eat and drink much more, thereby putting on a lot of weight and spending a lot of money.*
FACT: As long as you are eating a well-balanced diet (for your own benefit), all you need add for breastfeeding is approximately 600-800 calories a day, as well as additional liquids. This need not be expensive and can come from low-cost high-protein sources, such as beans, rice, cornmeal, enriched or whole-grain bread, peanut butter, wheat germ, etc., with vegetables and fruits or a vitamin-mineral capsule. As far as weight is concerned, if you continue to follow a diet that did not cause a weight gain before your pregnancy, you are more

likely to lose than to gain weight, because breastfeeding causes the body to burn additional calories.

MYTH: *If you have small breasts, you will not have enough milk.*
FACT: Breast size (which is determined more by fat content of the breasts than by mammary gland content) has nothing to do with milk production. Small-breasted women may well produce far more milk than other women whose breasts look large.

MYTH: *If you are the "nervous type," you cannot produce enough milk.*
FACT: If you are extremely nervous, this may interfere with your let-down reflex and may inhibit the release of milk. It will therefore seem that you have less than enough. If you have this problem and relaxation techniques do not help, your doctor can prescribe an oxytocin nasal spray which will help your milk let-down until you are relaxed enough to do without this spray.

MYTH: *Your breasts will sag and become pendulous.*
FACT: Your breasts will become pendulous if you are genetically predisposed toward pendulous breasts. Any increase in breast size occurs during and because of pregnancy, not breastfeeding.

MYTH: *You will be "tied down."*
FACT: You will be tied to feeding the baby, but that does not necessarily tie you down. Breastfeeding mothers can and do take their babies practically anywhere they choose to go. It is important for you to realize that unless you go back to work full-time, whether you breast- or bottlefeed, you will be spending most of your time with the baby anyhow. Even mothers who bottlefeed give most feedings themselves. When you do go out with the baby, a breastfed infant is more easily portable because you don't have to carry bottles of formula along with you. A breastfeeding mother can, just like a bottle-feeding mother, leave the baby with a sitter occasionally and get out by herself or with her mate if she so desires.

MYTH: *The new father can establish a closer relationship with the baby if he can bottlefeed him or her.*

FACT: The new father need not communicate his love and form a special relationship with his child only through feedings, but can do this through holding, bathing, changing, massaging, touching and talking to the infant. Studies have revealed the important role the new father plays in the development of the baby without his direct participation in the feeding process.

Arguments in Favor of Breastfeeding

●Breastfeeding is more economical: it avoids the expense of formula.

●Breastfeeding is less work. There are no bottles to wash, sterilize or warm. Early morning or middle of the night feedings can be accomplished with a minimum of disruption of sleep.

●Breastfeeding is healthier for the mother:

a) Studies have revealed a possible connection between breastfeeding and a lower incidence of breast cancer.

b) Breastfeeding women regain their waistlines sooner.

c) Breastfeeding causes the release of the hormone oxytocin, which stimulates uterine contractions, thereby lowering the incidence of postpartum hemorrhaging.

d) Breastfeeding causes the release of the hormone oxytocin, which is conducive to relaxation and "motherly" feelings.

●Breastfeeding is healthier for the baby:

a) Colostrum, the pre-milk substance the breastfed baby receives, provides temporary immunity from polio, coxsackie B virus, staphylococci, E. coli (an intestinal virus) and other disorders.

b) Breastfed babies receive protection from many diseases to which their mothers are immune, for as long as nursing continues.

c) A British study indicated that breastfeeding may provide nature's own medication for a baby who has an illness. It is theorized that exposure to the baby's germs causes the mother to produce antibodies which are transmitted to the baby through the milk. For the same reason, it is less likely that a breastfed baby will contract an illness from the mother. (Exceptions to this include tuberculosis and whooping cough.)

d) There is evidence to suggest that adults who were breastfed as babies have a lower incidence of heart disease, dental problems, and obesity than their bottlefed counterparts.

e) Breast milk is easier than formula to digest.

f) Colostrum aids in the maturation of the infant's digestive system.

g) Colostrum has a slightly laxative effect which helps eliminate meconium—the tar-like black substance in the newborn's intestinal system.

h) Scientists continue to identify substances in breast milk not present in formula that facilitate the baby's growth and development.

i) Babies who are breastfed have a lower incidence of allergies later in life. This is especially important in families where one or both parents are themselves allergic.

Arguments in Favor of Bottlefeeding

●A bottlefed infant can be fed by anyone, thereby removing the almost total feeding responsibility from the mother. She can more easily choose to go to work full- or part-time, to share the nighttime feeding responsibility with her mate, and in general will be less tied to the baby's feeding needs.

●Because formula is more difficult to digest, bottlefed babies tend to feed somewhat less frequently than their breastfed counterparts.

Disadvantages of Breastfeeding

●There may be minor physical discomforts, such as sore nipples and breast engorgement, which usually last only a few days.

●It takes time and patience for you and your baby to learn to nurse. During the first day or two, breastfeeding is not always as simple as putting a bottle in the baby's mouth. (But once the technique is established, there is nothing to it!)

•During the first two or three weeks, your baby may demand to be fed as often as every two hours (or even every hour at times) and you will be unable to leave the baby for any length of time during this period. It is possible that you may not feel like going out for several weeks anyway.

Disadvantages of Bottlefeeding

•Your breasts may become engorged several days after giving birth. This engorgement generally lasts a day or two and can be quite painful. This can be minimized with analgesics, cold compresses and/or binding the breasts.

•You must always provide a bottle of formula for the baby wherever the baby goes.

•Formula needs proper refrigeration and, according to some pediatricians, must be warmed before serving.

•You must wash feeding equipment; some pediatricians still insist that bottles and nipples be sterilized.

•All formulas do not agree with all babies. You may find that your baby does not tolerate a particular formula well and your doctor will recommend another. Occasionally a baby does not tolerate any formula and the mother is advised to locate a source of breast milk while she attempts to relactate.

•Formula, like any prepared food, carries with it the possibility of bacterial contamination and/or errors in manufacture.

•Formula is an additional expense. Moreover, any formula left over from a feeding should be discarded because it may spoil.

Environmental Pollutants Like PCBs and DDT in Breast Milk

We live in an era of environmental contamination and there is no way for any of us to escape this unfortunate aspect of today's technological society. Even while growing in your uterus, your baby absorbs contaminants present in the food you eat. These pollutants continue to be passed to the baby after birth through the breast milk if a mother nurses. While formula does not contain these contaminants, because they are fat soluble and because the fat in cow's milk is removed before the formula is processed, formula does, however, carry with it the possibility of *bacterial* contamination. When babies begin to drink pure cow's milk instead of formula and begin to eat solid foods from the table, they are exposed to these same environmental pollutants.

The long- and short-term benefits of breastfeeding are known and documented. Scientists continually come up with new reasons why women should nurse. We therefore feel these outweigh the hypothetical risks involved in exposure to environmental pollutants in breast milk. However, should you suspect that you have been exposed to high levels of environmental pollutants, the Environmental Protection Agency is a source of information on whether or not particular pesticides or chemicals are a cause for concern. For information about pesticides call 1-800-858-PEST. For information about other chemicals, 1-800-424-9065. To have your milk tested, contact the nearest large research hospital.

If you do decide to breastfeed you can restrict your intake of potentially harmful contaminants by

a) Peeling and washing all fruits and vegetables before they are consumed.
b) Eating lean meats and poultry and trimming all visible fat from them.
c) Avoiding freshwater fish.

Since environmental pollutants are stored in the body fat, it is wise to avoid crash diets while breastfeeding. Quick weight loss causes the release of larger amounts of these substances at one time than would occur during a more gradual weight-reduction program.

SUMMARY: While the arguments in all the literature are clearly stacked on the side of breastfeeding as nature's way of providing the best possible nutrition for the baby and some distinct physical advantages for the mother, we believe that the expectant mother must also consider her own feelings before making a decision. It's one thing to say breastfeeding is better for mother and child and another to want to feed your baby this way. Also, breastfeeding involves a commitment some women are unable or unwilling to make. While a breastfed baby can occasionally be left with a sitter who can feed the child a bottle of expressed breast milk or formula, the overwhelming majority of feedings must be given by the mother.

Many women find they feel a special closeness toward their breastfed infants and believe this is an especially beautiful part of motherhood. Mothers who have had occasion to breastfeed one infant and bottlefeed another can attest to this. Others find the idea of putting a breast into a child's mouth absolutely distasteful. And, while some fathers take pride in seeing their mates fulfill this part of their biological function, others don't want to share "their" breasts with anyone, even their children. It is important that both parents express and share such feelings before a decision is reached. The greatest asset a breastfeeding woman can have is a supportive mate who will help her over the rough spots. A new father who is not committed to breastfeeding will most probably encourage the use of formula whenever a problem occurs and thereby subvert the breastfeeding efforts of his mate.

The new mother who is negative, embarrassed, or uncomfortable with the idea of breastfeeding should not be coerced into it. There are enough pressures in the early weeks of new parenthood without adding the stress of an unwanted commitment to breastfeeding. A mother who breastfeeds even though she really would prefer not to, may communicate her negative feelings—in the form of tension—to the baby, who may respond by feeding poorly. In addition, a woman who truly does not want to breastfeed may very well be unsuccessful at it. Her reluctance to nurse may inhibit her let-down reflex, which will cause frustration on the part of the baby who sucks fruitlessly. The mother who will feel more at ease while bottlefeeding her baby should bottlefeed. She will relate her positive feelings through the relaxed and loving way she holds, looks at and speaks to her infant. They too will feel a special closeness.

Whatever your choice, don't permit anyone to influence you away from what you believe is right for you and your baby. Your best friend or sister-in-law can only discuss her feelings and experiences. They may be helpful, to be sure, but only you can evaluate your own situation and decide which method is best for you.

If you decide to breastfeed or have mixed feelings about it, we suggest you contact La Leche League International (9616

Minneapolis Avenue, Franklin Park, Illinois 60131) or a La Leche League group in your area. This is an organization of mothers who have breastfed and/or are breastfeeding their babies and who know practically everything there is to know about the subject. Through them you can locate books and films about nursing and you will most certainly be invited to attend a local La Leche meeting to get together with other women like yourself and have some of your questions answered. If you are undecided about whether to breastfeed, members can help you obtain information to give you a better basis on which to make your decision.

However, we will make one suggestion. If after doing some research and soul searching you honestly cannot decide, please give breastfeeding a try. You can always wean the baby to formula if you decide breastfeeding is not for you, but it is decidedly more difficult (although not impossible) to encourage the production and let-down of milk after you've bottlefed the baby over a period of time. (Also, see "Breastfeeding" and "Bottlefeeding" later in this book.)

FINDING A PEDIATRICIAN

An understanding pediatrician or general practitioner is a vital ingredient for a good postpartum adjustment period. Search out the services of such a physician who, in addition to being medically competent and concerned with the new baby, is understanding, helpful, and concerned with the new parents as well. Today it is not uncommon for expectant parents to shop for such a doctor. Why wait until after the baby is born to discover that you and the baby's doctor cannot have a good relationship because of basic differences about childcare theories or because of personalities that are totally incompatible?

Obtain the names of several doctors from friends and relatives and ask why they are being recommended. If possible, accompany a friend on a visit to her pediatrician with her baby to get first-hand knowledge of the doctor's personality and attitudes. Obtain names from your obstetrician, childbirth educator, La Leche League leader or any other individual in a medically related field and ask for an opinion of the other doctors already referred to you.

Once you have narrowed the field down to about three possibilities, call each pediatrician and ask if he or she can spend a few minutes on the phone with you or if you can call back at a more convenient time, or even better, if you can come in for an appointment to meet the doctor. No doctor should charge for such a telephone conversation, but you can expect to pay for a prenatal consultation visit (many do not charge for this service).

If you are put off by a cold or nasty nurse who doesn't care to understand your concern and refuses to let you speak with the doctor at any time, strike that doctor from your list. (You might let the doctor know in writing that you were put off by the nurse's attitude.) In most instances, it is probably true that whatever attitude the doctor's nurse or receptionist shows to patients is a reflection of the doctor's feelings.

Before speaking with the doctor, you should read all you can about infant care and nutrition and speak with other new parents about issues they consider important. By the time you speak with the doctor, you should have some idea of how you feel about breastfeeding, vitamins, when to start solids, weaning from breast or bottle, prepared baby foods, etc. Your opinion on most infant-care issues are just as valid as the doctor's, since many issues in the field of pediatrics are being disputed even within medical circles. Think about what you need in a pediatrician. Are you looking for someone who will present information in terms of options or who will tell you what to do? Remember to ask about the doctor's hospital affiliation. If the pediatrician is not affiliated with the hospital at which you will give birth, he or she may be able to examine your baby but cannot treat your child there. Can he or she practice at the hospital you would most likely take your child to in an emergency? Another thing to check is whether or not the doctor has a telephone hour—a time of day especially set aside for answering questions—or can you feel free to call with a question at any time? Who covers when the doctor is on vacation? Does he or she make house calls? (This may or may not be important to you because facilities in the doctor's office are more complete than in your home.) Can the doctor be reached twenty-four hours a day in an emergency? (Anything you feel is an emergency should qualify.) What is the waiting room like? Is it filled with toys and books for children to use while waiting? Is it bright and cheerfully decorated? Are there laboratory facilities available in the office, or will you have to go elsewhere for blood tests, throat cultures, etc., if they are required? If you plan to breastfeed, ask not only if the doctor is in favor of breastfeeding, but what percentage of his or her patients is being breastfed. What are the fees for office visits, house calls, immunizations? How many times will the doctor visit the baby while you're in the hospital and what is the fee for each of these visits? What, if any, parenting sessions are offered? Is information about community groups posted? What are the qualifications of the individual who answers the telephone, and other staff members: registered nurse, licensed practical nurse, nurse-practitioner, etc.? Such qualified individuals should be able to answer many questions, saving the time necessary to wait for the doctor to return your call. What are the office hours? If the new mother will be returning to work outside the home after the baby is born, will the physician be supportive of this? Does he or she offer evening and weekend hours for working parents?

If you detect annoyance, disrespect or indifference when you discuss these points, find another doctor. If the answers to your questions are curt, without adequate explanation or in language you cannot understand, forget about him or her. On the other hand, if the doctor expresses, by word or inference, understanding of your fears and feelings as an expectant parent and recognition of the special needs of new parents—fathers as well as mothers—during the postpartum period, you have found a special physician.

LEGALITIES: WILLS, INSURANCE

Parenthood brings with it the responsibility of making provisions for the welfare of your children. Have you made such provisions? Are both of you covered by life insurance? While the loss of her mate's income can be devastating to a new widow and child, think of what it would cost a widower to hire someone on a full-time basis to care for the baby. And with more and more women working outside the home, the possibility of the loss of the mother's income should also be considered. Whether one or both of you are working, when a baby is born, finances may be tight and there may not be much, if any, money for insurance policies. Check what coverage you each may have through your place of employment, evaluate your needs, then budget and decide what, if anything, you can spend on insurance. Speak to an insurance broker and compare several different plans before making any decisions. Resolve not to sign anything until you've given the matter some thought for at least a few days. This will prevent spending more than you can afford in response to a good sales pitch.

Now is the time to see an attorney and have wills drawn up. We believe this is a necessity at this time of your life. If either of you dies without a will, inheritance of any money or property is determined by the laws of your state. Under these laws a certain percentage of any money and property is generally given to the husband or wife and the rest placed in trust for any minor children. It may be difficult to invade this trust to obtain money needed for your children's food, clothing, education, etc., and your mate would be asked to justify any such invasion. We suggest you seek legal advice to determine what provisions should be made in your particular circumstances. Also, if at all possible, name a guardian for your children in your wills. In the event that both of you die, this will ensure that your children will be raised by the individual of your choice. If you do not name someone, a custody fight among members of your families might ensue. The guardian should be someone in whom you both have confidence and should be consulted to determine if he or she would be willing to accept this obligation. The fact that you name someone guardian does not legally oblige him or her to accept this responsibility.

Also, if you are not married, we suggest you learn the legal position of your child and the other parent should you die, regarding inheritance, guardianship, survivor's benefits under Social Security, etc. If the father dies, the mother may have to obtain a court decree stating that he was in fact the father of the child before the child would be eligible to collect any benefits under the law. She most likely would be unable to collect for herself, and any will he may have left bequeathing funds to her could be challenged by his relatives, who could claim that they are the rightful heirs. If the mother dies, the father may find he is faced with a legal battle over custody of the child, since the mother's relatives, particularly her parents, might claim guardianship. State laws vary. Avoid any possibility of legal problems later by getting legal advice now.

It is also imperative that both of you know exactly what your financial situation is—where any money, stocks, bonds, etc. are kept, to whom you owe money, etc. Trying to piece together this information after the death of a mate can be a trauma in itself. Make sure someone you trust—ideally the person you name as guardian for your children—would be able to gather this information quickly if necessary. Keep a list of all bank accounts, safe deposit boxes, insurance policies, etc., and the name and address of your attorney in a fireproof metal box in your home. Put your will in this same box, not in a safe deposit box. A safe deposit box which is jointly owned is routinely sealed when one of the owners dies, and for a period of time the contents may not be easily accessible, even to someone who legitimately requires it.

Few people like to think of the death of a loved one at any time, and especially not when feeling the joy that accompanies the anticipation of the birth of a child. But these are important considerations. Death is a fact of life. It's better to take care of these matters now and put them out of your mind.

2. After the Birth

PHYSIOLOGICAL CHANGES

Your postpartum experience begins as soon as the baby and placenta (afterbirth) are delivered. The process by which your body returns to its pre-pregnant state is called "involution."

Your body has made preparations during pregnancy for giving birth, building up to the point where the levels of the hormones estrogen and progesterone have risen very high; your uterus has grown large and strong enough to carry the baby, the placenta and amniotic fluid; your abdomen has stretched and grown enough to accommodate the uterus and its contents; your internal organs have been displaced enough to make the necessary room; and your vaginal canal has increased its stretching capacity enough to accommodate the size of the newborn during the journey from the uterus to the outside world. This nine-month process climaxing in the birth of the baby and placenta only takes about two or three months to reverse itself completely. The majority of these changes back to the pre-pregnant state occur during the first six weeks after delivery. Such dramatic changes in so brief a period are unknown in any other normal health situation.

The Uterus

After the baby is born, uterine contractions continue, assisting in placental separation from the uterine wall; this usually takes about five minutes. Separation of the placenta exposes the extensive vascular uterine bed through which feto-maternal biochemical exchange has been taking place. The continued contractions of uterine muscle fibers serve to constrict, compress and obliterate most of these blood vessels, thus preventing hemorrhaging. Having no placenta and baby within, the uterine cavity diminishes in volume. It continues to shrink in size by maintaining contractions and by breaking down and reabsorbing the muscle cells. The uterus becomes firmer and smaller as it begins to sink lower in the abdominal cavity.

If you breastfeed your baby, the infant's sucking triggers the release of oxytocins—hormones which contract the uterine muscles. Each time your baby nurses, you will be aware of these uterine contractions, which might or might not be painful. If they are painful, try using breathing and relaxation techniques. If these do not help enough and you so desire, your doctor might prescribe a mild painkiller such as acetaminophen (e.g., Tylenol) prior to each feeding of the baby.

To give you an idea of the magnitude of the uterine involution process, consider that before the birth the full-term uterus weighed approximately two pounds. The top of it, the fundus, could be felt just beneath your ribs. Within about a half-hour after delivery, the uterus can be felt as a hard mass, midway between your navel and your pubic bone and not much larger than a large grapefruit. It remains about the same size for the next two days. By about the third day after birth, the uterus descends further into the pelvic cavity, growing smaller and losing weight. By the fourth or fifth day, you might be able to feel it just slightly above your pubic bone. At approximately one week after delivery, it weighs about one pound. By the tenth day, the uterus has descended below your pubic bone and cannot be felt through the abdominal wall. It weighs about twelve ounces by the second week and returns almost to its pre-pregnant position and size by the sixth week—weighing only approximately two ounces.

Afterbirth Pains

Afterbirth pains, or afterpains, are most intensely experienced by mothers having their second or subsequent babies, although some first-time mothers may be aware of them also. These are caused by the extra effort expended by these previously stretched uterine muscles in order to contract effectively. While the uterus of the first-time mother usually remains firmly contracted after delivery, the uterus of the second-time or subsequent mother often contracts and relaxes at intervals. Because the musculature is more relaxed, the uterus works harder to contract, sometimes resulting in pain severe enough for the new mother to request medication during the first few days after delivery. Using Lamaze or other childbirth breathing and relaxation techniques during painful contractions can help minimize this for you.

Chills/Shakes

Soon after giving birth, while still in the delivery room, you might develop chills—so much so that your teeth may chatter and your arms and legs may shake uncontrollably. It may seem almost funny to you as you watch and experience this, except that it might be frightening if you did not know it is usually normal. Chills and/or "the shakes" may last for as long as thirty minutes. It is thought that these may be partially a result of the nervous reaction to and exhaustion from the birth process, your lowered body temperature due to the decreased blood volume now that the placenta has been delivered and your body's process of dealing with the extreme temperature change in a brief period of time. Also, because you may have perspired heavily during the exertion of the delivery stage, during your postdelivery relaxation, the relatively cool air in the room may chill you. You can ask for an extra blanket or two to be tucked closely around your body and you can try Lamaze slow chest breathing, which *sometimes* helps, but chances are that nothing except time and perhaps a hot-water bottle or heating pad will help. If the tremblings are excessive and nothing else helps, your doctor may prescribe a tranquilizer.

Hunger

You may feel ravenously hungry after the baby is born, and no wonder. Your stomach is no longer compressed and, more important, you have not eaten since labor began. Also, after working hard, which is what labor is all about, people do get hungry. You may desire and be given something to eat or drink in the recovery room.

Cervix

After delivery, the cervix becomes soft and flabby for a few days. By the seventh day, the cervix firms and narrows considerably.

Vagina

The vagina, which had been stretched to accommodate the baby's passage, begins gradually to reduce in size but does not usually return entirely to its pre-pregnant condition. Slackness in the vaginal supports may be helped by regular and continued use of the so-called Kegel exercises—contracting and releasing the vaginal floor muscles, approximately five contractions at a time, perhaps three or four times each day, building up to a total of about fifty contractions each day (see "Body Image").

The labia majora and labia minora become flabby after childbirth. The other birth-related structures—ovaries, Fallopian tubes and ligaments supporting the uterus—after undergoing such great tension and stretching, are now relaxed and take some time to return to what is close to their pre-pregnant size and position.

Abdominal Walls

The process of involution (the return of an organ to its normal condition) of the abdominal walls, takes about six weeks. If the muscle tone has been retained, the abdomen will gradually return to its pre-pregnant condition. But if the muscle tone has been lost, the abdominal organs cannot be properly supported and a woman will give the appearance of still being several months pregnant.

Very few women are able to fit into their regular clothes within the first few days following childbirth. Most find their abdomens are very much distended and flabby for three or four days. Still others take several weeks before they can adequately fit into non-maternity clothes. After subequent babies, many women find that it takes even longer to fit into their regular clothing.

Obstetricians disagree on whether abdominal exercise begun soon after delivery can minimize flabbiness. Some believe exercise is useless until the natural process of involution has sufficiently reduced the abdominal muscle fibers; this takes about four to six weeks. Others in the health care field believe in the advisability of early, gentle abdominal exercises (e.g., pelvic rock, abdominal tightening and releasing) to reestablish muscle tone and control. Still others believe that the special exercises taught in prenatal classes and practiced during pregnancy go far toward building up and maintaining tone even after delivery.

Many women are afraid to use their abdominal muscles during pregnancy, mistakenly thinking it will hurt the baby. They allow these muscles to become weak due to disuse. If a woman does not use these muscles during pregnancy, it will be harder for her to regain muscle tone after delivery. Muscle tone can be restored to some degree by proper diet, good posture and prescribed exercises. Do not, however, begin exercises—whether during pregnancy or after delivery—without your doctor's or nurse midwife's permission. During the postpartum period, begin only with mild excercises, building up intensity and frequency gradually in relation to your rate of recuperation. When you feel that you are really straining, you've had enough exercise for the time being. Try again several hours later or even the next day (see "Body Image").

Bloody Discharge

After delivery of the placenta, a bloody discharge called "lochia" begins to be expelled from the uterus and continues for about two to four weeks. Lochia is made up of blood from the site where the placenta was attached, particles of the lining of the uterus now being discarded and blood oozing from small superficial vessels. It takes six to seven weeks for the placental site to heal and half this time for healing of the rest of the uterine wall.

The color and consistency of the lochia changes from bright red (with some mucus and small blood clots) during the first three to five days, to a lighter reddish-pinkish brown flow over the next five to ten days. This then turns a yellowish-white and later becomes an almost colorless, watery discharge before it stops completely. You will be advised to wear sanitary pads rather than tampons during this period. The use of tampons blocks the free flow of lochia from the vagina, thereby providing an environment for possible infection. Since the cervix may not have fully closed, infection can more easily enter the uterus.

The quantity of lochia varies with each woman, but tends to be less heavy in breastfeeding women. It is usually more profuse in women having their second or subsequent babies. The first time that you get out of bed after delivery, there will be an increase in the amount of flow due to the accumulation of lochia while you were lying down. In some cases the duration of *red* lochia continues for as long as ten or more days; spurts of red lochia may recur during the weeks that follow. These episodes usually occur after urination, particularly in a woman who is not breastfeeding. If the lochia remains bright red for more than three weeks and if it becomes as heavy as the amount of blood lost during the first day of a menstrual period, your doctor or nurse midwife should be consulted. If lochia does not begin to taper off, it might indicate the retention of small pieces of the placenta, or that your uterus might need additional stimulation in order to contract more strongly and seal off more uterine blood vessels at the placental site.

It is normal for the lochia to stop completely for a few days and then resume. However, if it has begun to taper off and darken, or if it has stopped completely for several days and then suddenly re-appears as a heavy red flow or gush—or if your lochia has been discharging steadily and there is a sudden heavy red flow or gush—perhaps you have been too active, moving furniture or lifting heavy items, running up and down stairs too often or doing strenuous exercises. These can all interfere with the process of involution. If resting and cutting down your activities do not help, consult your doctor or nurse midwife. Bleeding should taper off, not increase.

It can be frightening to pass blood clots if you do not know this can be normal and quite common. Sometimes, several clots or one large clot several inches in diameter can be felt as they pass through the vagina. Often, this type of loose clot is formed by blood that has accumulated in your vagina while lying prone; when you get out of bed, it comes out. If it is not accompanied by active or persistent bleeding, it is usually nothing to worry about. However, if such clotting *is* accompanied by such bleeding, it *may* be a sign that something is wrong. It may also mean that the clot had been blocking the blood behind it from coming out. If you are breastfeeding, a good first-aid action is to try breastfeeding the baby to see if the resultant contractions of the uterus decrease the flow of blood. If this heavy bleeding and/or passage of clots occurs, whether you are breastfeeding or not, you should consult your doctor or nurse midwife. Meanwhile, remain in bed and check the number of sanitary napkins needed per hour. If you need more than one per hour, or if this heavy flow and passage of clots continues beyond six hours, you should consult your doctor or nurse midwife again.

After the lochia stops, you might notice the presence of a whitish or brownish mucus discharge which eventually lessens. Some amount of discharge keeps the vaginal mucus membrane moist and is normal in all women. However, if you notice a heavier-than-usual discharge, one with a foul odor, one that is yellowish, greenish or frothy, and/or you have vaginal itching, you might have an infection and require medical treatment. In such instances, it is wise not to douche without your health care provider's knowledge because, in some cases, douching can spread the infection higher up the vaginal canal and possibly (although rarely) into the uterus.

Breasts, Nipples and Lactation

During pregnancy, the breasts become temporarily enlarged and require a richer blood supply in preparation for lactation. This explains the swelling of blood vessels supplying the area. After delivery, the breasts remain about the same size for approximately two days. Meanwhile, colostrum—a thick, yellowish pre-milk fluid—is secreted. During pregnancy, the hormone prolactin, which is known to stimulate lactation, is present in your body but its effects are inhibited by high levels of estrogen and progesterone. The delivery of the placenta and the resultant complex hormonal changes initiate the lactation process. Colostrum is soon followed by milk which is bluish-white and appears thinner than cow's milk.

The day during which the milk "comes in" is, to some degree, determined by how soon after birth the baby is allowed to nurse for the first time and how often thereafter. Some claim that milk production can begin on the first or second day if the baby is put to the breast often and is receiving no other fluids. The reason that most people assume the milk does not come in before the third or fourth day is because most babies' feeding patterns are regulated by hospital nursery schedules, limiting the number of nursings and thereby postponing the mother's milk production. If the baby is encouraged to breastfeed soon after birth and often thereafter, milk may come in sooner.

The establishment of lactation is enhanced by the baby's continued sucking, which signals the pituitary gland to release more prolactin. The more the baby sucks and empties the breast, the more milk is produced. As the lactation process establishes itself, the breasts may become larger, extremely sore, hard and warm or hot to the touch. Known as engorgement, this might last twenty-four to forty-eight hours and is caused by the pressure of increased blood in the area and increased milk in the ducts. Painful engorgement, which, according to some breastfeeding authorities, is caused by the four-hour hospital feeding schedule, can be relieved by manually expressing some milk from the breast. If engorgement advances to the point that it is accompanied by a headache and fever, it might be a sign of a breast infection and the doctor may prescribe an antibiotic (one that is not harmful to the baby) for a few days. While the mother takes such medication, she can and should continue nursing.

If you do not breastfeed, the lactation process will start by itself—even without the encouragement of a sucking baby—and you may find that your breasts engorge on or about the third or fourth day for twenty-four to forty-eight hours. Because there is no stimulation from the baby's sucking, milk production usually ceases within a few days. However, some health care providers think it would be wise for you to decrease somewhat the amount of liquids you drink because liquids encourage milk production. Do not, however, stop drinking entirely!

Since engorgement can be very uncomfortable, doctors recommend that you wear a firm supporting bra during this period. If you are not breastfeeding, binding the breasts and/or applying ice packs for brief periods of ten or fifteen minutes are often prescribed.

If you had received an antilactogenic hormone to "dry up" the milk, either by injection or pill, you may or may not be spared the discomfort of engorgement. Sometimes it works, sometimes it doesn't. If you were given this hormone in the form of an injection in the delivery room, you will probably be very aware of having received it because your hip area will feel extremely sore for days afterward.

After deciding not to breastfeed and experiencing the fullness of your breasts and resultant leaking, you may have mixed feelings and wonder if your decision not to breastfeed was right after all. Should this occur, you can still change your mind, even after having received an antilactogenic hormone. Put your baby to your breast and the sucking will stimulate lactation. (Contact your health care provider regarding the interval necessary before initiating breastfeeding after the administration of an antilactogenic.)

Breastfeeding is a supply-demand situation. Babies who are given additional bottle feedings (either water or formula) have reduced need for sucking at the breast. This diminished amount of breast stimulation results in the decreased production of milk. Milk production is also affected if a woman fails to eat a well-balanced diet, does not drink adequate amounts of fluids, is under great stress, etc.

The supply of breast milk also depends on another factor. Although the milk is produced in the glands of your breast, it must be released from these glands into the collection area behind the areola (the dark area surrounding the nipples) and then out through the nipple. This release is known as the let-down or milk-ejection reflex and is essential to the nursing process. If your milk does not let-down, the baby will be unable to obtain all the milk you have produced. Because, in the early weeks, the let-down reflex can be affected by too much activity, fatigue or aggravation, it is important to limit your activities. Rest! While nursing, put your feet up, or, even better, lie down and relax. Don't worry about everything that has to get done. It will—in time. Breastfeeding women needn't become bedridden; they just must be sensible about getting rest and not overtaxing themselves.

Dried milk or colostrum which may accumulate on your nipples can cause irritation. Therefore, it is suggested that you rinse the area with warm water (no soap) before each nursing, or at any time that there is such an accumulation, whether or not you are breastfeeding.

Urination

Urinating after you give birth may feel somewhat strange. If you have had a regional anesthetic (caudal, spinal, epidural, saddle-block), you might be less aware of a full bladder and you may find it difficult to empty it completely until your sensitivity returns. If you are unable to urinate after several hours (time varying from hospital to hospital) a nurse will insert a catheter through your urethra into your bladder to withdraw urine. If you try contracting and releasing your pelvic floor muscles (Kegel exercise) a few times every fifteen or twenty minutes, you might succeed in stimulating urination without the need for catheterization. If using a bedpan, be sure to sit upright with your feet over the side of the bed—in your normal urinating position—for more chance of success.

Urinary Tract Infections

These occur often enough to warrant mention of their symptoms, which you should report to your doctor or nurse midwife. They are chills, fever, pain or burning sensation while urinating, urinating often and in small amounts, back pains or lower abdominal pains.

Bowels

Do not expect to have a bowel movement until the second or third day after delivery, at which time you might feel as though you are constipated. This may be because you had an enema during labor or hadn't eaten for several hours before the delivery. Also, after childbirth the intestinal and abdominal muscles are relaxed and do not assist efficient evacuation of intestinal contents. In addition, you might be avoiding a bowel movement, fearing it will be uncomfortable or put stress on your episiotomy sutures; this avoidance can lead to constipation. To prevent straining, we recommend that you drink more liquids. Since liquids stimulate milk production, you might want to encourage bowel function by eating fresh or cooked fruits, prunes, dates, raisins, figs, whole-grain cereals, bran or leafy vegetables. Or, your doctor or nurse midwife might prescribe a bowel softener (this is not a laxative) to be taken perhaps the evening of the second day after delivery. This softens the movement so there's no need for straining.

Hemorrhoids

The presence of hemorrhoids is a possible, although not probable occurrence after childbirth. Hemorrhoids are enlarged blood vessels which can pop out of the anus from the enormous pressure the baby exerts against the pelvic floor as uterine contractions push the infant through the birth canal. Hemorrhoids, which look more like swollen lumps of flesh than veins, can occur in a woman who is sedated during delivery and not actively bearing down, as well as in a woman who is awake and adding her own conscious bearing-down efforts to help deliver the baby.

If hemorrhoids do appear, you must be sure to avoid straining during bowel movements. Not only can straining cause more hemorrhoids to pop out, but the harder the bowel movement, the more it will irritate the existing swellings. Hemorrhoids can be extremely painful and several treatments are recommended by most health care providers: 1) Soak your entire bottom in the warm sitz baths available in the hospital. This is very soothing and promotes healing. 2) Tuck the hemorrhoid(s) back into the anus with your lubricated fingertip (be sure your fingernail is not too long or sharp) and contract your vaginal and anal muscles five to ten times. 3) Apply an anesthetic ointment. 4) Apply a special hemorrhoidal ointment. 5) Apply specially treated gauze pads available in pharmacies specifically for the treatment of hemorroids. 6) Apply your own gauze pads soaked in witch hazel. Some health care providers recommend comfortably hot or warm sitz baths or applications; others advise cold witch hazel solutions. In most cases, the hemorrhoids will regress about ten days after delivery.

Weight Loss

The amount of weight you can expect to lose immediately after delivery of the baby and placenta is approximately twelve pounds: about seven pounds of baby, about one and a half pounds of placenta, about one and a half pounds of amniotic fluid, and about two pounds of other body fluids and blood. You will lose approximately three more pounds in the following week as body tissues rid themselves of excess fluids. Approximately another two pounds will have been lost by the time the uterus returns to its usual two-ounce prepregnant size. After the initial six weeks, weight loss continues gradually, depending on how carefully you eat and how much you exercise.

Hot Flashes

During the first few days after delivery, you may feel your face becoming red and hot. Called "hot flashes" or "hot flushes," this condition is caused by the hormonal shifts occurring within your body.

Swelling of the Perineum

If you've had stitches to repair an episiotomy, we recommend that while you are in the recovery room you request an ice pack to be placed directly on your perineum. You may leave the ice pack in place for about ten to fifteen minutes, take it off for fifteen minutes and then repeat the procedure for the first few hours; then apply it every hour or so for fifteen minutes during the remainder of the first day. This helps to prevent the swelling of the perineal tissues which causes tension on the sutures and pain or discomfort for days or even weeks. We also suggest that you ask your doctor or nurse midwife, before you give birth, that permission for the application of ice be recorded on your chart, so you will not possibly be told by any nurse, "Sorry, it wasn't ordered for you."

We suggest that you try doing a few Kegel exercises in the recovery room, every fifteen or twenty minutes, to promote healing of the episiotomy by stimulating blood circulation in the affected tissues. It may be difficult to do at first, because the area may feel numb and/or weak, but that does not matter. Any mobilization of these muscles will help and the more you try to exercise, the more strength and ability you will develop. Do not strain yourself. Concentrate on tightening your muscles a little at a time, resting for fifteen or twenty minutes and then doing it again two or three times more, if you are comfortable. Remember—do not strain.

Stretch Marks

After having a baby, some women are left with brownish or reddish stretch marks—called striae—on their abdomen, breasts, buttocks or thighs. These gradually shrink and become paler within four to six months postpartum but remain to some degree as pearly-white scars in white women and dark scars in black women. Striae are more noticeable in some women than in others.

Pigmentation

Increased pigmentation caused by heightened hormonal levels is common during pregnancy and might intensify the color of already dark areas of your body such as the genitals and around the nipples and the navel. You may also have developed some freckling or dark patches on your face, or, if you have any recent scars, you might notice they have become darker. Within a few weeks after delivery, when your hormonal levels decline, most of this pigmentation fades. Linea nigra—the dark line which appears on the abdomen during pregnancy and extends from the navel down to the pubic hair —also lightens in time.

Skin Changes

During pregnancy it is also possible that you have noticed "spiders"—bright red, branchlike skin markings—on various parts of your body. These are actually distended capillaries just beneath the surface of the skin. They usually regress within two months after delivery.

"Skin tags"—pinhead-sized bumps that sometimes appear on the breasts, neck or underarms during the prenatal period —grow a bit larger with each pregnancy and do not disappear. However, if necessary, they can be removed surgically or by cauterization (destroying them with an electric needle).

The redness of palms and soles of feet which may occur during the last three months of pregnancy and which becomes brighter after delivery is caused by increased blood volume and enlarged blood vessels. This usually disappears within two weeks after birth.

Hair

Increased hormonal levels might also cause unwanted hairiness on the body, which usually disappears within the first three months. About four to six months after delivery, many women experience the phenomenon of excessive hair loss from the scalp which is caused by the natural imbalance of hormone levels in the process of returning to the non-pregnant state.

Emotions

The hormonal changes occurring immediately after delivery affect you emotionally as well as physically. Each woman who is awake and aware reacts differently at the moment of her baby's birth. Reactions vary depending on the hormonal shifts which occur and the sentimentality attached to being witness to and active during the birth event. A part is also played by the kind of labor and delivery she experienced. For example, simply the relief that labor is over may bring a flood of tears.

On the third or fourth day after delivery, many women feel "let down," "blue" or slightly depressed. During the period of time following delivery, possibly even until your first menstrual period, you may experience swings of emotions from great heights of joy to great lows of sadness. Be assured that reasonable emotional extremes are normal and are brought about by the dramatic hormonal changes which have been taking place within your body. There need be no other explanation if anyone comments on your being moody, and you need not analyze the situation any further. (See "Postpartum Blues.")

Menstruation

After childbirth, when you resume menstruation depends on several factors. Most non-breastfeeding women menstruate six to eight weeks after giving birth. A breastfeeding woman will probably not menstruate for as long as she *totally* breastfeeds her child and gives no solids or formula. In addition, since ovulation is suppressed by total breastfeeding, it is unlikely, although not impossible, that she can become pregnant. Some women do resume menstruation even while totally breastfeeding their babies; therefore, there is a chance that ovulation—and pregnancy—may occur.

If menstruation does resume while you are breastfeeding, it has no effect on the quality of the milk, as some people believe. However, some babies have been known to be temporarily "turned off" to nursing while their mothers are menstruating, perhaps due to a subtle taste or scent change they detect in the milk.

While most women find their menses return soon after solids are introduced or the baby is weaned to a bottle, others do not menstruate for several months thereafter. It is also possible for a breastfeeding woman to menstruate and then skip a month or two. The menstrual cycle may be different from what it was before the baby. This irregularity generally occurs in a woman whose baby has just begun solids and whose output of breast milk varies. As solids are increased and breastfeeding is decreased, more normal menstruation resumes. If the baby gets sick or has teething pain and refuses solids, temporarily increasing the number and duration of nursings, menstruation may be temporarily suppressed once again.

The type of menstrual period you have the very first time after childbirth will depend on your rate of hormone production. Some women experience a comfortable bleeding-as-usual menstrual period; many others have a very heavy flow for several days, with or without severe cramps. If you are not sure whether or not your menstrual bleeding is excessive, try resting in bed for a day and keep track of the number of sanitary napkins you need per hour. If the heavy rate of blood flow continues past six hours, or becomes heavier and requires a change of napkin more often than every hour, it is advisable to consult your doctor or nurse midwife.

POSTPARTUM EMERGENCIES: WHEN TO CALL FOR HELP

•Sudden heavy gush of red blood from vagina after flow has been stabilized, decreased and changed in color

•Vaginal bleeding requiring more than one pad per hour for several hours

•Large amounts of clots, all sizes, with accompanying heavy flow

- Faintness
- Dizziness
- Extreme fatigue; exhaustion
- Severe back pain
- Severe pain in the chest, lower abdomen or legs
- Malodorous vaginal discharge
- Severe headache
- Chills
- Temperature of over 101°F

If Breastfeeding:
- Sensitive or inflamed lumps in breast
- Flu-like feeling accompanied by fever over 100°F, possibly engorgement and red areas on breast
- Sore nipples that last more than a few days
- Bleeding nipples
- Pain during nursing that extends from the nipple into the breast and does not go away when the milk lets down

WHAT TO EXPECT AS NORMAL: HOW TO DEAL WITH IT

- Chills, trembling immediately after delivery and perhaps lasting as long as thirty minutes (use warm blankets, hot-water bottle, Lamaze slow chest breathing)
- Fatigue (get plenty of sleep)
- Swings of emotions (accept your feelings)
- Body aches (take warm showers and massage)
- Backache (massage)
- Heavier-than-usual lochia flow, if more than usual activity (rest)
- Leaking breasts, whether or not you breastfeed (wear gauze pads in your bra)
- Burning or itching at episiotomy site, especially if you were shaved (warm air from blow-dryer, cold witch hazel applications or ointment prescribed by your doctor or nurse midwife)

●Numbness in area of I.V. infusion (warm, wet compresses)
●Bruises from I.V. infusion (warm compresses)

PROCEDURES INVOLVING THE MOTHER

Note: If your baby has been born in a birthing room, all procedures normally done in the delivery and recovery rooms, as described in this chapter, will take place in the birthing room.

In the Delivery Room

DELIVERY OF THE PLACENTA. Immediately after the delivery of the baby, the doctor, nurse midwife or nurse will feel your uterus through your abdominal wall to be sure it remains firm. Next, you will be watched for signs that the placenta has separated from the wall of the uterus; this occurs with the aid of continued uterine contractions. Signs of placental separation are a firmer, globular-shaped uterus, a sudden gush of blood, the rise of the uterus into the abdominal cavity as the separated placenta descends into its lower part and farther down into the vagina and the protrusion of the umbilical cord farther out of the vagina. These signs sometimes occur within the first sixty seconds after the baby is born, but more usually within five minutes. As soon as it is determined that the uterus is firm, you may be asked, if you are awake, to "give another push for the placenta." If you are not awake or if you have been given a regional anesthetic, the doctor or nurse midwife might press on your fundus (the top part of the uterus) through the abdominal wall, to urge the placenta down into the vagina. An oxytocic drug may be given to you to stimulate contractions of the uterus and aid the delivery of the placenta. This may be given through an injection or the intravenous catheter.

Usually, if an I.V. has been set up prior to this moment, this is the route chosen.

After the placenta is expelled, it will be examined closely to be sure that no part of it has broken off and remained inside the uterus, a situation which can cause hemorrhaging. If there is any doubt, or if it is the doctor's or nurse midwife's practice to routinely do so, he or she will perform a quick examination of the inside of the uterus and if any piece of placental tissue is there, will remove it.

SUTURING OF THE EPISIOTOMY. If you have had an episiotomy (incision into the perineum beginning at the rear of the vaginal opening), the doctor or nurse midwife will begin suturing it at this time, if the procedure was not already begun before the placenta was delivered. If you are awake and have had an epidural (regional anesthetic) or a pudendal block (extensive local anesthetic) prior to delivery, it will still have its numbing effect. If you did not receive either, the doctor or nurse midwife may administer a local anesthetic into the perineum (area between the vaginal and anal openings). This injection will be felt as a burning sensation and will numb the area for the suturing. Sometimes the anesthetic is not as effective as one would like and you might feel some of the suturing. If you do, try to release all your muscles and use breathing techniques to minimize your discomfort.

Suturing techniques vary. Some physicians and nurse midwives use a "running stitch," leaving the beginning and end of the suture loose and unknotted, on the theory that such technique allows for normal swelling of tissues without undue straining at the sutures (which causes later pain). Other physicians and nurse midwives use the stitch-and-knot method of tying off individual sutures. Whatever the technique, sutures dissolve in about ten to twenty-eight days.

New mothers often ask the number of sutures used because they believe this is related to the size of the incision or the discomfort afterward. The number of sutures has no bearing on the size of the incision; some doctors and nurse midwives use more, some fewer, sutures per given area. The number of sutures also does not always relate to later discomfort; all you need is one tight stitch to have pain. The length of the incision, the direction in which it extends, how tightly the stitches were made, and how much swelling there is have more to do with later discomfort than the number of sutures used.

During the suturing, keep your vaginal muscles as released as possible. If you tighten these muscles during the suturing, the normal swelling of the perineal tissues the next day may pull against the stitches and cause you more discomfort than necessary.

After the suturing has been completed, your vaginal area will be washed with an antiseptic solution or soap and water. The lower end of the delivery table which had been pushed down and "broken" under for the birth will now be replaced. The surgical drapes will be removed, both your legs will be lowered from the stirrups slowly and at the same time, a sterile perineal pad will be put into place.

If the new father has been present for the birth, he may remain in the delivery room during the expulsion of the placenta and whatever suturing may be necessary. He can stay at the head of the table with you and together you can admire your newborn, who might be placed on your chest, in your mate's arms, or in a heated crib or unit nearby.

ANTILACTOGENICS. During labor you may be asked if you will be breastfeeding or not. If your answer is "no," and if this is the procedure at your hospital and used by your doctor, you will be injected with an antilactogenic hormone to "dry up" your milk without painful engorgement. This is routine in some hospitals. The injection is given in your hip area, is frequently described as painful and you may feel soreness in your hip for days afterward. If your doctor prefers to use an antilactogenic hormone in pill form, you will be given this later on in your room. Antilactogenic hormones do *not* invariably prevent painful engorgement, however. It seems to be more effective if given earlier in labor than just prior to delivery, as was done in the past.

It is important for you to know that this hormone is optional. If you prefer not to take it, speak to your doctor in advance and remind him or her about it in the labor and/or delivery room. The routine administration of antilactogenics is controversial and is not as widespread today as it was a few years back. Some physicians still favor its use; others prefer non-medical techniques to stop milk production, such as ice packs, binders and reduced intake of liquids.

RH FACTOR. If you are Rh negative and the father of the baby is Rh positive, you should be given an injection of Rho-GAM (unless there is a contraindication for this) within seventy-two hours after delivery. RhoGAM is an immune globulin containing a concentration of Rhoantibodies. This serves to protect future babies by preventing maternal Rh antibody production. There are situations in which RhoGAM cannot be given or may not be helpful, so it is advisable for you to discuss all possibilities with your doctor in advance of delivery.

From the delivery table you will be asked to shift yourself onto the stretcher or bed which has been placed alongside it. You will be covered with a blanket, which may or may not be enough to warm you if you experience postdelivery chills. We suggest you try doing Lamaze slow chest breathing (slow inhalation through the nose, slow exhalation through the mouth). This sometimes helps.

In the Recovery Room

The recovery area or special recovery room will be your next destination. There you will remain for an hour or two, depending on your hospital's procedure. If your hospital does not have a separate recovery room, you may remain in the delivery room for this period. If you are awake and there are no medical contraindications, your mate and baby may remain with you for a while—approximately fifteen minutes or longer—depending on your hospital's policy, your physical condition, your baby's condition, how much and which kind of medication you had received, and during which nursing shift you happen to have given birth! If you want to breastfeed your baby and have not already done so in the delivery room, you might do so in the recovery room. Be prepared to experience uterine contractions resulting from the baby's sucking at your breast.

If you are asleep or otherwise in no condition to hold your baby, he or she is taken to the nursery to be cleaned, weighed, and measured (if this has not already been done in the delivery room) and the new father may be able to watch these procedures if he so requests.

While in the recovery room, your pulse and blood pressure will be checked. If your membranes had ruptured prior to admission to the hospital, the nurse will be especially alert to pick up signs of possible infection. Your temperature will also be taken.

FIRMING THE UTERUS. Your uterus will be checked through the abdominal wall to be sure it continues to contract, becomes firm and begins to descend. If your uterus is not firm enough, an oxytocic drug may be given to you to stimulate stronger contractions and the nurse will help it along a bit by massaging the uterus through your abdominal wall. This feels uncomfortable to some women and downright painful to others. However, the procedure only lasts a few minutes and can be made more tolerable if you use some relaxation and breathing techniques. It may be difficult for you to muster up the necessary concentration to force yourself to do a special breathing pattern (such as Lamaze slow chest or slow panting described in "Body Image—Exercise and Diet") and to release your arm, leg, and abdominal muscles, but this does help.

As a result of the abdominal pressure applied by the nurse, you will feel oozing of blood and possibly passage of some clots from your vagina. This will be caught in the large, disposable bed-pad beneath your buttocks, which the nurse will remove from time to time as it becomes necessary. She will also check your bloody discharge (lochia) by observing your sanitary pad approximately every half hour for the first two or three hours after delivery and perhaps once a day thereafter to be sure there is no abnormal bleeding or clotting.

The intravenous usually started in the labor room has followed you through delivery and into the recovery room, affording the medical team easy and prompt access to your veins in case of need. In some hospitals, an oxytocic drug is routinely administered through the I.V. to ensure continued uterine contractions and prevent hemorrhaging. If no I.V. had been set up, you might be given this drug by injection. If you are planning to breastfeed your baby, you might discuss in advance with your doctor or nurse midwife the possibility of breastfeeding immediately after delivery, which is nature's way of causing the uterus to contract. Your baby's sucking triggers the release of natural oxytocins, hormones which con-

tract the uterine muscles. Perhaps you can prearrange a wait-
and-see policy and if your uterus is contracting well enough
from breastfeeding, you can forgo the additional medication.

PERINEAL CARE. Your perineum will be checked for signs
of infection at the episiotomy site. It is slowly becoming accepted procedure in more hospitals to apply an ice pack to the
perineum as a preventive *before* swelling occurs. A routine of
alternating ice applications fifteen minutes on and fifteen minutes off while in the recovery room is usually effective. (Note:
You might need your doctor's or nurse midwife's advance permission recorded on your hospital chart in order for the nurse
to give you an ice pack.)

URINATING. You will be urged to urinate into a bedpan
while still in the recovery room. If you have difficulty urinating, some nurses will wait until you are able to walk around a
bit in order to stimulate natural urination but will usually make
every effort to have you urinate no later than four hours after
delivery. If you have received a regional anesthetic, you might
not be aware of a full bladder due to the numbing effect of the
medication. If you received or are still receiving intravenous
fluids, there is even more likelihood that your bladder will be
full and therefore must be emptied. If permitted, sit upright on
the bedpan with your feet over the side of the bed so gravity
can help you. If you cannot urinate by yourself within several
hours, it is common for the nurse to withdraw urine from your
bladder through a catheter inserted into your urethra. This can
sometimes be an uncomfortable procedure and may possibly
be avoided if you encourage the passage of urine by contracting and releasing your vaginal muscles several times every
fifteen or twenty minutes. These Kegel exercises are often
difficult to do soon after childbirth because you may not have
full sensation in the vaginal area due to the extreme stretching
of the tissues by the baby during delivery and/or the local
anesthetic you may have gotten for suturing of the episiotomy.
If you've had an epidural, you will find it difficult to use these
muscles until full sensation returns. (If you've had epidural
anesthesia, you will be routinely catheterized during and after
delivery.) When you are requested to urinate, try using your
vaginal muscles to do the Kegel exercise, no matter how weak
your muscles seem at the time because this may encourage
urination.

After the Recovery Room

In some hospitals the nurse walks with you on your first trip from the bed to the bathroom and remains posted outside the open door to be sure you don't become faint and fall. In some hospitals, your output of urine is observed and/or measured for twenty-four hours by having you urinate into a special pan within the toilet bowl.

If urination is accompanied by a burning sensation, it might be a sign that your urine needs diluting before it passes through your urinary tract, which is especially sensitive and swollen after the stress of the birth process. Your doctor or nurse midwife may advise you to drink at least two quarts of water each day. This usually helps the burning sensation to go away after twenty-four hours. If burning persists or if you develop a fever, consult your doctor or nurse midwife; you might have an infection.

Urinating may feel strange at first, but each day it will become easier. In fact, you will probably notice a frequent need to urinate as well as heavy perspiration by the second or third day. This is your body's way of ridding itself of excess fluids during its return to the pre-pregnant state. You might want to take a shower and wash your hair soon after delivery and there is usually no reason why you shouldn't, except for the possibility of your feeling weak or faint. This is why most nurses try to postpone your first shower until the second day after delivery when you have more strength.

On your first trip to the bathroom you may be given a "peri" (for perineum) or "irrigation" bottle—a plastic container holding an antiseptic solution. After urinating or defecating, while you are still seated on the toilet, this liquid is to be poured over your vagina and perineum. This is to prevent the possibility of infection reaching the uterus, which is still highly susceptible to invading organisms. In some hospitals, another plastic bottle containing water is used to wash off the antiseptic.

When patting dry or wiping the area after defecating, always remember to do so from the front toward the back—from the vagina toward the anus—never the other way, and drop the paper into the bowl after its use; if more wiping is necessary, use a fresh piece of paper each time. If you do not already have these very important habits, start today to develop them. This prevents the introduction of infection into the vaginal canal, which is always a possibility at any time in a woman's life, not just during the postpartum period. It is wise to teach your daughters to develop this habit while they are young.

If you do not have a bowel movement by the end of the second day after delivery, the doctor or nurse midwife may prescribe a bowel softener (not a laxative) to encourage normal bowel function before you leave the hospital. If you have added fresh or cooked fruits, vegetables, prunes, figs, dates, whole-grain cereals, or bran to your diet, chances are you will not need other aids. If you are hesitant to strain while moving your bowels for fear of adding stress to your perineal sutures, you might be more comfortable if you hold a piece of sterile gauze pad against your perineal area. The external pressure you apply will give your pelvic floor support while you defecate. After, drop the gauze into the toilet bowl and follow the usual hygiene routine—wipe or pat dry (from front toward back), rinse with peri bottle solution, etc.

You will be encouraged to get out of bed within the first twenty-four hours after delivery. Early mobility helps you regain your strength and encourages bladder and bowel function. Until then, while you have been reclining, blood probably will have accumulated in your vagina. Therefore, when you stand up, you might feel a sudden gush of blood which can be frightening if you are not prepared for it. You will be wearing the hospital's sanitary napkin which, although larger than the usual size available in retail stores, may not be adequate for this accumulated flow. As a precaution, therefore, we suggest that you place the disposable bed-pad between your legs, diaper-style, before getting to your feet.

Another word of advice: Do not attempt to get off the bed or walk to the bathroom the first time without assistance! You *might* feel weak or faint from the sudden blood flow, especially after having been reclining for hours; it is usually wise to have a nurse at your side at this time.

Some hospitals provide sanitary napkins which must be worn with panties to which they will adhere when you remove the specially designed strips. Be sure to bring panties you don't mind staining. If the hospital does not provide the self-adhering napkins, you will need a sanitary belt—which some hospitals provide—to keep pads in place.

It is important to follow the doctor's or nurse midwife's instructions concerning sanitary napkins versus tampons. There is less chance of uterine infection if a free flow of blood is permitted; tampons might restrict this flow. When you are *eventually* permitted to use tampons instead of napkins, you may find them difficult to insert. You might want to try applying a small amount of lubricating jelly (such as KY) on the tip of the tampon to solve the problem. Remember to change tampons frequently and do not use overly thick tampons which restrict outward flow and dry the vaginal walls. Be aware that toxic shock syndrome (TSS), a rare and sometimes fatal disease, has been associated with tampon usage. Some symptoms are sudden high fever of 102 degrees or more, vomiting, diarrhea, dizziness, a fine rash that looks like sunburn, fainting or near fainting when standing up. Refer to the tampon package insert for more specifics before using.

It is recommended that you wear the hospital's nightgowns to sleep in so you will spare your own lingerie from the possibility of being bloodstained. Or, you might prefer wearing your own short nightgowns for the same reason. If you prefer wearing longer nightgowns when visitors are expected, be sure to lift the bottom when you sit!

The sutures will dissolve in about ten to twenty-eight days. Do not be alarmed if you notice what appear to be black, string-like fragments in the toilet bowl after voiding; these are pieces of sutures that fall out of your perineum before dissolving completely.

To prevent the possibility of infection of the episiotomy site and to promote healing, be sure to keep your vaginal and rectal areas as dry and clean as possible. Shower daily and change your sanitary napkins often. You might ask your doctor or nurse midwife about using special antiseptic swabs or continuing to rinse with an antiseptic solution after urination and bowel movements when you are home from the hospital and for how long to do so thereafter.

If your episiotomy sutures are causing you a lot of pain, there are ways you can make simple acts like sitting down and standing up much less of an ordeal. If you are sitting and wish to stand up, you should tighten your vaginal, rectal and buttock muscles and hold them tightly while you stand up. After you are on your feet, you can slowly release the muscles and go about your business. When you are ready to be seated again, you should tighten the muscles and sit down while they are still contracted. Once seated, you can slowly release these muscles. You will be surprised at the difference this kind of control can make. Sitting on pillows or rubber tubes only prolongs your inability to sit comfortably without them.

For relief of pain in the perineal area, you can choose from several treatments recommended by many physicians and nurse midwives: 1) Apply ice packs, on for fifteen minutes, off for fifteen minutes. This relieves and hopefully will reduce the swelling. 2) Soak your entire bottom in warm sitz baths several times each day (continue this at home). Some health care providers recommend this even when there is no swelling in the perineum, since it is soothing and promotes healing. 3) Set up a heat lamp a few feet away from your perineum. Keep the heat on for only ten or fifteen minutes at a time. When you are permitted to take regular tub baths, be sure to use clear water with no bath crystals or powders added; these can irritate your genital area if the episiotomy site has not completely healed. 4) Apply gauze soaked in ice-cold witch hazel.

If sanitary napkins cause discomfort or pain by pressing or catching at your stitches, ask if you can use a cream or alcohol compress to soothe the area. Some women find the napkins that adhere to their panties more comfortable than those that are attached to a sanitary belt. Remember to find out if your hospital supplies sanitary belts or if you must bring your own or if the hospital uses self-adhesive napkins. After coming home, while your blood flow is still heavy, you can purchase hospital-size napkins at many pharmacies.

If you are not breastfeeding, you can help stop milk production by reasonably limiting your consumption of liquids (do not stop drinking altogether). If you ordinarily would drink more water to aid your bowel movements, you can substitute fresh fruits and other such foods to stimulate bowel function. You may be advised to wear a tight bra or "bind" the breasts with a towel, sheet, pillow case or diaper wrapped firmly around your chest for about twenty-four to forty-eight hours. Many doctors and nurse midwives prescribe ice packs to be applied alternately for fifteen minutes on and fifteen minutes off and/or a mild painkiller such as acetaminophen (e.g., Tylenol) if you are in pain.

During each day of your hospital stay, a nurse may check your breasts, episiotomy and uterus. In most cases, you will be leaving the hospital on the third or fourth day after a vaginal delivery and on the fifth to tenth day after a cesarean delivery.

The actual coming home from the hospital, with all it entails—dressing yourself and the baby, saying goodby, leaving the building, entering the car, the ride home, the walk from the car to your house—is surprisingly exhausting. It is advisable that you and your baby both go to bed and rest after you are home.

During the first two weeks of your recuperation, climbing steps should be avoided or extremely limited. Lifting heavy objects or moving furniture around should not be done at all. Tub baths are approved by some health care providers only when about four inches of water are used. Douching is *not* advised unless specifically prescribed by your doctor or nurse midwife.

THE POSTPARTUM EXAMINATION

Obstetricians and nurse midwives vary on how soon they want you to return to their office after the baby is born for your postpartum check-up. Some ask you to come in when the baby is six weeks old; some when the baby is four weeks old and again at six weeks; and we know one obstetric practice which sees patients at two, four and six weeks postpartum. You will be checked for general physical condition, weight, blood pressure, urine and possible anemia. Among the other things checked are the size and location of your uterus, the condition of your abdominal wall, whether or not your cervix has closed and whether there are lacerations of the cervix. Your vaginal walls and genitalia will be examined to be sure any tears, abrasions or lacerations are healing and, if you've had an episiotomy, you will be checked for proper healing there. If lochia is present, its color and consistency will be observed as well as any foul odor, which would be a sign of infection. A

Pap test may be taken, although it is not routinely done at the six-week check-up because the cellular structure of the cervix may not as yet be back to normal. This therefore is the reason you may be asked to return six months later for a Pap test. If a test is taken at six weeks, and shows some abnormal cell structure or inflammation, do not be alarmed. This is a common occurrence. A later test will most likely produce normal results.

Your breasts may be examined for lumps that should not be present if you are not breastfeeding. Nursing mothers often notice lumpy areas where milk has accumulated. For the most part, these are perfectly normal. Your nipples should be examined for cracking, bleeding or infection. If contraception has been discussed and a diaphragm or I.U.D. decided upon, this is usually the time for having it fitted and/or inserted.

Once the uterus has involuted, the cervix has closed satisfactorily, bleeding has ceased, the episiotomy (if present) has healed, there are no vaginal or cervical erosions, tears or infections, your breasts and nipples are normal, you are not anemic and the subject of contraception has been discussed, you are usually pronounced healthy and sent on your way with congratulations, good wishes and permission to resume sexual relations. As far as your doctor or nurse midwife is concerned, the postpartum period is over and involution is practically complete.

PROCEDURES INVOLVING THE BABY

Umbilical Cord

As soon as your baby's head is delivered, the doctor or nurse midwife will usually feel for a loop or more of umbilical cord which may be around the infant's neck. Loops of cord occur in approximately twenty-five percent of all deliveries. If it happens and if the cord is loose enough, the doctor or nurse midwife gently maneuvers it out of the way and tries to slip it over the baby's head. This procedure is done to prevent interference with the infant's oxygen supply, which could result from pressure on the cord. However, if the cord is too tight, it must be clamped and cut *before* the shoulders are delivered and the baby must be delivered immediately, since the cord will no longer be supplying oxygen.

Cord Clamping

After the doctor or nurse midwife has seen to your baby's immediate welfare, the infant may be placed on your chest or abdomen with the head kept low (for drainage of mucus) and the body covered (to prevent chilling). The umbilical cord is then clamped in two places near the baby's abdomen and cut between two clamps. The exact moment of clamping varies among both doctors and nurse midwives; some clamp within the first forty-five to sixty seconds after the baby is born; others clamp from one to three or even five minutes after birth; still others wait until cord pulsation stops. The pros and cons of early and late clamping continue to be argued in medical circles. (See "Leboyer Method" on page 70.)

In most hospitals, the cord stump is not covered by a gauze dressing but is left exposed to promote healing. The umbilical cord at birth is bluish-white and moist-looking but its stump will darken as days go by, until it appears almost black before it falls off, on or about the seventh day.

Draining of Mucus

When your baby is born, he or she is usually held with the head lower than the body to encourage the clearing of mucus and amniotic fluid from the upper respiratory passages. In order to prevent inhalation of this matter, the nurse or doctor promptly clears the baby's nose and throat by using either a small rubber syringe (which is squeezed by hand) or a soft rubber suction catheter (one end of which is attached to a mechanical suction aspirator or placed in the practitioner's mouth). If there seems to be a lot of mucus present, the baby may continue to be held with the head down to encourage more mucus to drain from the passages. If the baby has not cried by this time, he or she usually cries or gasps as soon as the mucus is removed. The act of crying can itself aid in the expulsion of mucus.

Breathing and Crying

Since the placenta begins to separate from the wall of the uterus soon after birth, the blood and oxygen supplied through the umbilical cord will soon stop and the baby must get oxygen by way of his or her own lungs. Therefore, if breathing is not initiated on its own or by immediate suctioning procedures, it is usually further encouraged by gently rubbing the infant's back or tickling the soles of the feet. If the baby does not breathe, cry or cough within thirty seconds, additional resuscitation procedures are undertaken. If within a few minutes these attempts do not get the baby to breathe, oxygen must be administered.

Years ago, physicians vigorously slapped the baby's buttocks or the soles of the feet to induce crying. Today, this is considered too shocking to the infant and is no longer routinely practiced.

Skin Tone Indications

If the baby's color appears *extremely* reddish-blue at birth, this may mean that body temperature is too low and the baby needs warming. The baby will be placed in a special heated unit or warmer, or on a table with an overhead heating lamp.

Apgar Scoring

Notation is made of the time of the infant's first breath and cry. The baby's condition at one minute and again at five minutes after birth is evaluated by means of the Apgar Scoring System, developed by Dr. Virginia Apgar. The infant is rated on a scale of 1 to 10; the higher the score, the better the baby's condition. If a baby received scores of 7 to 10 at five minutes after birth, he or she requires no special treatment. If, however, the five-minute score is less than 7, special treatment is necessary. The degree and type of treatment is determined by the seriousness of the baby's condition.

The Apgar Scoring System rates five vital areas: heart rate, respiration, muscle tone, reflex irritability (cry) and color (blood circulation). The infant is given a score of 0, 1 or 2 in each of these areas.

Heated Crib

After clamping of the cord, attention is then given to the delivery of the placenta. If you are awake, your baby may remain with you during this third and final stage of labor, or may be taken by the nurse to the heated crib or table with an overhead heating mechanism which has been set up in the delivery room. The baby is usually placed with the head slightly lower than the rest of the body to aid further drainage of the breathing passages.

At about this time, you may notice that the baby's crying has stopped or decreased. This is normal and nothing to be concerned about.

Suctioning

It may be necessary for the nurse to further suction mucus from the baby. If so, the electric infant resuscitator, the bulb syringe, or the rubber catheter suction apparatus may be used. If mucus is obstructing the nasal passage, the nurse may insert a special small suction catheter into each of the baby's nostrils.

Vitamin K

Many doctors prescribe the administration of Vitamin K to the baby soon after delivery to enhance coagulation. This procedure is routine in most hospitals.

Eye Treatment

If gonorrheal organisms are present in the mother's birth canal, blindness can afflict the newborn. Therefore, state laws provide that the eyes of *all* newborns (including those born by cesarean) be treated with either silver nitrate (followed by rinsing with a warm salt solution) or with an antibiotic ointment such as penicillin, tetracycline or erythromycin. The latter is often preferred because it is not only effective with gonorrhea but with chlamydia infections as well.

Silver nitrate might cause swelling of the eyelids, redness and discharge from the infant's eyes for twenty-four to forty-eight hours. Antibiotic ointment is often preferred over silver nitrate because the incidence of irritation is much lower and, if present, is usually milder. To lessen the possibility of allergy to penicillin, the antibiotic tetracycline or erythromycin is sometimes used instead. It is worth noting that it is mandatory in many states that silver nitrate be used, although antibiotic ointments are preferred by many physicians and nurse midwives. People in the health care field believe the statutes should be changed to include the use of antibiotics. In some states in the country, this change has been made.

Eye Contact and Bonding

Eye treatment is usually done in the delivery room but can be safely delayed for one hour until the baby is taken to the nursery or after the mother, father, and baby have had some time to "look" at each other and some degree of bonding has taken place. Studies have suggested that the newborn can see and look directly at you within the first few minutes after birth and that this is a part of the natural process which helps establish the important bond or attachment between parent and baby. This is nature's way of helping you identify emotionally with your baby. If eye treatment is given during those early minutes, it may blur the baby's vision, making eye contact difficult during the first forty-five minutes after birth—considered by some to be the optimum period of time for bonding to occur. If it is important to you to have the eye treatment delayed and if you plan to be awake for the delivery, discuss it in advance with your doctor or nurse midwife and then remind him or her about it in the delivery room. Of course, if the mother is asleep at the time of delivery or if the baby's eyes remain closed, maternal-infant bonding is delayed. This does not mean that you will not "bond" with your baby; it simply means the process is delayed. If the father is present, paternal-infant bonding can take place.

Infant Massage

In some hospitals, new parent and/or the nursing staff are encouraged to massage the newborn immediately after delivery. Maria Cotty, R.N., co-founder of Special Delivery/Special Handling in New York—an organization formed to teach the benefits and application of infant massage to parents and professionals—reports that a growing number of hospital nursing department directors are requesting information and instruction for their obstetric and pediatric nurses. The staff is taught how to incorporate massage techniques into routine infant care in the delivery room and newborn nursery. Although several minutes of massage several times a day is ideal, no special blocks of time need be set aside for infant massage, according to Mrs. Cotty; it can be accomplished by using specific techniques while holding, diapering, washing or drying the infant. Massage is credited with soothing and relaxing crying babies and minimizing colic, constipation, gas and the necessity of suctioning mucus from the nose and throat. For more information contact Special Delivery/Special Handling, 147–32 15 Dr., Whitestone, N.Y. 11357; or read *Loving Hands* by Frederick Leboyer, M.D. and *Infant Massage* by Vimala Schneider.

Leboyer Method

If you have arranged for a Leboyer-style delivery, the bright delivery room lights will be dimmed moments before your baby's head emerges and the doctor will work with indirect lighting. Imagine what it is like to be in darkness for months and then to be thrust into extreme brightness and you can see why Dr. Frederick Leboyer, French obstetrician and author of *Birth Without Violence,* advocates subdued lighting for the baby's first encounter with our world. Bright lights cause babies to squint or close their eyes; dim lights allow their eyes to remain open and make contact with the people around them.

Following the Leboyer method, your doctor or nurse midwife may encourage a quiet environment for the moments of birth, with those present requested to speak very softly and to minimize metallic and other sounds as much as possible. Your baby will be handled especially gently and his or her back will be allowed to straighten from the curled fetal position slowly, at its own pace. Dr. Leboyer believes it is wrong to hold the newborn upside down by the heels with the back straight. Such abrupt straightening of the back after being in the curled fetal position for so long, he believes, causes trauma to the spine.

When the infant's breathing is established, he or she may be placed on your abdomen or chest, skin-to-skin, and you may be encouraged to soothe the baby, gently massaging the back while the infant gets acclimated to the new environment.

If yours was a cesarean delivery and if you are awake, some hospitals will permit the free use of one or both of the mother's arms to hold the baby skin-to-skin at her shoulder.

A warm bath may be set up near you in the delivery room and the baby will be gently dipped into the water (usually by the father) and held there in an attempt to simulate conditions in the amniotic fluid within the uterus. This, Dr. Leboyer claims, gives the baby a sense of security, because the feeling of being immersed in liquid is a familiar one.

Dr. Leboyer's concepts are quite controversial. Most doctors in the United States refuse to dim the lights, claiming they need all the light they can get to properly evaluate the baby's condition; doctors sympathetic to Leboyer's thinking claim there is no need for the usual glaring delivery room lights and that the indirect lighting they do use is adequate for safety.

Leboyer believes there is no need for the newborn to cry; the usual shock of birth in traditional delivery procedures, he believes, is the cause of most newborn crying—because of the insensitive handling of the baby. A full-grown healthy adult from Earth thrust through space and onto a foreign, cold planet would be shocked, frightened, panicky. And so, new babies, reasons Leboyer, thrust from their warm, wet, quiet, dark, secure environment into the dry, cool, noisy, bright and alien world, are downright shocked. Of course they will flail and kick and scream! Of course, they will shut their eyes to the brightness, etc.

Most doctors in the United States believe that for proper lung development it is a physiological necessity for the infant to cry after delivery. Further, in contrast to Leboyer's belief in delaying the cutting of the cord so the baby will get as much of the placental blood as possible for a good start in life, most U.S. doctors believe the increased blood supply is too much for the young liver to handle and might be a cause of newborn jaundice.

Whether to cut the cord early or late is always a subject for argument. By holding the newborn at or below the level of the placenta and delaying the clamping of the cord, an amount of blood equal to approximately one third of a fetus' entire blood volume is added to the baby's system. Called "placental transfusion," one benefit is that the infant receives additional iron, which *may* reduce the chance of iron deficiency anemia later in infancy. However, this is sometimes believed to be detrimental, as in the case of premature infants. Some doctors believe that *too early* clamping of the cord—before respiration is well established—may be a cause of respiratory distress syndrome (RDS), not an uncommon problem.

As for the immersion in water, most doctors think it a waste of time and confusing instead of soothing to the newborn. After being in the watery environment of the amniotic sac, the baby is exposed to the dry air and is kept in our dry environment while being massaged on the mother's abdomen and while the cord is being cut and *then* is placed in the warm water tub, after he or she has already had some time in our atmosphere. Further, many doctors believe this adds to the risk of chilling to the newborn, whose body temperature is unstable. Others argue that if the water is warm and the baby is covered and dried immediately after the bath, there is no greater risk of chilling than that after leaving the warm womb!

Breastfeeding

In some hospitals, breastfeeding can take place immediately after the birth in the delivery room, if you so choose. In other hospitals, this is delayed until you are settled in the recovery room within approximately thirty to forty-five minutes after delivery. If you've delivered in a birthing room, you stay right there and breastfeed if you like. The father, baby and mother spend time getting to know each other during this early postpartum period.

Some babies take to the breast very easily and immediately upon delivery, while others are not interested and will begin to nurse later on. When trying to interest the baby in your nipple, keep in mind the rooting reflex. If the infant is touched on the cheek or the side of the mouth, the instinctive reaction will be to turn the face in the direction of the touch—nature's way of helping the baby find food. If, in your well-meaning desire to induce sucking, you hold the baby's face in such a way that *both* sides of the mouth or both cheeks are touched at the same time, he or she will be confused and frustrated. Also remember that if you have had any medication during labor, even a minimal dosage of Demerol, sucking may be lazy or delayed. Just relax, let the baby relax, and try again later—perhaps while in the recovery room.

Identification

While still in the delivery room, a footprint (and sometimes palmprint) of the baby and fingerprint of the mother are taken for identification purposes. Should there be any question of identity afterward, this procedure can always be repeated and prints checked.

Before the baby leaves the delivery room, another method of identification is used. Some hospitals use linen tapes marked with the mother's name and hospital number, fastening one to the mother's wrist and the other to the baby's arm or ankle. Other hospitals use a bracelet made of beads spelling out the mother's name; this is placed around the baby's wrist or ankle and sealed with a lead bead; the bracelet must later be cut in order to be removed.

Most hospitals have a special identification apparatus which produces plastic strips previously imprinted with identical numbers for each mother and baby; these are fastened with a permanent lock around the mother's wrist and the baby's wrist and/or ankle—and must be cut to be removed.

Whatever method is used, the baby's identifying bracelet is not removed until the moment the baby leaves the hospital, preferably by the mother, as she identifies the baby as hers.

Recovery Room or Birthing Room: Togetherness and Breastfeeding

In most hospitals, mother, baby, and father can spend some time together in the recovery room or birthing room before the baby is taken to the central nursery. If breastfeeding is desired, the nurse will help you. Some babies will breastfeed at this time, while others will not be interested and in fact will prefer to sleep off their exhaustion after having been born.

If the baby has a fever or is in any way in need of close attention and care, she or he will not be permitted to remain with you during your recovery period. If *you* have a fever, you and the baby will be separated until your temperature is normal.

In some hospitals, there is automatic separation of baby and mother after a cesarean delivery. The baby is taken to the nursery and placed in a warmer and watched for possible signs of infection and respiratory problems, which are more likely to occur in cesarean babies. There are some attempts being made to forgo such automatic separation and to replace this procedure by treating each case on an individual basis. (See "The Cesarean Baby.")

The Nursery

When it is time for the baby to go to the nursery, she or he may be transported through the hall in a warmer. Its use does not indicate any serious condition of the baby.

In some hospitals, the newborn is weighed and measured while still in the delivery room, while in other hospitals this is done in the nursery, where further cleaning of the infant takes place.

Early Feeding Procedures

In many hospitals, the baby is given glucose water when taken to the nursery after birth. This practice is currently being questioned by a growing number of breastfeeding mothers because they believe it is unnecessary and decreases the baby's appetite, thereby minimizing sucking, which in turn postpones the mother's milk production. Besides, the baby benefits more from the colostrum in the mother's breast than from glucose water.

Some pediatricians are beginning to agree with these mothers, while others continue to claim that this "test feeding" of glucose and water (or just water, if requested by the mother) is important to determine the infant's digestive abilities. Colostrum, argue believers, is nature's magic formula which actually *aids* the maturation of the digestive system and helps clear the tract of intrauterine digestive matter.

Later Feeding Procedures

It is the procedure in most hospitals to designate feeding times at four-hour intervals. This is most convenient for the staff. When it's time for feeding, the babies are brought by the nurses to the mothers' bedsides. No visitors are allowed on the floor at these hours, to protect the babies from possible infection. Many hospitals have liberalized their policies to permit fathers to visit at special times (in some hospitals, all day).

If you are breastfeeding, it is recommended that you feed your baby whenever she or he is hungry and not wait for prescribed feeding hours. The reason for this is to allow as much sucking as possible on your breast in order to stimulate the production and let-down of your milk. If the nurses are not willing to bring your baby to you whenever she or he is hungry—assuming this is your preference—you can offer to come to the nursery yourself to feed the baby, provided, of course, you are notified that your baby needs you. If this is difficult for you to arrange, your pediatrician may be willing to ask the nursing staff to cooperate with you.

It is also recommended that you request that the nursery staff not feed your baby the glucose water or formula between regular feedings because this will tend to fill the baby up. Then, when regular feeding time arrives, the baby may not be interested in what you have to offer. This can be one of the greatest deterrents in establishing your milk supply. Again, if you cannot make this arrangement with the nursery, ask your pediatrician to arrange it for you.

Rooming-in

If your hospital offers rooming-in, this usually means that your baby can share your room during specified hours. In some hospitals, you can have your baby in your room night and day. However, most hospitals have modified rooming-in arrangements whereby the baby can stay with you all day but is returned to the nursery during visiting hours, for the night, and any other time you choose. These rules protect the baby by not exposing him or her to visitors and by affording nursery observation and care while you are asleep or out of your room. They protect you by allowing you as much rest and sleep as possible without the responsibility of caring for the baby during certain periods.

Some hospitals offering rooming-in facilities have special mini-nurseries, each housing four babies. Each nursery adjoins a four-bed room for mothers and is staffed by one nurse. This allows each mother to observe her baby at any time through the adjoining nursery window and she may take her baby out of the nursery to feed and hold at any time.

Circumcision

Whether circumcision of male newborns is necessary continues to be a topic of controversy. This operation consists of removing the foreskin—a thin piece of skin which covers the glans, or head, of the penis. If the foreskin is not removed, urine and a substance called smegma can collect beneath it and, if the area is not adequately cleansed, can cause infection. Some religious groups (Jews and Muslims, among others) require that all male infants be circumcised. Aside from religious indications for this procedure, some health specialists believe that circumcision may decrease the likelihood of penile infection and cancer in later life. However, some people choose not to have their sons circumcised because of the small possibility of infection or hemorrhage due to the surgical procedure, because they believe it is painful for the baby and/or because they think that proper hygiene will prevent other difficulties. Some parents make the decision based on what is commonly done in their community, and also, more importantly perhaps, whether the boy's father is circumcised. Growing boys compare themselves to their fathers and older boys compare themselves with others in the locker room.

If you decide to have your baby circumcised and your religion does not prescribe that it be done ritually, the procedure will be done by your obstetrician in the hospital. Within two to four days, if the baby is in good health and weighs at least six pounds, you and the baby will be discharged. Your doctor will give you instructions on the care of the circumcised penis, which usually involves keeping the area covered with sterile gauze pads and antibiotic ointment for several days.

Immediately after circumcision, the penis will appear red and sore. The redness soon disappears and there is rapid healing. Sometimes the wound may be irritated by the baby's diaper and you may notice a bit of blood; this is normal.

PKU Test

Usually on the third day of the baby's life, a special blood or urine test is routinely taken in all hospitals to test for Phenylketonuria (PKU). This is a metabolic disorder which, if undetected and ignored, leads to brain damage. If PKU is present, the baby is put on a special diet which prevents the debilitating effects of the disease from occurring.

Hypothyroid Test

This test is taken from the same spot of dried blood used for the PKU test. It is not yet routine in all states but there is a movement in that direction. This test can prevent severe mental retardation, stunted growth and coarse features due to low thyroid levels, and the condition should be treated before the infant reaches three months of age, or else there is irreversible damage. Hypothyroidism affects about one baby in 5,000 (making it two or three times more prevalent than PKU).

CHARACTERISTICS OF THE NEWBORN

Although a physician will examine your baby several times during your hospital stay, it is a good idea for you to perform your own examination of your newborn. Strip him or her naked, count fingers and toes and reassure yourselves that everything is fine. Have a pad and pen handy to note anything that appears unusual to you. When your pediatrician comes to see you before you go home, ask him or her about the items on your list. Of course, your pediatrician should take careful notice of your baby's appearance, but he or she might not even mention any of the characteristics that are quite common in the newborn but may seem strange to those who have never seen a newborn before. Asking prior to leaving the hospital will spare you anxiety when you arrive home. This chapter can be used as a guide when you perform an examination.

The first sight and sound of your newborn may be very surprising, especially if you had a preconceived idea that your baby would look like you, your mate or the older babies prominently displayed in magazine ads and television commercials. Being prepared for what the newborn will look like can remove unnecessary anxieties during the early postpartum period.

In their first days, babies recover from the experience of birth and learn to deal with living in our world. All their systems must change from intrauterine dependence to extrauterine independence. They must now breathe, eat, digest, eliminate and stabilize their circulatory system, body temperature and hormone levels on their own.

Crying and Breathing

Some babies cry immediately upon exposure to the air— even if only their heads are outside the mother's body; other babies take several seconds longer. Some make very loud announcements upon their arrival; others cry softly. Still others emit a few cries—loud or soft—broken up by long stretches of silence. Some cry a lot within the first few seconds of birth and then suddenly there is no sound of crying for hours. You may notice extreme quivering of the baby's lower lip when he or she cries. If the baby cries hard, you may notice the veins beneath the skin of the head swell. However, no matter how much the newborn cries, you may not notice tears for several weeks.

The baby's first breaths of air take much more effort than what is necessary for normal breathing. This extra effort is required to expand the alveoli, thousands of uninflated sacs in the lungs. Crying soon after birth serves as an effective means of clearing mucus and fluids from the passages. Gradually, by the third day of life, the baby's breathing becomes easier, although inconsistent breathing patterns continue for several weeks.

Each baby has a distinct personality. Some are criers, loud and gusty, eat heartily and noisily, and are very active. Others cry softly and rarely and are generally very quiet and relaxed. When in need, they may whimper and frown, not cry a lot.

A newborn's heart beats about 120 times a minute—twice as fast as an adult's. He or she takes about 33 breaths a minute, also twice as fast as an adult. Breathing and heartbeat can vary widely, depending on the baby's degree of activity and excitement.

Sleepy Babies

The type and dosage of pain-relief medication given to the mother, when and how it was administered during labor and delivery and for how long, all have a bearing on whether or not the medication will influence the baby's condition at birth. Therefore, babies whose mothers were excessively sedated may have more difficulty in establishing good respiration. In some extreme cases, emergency resuscitation efforts must be made. In addition to respiration, the baby's other reflexes (e.g., sucking) may be affected by certain pain-relief medications administered to the mother during labor and delivery. Whether or not their mothers received such medications, many newborns fall into a much needed sleep within fifteen minutes of being born. Others are wide awake for as long as two hours after birth. In the beginning the newborn sleeps about fourteen to eighteen hours each day—hours not necessarily coinciding with *your* sleeping and waking hours.

Weight

The average newborn weighs approximately seven to eight pounds and measures eighteen to twenty-two inches in length. Boys tend to be larger than girls. Because the newborn excretes more than he or she takes in (probably as a result of hospital feeding schedules) during the first three or four days of life, some newborns lose weight. By the tenth day, however, if the baby is eating properly, the birth weight is usually regained.

Head

The head of the newborn is disproportionately larger than the rest of the body, comprising about one-fourth of its entire length. It may appear lopsided, pointy or flattened. This is caused by "molding" of the baby's skull to conform to the confines of the birth canal. The four large bone plates of the skull are not attached to each other; they therefore can be pushed together by the pressure of the birth canal, enabling the baby to fit through this narrow passageway. During birth the bones may even overlap each other, which may explain why some babies appear to have ridges on their heads.

You may notice or feel two soft spots on the baby's head —one above the brow, the other near the crown—where the bones of the skull have not yet fused together. It can take as long as two weeks for the head to assume a normal shape and about eighteen months for the skull bones to fuse together.

If your baby tends to lie in the same position most of the time, one side of the head may become flatter than the other. If the baby is bald, you may notice that the skin of the scalp may be surprisingly loose and the brow may be wrinkled.

Hair

Some babies are born with a thick crop of hair, while others are born completely bald. The fact that your baby has dark thick hair at birth does not mean that it will remain that way. Permanent hair growth at about four or five months may even be blond—and thinner.

Cheeks, Nose, Chin, Forehead and Mouth

"Sucking pads" inside the baby's cheeks may make it appear that the face is somewhat swollen. The newborn has a broad, flat nose and receding chin and jaw—all of which facilitate breastfeeding. The chin and lips often tremble soon after birth.

There may be small raised white spots on the cheeks, chin or forehead. Called milia, these are accumulations of natural oils in the gland ducts. As the glands mature and function more completely, these will disappear.

Eyes

The eyelids may be reddish and swollen due to the pressure of the birth process. The swelling usually disappears in two or three days. In addition, there may be patches of red or purple on the eyelids. These too will disappear in time.

The color of a newborn's eyes is usually grey-blue, although some babies of Negro, Mediterranean or Asian descent may have brown eyes at birth. Permanent eye color usually sets in within the first six months, although it may take longer. Your baby's eyes may appear bloodshot or have a small red spot in the white area of the eye, caused by the breaking of tiny blood vessels during the birth process. This usually disappears in a few days. If the baby's eyes were treated with silver nitrate, as opposed to an antibiotic ointment, you may notice a clear or whitish drainage coming from the eyes. This should be brought to the nurse's or doctor's attention. Simple rinsing with clear, warm water generally clears this up.

One or both eyes may turn and appear crossed or wall-eyed. This condition is normal and usually disappears as eye muscle strength and coordination mature. Newborns *do* see. New babies can focus on a bright red or soft yellow object about eight to twelve inches away. When their eye muscles are more developed and do not easily cross or go outward, babies will stare at and show interest in any object for a while. If the object is moved *slowly* in front of them, they will try unsuccessfully to follow it with their eyes, moving their heads from side to side or up and down. Newborns can tell the difference between shapes and patterns. They usually prefer looking at a pattern rather than solid colors, whether they are bright or dull. And the patterns they dwell on longer are stripes and angles rather than circular shapes. Their focusing on patterns helps them discern between various human faces—each of which has a different facial pattern, but basically the same shape head.

Newborns' eyes are sensitive to light. They squint if the light becomes brighter and shut their eyes tightly and keep them shut if they are suddenly faced with extremely bright light.

Neck

The newborn's neck is short and the muscles are not yet well developed. The head must be carefully supported when the baby is lifted or carried. The nape of the neck may have patches of red or purple which go away in time.

Trunk

The circumference of the newborn's *chest* is smaller than that of the head. Due to the weakness of abdominal muscles, the *stomach* may appear surprisingly large and rounded compared to the very small hip and buttock area.

The *umbilical cord* is shimmery-moist and bluish-white at birth. After it has been clamped and cut, the remaining stump dries and becomes almost black within twenty-four hours. It shrivels and blackens completely by the time it drops off—painlessly—about seven days after birth, at which time you may notice some bloody discharge at the site. If, instead of alcohol, an antiseptic purple dye was used on the stump to prevent infection and promote drying, the surrounding skin may take on a purplish stain.

If the baby is a boy, you may notice an erect *penis* and immediate urination soon after birth. Both are good signs. The *scrotum* may seem especially large in relation to the rest of the baby and some boys are born with one or both testes as yet undescended.

A brownish-red or white cheesy discharge may come out of a baby girl's *vagina* and her *clitoris* may be swollen.

Swollen *breasts* and *genitals* on girl and boy babies are common and caused by the mother's hormones, still in the infant's bloodstream. In addition, the hormone estrogen, which is present in the mother's bloodstream at the time of delivery, may cause a milky substance to appear from the nipples of a girl or boy. Called "witch's milk," this usually lasts for a few days, although it can continue for as long as six weeks. Baby girls may have a bloody vaginal discharge beginning on about the fifth day, lasting for several days.

Because of the restricted space occupied by your baby in the uterus, the *legs* are somewhat bowed at birth and may remain so for many months. Both legs and *arms* are short in relation to the entire body length. Many babies remain in their curled-up fetal position for several days with their arms and legs kept close to their bodies and fists clenched. In their own time they straighten out.

The baby's *fingernails* may be very long and sharp. In fact, some babies are born with scratches on their faces, caused by their own nails while inside the uterus. Sometimes a newborn's thumb is red and wrinkled, indicating that he or she sucked the thumb while still in the uterus!

The newborn's movements are usually jerky and twitching, especially so if he or she was born prematurely. The more mature the baby is at birth, the more smooth the movements.

The newborn responds more often to a high- rather than low-pitched voice. It has been noted that many new mothers

instinctively coo to the baby in a high-pitched tone, to which
the infant responds with body movements in matching rhyth-
mic patterns.

Skin

The skin of many newborns appears almost transparent,
with veins quite visible beneath the surface. Sometimes there
is blood on the skin, especially on the head or buttocks,
whichever part was born first, usualy picked up from the
mother's episiotomy site as the baby passed through the vaginal opening. Some babies have more blood on them than
others.

Sometimes the baby's skin is covered with *vernix caseosa*,
a sticky white substance made of dead skin cells mixed with
secretions from the oil glands. This lubricates and protects the
baby's skin from the constant exposure to the amniotic fluid
while in the uterus, and some believe its greasy character
helps the baby slide more easily through the birth canal. Vernix is thicker on some babies than on others and may not be
apparent on many. Usually, smaller infants have less or none,
while "older" babies who have spent more time in the uterus,
perhaps past their due dates, tend to have more vernix. Depending on the routine of your hospital, the vernix may or
may not be removed entirely; only the excess and whatever
blood and meconium (the blackish first stool) might be present
is wiped off or washed off later in the nursery. Whatever vernix is left becomes absorbed by the baby's skin within the first
twenty-four hours. During the next few days, you may notice
the skin peeling as the result of dryness.

The baby's body may be coated with fine downy hair,
called *lanugo,* which may not even be seen on some babies,
while on other babies may be quite thick and very noticeable,
particularly if it is dark. Lanugo is usually more evident on the
baby's shoulders, back, forehead or cheeks and sheds during
the first few weeks. The presence of lanugo or its thickness
does not mean your baby will be "hairy" later on in life.

Pigmentation

Before the baby's first breath, he or she may appear lifeless, almost like a child's rubber doll, without movement or normal pigmentation in the skin. As soon as breathing begins, however, the skin tone begins to change from a greyish-blue or a mottled red to pinkish or a ruddiness starting in the face and traveling to the rest of the body, although not always to the hands or feet, which may remain bluish for several days. Sometimes a baby's skin tone at birth is purplish or bluish; some have a soft pink tone at the moment of birth.

The natural pigmentation of Negro, Mediterranean or Asian babies does not usually appear for several hours or days. Many of these babies, born with relatively light skin, have areas of dark bluish-black pigmentation, called Mongolian spots, on their backs and/or buttocks, which may last for months or even years, sometimes until the child reaches school age, when they blend into the rest of the skin tone or disappear. Sometimes these spots are present on Caucasian babies but will disappear in time also. Mongolian spots have no relation to Mongolism, a form of mental retardation.

Bowels

The baby's first bowel movement (which might occur in the delivery room) will be a blackish tarlike substance called meconium. Its presence indicates that the baby's intestinal tract is in good working order. If you do not have rooming-in and therefore do not change your baby's diaper during the first three days, you may not ever see meconium, which is usually completely excreted by the second or third day. If the newborn does not eliminate meconium and/or urinate within twenty-four to forty-eight hours, something may be wrong.

As feeding becomes established, the color of the stool changes from black to green-black to green-brown to brown-yellow to soft yellow (if formula-fed) or golden yellow (if breastfed). Bowel movements are loose in newborns. In a few days, the stools of formula-fed babies take on a more characteristic shape and odor, while the stools of breastfed babies remain the consistency of thick soup and have a more acceptable scent.

The baby may have several bowel movements each day. Bowel schedules of individual babies vary widely—some babies have a movement with each feeding; others have one or two a week!

Reflexes

All infants are born with several reflexes which help them to survive and adapt to life outside the womb.

ROOTING. When the baby's mouth or cheek is touched, the head turns toward the side that is stimulated and the mouth opens. This is an instinctive way to seek food. If, however, someone touches or grasps both cheeks at the same time, perhaps trying to turn the newborn's face in a particular direction, the infant may become frustrated and confused. The baby may draw his or her hand up toward the mouth and suck on the fist or finger for several minutes at a time, sometimes even as long as fifteen minutes. This may not be new to him or her; hand-to-mouth activity and finger sucking while in the womb have been observed via ultrasound techniques.

STARTLE or MORO REFLEX. The newborn reacts to a loud noise or quick movement by throwing both arms and legs outward, with fingers and toes spread apart and then bringing them together toward the body. The baby also may begin to cry. If crying is the result of being startled, the baby can be calmed by being turned on the stomach.

STEPPING. If held upright with feet touching a flat surface, the newborn will appear to be trying to walk, making stepping motions. This reflex may remain for about six weeks whereupon is disappears. The baby's legs are not yet nearly strong enough to support his or her weight and should not be encouraged to do so.

GAGGING. The newborn will gag reflexively if too much liquid is taken in. The infant will also spit up mucus to clear breathing passages.

SNEEZING. An irritation in the nose may cause the newborn to sneeze.

DOLL'S EYE. If babies are turned to one side quickly, their eyes will turn in the opposite direction and will then slowly move in the direction in which they have been turned.

GRASP. The baby's hands are usually clenched tight. If an object or a finger is placed in the infant's hand, he or she will reflexively grip it. The strength of the grip may surprise you. If the sole of the foot is touched, the toes will curl downward.

Other Sense Reactions

By the third or fourth day of life your baby will let you know that his or her taste buds are operating—that he or she likes sweet stuff and doesn't care at all for bitter flavors. As early as the fifth day of life a baby will react to strong offensive odors by turning the head away and crying. A newborn's hearing is very acute and he or she can even turn in the direction of a sound as early as ten minutes after birth.

If the baby's foot is uncovered and exposed to cool air and the rest of the body becomes cool as a result, the baby pulls in the legs to warm them; if cold enough, he or she cries and begins to shiver, which increases the blood circulation, helps raise the body temperature and lets you know that he or she is in need of some help. If a blanket or other object covers the face and is causing difficulty in breathing, the baby twists the head from side to side in attempts to remove it.

Jaundice

Newborn babies often develop what is known as physiologic jaundice on the second or third day of life. All babies are born with more red blood cells than they need after birth. As red blood cells die and are broken down by the body, they give off a by-product known as bilirubin which must be excreted. If the liver is not mature enough to filter this waste product from the blood, the skin takes on the characteristic yellow appearance of jaundice. Within a few days, as the infant's liver matures, normal skin pigmentation returns, usually without special treatment. Physiologic jaundice is more common in premature than in full-term infants.

Pathologic jaundice, a more severe condition which may appear within the first forty-two hours after birth, is most often caused by an incompatibility between the blood types of the mother and baby. This must be watched more closely and is more likely to require treatment.

Treatment for jaundice consists of placing the infant under a bright fluorescent lamp—called a bilirubin lamp—for several hours, or even days, with the body completely exposed and the eyes protected by gauze bandages or an eye mask. This lamp helps destroy the bilirubin which the liver cannot yet handle. If your baby is jaundiced, your pediatrician may recommend that water be offered between feedings to help "flush out" the excess bilirubin. In the case of physiologic jaundice, many experts believe that if the mother is breast-feeding, additional fluids are unnecessary. Because physiologic jaundice usually resolves by itself, they believe that encouraging frequent feedings to facilitate the establishment of lactation is more advantageous to the baby than offering water, which may interfere with breastfeeding. In the case of pathologic jaundice, however, additional fluids may be helpful. In the most extreme case of hyperbilirubinemia an exchange blood transfusion may be necessary.

Occasionally, breastfed babies develop a rare form of jaundice which appears towards the end of the first week or during the second week of life. Called breastmilk jaundice, this condition is caused by a substance present in the milk of some nursing mothers. While breastmilk jaundice can last for several weeks, it is thought to be a harmless condition and usually resolves without treatment. Some pediatricians who suspect breastmilk jaundice recommend that the mother stop nursing for twenty-four hours to see whether this causes the bilirubin level to drop, thereby proving the diagnosis. Others prefer to monitor the level of bilirubin and possibly do tests to rule out other causes of prolonged jaundice. In either case, temporary weaning may be recommended as a treatment if the bilirubin approaches dangerous levels.

Early Infant Behavior

Many parents feel guilty when they believe they are not effectively identifying and meeting their baby's needs. A baby who is difficult to soothe, a baby who is jumpy and cries whenever the telephone rings, a baby who makes his or her demands known by loud intense screaming can make life miserable for his or her parents if they do not realize that they are probably not at fault for the baby's response and their inability to change it. The key to resolving some of the difficulties encountered during the postpartum period can sometimes be an understanding of the range of infant responses and how to apply this knowledge to your particular baby and situation.

It is important to know that your baby's characteristic response pattern during the first three months is not necessarily indicative of how your infant will react when he or she is older. For example, some newborns have a low sensory threshold. They are so highly reactive to sensations that common things in the environment like the telephone or doorbell ringing, the texture of a blanket, and the aroma of onions or even perfume cause the baby to feel extreme discomfort. As they gain in experience with their surroundings, many babies get used to and can therefore deal with these sensations.

Newborns also vary in the intensity of their reactions— how frequently and how strongly they cry; how tightly they tense up their bodies and faces to indicate displeasure. As they begin to recognize that there are people around who will help them and as they begin to feel more comfortable about their own bodies, many babies become more relaxed.

How quickly your baby overcomes any initial difficulties is one indication of your baby's flexibility or adaptability. Remember, the world outside the uterus is new for the baby. Some babies adapt more easily than others to new situations.

In the beginning, it's often better for all concerned to identify and accept your newborn's behavioral style and say, "This is the way he or she is *now*. Over time, things will probably get better," and to work to identify and meet whatever additional needs for assistance and support you may have if you are dealing with a difficult situation. Accepting and appreciating your infant as a unique individual is an important first step in being a responsive, effective parent.

It is also important to realize that your reaction to your baby is in part determined by *your* adaptability. If you are a very flexible individual and your baby is inflexible, it may not be difficult for you to conform to the baby's need for a routine that he or she determines. Someone else who is more rigid and intense may have a great deal of difficulty with an inflexible and intense baby. If you are a very quiet, low-key, calm person dealing with a highly reactive baby who in addition is very intense, who cries frequently and loudly (this could be called colic), you may experience less stress in dealing with your child than would another, more intense individual. Again, it is important to realize that your baby cannot be expected to change easily at this early stage of development. While it may be difficult to accept your baby the way he or she is, it is important that you try to do so.

Also, thinking about your baby's individual characteristics can help you make effective decisions about when and how to introduce your baby to new experiences. For example, if your baby is highly reactive, soft lights and a quiet household atmosphere may help. If your low-sensory-threshold infant does not seem very adaptable and is very intense in his or her response, a trip to the circus (or Thanksgiving dinner at your in-laws' with all the aunts and cousins) is not likely to be successful. We're not suggesting you forgo the activity. If it's important to you to go, perhaps you should leave this type of baby with a sitter until he or she is older and can more gradually be introduced to new situations.

Common advice given to new parents to run the vacuum cleaner near the baby's crib to get the infant used to loud noises may or may not work for you depending on your baby's reactivity. If your baby is not highly reactive, loud noises may not be an issue at all. If, however, your baby has a low sensory threshold, the noise may pose some initial difficulty. If, in addition, the baby is adaptable, he or she may gradually get used to the noise and no longer find it disturbing. The advice in this case, to run the vacuum cleaner near the crib, may be effective. However, if your low-sensory-threshold baby is nonadaptable, adjusting to the noise may take longer, if it is ever accomplished at all.

While you can begin to make observations about your baby based on his or her response to being born and reactions in the hospital, be aware that many babies are sleepy for a day or two after birth, even if their mothers received no medication during labor and delivery. This is nature's way of allowing newborns (and their mothers) to recuperate from the rigors of the birth process. Some parents who described their babies as easy-going and flexible in the hospital were surprised to find that the opposite was true once the baby had a chance to "sleep it off." Conversely, some babies find the hospital environment, with its bright lights and constant sounds, so irritating that they cry and thrash. When they arrive home to a quieter, more modulated environment, their parents discover that these babies may be quite capable of settling down and sleeping or observing the world quietly.

CHANGES: IN MOTHERS' FEELINGS, LIFE-STYLE, ROLES, RELATIONSHIPS

Your baby has been born. The pregnancy you may have felt would last forever is finally over. Labor and delivery, experiences you could previously only speculate on and wonder about your ability to handle have been faced and put behind you. The nine-month build-up of anticipation has climaxed.

Some women who were awake for the births of their children experience quiet satisfaction after a job well done are relieved that it is over with and are ready for sleep. Others feel great joy and excitement, are exuberant, bubbly, sometimes giddy, and very talkative—not at all interested in sleeping. Some cry—sometimes from joy, sometimes from relief of tension and/or discomfort, sometimes from a combination of these.

"I was very emotional. I cried a lot and could not believe this beautiful child was all ours."

"I don't know why, I can't explain it, but I just welled up with tears and sobbed. I was so happy, but I couldn't stop crying for several minutes, and even then, I was feeling very emotional and teary-eyed and shaky."

Some new mothers who were sure they knew what they would feel were surprised at their actual reactions.

"I always thought that at that moment I would become very emotional—but was literally speechless. Mark and I both stared at our baby in disbelief, unable to say a word. My first comment was something about how beautiful the umbilical cord was! Once these first moments of shock were over, there was a rapid release of tension that permeated the delivery room."

"Mostly, I was surprised by my lack of emotion—something my Lamaze instructor had warned me about, but which I hadn't really anticipated happening to me. My husband felt the same way. We were very tired and happy that the hard stuff was over and kind of numb—not a bad feeling, just not much of one. It wasn't until the next morning that we really became excited."

If you were awake for the birth of your child and had the support of your mate through labor and delivery, quite possibly you were filled with feelings of joy, excitement, and wonder!

"I was really in awe. Just amazed and shocked!"

"I was totally amazed. Couldn't shake the feeling that this baby was mine."

Some new mothers experience feelings of immediate love for the baby.

"I instantly fell in love with my child and all new maternal feelings arose quite naturally at the first glimpse of my child on the delivery table."

If labor was exhausting for you, you may not feel so exhilarated or have the energy to give anything of yourself for a while.

"I was so exhausted that I didn't even feel like holding the baby—even though I was so happy, since she was a girl after two boys."

Others experience mixed emotions:

"I knew I was saying goodbye to a part of myself. I was no longer a girl and a wife; I became a mother, too. I was sad and yet happy, for a new life was beginning, not only my baby's, but my own and my husband's."

If you were not particularly excited about becoming a mother in the first place or are not happy about adding another child to the family, you may not have adjusted before delivery to the idea of having this child. Your feelings after delivery therefore may be of sadness, quiet and disinterest. Your thoughts and comments may focus on an event unrelated to the baby—like an upcoming move or a planned vacation. This is usually temporary and after you've had time to look at, hold, and get to know your baby, feelings for and acceptance of the child will probably come.

If you've had a long and difficult labor and delivery experience, forgive yourself if you are not overjoyed and immediately interested in the infant who you may consider the cause of it all. Later, in your own time, after you've had a chance to recuperate from the stress of the experience, your interest in the baby will develop.

If you were sedated during the birth, your first recollection of the post-delivery period may be of a figure standing beside your recovery room bed, trying to wake you up. Through the fog of sedation you may recall hearing a voice that seemed to shout at you, telling you the gender of your new baby. "Baby? Did I have the baby yet?" You may have felt a sense of disorientation. "Where am I? What happened?" Because of your medication, you may not even recall a few moments later that someone had attempted to communicate with you and may in fact later complain, "No one even bothered to tell me whether the baby was a boy or a girl."

Many women who were asleep through labor and delivery comment that they feel a time gap—a space in their lives they cannot account for and were not a part of.

You might find yourself asking, as one woman did, "How did I get this baby? Where did she come from?"

You may even wonder if the baby is really yours, knowing full well that there are hospital procedures to prevent accidental switching of infants. For women who did not expect to be sedated, the awakening is more shocking than usual:

"I awoke with a flat tummy. I was confused. What happened to me? Did I have a baby? Two nurses came into my room. One asked me to urinate and the other asked me whether I wanted to feed the baby. I remember thinking, 'I guess I had a baby.' I took the baby in my hands and then I had to ask the nurse if it was a boy or girl! Then I felt guilty: Why didn't I know the gender of my own baby? I could not believe that I had a girl. I even thought that the nurse brought me somebody else's baby. I tried to bring back my memory, but all I remembered was being in the labor room with my husband."

Feelings of disassociation may be highlighted when, upon leaving the hospital with the baby, you must sign a piece of paper stating that you recognize the baby as yours. Of course, the numbers on your ID bracelet match those on the baby's, which logically means mother and baby were identically braceleted before leaving the delivery room. Nevertheless, you may not *feel* the baby really belongs to you. Since there was no opportunity for immediate bonding with your infant because you were asleep, it may take you longer than a non-sedated mother to feel and develop a sense of attachment and belonging to the baby.

Even if you were awake throughout labor and delivery, there may be bits and pieces of the experience which you cannot remember at all, while other segments are very vivid and will probably remain with you always. Many women try to reconstruct their experiences by asking whoever was present—the nurse midwife, a nurse, the doctor, their mate—detailed questions like "What did I say when the baby was born? Did he cry right away? What happened next?" and making statements like "I can't remember being wheeled through the hall or getting onto the delivery table or being in the recovery room or what the doctor said about the baby."

If you are concerned or upset about any part of your labor or delivery, discuss it with your mate and your doctor or nurse midwife. Ask any questions you may have about exactly what happened and why. Any occurrence that was even remotely upsetting should be talked about. Don't let your questions build into fears; ask them and clear your head.

"It took me six months of suffering by myself to get up the nerve to ask my obstetrician if the temporary drop in my baby's heartbeat toward the end of labor meant that he could possibly be brain-damaged—even though he appeared normal and was developing nicely. I was assured that what had happened was usual for that stage of labor. Why did I wait so long to ask?"

"I was embarrassed to ask my doctor questions. He knows I'm a nurse and assumes I know everything. If I had asked why did this happen or why did that happen, I was afraid he'd think I was dumb."

The first time you see your baby, you may be disappointed in his or her appearance, having expected a much better or at least different looking baby. Your fantasy version of what a newborn baby or your baby should look like may not match the real product. The shock may dilute your overall excitement and make you wonder how you really do feel about this new person. It may take a while for you to get accustomed to your baby's face and accept him or her as truly yours.

Feelings of disappointment over the sex of the infant can take away from the joy and excitement of the event of birth. Sometimes there are so many pressures from one's family or mate in the form of openly expressed desires for a child of either sex ("I want a girl...I'll be so disappointed if it's a boy..."), blatantly expressed demands ("You'd better give me a boy..."), or simply assumptions that the baby will be one sex or the other ("It's going to be a girl. I'm sure of it. Look at the way you're carrying...").

If you were under pressure to produce a child of a particular sex, do not take the blame for not coming through. Remember that you are not responsible for the baby's gender. As a matter of fact, physiologically speaking, the father determines the baby's sex and while several books are available that promise their method will increase the odds of producing the gender of choice, to date, science has not discovered a foolproof way to ensure you will conceive the boy or girl you might prefer.

During pregnancy, many women think of the baby as either a boy or girl. This helps give a sense of reality to an individual as yet unknown.

"Sometimes I thought of my baby as a boy and dreamed about the things we'd do together. Other times, the baby was a girl and I thought about how that would be."

If you have allowed yourself to *expect* a child of a particular sex, however, you stand a 50 percent chance of being disappointed. You also may be very disappointed if you have just given birth to your second, third, or even fourth child of the same sex and desired a child of the opposite sex. It's important for you to see the baby for what he or she is: an individual with a distinct personality, a human being who has come into your world to be reared, loved and enjoyed, and who really doesn't know what all the fuss about sex is, anyway. The baby's gender and physical appearance do not change the fact that this child is yours and *needs* your care and love.

Some women experience a feeling of loss in the days following childbirth. Even though they know quite rationally that they have actually gained a child, there *is* a loss after birth—of bulk, of weight, of the live being which they had carried within them during the months prior to delivery. They may miss feeling the baby move inside them and the exclusivity of the relationship they had with their child while it was in the womb.

If you had a comfortable and happy pregnancy, you might especially feel this sense of loss and miss the extra attention your pregnancy had brought from your mate, friends, relatives, doctor and even strangers. You may miss the feelings of anticipation you had before giving birth, the telephone calls from interested friends and neighbors.

All too often after delivery there is a shift in the attention of others away from the new mother to the new baby—at a time the new mother especially needs to feel a continuation of the loving care and concern she felt during pregnancy. Visitors rush to the hospital nursery to admire the baby after briefly congratulating the new mother, and although most new mothers do enjoy unwrapping and admiring presents, they are, in the final analysis, gifts for the baby.

To some degree, your emotions are affected by your hormones, and after having a baby your hormonal levels are "out of balance" for some time. Until leveling off is achieved, while in the hospital and even after you come home, they may play havoc with your emotions. You may find it difficult to deal with the resultant sudden changes in your mood at unexpected times. From feelings of joy and contentment with your new baby and the role of motherhood, you may swing to feeling sad or teary-eyed or even break into crying jags without warning or explanation. Minor happenings may assume gigantic proportions to you. The smallest upset may bring floods of tears. Even a happy event may set you off in sobs.

Understand that a word, gesture, statement or even your own thoughts—which ordinarily would pass almost unnoticed—now, during postpartum, may trigger exaggerated responses.

"In the hospital I cried a great deal. The whole painful

experience was just overwhelming. I more or less expected it, since I was depressed the first two times also."

You might feel embarrassed at these sudden outbursts and not know how to handle the situation. You may be completely at a loss to understand or explain your strange behavior and, as a result, feel frustrated, out of control and foolish on top of it all. You may think you are losing your mind, recalling horror stories of women who did just that after having a baby. You are *not* losing your mind, just losing your cool, if you start taking this behavior seriously. The horror stories you may have heard about women after childbirth were probably about isolated cases of severe postpartum psychosis—not the normal baby blues or waves of depression which commonly occur to many women. Postpartum psychosis is another matter and occurs so infrequently that it is unlikely to happen to you. The best thing to do about postpartum emotional swings is just to let them pass.

Perhaps you can get into the habit of saying aloud or to yourself, the next time you feel weepy or whatever: "Here we go again. As soon as it passes, I'll be back to myself." And as soon as it passes, do go about your business. If it takes a little longer to pass, help it along by calling a friend, getting out of the house, or doing whatever you can to elevate your mood. If you dwell on each incident—in your own head or in discussions with others—it only tends to make matters worse. Accept the fact that you need no particular reason for your reactions. It does not necessarily mean that you're unhappy or miserable. It probably and very simply means that your hormones—those very powerful and influential substances within you—have not yet returned to their pre-pregnant levels.

While still in the hospital, you might find yourself thinking more about your physical discomforts and recovery than other aspects of new motherhood. The full realization of being a mother and all that goes with it has probably not yet reached you because the *total* responsibility of the new child is not yet yours. There are still nurses and doctors twenty-four hours each day in whose charge the baby is. In fact, you *and* your baby are in the care of others. When you arrive home, babe in arms, that blanket of security is lifted and you are then more likely to fully digest the reality: "This is it; the baby is all mine; I have no one else to run to." If you have the help of a baby nurse or other person for a week or so, these feelings may occur when she leaves.

"It hit me that if I can't stop her crying, or get her to drink, I can't just ring a bell for a nurse to help me!"

The sudden shock of total responsibility for every decision you will make regarding this baby—knowing how to handle every possible situation—can seem overwhelming.

"I am responsible for this brand-new human being who is totally dependent on me!"

Or, the reality of an additional child in your realm of responsibility can seem overwhelming: "I thought she was beautiful and precious but was scraed to death realizing that I had three children who depended on me."

Many couples today share the responsibility of childcare whether or not the mother works outside the home. Accepting the responsibility together and sharing their reactions to being totally responsible for another human being gives these couples the advantage of being able to understand and support each other through this adjustment period.

While initially you might react with feelings of warmth, love and the desire to care for and protect your child, as the days pass and you realize what caring for the baby involves, you might be surprised at some nagging feelings of resentment rising within you. Such total dependency means you must sacrifice some portion of your freedom. You will be called upon to give of yourself, your time, your resources, in order that he or she will thrive—quite a challenge! In addition, there may be fear: "Will I be a good mother? Will my baby love me? Can I adequately care for the baby? If something happens to me, who will care for the children? If I go back to work, how will I manage everything?" Being a mother, having to give of yourself when you're least likely to feel physically up to giving because you're so exhausted can be very difficult. You may resent the baby's need of mothering. "I know she needed to be held and cuddled and soothed. But I had this strong feeling, as I was rocking her in my arms, that *I* needed to be held and rocked, too!" New mothers need mothering themselves, during the early postpartum period.

And in return for all your giving and caring, during those early weeks, you receive very little response from the child in return. The baby may cry a lot, sleep a little, and completely confuse you about his or her nutritional needs. When you finally figure out what's wrong and the crying stops, the baby doesn't even smile to thank you. The problem with this is that most of us are used to a lifelong system of almost immediate rewards. We get good marks on tests, "A's" on report cards, raises and promotions for our efforts in the work world, or at least pats on our backs from our employers. Even the Mayor of New York City needs to be patted frequently as Mayor Ed Koch's famous "So, how am I doing?" plea for applause indicates. It's a question we all need answered but the final results on our parenting efforts are not in for *years*. Furthermore, the baby continues to get the gifts, the attention, the company and the love. People are visiting the baby, and asking how well the baby is doing, not you. Even your mate may come home, scoot right past you with a quick, "Hi," and head for the baby! Although he may try to give his love and attention to the woman who has just brought forth this new person, amidst the kissing and kudos for her part in this, his attention is understandably drawn to his issue: the new baby!

Feelings of jealousy toward my own child? you might ask yourself in horror. Yes, possibly. And more common than you might think.

"I wasn't pregnant anymore. That was over. Finished. Not being pregnant put me in a different category. I wasn't the star anymore. The baby took center stage."

"I'm the mother of the child everyone is so interested in. I'm the one who carried him in me all those months and just went through the physical and emotional stress to give birth. Don't I count anymore?" If you are experiencing such thoughts and feelings it is wise to express them directly, instead of harboring them within you and letting resentment and hostility build. Set aside time to sit quietly with your mate and tell him what your feelings are without laying blame. For example, try saying, "I feel left out of your life. I feel neglected and unloved and uncared for," instead of "You don't care about me. You ignore me. All you care about is the baby." When words come out in an accusatory way, your mate's reaction will usually be one of self-defense instead of feelings of caring about you.

Perhaps your mate goes to the other extreme and ignores the baby entirely. He may want to sit and unwind a bit after returning from his day away from home before going to the crib and may not appear to be as interested in all aspects of the baby's care and development as you are. He may not hold or play with the baby frequently and you may view that as a rejection of your child and maybe even of yourself. Perhaps he is the kind of individual who finds it difficult to respond to a baby until the baby is older and more responsive. It is quite possible that when your child begins to smile, lift his or her arms to be picked up, or begins to walk and talk, your mate will become more involved.

"I couldn't stand the fact that he'd come home, put his feet up and ask about dinner. Before the baby was born and I was still working, we got to unwind together. I need time to relax too and I resent feeling less important than he is."

"One thing I had to cope with after the birth of our child was my husband's not being as excited with the day-to-day achievements of the baby. Since I am involved twenty-four hours a day, I see every little new thing the baby does, but the father is much more removed. I had feelings at first that maybe he didn't love the baby as I did, but now I feel that he just needs more time to get to know the baby."

It is important to tell your mate that you are concerned about his lack of attention to the baby and discuss what you are both feeling so you can avoid misunderstandings.

"When my husband first came home, all I wanted to do was hand him the baby and rest for a while. All he wanted to do was read the newspaper. We realized that we both needed "unwind" time after a long day. After all, I was working as hard as he was even though I was at home. We agreed that he would get time to relax first and that after dinner, he would take over completely—the baby, the dishes, etc. to give me a chance to unwind."

You may be aware and perhaps surprised that your mate is feeling jealous of the baby and is resentful of all the attention the infant is receiving from you!

"My husband, who was so excited about having a child became jealous and angry."

This is a very common reaction from new fathers and is quite understandable. Now that the baby is part of your life, the time you spend with your mate has to be lessened to some degree. It may be difficult for you to deal with his feelings of jealousy. You may find yourself trying to justify the time you spend with the baby and feel upset that your mate is jealous of his own child who needs the attention for survival.

"Why am I having this additional hassle? It's bad enough that *I* resent all the extra time taken away from the two of us. Who needs *him* to be jealous on top of that? Besides, the baby is *his* child as well as mine!"

"Caring for my baby comes easy, but there is jealousy on my husband's part, which I do understand somewhat. The baby does demand much of my time and attention, which my husband had dominated before. We talk about his jealousy and try as best we can to change his feelings."

"I resent my husband's jealousy, but I realize that I had time to prepare for my child during pregnancy—feeling the baby grow, visiting my doctor, and experiencing the actual physical emergence of my child. My husband, although he was actively involved in my pregnancy and childbirth, could not quite grasp the feelings that I, the female carrying the child, could. He was first faced with the responsibility at our child's birth. There was a sudden shock. Being a male in our society, he was not as prepared as I was for parenthood."

On the other hand, you and your mate may spend much time *together* playing with and observing the baby's actions and expressions, marveling at the miraculous work of art you both took part in creating. Nothing seems as beautiful as the sight of a sleeping child (especially to exhausted parents) and the knowledge that you are bringing him or her contentment and survival. All your baby's achievements—the first smile, rolling over—are eagerly anticipated and shared.

It's only natural that topics of conversation between you and your mate will revolve around the baby's daily growth and development, eating and excretory habits, sleeping and crying period, likes and dislikes. Other topics will probably include your lack of sleep, your mate's lack of sleep, your feelings of frustration and resentment, and your reactions to the baby's grandparents' advice, concerns and grievances! For variety, there might be mention of baby photographers, diaper services, disposable diaper prices, convertible baby furniture, and whether or not to hire a babysitter and, if so, which one —and if none is available, what to do. And even when you find other topics of conversation, you'll probably find yourselves inevitably talking about the baby again. This is to be expected; for the first few months the baby becomes the focal point of your lives. Realize though that as you both adjust to new parenthood it is important to begin to get back in touch with old interests and/or develop new ones in addition to your interest in the baby. As the baby gets older, you will be able to resume more of your usual pursuits. For now, identify the one or two outlets that are integral to your sense of self and develop strategies to include them in your life. You may find that in the early months juggling time to include the activity selected involves giving something else up, but if you choose wisely, it will be worth it. And as a side benefit, your conversations will broaden to include your other interests as well.

"When the baby started sleeping through the night consistently, I resumed swimming. I had to get up early in the morning to be back before my husband went to work—but it was worth it. I feel so much better about myself."

"I had always wnated to learn another language. I registered for a Hebrew class at my local adult education school. It was only one and a half hours away from the baby each week, but I found a tremendous carryover of good feelings. I found it easy to practice what I learned as I went about my routine the rest of the week and felt very accomplished at each class."

Preparing and enjoying a simple dinner with your mate will not be the cinch it was before. You may both have to accept cold soup and dried-out steak in the early weeks as a matter of course or resort to sandwiches. One of you might hold the baby while the other eats and vice versa—hardly the epitome of togetherness, and certainly grounds for frustration. Some babies choose to be fed every night at their parents' dinnertime. Even changing the dinner hour does not fool them. One new father we know had to cut his mate's food so she could eat with one hand while supporting the baby with the other. He was lucky; his mate was breastfeeding and had one hand free. If she had been bottlefeeding while she fed the baby, he would have had to feed her!

The home you may have taken such pride in furnishing may begin to resemble a laundromat with clean clothing on one chair, dirty on another. There simply may not be enough time in the day to care for yourself and a newborn, keep a spotless home, plus sort out laundry. You'll both have to temporarily adjust to the fact that only the most essential (if any) housekeeping should be done during your first weeks at home.

The subject of resuming sexual relations can be extremely difficult to handle. Even after you've been given the "go-ahead" by the obstetrician, you may not be ready to do so.

For several weeks or months following childbirth, and possibly until after your first menstrual period, your sexual desire may be absent or minimal because of the lowered estrogen levels in your body. Lower estrogen levels are also responsible for the decrease in vaginal secretions, which can cause sex to be very uncomfortable or even painful. Fear of pain may cause your vaginal muscles to constrict instead of relaxing for easier entry. This combination—lack of desire, lack of secretions, constricted vaginal muscles—may cause you to worry about your sexuality. Because it is known that sexual desire triggers the release of vaginal secretions, you may mistakenly presume that the lack of secretions means you no longer desire your mate. Your ability to achieve orgasm may also be delayed several months—possibly even a year.

"I wondered what was wrong with me. I wasn't particularly interested or passionate, but I wasn't exactly disinterested. Yet I was dry. So how interested could I be? I worried about this until I found from talking to other mothers that they had the same problem."

"I lost my ability to respond. When he used to just touch me, I'd get all tingly and wet. Now, he can do all sorts of things and I just lie there feeling so guilty and hoping I can drum up some reaction."

Be assured that vaginal secretions are governed by the hormonal balance in your system and will return to normal after estrogens and progesterones level off. This may take several weeks or months and generally lasts longer in breastfeeding than in bottlefeeding mothers.

Your doctor may prescribe an estrogen cream lubricant or you can purchase a tube of surgical lubricant (such as KY jelly), which is clear, odorless and water soluble, prior to resuming relations. Applying some to the penis and vaginal opening will ensure more comfortable and relaxed relations until natural secretions return.

You may be sore and fear that the first sexual experience after delivery will be painful or uncomfortable, especially if stitches had been used to repair an episiotomy or tear in the perineum after the birth process.

Some women experience extreme pain when attempting intercourse. This may be caused by an accumulation of nerve endings inadvertently brought together by the suturing of the episiotomy. It may take several weeks until the supersensitivity disappears. In extreme cases this condition may require surgical correction. More frequent intercourse helps desensitize the area, but because the initial entry is so painful, patience and understanding are essential from both partners.

"At first after the birth I was afraid. I still am, but then I take hold, relax, forget and enjoy. Because of the sharpness of his entering me, it hurts, but only if I expect it to and tense up." (Three months postpartum)

You may be putting off the first postpartum sexual encounter because you believe that your vaginal tissues were so stretched by the birth of your baby that you are too loose to satisfy your mate or be satisfied yourself. You can help the situation by doing the vaginal tightening and releasing exercises (Kegel) several times a day (about five to ten contractions at a time) to improve muscle tone and control. During intercourse you can use your ability to contract these muscles for greater mutual pleasure.

You may worry about becoming pregnant so soon after giving birth or about not being healed enough for intercourse. You may be reluctant to resume relations during the time you still have the lochia flow. Your breasts may be heavy and very tender and you may feel embarrassed if your nipples leak during intercourse. You also may worry that your child will awaken and interrupt you—not a groundless fear.

"The baby has radar. She knows when to cry."

If your baby sleeps in your room, you may be concerned that your lovemaking will awaken him or her and that it might be damaging for the child to witness you having intercourse. If you have these fears, consider making love in another room. There is no known reason to limit lovemaking to bedrooms. If, however, there are other children in the house, and there is no other room in which you could have guaranteed privacy, it might be wise for you to move the baby to another room while you relax and enjoy lovemaking in your bedroom.

If you are breastfeeding, you may have mixed feelings about your mate fondling or orally stimulating the breasts which now provide nourishment for your baby. You may have a conflict between the pleasurable sexual feelings that accompany nursing and the sexual feelings accompanying your physical relationship with your mate. Some women, breastfeeding or bottlefeeding, feel it is "wrong" or "dirty" to use the same passageway the baby came through, for sexual gratification. Your inner conflicts may not be simple to put into words, but may be related to a sense of right and wrong, good and bad, clean and dirty. Motherhood and sexuality may not, in your estimation, mix. They may represent entirely different things to you. If you feel this way, be assured that as you adjust to new parenthood these feelings usually change.

You may not understand how your mate can desire you sexually; you may feel unattractive and not sexy at all. Not fitting into regular clothes during the first weeks after delivery can be very demoralizing. The flabiness of your abdomen and the fear that you will never look attractive again may not be conducive to good feelings about your body. Explaining your feelings to your mate can go a long way toward easing the tension between you, if resuming sexual relations is being hampered by your self-image at this time. If your sexual drive is diminished and he knows that your lack of interest is in part due to your negative feelings about your own body and not wanting to be seen by him as yet, he can better handle an extended waiting period. He would understand that your feelings have nothing to do with him and he could help you through this period with warmth, understanding and dimmed lights.

Your decreased interest may simply have a lot to do with just plain fatigue. Exhaustion from a demanding day with a new baby, plus the emotional stress that accompanies new motherhood and the knowledge that your sleep will be interrupted during the night ahead, is hardly a basis for sexual desire. All your creative energies will probably go into devising ways to catch up on sleep. Sex may not be a viable priority until you are feeling more rested. Some mothers also find that on some days they have given so much of themselves physically to the new baby—holding, rocking, nursing, etc. —that they are all "touched out" and want their bodies to themselves for awhile. Holding and cuddling their mates may not even seem appealing.

Whatever your feelings, it is important to discuss them with your mate. Be sure to explain why you feel the way you do so you can help alleviate feelings of rejection on his part and he can better understand what is really happening.

"He really thought I lost all interest in him and that it was all over between us. I found it hard to tell him that I was scared that sex would hurt. I thought he'd think I was just making up excuses."

"I was embarrassed to tell him that I didn't believe he

could still be sexually interested in me after seeing our baby born. He told me that he wants me more than ever now."

"I felt so ugly with my flabby stomach and my stretch marks that I didn't want him to look at me. It was a turn-off to me and I thought it would turn him off. When I finally was able to explain my feelings, he convinced me that he loved me and didn't give a damn about my stretch marks. I loved him for it."

"There was still some vaginal discharge several weeks after delivery and I felt uncomfortable, actually embarrassed about it and unsexy because of it. Luckily he pressed me into talking about it, telling him what really was holding me back. What a relief, he understood my feelings."

Even if you feel rested and interested enough, there remains the question of when!

"I always have and still do enjoy the sexual relations we share. Only problem is finding time to do it!"

"By the time the baby is off to sleep for the umpteenth time, the dinner dishes are finally cleared away (at midnight), the half-sorted laundry is pushed from our bed onto the floor, and I plop under the covers and breathe a sigh of relief—who has the strength or the interest or the physical desire for sex? There is just nothing left for me to give, or want, except sleep!" (Three weeks postpartum)

"After several weeks of 'wanting' but not finding time for sex due to exhaustion, the baby crying, etc., my husband and I met en route to the bathroom one morning at 3 a.m. I looked at him and said, 'What do you know? We're up and he's asleep. Let's go!'"

Many other women find that they feel much closer to their mates after childbirth. This closeness is accompanied by a strong desire for physical expression and some women find that lovemaking has never been more frequent or more satisfying than since childbirth.

"I feel sexier somehow and more of a woman. And sex is absolutely fantastic. Our lovemaking was always rewarding but now it's a total experience." (Eleven weeks postpartum)

After a broken night's sleep and a 6 a.m. awakening, you may crave an hour to go back to sleep and if you are not working outside the home, you may be fortunate to be able to do this. You may consider yourself more fortunate than your mate in this respect because he cannot go back to sleep; he must get out of bed and get to work. On the other hand, you might find yourself plagued with jealousy for his being able to leave the house each day without the baby and assorted paraphernalia, without being responsible for the baby's needs all day and without feeling confined, limited and cut off. He gets a daily dose of a change of environment, a relief from baby care and escape. He might not be overjoyed at the thought of going to work each day, but you may be jealous of what you view as a more interesting existence. You may feel angry as the door closes after him and you are left with a sense of abandonment as you face the day's cares alone. You may feel bad about not having the time or energy to fulfill your mate's needs, not to mention your own. You may feel torn apart by "all the people" who need you: the baby, the baby's father, your other children and of course, yourself! Sometimes the tension can be overwhelming.

"When I go through a whole day with not even five minutes to myself, that's the day I just sit down and cry my eyes out. I feel so helpless, stuck, frustrated."

"How can I make everyone happy and still save some happiness for myself? I can't do everything: feed the baby, diaper her, wash her clothes, love her, sing to her, walk with her, clean the house, shop, cook the meals, mend the clothes, wash, iron, spend time with John, have sex with John, go out with John, and take care of myself and my needs like shower, dress, eat, wash my hair, put on cosmetics, read, pursue hobbies, socialize. It's too exhausting."

If you are staying home to care for the baby, you may find you are resentful because your mate who works outside the home does not understand why you are so exhausted and can't finish everything you want to get done each day. Try to understand that it may be difficult for him to imagine exactly what your day is like without having experienced it himself. Hearing about and living through are very different experiences. Some mothers find that if they leave their mates with the baby on a weekend or holiday and take a "day off," their mates gain a renewed appreciation for what happens at home in their absence.

It is possible that at this time you may even be having doubts about your relationship or marriage. If you are having second thoughts, be assured that this happens to many couples at this time. Emotions run high in both new parents. There are excessive and sudden pressures and concerns descending upon them within a brief time span. The baby's cries can be irritating and the demands unceasing. And much as you may want to talk to your mate, you may not have much uninterrupted time for discussing problems. All this in addition to the physical realities of your recuperation process and prevailing exhaustion do not provide the best possible circumstances for good feelings to thrive.

If you find yourself thinking your relationship is one huge mistake, try to postpone any further thoughts about it. This is not the time. Allow yourself at least six months to get past the initial adjustment period. No one should make judgments or decisions about major issues when in a depressed or agitated state of mind.

"I wanted to leave but I had no place to go. I felt that he was inconsiderate, uncaring, unhelpful and downright nasty. I felt all alone in my concerns and caring for the baby—our baby—and felt that he couldn't care less! But now that the baby is over two months old, things have gotten easier. I can see now that a lot of my feelings had to do with not getting enough sleep and both of us were irritable. And I can understand now that he had some strong emotions working on him too! I'm glad I didn't leave; it would have been a mistake."

We believe that the postpartum period is one of the crises of life. Relationships can be on very shaky ground. Major decisions should be postponed until solid ground is restored. Then, when hormones have leveled off, when the baby is letting you sleep more, when the shock of new parenthood is past, when the pressures are reduced, when you're feeling more mobile and self-assured and after you've both read this book, perhaps participated in some postpartum discussion sessions and gotten past the critical period, you can better discuss your differences, your feelings, your relationship and your future.

On the other hand, many couples say they have never been closer than since the baby's birth. They express feelings of love, closeness, togetherness and oneness which they attribute to having shared in the creation and the birth of the child—especially those couples who witnessed together the first moments of their baby's life.

During the first days home you may discover that your baby cries and we mean cries—not only when hungry, but even after being fed, diapered, cuddled, soothed, rocked, and loved. He or she may cry at the same time every day (often in the evening) or at different times each day. As a new parent, you may find that even when your baby is not crying, you have become so accustomed to hearing cries that you imagine them. You may discover that you can't even enjoy a shower because you think you hear the baby. However, if you check, more often than not, the child will be fast asleep.

If your baby cries a lot, your feelings of concern and sympathy can lessen as your stress tolerance is reached. It is well known today that continual noise pollution from airplanes, electronically amplified music, loud motors, etc., is bad for your ears and entire organism. It can affect your state of mind and your digestive processes. Crying is noise; incessant crying is constant noise and a constant source of stress to those present, usually the parents. If, in addition, there are other causes of stress occurring at the same time—a dog barking, the telephone ringing, the T.V. blaring, other children crying, yelling, whining, talking, demanding attention—the recipient is unquestionably under a lot of stress. Since stress tolerance levels vary, each individual reacts differently to a given situation. But a woman who has just undergone childbirth and whose hormones are out of balance, who is fatigued from the birth process and lack of sleep, who may be overwhelmed by being responsible for a new human being and possibly is shocked by the dramatic changes in her life-style, who is perhaps unsure of her abilities to cope, who is possibly being pressured by relatives to do things their way, whose bottom is sore and back is achey, and whose body image is not what she'd like, may not have a high level of resistance to the stress of noise. You may find you especially cringe when the baby cries in public or when friends or relatives are visiting. "I used to worry that people would think that I wasn't a good mother if I couldn't get him to stop crying."

It might help you to think of the baby's cries as pleas for help, an indication that he or she is hurting and unhappy, not just being difficult. Tuning in to what the infant's feelings may be, what the cause of the crying may be, or where the pain or discomfort is located can help to diminish your annoyance and increase your care and sympathy, which in turn can lead to quieting his or her cries.

Many new mothers find the most difficult thing to deal with is a baby who cannot be soothed and continues to cry for long periods of time. After trying all she possibly can on her own, perhaps consulting with other new mothers and perhaps even calling her own mother, she usually, eventually and quite reluctantly, calls the pediatrician for advice. Such advice varies with the physician's philosophy on child rearing. After establishing there's probably nothing physically wrong, some say, "Let the baby cry for twenty minutes; pick up the baby; check the diaper; give the baby some water; try holding, rocking, cuddling again, and then put the baby back and ignore the crying or you'll have a spoiled child!" Others blame nutrition: "Maybe the baby's not getting enough nourishment. Let's try solids." Where does the new mother place blame? Usually on herself. "This is my child. Why can't I figure out what's wrong?" There's nothing quite like the feeling of guilt and frustration the mother of a constant crier experiences even though intellectually she knows the crying is not her fault. After all, she's done everything she can.

If the situation continues, day after day, night after night, either constantly or on and off, the incessant crying and loss of sleep take their toll on the new parent. If she follows the advice to let the baby cry it out, she may be unable to go about her business, sleep, eat or even think while her baby wails. If she holds the baby constantly, she may worry that she is "spoiling" him or her. In either case, she may become nervous and upset. Her helplessness at being unable to soothe her own baby may even turn to anger and many a new mother reports having yelled at her baby, "Why don't you stop crying! Stop it!"—some while holding the baby and angrily shaking him or her. Some feel an urge to strike the baby. Then come the feelings of guilt or shame for having behaved this way toward a helpless and innocent child.

"There I was. I couldn't believe it was happening. I was hovering over this poor creature and yelling at her to shut up and be quiet and stop crying! All the while I knew how ridiculous it was. My screaming only frightened the poor little thing and she cried more, this time in terror! Of me! A wave of guilt and pity came over me and I picked her up and held her tight and we were both crying."

"I couldn't stand the crying after a while. I wanted to throw him out of the window! But I didn't, of course. And what prevented me was being able to tell my husband, not holding the feelings in."

If you ever have feelings like these, understand that they

are normal manifestations of anger. Know that there are self-help groups such as Parents Anonymous, consisting of parents who have had the same destructive feelings toward their children. They want to help you redirect your anger away from being hurtful to your child. While it is normal to have occasional destructive feelings toward your child, it is not normal to act on them by abusing or neglecting your baby. Also, vigorously shaking the baby may be harmful. Because no one can really know if and when he or she will ever need to use it, we advise that you have the phone number of such a group easily accessible, even posted near your telephone. If you ever feel you may actually take out your anger directly on your child, call the number at any hour, twenty-four hours a day; no one will ask for your name. Your call can be a lifesaver.

Such groups help you to understand that you are not a bad person for having negative feelings toward your baby. They help you learn to get your negative feelings out in ways that do no harm to the child or to you. The simple act of letting off steam to the person at the other end of the phone, even yelling and crying out your frustrations in total confidence, can do wonders for your family life.

You may find yourself very concerned and possibly feeling guilty about the conflicting emotions you might be feeling toward your new baby. "I love him so much and then wish him out of my life. How could I really love him if at times I resent him so much?" You may be having second thoughts about whether or not you made the right decision about starting a family after all and now that you've had the baby, it's too late to change your mind. This gives rise to feelings of being trapped within a situation that's out of your control. After all, you cannot change the fact of the baby's existence. You cannot change the fact of motherhood; you are a mother! Such conflicts are very common. It might help if you reflect on the range of feelings you experience in your other relationships. For example, you don't constantly feel the same emotions day after day toward your mate, close friends or your own mother. The feelings may range from love to annoyance to anger to love again and each emotion may have different intensities at various times. This is also true in your relationship with your new baby.

Some new mothers have frightening dreams or fantasies involving harm to their babies.

"I used to dream about leaving her at the supermarket in a

carriage parked outside and just walking away."

It is common for women to experience negative feelings toward their babies at one time or another. After all, it is precisely the baby's entrance into the world that changes a woman's life so drastically and causes some degree of inconvenience and discomfort.

You cannot constantly feel only love and warmth toward your child. You can, humanly, feel other emotions as well and still be a caring and loving parent. After all, how can you feel love toward someone who is depriving you of sleep, interrupting your meals, demanding your constant attention, playing havoc with your relationship with your mate, etc.?

Usually, the loving feelings predominate and you somehow manage to get through difficult days and nights in a series of weeks which become better as the baby adjusts. Talking about your feelings with another mother who may feel the same way can do wonders to minimize your resentments and whatever guilts result.

You may even find yourself laughing about a tense situation: "You mean your baby was up at 3 A.M. also? They must have made a pact in dreamland to awaken and make us miserable!" Many things are accomplished when you are able to express your feelings to another woman in a similar situation. You are letting off steam and not hurting the child in any way; you can learn some new strategies to help handle problem situations; you will realize that you are not unique, that other new mothers have similar feelings and problems.

In the early weeks, feelings of inadequacy and insecurity are common. "Am I doing the right thing? Am I holding him correctly? Will she slip from my hands in the bath? Will I be a good mother? Will I know when he's sick? Should I let him cry or pick him up? What gave me the idea I could be a mother? I can't handle all of this . . . I'm not ready." These feelings are often intensified by advice and comments the new mother receives, not only from friends and relatives, but even from strangers on the street. How can you feel secure in your decisions about your child when, while strolling on one street, someone tells you the baby is overdressed and on the next, another stranger tells you he or she is underdressed? This can extend to a feeling of hesitancy to call the pediatrician with questions and problems that can arise. "I was afraid to sound stupid." "I hated to call and ask a question I knew the doctor had been asked a hundred times." When in doubt, call!

Infant care and parenting are not inherited abilities. We all must learn the skills involved. As a new parent, you may never before have been exposed to new babies. You may have to learn how to care for a baby by caring for your own. Pediatricians should recognize this and expect extra calls from new parents. If your pediatrician belittles your concerns or in any way makes you feel foolish for calling, you are using the wrong pediatrician. After all, could you drive a car the first time you tried? Similarly, don't expect to be an expert diaperer, bather or burper the first few times you try. You need time and practice. You will have questions and make mistakes along the way, but this should be expected.

"On the fifth day I felt really down. I felt insecure about everything. I wasn't sure of being a mother. I wasn't sure of being a wife. Just all depressed."

"I put myself into a tizzy wondering if this is right or that is right. It is incredible, though, how easy the actual care of the baby is. I was quite concerned before his birth about bathing, dressing, when will I know he is ready for shoes, etc. But it has been relatively easy. This may sound really silly, but I was even worried about when do I send him to school. Do the school authorities notify you or tell you in the papers?"

Some parents are overly concerned with following "the rules" and doing everything "the right way." One couple put it very well: "Babies should come with instructions." Both husband and wife are highly trained professionals who believe their education and experience prepared them to feel competent in making decisions in the business world. The world of babies was another matter! No one offers "licenses in parenting" and some of us become parents having had very little contact with infants and children. Despite some of the disadvantages of life a generation or two ago, the presence of the extended family provided love, support and the opportunity to "apprentice" as parents by observing other close family members. For the most part today, we no longer have this opportunity.

Some parents become so concerned with "getting it right" they forget to relax and follow their instincts. In their tensions, they lose many of the feelings of joy and wonder which could reward them for the anxiety and sleepless nights of new parenthood. If you truly need a "new parenting rule" to guide you, the only reasonable one we've come up with is this: If the decision you are about to make is motivated by love for your baby, if it's not physically or emotionally harmful to the baby or family members, and if it might work, it's probably the right thing to do! Don't worry about "shoulds" and "shouldn'ts." The only "should" is "Love and respond to your baby to the best of your abilities."

Another feeling often expressed is a new mother's reluctance to admit that she needs help to get through the early weeks. "What's wrong with me? Why can't I handle this? My mother was able to do everything herself when she had me and my brothers and sisters!" Don't compare yourself to anyone else. Your abilities and needs are yours alone and if you need assistance, accept your need as a fact—a need, by the way, that most new mothers share.

Some individuals need to lead highly structured lives in order to feel comfortable. For them, the inability to control the environment and make daily procedures conform to how things "should be scheduled" can cause great anxiety. However, the frequent occurrence of unpredictable events and the inability to rigidly schedule the day are common characteristics of the postpartum period. Babies cannot be regimented.

Whether you are highly structured or flexible in your approach to life, if you're feeling "out of control," it's important to take the time to categorize the things you *can* change about your new life-style and the things you will have to accept. For example, if you are feeling anxious because it is vitally important to you to have an orderly home and you can't manage this without help (few can in the early weeks), if at all possible, hire someone you can supervise to do at least some, if not all, of these chores. Identifying and taking charge of what you *can* control may help you to accept the aspects of your life you cannot directly influence (like the baby's behavioral style).

There is no reason for you to prove to anyone, least of all yourself, that you can do it all alone. By determining to so prove yourself, you will be fighting against great odds. In your efforts you can overburden yourself and therefore be even less able to cope. This can lead you to feel you are incapable of handling your responsibilities and make you unsure of yourself as a person, leading to depression.

You may be surprised at all the energy and time this tiny little being takes out of you and you may find it difficult to reconcile your expectations during pregnancy of what life with a baby would be like with the realities of new parenthood.

"How can one five-pound, eight-ounce bundle be the cause of such disorder, disharmony and exhaustion? It's unreal."

"After working twelve years and being thrown into the baby world: Shock! Other mothers somehow don't admit they're unhappy or walk the floors with their baby! I wish I had some hint that there's another side to the buttons and bows and booties. I'd have been better able to handle it."

"All during my pregnancy people would only say pleasant things about raising children. I am not complaining, but I just didn't know about the difficult times."

Your baby's behavioral style probably has a lot to do with your feelings toward him or her. If the infant sleeps a lot, wakes up for feedings and goes back to sleep without much fuss, why wouldn't you be delighted with your new parent role? Such babies seldom disturb their parents' routines and when they do, their simple needs are easily satisfied and the parents in turn are pleased with their ability to cope.

You may even be able to follow the maxim that says, "Sleep when the baby sleeps" and be fairly well rested. But, on the other hand, you may discover that newborn babies do not sleep all the time. In fact, your baby may sleep for surprisingly brief periods of time, hardly enough for you, the new mother, to lay your weary body down for a rest, close your eyes and begin to drift off before there are cries demanding another round of attention. And even when the baby does sleep, how can you nap when every insurance company, baby photographer, friend and relative calls to offer services and congratulations. And if you have a toddler around in addition to the new baby, there is certainly no way for you to sleep when the baby sleeps. At night, when the baby is finally asleep, the laundry folded and the dishes done, you may find you're so tired that you're not interested in anything at all. You may just want to go to sleep.

Babies who sleep away the days are likely to be up at night. During the first six weeks or so, it is unusual for new parents to sleep through a night without awakening several times to respond to the baby's cries. And once you do fall asleep, it might be so lightly that if the baby's breathing pattern changes, you may find yourself wide awake and dashing to the crib to see if everything is all right. Many new parents, especially new mothers, seem to wake up several times each night during the first weeks just to check the baby. Breastfeeding mothers often awaken moments before the baby in anticipation of an early morning feeding; and if the baby is bottlefed, someone must get the bottle, perhaps heat it and feed the baby. You can see, therefore, why we continue to emphasize the importance of getting your rest whenever you can.

If your baby is costing you a large part of your most prized postpartum possession—your sleep—you may be surprised at the intensity of the negative feelings you have for him or her. As you drag your weary body from your warm bed for yet another time during yet another night to answer the impatient cries, do you feel only great love and desire to please? Or is it possible you're feeling some degree of annoyance, resentment or anger? And when you do, do you feel guilty?

"Sometimes when I get very upset with the baby, I feel ashamed because, after all, what if something happened to him, it would be on my mind the rest of my life that I complained about him. I think one of the most important things would be for parents to understand their feelings of anger, despair, etc. are normal and that everyone experiences them. It's how you deal with them that's important."

Being extremely fatigued is a common complaint of new parents. When you are too tired to think or do things that you ordinarily could do very well, you may begin to lose faith in your abilities. You may think you'll never be able to handle the task of motherhood in addition to your other responsibilities and find time for yourself and your interests. Understand that during this period any estimation you make of your capabilities is being made on the basis of your tired, lackluster, perhaps physically uncomfortable self. You must keep in mind that fatigue is a state which may last several weeks or months but does improve when the baby, according to his or her own timetables, begins to sleep through the night, and you and your new baby get to know each other and settle into a routine. By the baby's sixth week, many new parents report a welcome change to greater normalcy and rest and most parents feel "settled in" by the time their baby is three months old.

Any change in your life requires a time for adjusting to it; so it is during the postpartum period. As time goes on, you will become better organized. You will be able to accomplish more. For now, rest when you can and do *only* the bare minimum of housekeeping or none at all!

The first few times your baby does sleep through the night you may awaken with the frightening thought, "Was I so tired that I slept without hearing her cry?" or even "Is the baby okay? Why is she so quiet?" Breastfeeding women often awaken painfully aware that they missed a feeding during the night. The engorgement and wet nightgown due to leaking breasts are signals that something different has occurred. Of course, concern turns to relief when you realize what really happened and that your nights will gradually be more peaceful from now on.

With time, the continued release of your tensions and frustrations and the baby's settling into a better schedule, you will probably find yourself feeling resentful less and less frequently. Some mothers marvel at how much more they enjoy their babies when they are two or three months old and recall how differently they felt during the early weeks.

"My feelings about the baby keep getting stronger. It's hard to believe you can love someone so much."

"I seem to love her more each day. It's a growing thing."

"I enjoy every waking hour and miss the company when she is sleeping."

Although it is important to get out of the house as a family and as individuals to help avoid the negative feelings of isolation and resentment, going out to a movie, restaurant, visiting or even shopping is no longer the simple process it was. You now have to consider the additional person in your midst— and the paraphernalia that goes along with him or her. Or, if you decide to go without the baby, you've got to hunt down a reliable babysitter. You can't suddenly decide to meet your sister for lunch and the theater in the city or your mate for dinner and dancing at your favorite restaurant. You must consider the baby's needs as well. If you do decide to find a sitter, you may have to deal with conflicting feelings. You might think that wanting to "leave the new baby," or "get away from the baby" means you don't love the baby, don't like your new role of motherhood or are shirking your responsibility. These feelings might be reinforced by relatives or friends who pressure you by direct word or innuendo to be a "good" mother and not leave the baby with "a stranger" (i.e., anyone other than the person giving the advice!).

Your feelings of wanting to get away from the baby from time to time may be in direct conflict with your general desire to care for your child. "If I want to escape," you might ask yourself, "why did I choose to have this child in the first place? Maybe I made a mistake. Maybe I'm not cut out to be a mother."

Motherhood need not be an all-or-nothing role. You *can* be a mother, have other needs and require periods of time away from motherhood. In fact, such periods can work to enhance your positive feelings toward your baby by giving you relief from the responsibility of childcare.

Remember, the rearing of a child, although it has its joys and compensations, is nevertheless a difficult task. Most people working full-time jobs need time off, rest periods, coffee-tea breaks and vacations. Motherhood is no exception. In order to do your work the best possible way, you might need the same benefits most full-time jobholders need.

On your initial trip out, you might experience strong regrets and anxieties while you're away because you may believe that no one knows your child as well as you. But chances are when you return you will find all went well and your anxieties were groundless.

The social life you enjoyed before the baby also changes. Can you imagine staying out to the wee hours now, knowing that the baby will be up and waking you at 5 or 6 A.M.? What about entertainment expenses? Are you now in a position to afford the theater *and* a babysitter? And if it's difficult enough to arrange a simple home-cooked dinner for just the two of you, you might not want to chance having friends over to dinner.

After the baby your conversation with other adults may change drastically. Your childless friends may not truly be interested in the minutiae of childcare; yet in the early weeks you will probably have a need to discuss these things. Also, you may not have had the time to read a current bestseller, see the latest movie, read the newspaper or even watch television and therefore may find it difficult to take an active part in conversations.

Although there is a definite need for new parents to talk about their recent birth experience and the new baby, it is important to be aware that this tendency to talk only about parenting can become a habit and remain a part of you. If you don't want to fall into such a mold, make a conscious effort to develop other interests, partake of different activities and make new friends—all of which will help you have a more interesting and well-rounded life. If you so desire and it's convenient, take the baby with you. You and your mate will benefit from such new dimensions within your relationship, your growing child will gain from an interesting family life and you will feel more comfortable at social gatherings when you can converse on several topics in addition to childbirth and childrearing.

If you choose to stay home with your child and not return to work, you may find that some people look down on those in your situation, valuing only those jobs that bring financial compensation. When asked what you do, you may find yourself saying, "Oh, I'm just a housewife," apologizing and putting yourself down as a reflection of society's viewpoint.

This attitude deserves rethinking on your part. If you have chosen to stay at home and give most of your time to childrearing and homemaking because it feels right for you and meets your particular needs and beliefs about parenting, this is your choice—and if it is right for you and your family, it is the right choice.

On the other hand, there will always be people who look askance at those new mothers who choose or need to return to work. The implication is that such mothers can't be "good" mothers if they are away most of the day. Even a mother working part-time will occasionally hear someone say, "Well, at least you have *some* time with the baby." A common comment regarding any working mother is "Why did she want a baby if she couldn't wait to get back to work?"

There are several answers to this: She may for financial reasons need to return to work. She may have discovered, after the fact, that being at home caring for her baby and home on a full-time basis is not what she thought it would be and she needs other avenues of fulfillment in her life. She may have planned to return to work all along, knowing in advance that she wanted to combine childrearing with another career.

If you are pursuing outside interests and/or are working

full-time or part-time, you may find you have very little—
other than new-baby talk—to share with other women who
are staying at home and not leading your life-style. You may
in fact, find men's conversations more appealing and may be
aware of resentment from those women present who cannot or
do not join in your areas of conversation.

If you do decide to return to work, it is best, if at all
feasible, to postpone returning for several months, for a
number of reasons. First, this will give you and your baby the
best possible opportunity to establish the very important bonding process considered integral to the development of a close
mother-child relationship. Second, as we have said, the first
few weeks are not representative of what new parenthood is
all about. If your decision is not being made on the basis of
financial need, you would do well to wait until the chaos is
over and you've had some time to adjust to being at home
before you decide to go back to work.

If, however, you are committed to returning to your career
or feel strongly that staying home is unbearable, do go to
work as soon as is reasonably possible, but realize that it is
important to at least take the time to recuperate from the
childbirth process (six weeks to three months at a minimum).
It is equally important to arrange for good, consistent childcare—preferably an individual who shares your views about
childrearing issues or a day care center or day care home that
is open to the opinions and beliefs of parents. Whenever possible, you should ensure that the situation you arrange can
continue for several years to provide your child with a consistent caretaker.

Money is tighter after a baby is born, especially if one of
you leaves the nine-to-five world to stay home with your child
and suddenly you must adjust to living on one salary. You may
find yourself thumbing through cookbooks for new ways to
prepare hamburger instead of steak, and casseroles may become a new way of life. You may suddenly find your wardrobe doesn't reflect the latest styles. Dining out may be at fast
food places instead of fancy restaurants and you may become
an authority on the location of inexpensive movie theaters.
Your funds might be so low that you have to turn down invitations to parties because you can't afford the sitter and feel you
are imposing if you bring the baby.

The new mother who had contributed to the total family

income before the birth of the baby may be accustomed to having money available from her own salary to do with as she pleased. Now that the family income is coming from only one source—not her—she finds herself in a very uncomfortable position: that of having to ask for every dollar she needs. For a woman who is used to this as a way of life, it may or may not pose a problem. However, for a woman who is not used to it, this situation can be psychologically demoralizing and is a potential troublemaker in the relationship. It's like "going to Daddy" for money, perhaps even feeling obligated to justify the need.

Both partners should discuss this—preferably in advance —so that a suitable arrangement can be worked out to avoid the growth of resentments and hostilities. Now that the new mother is spending her time caring for their child, her investment in the marital relationship is not any less in value than his and its benefit to the family unit is unquestionable. Income—although brought in by one person at this time—is nevertheless *family income* and should be regarded as such. Perhaps an agreed-upon sum of $75 or $100 can be kept in one place in the house for easy access by either partner. Assuming the relationship is built on trust and fairness, each partner can feel free to dip in when necessary for daily expenses, gift buying or whatever and let the other know when funds are getting lower. This way, feelings of total dependency, inadequacy and inferiority—resulting from "having to ask"—are removed.

Many of today's women are entering motherhood at later ages than ever before—in their late twenties and early, mid and late thirties. Quite often this means that such a woman has been in the working world for five, ten or more years and has gotten accustomed to the particular life-style that goes along with it. Even so, many such women happily anticipate the change from "going to work" to "staying at home." They look forward to the change of pace which they believe offers a welcome relief. Many find peace and contentment and are pleased with their decision to stay home with the new baby.

"A major concern of mine was how I was going to react to leaving work after twelve years. I was not as upset as I thought I would be. Perhaps I was ready for motherhood."

"I never realized previous to motherhood what a joyful and

exciting and totally wonderful experience a baby is. I feel no regrets about the life-style I left behind. It was my choice to assume a new life-style and I have taken it on with all good feelings."

However, many other women are shocked by the enormous contrast between one way of life and the other.

"I must admit it is entirely different than I thought it would be. Much more difficult. I thought my time home with the baby would be similar to days I stayed home from work for whatever reason. On those days I would perhaps sleep a little later, read when I wanted to, eat lunch when I wanted to, go out when I wanted to. In other words, do whatever I wanted to, whenever I wanted to do it. Near the end of my working career, I remember telling everyone how I was finally going to be able to read the whole *New York Times* every day. Well, my son is several months old and I'm only now getting through part two of the local paper!"

"Once I realized that life was not going to be like it was before, I was okay. I had naively thought everything would be the same, but it wasn't. Again, once I relaxed and realized, hey, this is the way it's going to be, I was fine. I can't imagine life without him now."

One of the first realizations that things are different is the shock of being totally cut off from other adults. There are no people to talk to or work with, no mental stimulation as a matter of routine, no planned lunch hours or coffee breaks.

Some women complain of how easy it is to lose touch with the styles people are wearing, the latest controversial books and topics of conversation, etc. Feelings of isolation and abandonment are common.

"I had my first baby at thirty-one and I live all the way out in the suburbs. My worst problem is that I feel so stranded."

If most of your friends are still employed in jobs outside the home, your opportunities for telephone socializing to help break up your day (considered a necessity by most new mothers) are limited. You can't expect a friend to enjoy a friendly chat with you when her job demands her attention.

If you are new in your neighborhood, have no friends or relatives accessible and/or haven't met any other new parents in your community because you've been traveling to and from work until now, you probably will experience strong feelings of isolation. Being alone with your baby each day without adult contact for a period of weeks and months can contribute to depression and negative feelings toward the baby.

Perhaps you have adjusted easily to your new life-style because it suits your needs better than your previous way of living or because your previous way of living was more demanding and stressful or less fulfilling. But if your new life-style comes as too sudden a change and you have difficulty adjusting to the many differences between the old and new, you may question your intelligence or sanity for having chosen this way of life. You may spend parts of each day comparing your before and after daily life routines and find yourself longing for the old nine-to-five job (even if you hated it) or just one day of being able to go to work and not worrying about dinner and the baby when you get home, because life now is so much more complicated. This is a common reaction during the early weeks at home.

It is understandable occasionally to yearn for the times you were without the cares and responsibilities of new parenthood.

"I yearned for my working days, in the office, I mean, when I had a place to go everyday, get up, get dressed, put on makeup, feel like a person. My working friends envied me because I could relax (ha!) at home in jeans all day and do my own thing and not work for somebody else! Not work for somebody else? All I do is work for somebody else! And when I say all these things, I feel guilty because I wanted the baby and now that I have him, what do I expect? It's not his fault. I just didn't know what it would be like, that's all. If someone had told me some of the negative things instead of only the nice things about having a baby in your life, maybe it wouldn't have been such a shock!"

If you wish, you can return to work full-time or even mix motherhood with a part-time job, nights, weekends or whenever you can leave the baby with his or her father or other responsible person; or you can work from the house and not have to leave the baby at all. You can become involved in local organizations, take a course, join a club, see shows, visit museums, form or join a discussion group, with or without the baby, as you choose. Being an individual apart and in addition to being a mother can fill your need so that motherhood doesn't continue to give you "trapped" feelings and you can better enjoy the time spent as a mother.

"Working outside the home has made both jobs more rewarding. It makes motherhood more pleasant."

"Immediately after our daughter's birth, my husband changed jobs. I have found this very hard on me for his hours are long—twelve to fourteen hours a day—and when he comes home, he is tired. I understand this, but there are times I resent being home alone with the baby for such long periods. To combat this loneliness, I have joined a dance class and a bowling league. The contact with new and different people is invigorating. It's just returning home to an empty house and having to wait until seven or eight to see my husband that drives me up a wall."

It may hit you hard to realize that being a parent means you are no longer just a partner in a one-to-one relationship. You must adapt that relationship to include all that was before: love, sex, friendship, etc.—plus all that comes with a child. It may seem overwhelming and you may worry about your ability to achieve this. As long as you and your mate are aware of the goal—adding parenthood to your roles while keeping your original one-to-one relationship alive—you can strive toward it in your daily lives and eventually achieve a happy result.

At the same time, other relationships are being formed: between mother and baby, father and baby and possibly sibling and baby. As the relationship between the two original partners undergoes change, so do the relationships between the new mother and her parents and the new father and his parents. In addition to whatever roles the two of you have played in other people's lives—sister, brother, daughter, son, grandchild, friend—you are now looked upon as parents. Particularly outstanding may be your own realization that you are no longer just somebody's child; you're also somebody's parent! And while this may be a tremendous adjustment for you to make, it can be a huge adjustment for your parents as well.

Most new grandparents are thrilled at the birth of a grandchild. Three generations in a family give a comfortable feeling of continuity. Grandchildren can be enjoyed and then handed back to the parents when grandparents get tired, bored or fed up with diapers. They have the joy of seeing a child grow and develop without having to get up at 3 A.M. or deal with colic. However, sometimes a new baby so closely resembles the way you or your sibling looked as an infant that your parents have a sense of déjà vu. It can be hard to pry the spitting image of your brother from your mother's arms! Because many grandparents are so captured by the new progeny, they are especially concerned with every detail of his or her care. This frequently manifests itself in the form of comments, suggestions and demands to the new parents.

"Nothing I do is ever right," many new mothers complain.

Everyone feels older when a new generation gets its start, especially new grandparents. While the beginning of a new life is a momentous occasion, it also marks a milestone on the road toward the end of life. This may bring up issues and feelings you may have thought were long resolved. Know, for example, if one, or both, of your parents is no longer living, this loss will be felt more acutely during the postpartum period—by the remaining parent as well as by you.

"I wanted to tell my mother I finally understood what she had gone through when I was born and thank her for all the love she gave. But she's no longer here and although she died several years ago, I'm feeling her loss all over again."

Your parents and in-laws may tend to evaluate their own job of parenting by how many of their tenets you follow in raising your child. If your methods differ drastically from theirs, they may see it as a personal rejection. Although child-rearing methods change drastically over the years, it's sometimes hard for grandparents to realize that the methods they so strongly believed in and were encouraged to follow are just not being utilized today. To better understand your parents' feelings, try to envision your small newborn twenty years from now. He or she may welcome your advice, maybe even seek it out and you might have this same relationship with your parents, but your child will want to be as free to make his or her own choices as you do now. Give a few moments of thought to how you might feel about this. Will you quietly allow your children to make their own mistakes, as you probably expect your parents to allow you to do now, or will you follow the natural urge to warn them? We are not trying to make a case for grandparental control, just for an understanding that they are parents too and still have the same concerns about you and your baby that you feel toward your newborn.

You may believe your parents and in-laws are holding on to their image of you and your mate as children because to acknowledge that you've grown and are parents yourself would mean they've lost you or lost control over you. Many women, especially of previous generations, had no career beside motherhood and pursued no interests outside of the home and family. For some of these women to acknowledge the maturity and independence of their children means to acknowledge their own growing feelings of lack of importance. The new parents have a conflict: While they have a very strong need to feel accepted and respected as adults by their parents, they have an equally strong need to be nurtured and supported emotionally as well! While many new parents take offense at suggestions or advice that even hint at the idea that their parents see them as children, they still want and need expressions of love and concern from their parents!

"When I had my baby, I needed my mother more than ever before in my life—to hold me and comfort me and tell me I could handle being a mother. I needed her to baby me! But at the same time, I needed her to acknowledge that I was an adult and knew what I was doing. It was a crazy feeling!"

While many couples find their parents and in-laws "controlling," others have a different concern. "I was especially hurt when I heard other friends complain about how overbearing their parents were," commented one new mother. "Mine ignore us. They won't babysit—ever. They barely acknowledge the baby's existence."

Are these grandparents really disinterested? Maybe. Some admit to wanting to make up for lost time, to enjoy life now or to get back at the cause of all their deprivation. "*We* couldn't go out, so why should they?" What these grandparents fail to realize is that they're missing out on one of life's great experiences—helping a new family get its start, sharing the joys of new baby growth, experiencing love and adoration from and for their grandchildren. The most fortunate families have grandparents who strike a happy balance—helping out after the baby is born and remaining available for help, advice and love on a flexible basis thereafter.

It's important to have the freedom to choose your own way through new parenthood, but it's equally important to realize that new parenthood is fraught with new sensitivities and vulnerabilities. We are oversensitive at times because we are feeling insecure. We're short-tempered or intolerant because we're overworked and tired. Just as our parents fail to communicate their true sentiments at times, and we have difficulty interpreting what their comments really mean, so we too fail to let them know what the real issues are for us in nonjudgmental language. And all too often people are afraid to voice their concerns for fear of being intrusive or offensive, leaving grievances to build and tensions to mount.

And what about *your* grandparents? A fourth generation in the family is exciting, but it tends to draw attention away from the elders' problems and concerns, at least temporarily. In a society that tends to brush aside its older people, loss of attention is a serious concern. Great-grandchildren can also be the final confirmation that your grandparents are indeed old.

"When I was pregnant, my grandmother was afraid that I and other relatives and friends would become so involved with my new baby we would forget to visit her. She lives in a home for the aged and was accustomed to having me visit often. She realized that this might not be possible after the birth of my baby and felt fear and an increased sense of loneliness and isolation. Fortunately, she was able to tell me her feelings and I was able to reassure her that she would not be forgotten."

This grandparent's generation grew up in a period when the entire family lived nearby, spent much time with each other and consulted with the older family members before making decisions. Today's nuclear families seem alien to those of her generation.

If you have brothers and sisters, especially if they are significantly younger than you, they may view the baby as an intruder in a close and special relationship which had developed with you over the years. They may fear you'll no longer be available for long talks and spending time with them. They may resent the extra attention the expectant mother gets and feel jealous of the gifts later showered on the new child.

"During my pregnancy, my sister openly admitted she was jealous. She is seven and a half years younger than I am and was concerned she wouldn't be special to me anymore, after the baby was born. She was reluctant to relinquish her role as the youngest in the family. Fortunately, we could talk about it!"

It is also important to realize that all your relatives may not be overjoyed watching your baby hold court at a family gathering. New babies certainly are appealing and new parents feel a strong sense of pride watching their offspring goo-gooed at, but your recently engaged cousin who wants to show off her ring and discuss wedding plans or the cousin whose four-year-old is saying and doing the cutest things is likely to feel left out and even annoyed.

If you sense feelings of anxiety or concern from members of your family, try to let them know that you're aware of and understand their feelings. The granddaughter mentioned earlier told her grandmother how excited she was about the impending birth because she was thrilled her grandmother was still with them to watch her new child develop. Letting jealous relatives know in advance that you'll still be concerned for their needs and giving them a sense of importance can do wonders when your schedule does become tight and you can't fit in a visit. If this does happen, you might tell your brother or sister how much you yourself miss the time you used to spend together. By all means make your own decisions about whom you'd like to visit or invite and how often, be true to your own needs, but keep in mind that a little understanding will go a long way toward keeping family resentments to a minimum.

If you are exposed to petty family squabbles, your stress level may be reached earlier than usual. It may be necessary for you, for example, to announce to your family that you do not want to hear any of their arguments, that you refuse to play the role of mediator or judge, and that you insist on having peace and quiet in your home. Your physical and emotional welfare depend on it. "Even after the name was already on the birth certificate, I still had to hear their arguments about which side of the family to name the baby after."

Your welfare and your family's welfare also depend on your not overextending yourself by taking on additional responsibilities such as the care of another person—perhaps an ailing or older relative—during your postpartum period when *you* need to be cared for! If at all possible, temporary arrangements should be made for this person's care.

As new parents, you both may have conflicting ideas and feelings regarding childcare. If each of you have been brought up under widely differing doctrines of childrearing, there are bound to be discussions and probably arguments and hurt feelings, especially if there is pressure from family and friends to do things their way. Keep in mind the supersensitivity of the postpartum period and postpone heavy discussions and decisions concerning childrearing with your mate. Whatever decisions must be reached—involving immediate care such as holding or feeding the baby, whether or not to let him cry, etc.—they must be discussed at a quiet time (not while the baby is screaming or when a third person is presenting his or her views) and in soft, loving, understanding tones from both partners.

Thoughts of having a baby in your life usually evoke the happiest of images: holding, cuddling, feeding, dressing up, the first smile, growth, changes, sitting up, the first step, etc. But rearing a child, just as with other things in life, has its own set of negatives to go with it. Each important or gratifying job or career has many assets, but also many difficulties, hard times and dirty work. The same is true of parenthood. There are many joys, pleasures and benefits to be derived from and during the rearing of children, but there are many difficult and frustrating roadblocks along the route. Most parents are not sorry for having traveled it.

"Parenthood is a blessing and I enjoy it totally. Both of us wanted to be parents and our baby was a planned happening. She has added so much warmth and love to our lives that it is impossible to express fully. We waited four years for this event and I'm glad. I am now ready to give up one life-style and begin a new one which can only add a new dimension to my life."

"I feel attachment, love, concern, affection. These feelings have increased, doubled, tripled! And he's a very important part of my life. I am very happy being a mother!"

"I had a happy childhood myself, with great parents. They always made me feel that children were a pleasant experience. I grew up this way and hope to pass this philosophy down to my children."

FATHERS' FEELINGS

Postpartum blues do not occur only to mothers! You, the new father, have your own set of adjustments, fears and concerns, as well as joys, during the postpartum period. You also had some share of the spotlight during your mate's pregnancy. Friends and co-workers may have been asking how your mate was feeling and if you arrived late at work one day, you may have found that everyone assumed she had just given birth.

"It was amazing. Even people who didn't know my name knew that my wife was going to have a baby."

"Every phone call from my wife was thought to be a call to take her to the hospital!"

The new father continues to attract attention after the baby is born as he spreads the word to assorted friends and relatives. Excitement and pride run high as he relates every detail of the ride to the hospital. If he was present for the birth, undoubtedly he tells everyone about his exciting experience.

"It was a compulsion. I had to share every detail with everyone I knew. It was like the whole thing wasn't real and talking about it convinced me that it really did happen."

"I saw my daughter being born. I held her before my wife did and I wanted to shout our joy to the world."

But as excited as you may be about the birth, you may have mixed feelings about the labor/delivery experience if things didn't go as you'd planned. Perhaps your mate required a cesarean and you were abruptly asked to leave. You may have spent hours in the lobby waiting for some word from the doctor, not really understanding why the cesarean was necessary and worrying about your mate and your baby.

"A baby was wheeled out from the delivery room. It was a girl. I didn't pay any attention to her. I was so worried. Besides, everyone had told us we were having a boy. Finally, the nurse came over and told me she was my daughter. I didn't care. I wondered what had happened to Barbara and was she all right."

You may have planned on being present for the delivery, but perhaps your mate requested sedation or there were medical reasons why sedation was necessary and you could not stay with her.

"I took classes with my wife, expecting to be with her for the delivery, but she just couldn't handle it after two hours and asked to be put to sleep. I know I should be more understanding, but I'm angry and disappointed in her. I feel cheated."

It is important that you discuss what happened during labor and delivery with your mate and the doctor. Clear up any questions you may have about why any medication was given, why a cesarean was necessary, why you were asked to leave the room at any time. It's important for you to be supportive if your mate requested sedation, even if you feel you missed out on an experience in which you had planned to share. You cannot know the intensity of the discomfort she may have been feeling, the depth of her fear, or whatever prompted her to change plans at the last minute. Any decision she made was in her best interests at the time and had to take priority over your expectations. By making judgmental or accusative statements you are not helping the situation. She may already feel guilt because she too looked forward to having you share this experience. While you're entitled to feel disappointment, expressing dissatisfaction with your mate about something that has already been done and cannot be changed is useless and can only be destructive. A new mother recuperating from childbirth needs all the support she can get.

You may have to reconcile your dream image of a baby with the real one. Newborns do not smile, goo-goo, or reach out their arms to be picked up. All newborns do not have thick crops of hair, nor are they all beautiful! What's more, you may have planned on a son and envisioned playing catch, taking him to a ball game, and teaching him to repair a car; now you may wonder what you can possibly do with a daughter. (Current thinking on nonsexist childrearing would urge you to play catch, take her to a ball game and teach her to repair the car!) Or, if you really wanted a "delicate, pretty little girl" to show off to all your friends, and now have to adjust to the fact that you have a son, you may feel somewhat let down. As you get to know your child, your disappointment will probably fade in time.

"I really wanted a daughter so we could name her after my mother who died when I was little. But when my son was born I realized that instead of a miniature version of my mother, I now had a small copy of myself. I felt proud."

"My first thought was—there are so many girls in my family already, why did I have to have another one? But as soon as that baby was in my arms and she looked at me, it was all okay!"

While your mate and baby are still in the hospital, you may begin to notice that people are more interested in seeing the baby and talking to the new mother than saying much more than a quick "congratulations" to you. As you exhaust the list of people you can share your experience with, the spotlight shifts to the new mother and baby and then almost entirely to the new baby. This may not be a cause of unhappiness to you initially, since they are the center of your concern as well. However, as time goes by and you realize how much your life has changed, you may resent the fact that no one is concerned with *you: your* achievements, *your* inconveniences and *your* feelings. And when you become aware of the fact that even your mate's attention is focused almost entirely on the baby's needs and accomplishments while yours have been sidelined, you may even begin to feel jealous!

"I guess I know the baby needs her, but I do too!"

"I got a promotion I had really sweated for and all my sister said was 'That's nice. I hear the baby's sleeping through the night.'"

"I had just gotten a raise. I bought some flowers and wine to celebrate and came bursting into the house all excited. All Susie said was 'Shhh, you'll wake the baby.'"

"It's really something. All of a sudden no one cares if I'm around so long as I bring in a paycheck. Everything's the baby, the baby, the baby."

It is important to realize that it will be impossible for the new mother to give you the same amount of time she did before the baby. She will have to focus most of her attention on the new baby—feeding, holding and otherwise caring for the infant. Your understanding and willingness to share her attentions with your new child will benefit all of you: the baby, by having a relaxed, loving, attentive mother; the mother, by not being torn between your demands and the baby's; you, because your mate is more likely to have warm, loving feelings for you because of your understanding and willingness to give up some time that would ordinarily be yours alone.

If you are feeling jealous of the baby, think about whether or not your mate has much time for herself—for her needs and her interests outside of motherhood. If she is working outside the home, her time is even more limited. Try to realize that it is often difficult for a new mother to be responsive to the needs of her mate when she has no time to attend to her own. Many fathers today share childcare and housekeeping with their mates. Working together can increase the amount of free time you both have and it can also help you feel closer to each other.

If you still feel left out, ignored, uncared for and that "all she thinks about is the baby," discuss these feelings with her. Try to use the *"I feel"* instead of the *"You are"* approach: *"I feel* left out ... unloved ... ignored. *I feel* unimportant and that only the baby really matters to you and everyone else." This form of expression usually will stimulate your mate's concern for what you are feeling because it is not phrased as an attack on her actions. She is under enough pressure trying to adapt to the drastic changes in *her* life-style since the baby's birth; your attacking will only add to her stress, which can build to explosive heights. While you are expressing your feelings, be sure to let her know that you are aware of the adjustments she is going through. Together, seek ways to minimize household and childcare tasks and maximize your togetherness.

Realize that she needs love, attention, understanding and support too. During her pregnancy, she probably received a great deal of attention and pampering. The monthly appointments with the obstetrician or nurse midwife, the comments and questions from family, friends and even strangers and, of course, your own excitement and interest all enhanced her feeling that she was special because she was carrying a new life.

One new mother commented, "While I was pregnant, I was really surprised at how my mother-in-law reacted. Usually when we had dinner at her home she offered everyone second helpings and ignored me. When I was pregnant, she offered me thirds!"

An awareness of her responsibility for the life she was carrying affected every decision she made: what to eat, whether to have a cocktail or even a cup of coffee, whether to jog or walk, etc. Her attention and concern were focused on her body and the new life.

Suddenly, the nine months are over and the baby is here. While it is a shock to the new mother to find that she's no longer the center of everyone's attention and the spotlight shifts to the baby, it can come as an even greater surprise that she no longer has the opportunity to focus on her own needs. In fact, she may have to sacrifice a great deal of what she probably concentrated on as important during pregnancy, such as adequate sleep, well-prepared balanced meals, pacing her activities during the day, putting her feet up when she got tired, moderate exercise, etc.

Fathers who make an effort to pamper their mates and help them recapture the feeling of being special are frequently rewarded with more attention, appreciation and stronger feelings of closeness than ever before from their mates. Bring her flowers or something else you know she will especially enjoy —something you may not usually bring her. Tell her she's doing a great job and that she's a terrific mother. Call her from work and tell her not to bother about dinner; you'll bring dinner home. Include wine and candles. Express concern about whether she's eating well and getting enough rest. Tell her she's beautiful and you love her . . . even on days she hasn't had the time to shower or fix her hair. Understand that she has had to sacrifice some of her needs in order to focus her attention outside herself on the new baby during this period. If you respond by sacrificing some of *your* needs and focusing on her and the new baby, you will strengthen your relationship and facilitate the transition from couple to family.

If your mate is breastfeeding, you may feel even more left out. Some new fathers feel useless if they cannot feed the baby.

"The baby looks at Kim with such love. I want him to look at *me* that way."

"How can the baby get to know me? I mean there's such closeness, such a oneness when she nurses. I feel left out of that."

It is a common assumption—spoken or felt—that food is love. Doting mothers, grandmothers, and aunts want to feed us. And many of us tend to stuff our own mouths with food to fill the need for love, all of which confirms the myth. Hunger is an urgent need in a baby and it is understandable that the first feelings of affection will be felt toward the person who fulfills that need.

Be assured that feeding the baby, although it is a loving act, is not the only way to show love to your baby, or to establish a bond between the two of you. You can give the baby a bath, followed by a gentle massage, while you also communicate your love verbally. You can even recite poetry while changing a diaper. You might take advantage of a papoose-like carrier which straps the infant securely to your chest for maximum support as well as body warmth, closeness and eye contact as you go about simple activities. Your bond with the baby grows through your contact with him or her. Feeding is only one avenue of contact. Granted, your child may not respond to your efforts immediately, but he or she will gradually learn that there's someone around who feels and sounds and smells different from Mommy and who plays differently too—another someone who's nice to be with, who feels good and makes him or her feel good. When your child begins to recognize people, you'll get your share of smiles and, later on, hugs and kisses.

Some new fathers wonder if the infant's suckling sexually stimulates the mother. Sometimes this does occur and it is important for you to know that this is purely a physiological reaction. This does not mean the mother will sexually desire her infant. Understand also that she may be having conflicting feelings about what she's experiencing. It may seem incongruous and morally wrong to her to have pleasant sexual feelings while nursing her baby and then follow this by having intercourse with you.

After having a baby, many women, breastfeeding or not, have a decrease in sexual desire. This is temporary and more often than not is misinterpreted as rejection by her mate.

"Now that she has the baby, I guess she doesn't need me anymore. She holds that kid more than she holds me."

"Sex? What's that?"

"I can't turn her on any more. It's like whatever we had—and it was good—is all over."

"How can she be so tired? She's home all day. She can take a nap. It's simply that she's avoiding me."

"When I want to make love, she acts like it's a big imposition. I hate what our relationship is becoming."

Decreased sexual desire can be caused by one or more of the following: hormonal changes that affect the emotions and decrease vaginal secretions, which can make intercourse painful; fear of pain in the episiotomy area; embarrassment about stretch marks and her still flabby abdomen; worry that her vaginal canal is too large since the birth; fear of another pregnancy too soon; embarrassment about the lochia (vaginal discharge that occurs after birth) or just plain fatigue.

It may be helpful for her to know if some of her fears are unfounded. For example, a new mother may believe it's impossible for her mate to truly desire her soon after the birth of the baby, but many a new father claims to be *more* interested in sex than ever.

"I am more interested now and more in love and this has increased sexual expression."

"Being with Nancy through labor and knowing what birth is all about, I have more respect for her and more feelings than ever before."

If exhaustion is her complaint, it may be difficult for you to comprehend this. Perhaps she *is* still asleep when you leave for work; but remember, she may have been up several times during the night to care for the baby and she's exhausted. When her day finally does begin, no sooner is the baby fed and possibly back to sleep than there are dishes to be done, beds to be made, dinner to be planned, the phone to be answered, the baby awakening again just as she has decided to try to catch a nap. Maybe she had planned on going shopping but when she tried to get ready, the baby started screaming and had to be held and soothed for hours. Result: no nap, no shopping. Perhaps she gulped a container of yogurt for lunch while folding the laundry and thinking about how simple life was before the baby was born; and then in the late afternoon there was dinner to prepare (minus the items she never managed to buy), but the baby's up again and even rocking doesn't seem to help and her mother calls and hears the crying and wants to know what's going on and you're due home in an hour and she's still in her nightgown! When the baby's finally asleep after a dinner that may have been no more than a quick omelet, the laundry is put away, dinner dishes are cleared, is it likely that she'd be interesed in sex? Or is it quite possible that she might view it as *another* imposition on her time? When a person is totally exhausted and hasn't had time to care for herself, it is pushing things to expect her to turn on the romance. And the fear of another pregnancy in the immediate future may evoke nightmares. Besides, if she has trouble sitting comfortably, it is naive to think intercourse would be tolerable, much less pleasant.

Expressing your feelings is one way to deal with this situation, again in the *"I feel"* context: *"I feel* like there's something wrong with me because I can't interest you anymore . . . *I feel* that now that you have your baby you have no use for me . . . *I feel* bad about not having sex. I miss you in bed." Her knowing your feelings is a step toward her understanding them and reassuring you that you are not the cause. The fact that you are both close enough to openly communicate on this touchy subject goes a long way toward making you close enough to physically express your feelings for each other. Being insistent only puts another pressure on your mate and tension is certainly not conducive to making love. She needs tender loving care and understanding from you. The more she gets, the more she'll feel loving and close to you— which can lead to intercourse. Until then, there is great advantage to hugging, cuddling, kissing, fondling—which in themselves communicate tenderness, caring, warmth and love —all vital to the successful postpartum relationship.

Be assured that her decreased desire is a temporary situation. When her hormone levels return to normal and her sore bottom has healed and her sleep needs are met and her baby's schedule has become more predictable and you have been patient and understanding, her desire will return—perhaps with even greater ardor!

On the other hand, the new mother may want to resume sexual relations before *you* feel ready. If so, it is important to discuss your feelings to clear the air. Some new fathers find it difficult to associate their mates' bodies with sexual relations after the process of childbirth. In some cases this is true for the father who was present at the delivery and was witness to the extreme stretching of the vaginal canal during birth. His mental image of the baby's emergence may conflict with the sexual associations he has with the vagina. He may worry that the vagina has stretched too much to be satisfactory during intercourse. These concerns are understandable and can interfere with the resumption of sexual relations. It might be helpful to keep in mind that there is nothing wrong with you for feeling this way and that this, too, like many other postpartum feelings, will pass in time.

Sometimes a new father is reluctant to approach his mate because he worries about hurting her. If you express your concern to her, she will be appreciative. Whenever she feels ready to resume relations, she will feel secure in the knowledge that your concern for her comfort is at least equal to your interest in sex and this will help her relax for easier entry and a more enjoyable sexual reunion.

Mothers who desire sexual relations very soon after the

delivery of the baby are cautioned by their obstetricians or nurse midwives against intercourse before being examined to determine if proper healing of the birth area has taken place. After such an examination, some practitioners approve the resumption of sex as early as two to three weeks postpartum. Even after you receive medical "permission" to have intercourse, the final decision belongs to the couple involved, not the health care provider. If the new mother is fearful or sore, her feelings should be respected. If the new father needs to wait, his sentiments should be considered as well.

At times both new parents may feel overwhelmed by the changes the baby has brought to their lives. If the new mother has left her job and plans to remain home to care for your child even temporarily, you may worry about the financial responsibility which now is totally yours. You and your mate may have been managing well enough on both your salaries, but now there is another person in the family and only one source of income. Initial expenses related to the baby's needs are very high and, in the event of a complicated birth or an ill baby, the outlay is much more than ever anticipated. If health and hospital insurance is minimal or lacking the pressures are even greater. With or without such extra costs there is the daily expense of rearing a child.

The responsibility of being the sole wage earner, even temporarily, can seem overwhelming. You may feel less free to switch jobs or take a chance on a new business venture for fear it will lead to a decreased income. Even men who enjoy their work sometimes say they feel "trapped" after a baby is born; it's no longer a question of doing something fulfilling in addition to bringing in an income; they *must* go to work to support their family.

"I came home from the hospital after Sue had given birth and stood for a moment in the darkened house. I suddenly felt a surge of responsibility land on my shoulders. It was a very physical sensation."

The pressure to achieve financially via raises and promotions also increases, because as long as the father is the sole wage earner, this is the only way the family's standard of living can be raised, or in a time of inflation be maintained. Even if his mate does return to work outside the home, it is amazing how much of her income will have to go toward childcare and related expenses. And for your increased efforts and tensions, you may find your favorite foods missing from the table, your favorite clothing styles financially inaccessible and your favorite vacation and recreation spots totally out of the question.

"I'm entitled to a good steak, an occasional movie—why else do I work so hard?"

"The thought of hanging around the house all week during vacation is unbearable. What will I do? But we really can't afford to go away!"

The pressures felt by you, the new father, should not be minimized and should be expressed so that your mate can understand what you are going through. Let her know *your* pressures—without laying blame. *"I feel* scared about being able to support my family . . . I'm worried about being a good father . . . If I can't get a good night's sleep tonight *I'm afraid* I'll lose my job . . . *I worry* about where we'll live next year." This type of approach is a better way to attract her sympathies for your feelings than by accusatory-type statements such as "A lot you care about how we'll make ends meet; that's my problem . . . Because of his crying I might lose my job!"

Letting her know how you feel and what your pressures are, as well as acknowledging concern for the difficulties she is experiencing, will do much toward strengthening the bonds of your relationship during this period.

Some new fathers have the notion that if they are the wage-earning half of the couple, the money is theirs to spend and make decisions about. If this is your belief, your mate may be resentful. If discussions about family finances are punctuated with the statement "But you're not working!" aimed at your mate who may have put in a much longer day than you (childcare is a twenty-four-hour responsibility), you might even be the recipient of open hostility. In the area of money matters it is especially important that you both discuss exactly what your financial situation is and that you make financial decisions together. For many couples today, marriage means sharing all responsibilities. Work done inside the home, including the upkeep of the household and the rearing of the children, should be thought of as a full-time job and as valuable as work done outside the home, no matter what the wage earner's occupation. Just because one job is rewarded with financial remuneration does not mean it has more value or took more time and effort than the other. Marriage is a partnership. Both partners, one working inside, one working outside, are nevertheless working—for the continuance of the relationship, for the benefit of the family—at equally demanding tasks.

And what of your home—your refuge from the pressures of the outside world? You may have a very tiring, demanding, stress-filled day at work and look forward to coming home to your "house-bound" and supposedly less-strained mate who will soothe your wounds with loving words. You may crave some time to unwind in front of the television or with a newspaper before doing anything else, but your mate may have had an equally tiring, demanding, stress-filled day and look forward to your arrival as the chance for her to unwind. She may wonder why you should have the right to come home and relax for a while when she hasn't had a few minutes for as much as a shower. Some men wonder why their mates are "already" in their nightgowns before dinner, failing to recognize they never had a chance to get dressed in the first place!

"I mean, what does she *do* all day? Why can't she get her act together?"

"I hassle all day at the office . . . push and shove on the subway . . . I come home to more pressure!"

It is important for you both to discuss how and when each of you will be able to unwind at some point in the evening. You both need a break!

Although you may feel and profess love for the new baby and are not sorry that he or she is in your life, at times you may find yourself extremely resentful of your offspring's part in inconveniencing you. There is a marked change in your life-style: your time is infringed upon, your sleep is interrupted, your mate is not always available when you would like her to be for making love or even quiet conversation. Despite both your efforts, dinners are no longer what they used to be or when they used to be, if at all; the laundry may be dirty, late or missing; the bed may not be made; the bedding may not be changed. Your creature comforts have been disrupted.

"Who ever expected that the tiny little creature would take up so much of her time? By the time I get home, she's so exhausted from the baby that she's got nothing left for me."

"I know she can't help it, spending all that time with our son, but I can't help feeling jealous and left out."

After the birth of a second child, you will be even more

acutely aware of the extra work and time involved. The time your mate spends in the care of the baby, the older child, the housework, etc. has to cut into the time she would be able to spend with you.

"Whenever I see her, she's feeding the baby, putting my older daughter to bed, doing a wash, washing a floor, or sleeping! She doesn't take the time to comb her hair or look decent!"

She may not *have* the time, believe it or not, and when and if she does, she may be too exhausted to care. She needs the sleep more. If you have not already "pitched in," perhaps you can relieve her of some of the workload so that she can spend the "saved" time with you.

If you are last on the priorities list, of course you may have negative feelings about what is happening. Who enjoys inconvenience and disruption? Your feelings are based on real happenings. You have a right to be upset, but so does she. It may help, though, to know your reaction is normal, that chaos will not be a permanent member of your family and that your needs will once again be considered important when your mate feels more confident and in control of the situation. It may also help to realize it is truly impossible for a new mother to handle every aspect of home and childcare completely and still be attentive to the relationship between both of you. Something has to give! Try to see things in terms of true priorities. What's more important: human care or household chores? If you would like to see a good mother-child relationship develop, along with a continuance and bettering of your relationship with your mate, be willing to sacrifice orderliness. If you prefer everything in its place, including dinners, be ready to do a lot of the work yourself, hire someone to do it or sacrifice your relationship.

Some women have cited their husband's lack of help with the baby as a factor that strongly contributed to their decision to end the marriage. Other stresses may or may not have been equally important to these women, but a common comment was "Look, I did it all myself—even when the kids were first born—housework, childcare; I even held down a job. Who needs him? I can do it all myself!" Certainly all women do not feel this way, but it is certainly worth thinking about before refusing to help.

Every relationship is different, but in most families it is the woman who takes responsibility for everyone's needs and who apportions tasks (if her mate is willing to share) or accomplishes them herself (if he's not) to ensure that at least the basic chores necessary to the continued functioning of the family are accomplished. While some women accept this responsibility as part of their role, others find that thinking about what has to be done and planning ways to do it themselves or asking their mates to do specific tasks are stress provoking.

"How does he think the casserole gets from the cans and into the oven? A magician appears and waves a wand?"

"For once I wish he would take the list and do the shopping without being asked!"

While many men do take on a good deal of responsibility for the housework, others express confusion at exactly what is expected of them.

"How much should I help and with what?"

"My wife complained that I never helped with the laundry —that a pile of dirty underwear could be right in the middle of the floor and I'd walk right past it or step over it, instead of doing something about it! I tried to explain that I literally didn't even see it! Of course, I knew something was there; but I grew up not taking notice of dirty laundry as something to do anything about because it was always taken care of by someone else—my mother. And when we were first married, my wife took care of the laundry, even though we were both working. I never stopped to think about what had to happen between the time I placed dirty clothes in the hamper and they reappeared in my dresser. It wasn't until I opened the closet looking for a shirt and didn't find one there that it even occurred to me to think about 'doing the laundry' as a task that I might have to help with."

Perhaps you can suggest that you both discuss what the household tasks are and how to accomplish them. Admit to your mate that you would like to share the work and perhaps even take on part of the burden of planning, but you are unsure of what needs to be done and who can best do it. Look around your home and ask yourself, "How can I help?" If the bathroom should be cleaned but you've never scrubbed the tub, ask your mate what products she uses and where they're stored, if you don't already know. If you've never done laundry, have her teach you how to use the washer and dryer and check the hamper on a regular basis. Be sure, however, to convey to her that your desire is to help, not to express criticism of her for not being able to get everything done herself.

If you do not believe that sharing the housework is part of your role or you truly do not have the time to help and you can afford outside help, you might suggest to your mate that she hire someone. Again, it is important that the message be that you love and value her enough to provide for some relief and assistance, not that you're disgusted because she can't cope on her own. Few can in the early weeks.

(The issue of who will do what around the house is even more important if the new mother returns to work outside the home.)

You may feel put upon if asked or expected to share in the workload or provide outside help when she has been "home all day." The presumption in this attitude is that she has been lounging around the house all day while you've been hard at work, so why is she so tired!

"I work all day and go to school at night. How can she expect me to help her? That's her job; I do mine!"

Realize that other cultures do provide automatic support and assistance for new mothers in the form of other women who assist with the birth itself or arrive soon thereafter to assume the new mother's household responsibilities while she recuperates. Try to understand, first of all, that having a baby —going through labor and delivery—is tiring. Caring for a baby—being "on call" all day—is wearing. Having your sleep continually interrupted is exhausting. Emotional strains from worries, pressures, postpartum hormonal imbalances and physical discomforts take their toll on her energies. She has every reason to be tired. So do you. Your job pressures, plus your interrupted sleep and your emotional strains, are quite real. But comparing point for point on whose job is more tiring and asking why she is so tired serves no purpose. What does matter is your realization that whether or not you're tired, she is too. And in order for her to be able to continue functioning, she must have help and rest. So, although you may feel quite justified in your annoyance of being asked to do more work after your day "has ended," she is justified in asking you to share the workload *still remaining*—from *her* day which has not ended. If you pitch in, you'll *both* have time to relax later in the evening.

On the other hand, you may miss your family all day and may rush home to see and help care for the baby. You may resent the fact that your mate spends her entire day with the baby and your time with your child is restricted to before and after work. Some men feel more capable of caring for their babies than their mates; some are even taking paternity leaves to stay home and care for their children while their mates go to work outside the home, full-time. While some men who want to have a large share in caring for the baby and in decision-making find their mates expect and appreciate the help, others find their efforts are resented by mates who want to assume the full responsibility themselves. It is important to discuss exactly what your roles will be in the areas of childcare and come to a mutually acceptable compromise if necessary.

"I am very involved with my baby's care. I wouldn't have it any other way. But not everyone is accepting of fathers. When my son was sick I called the pediatrician to ask his advice, only to be told, 'Let me speak to the mother!' I was furious!"

While most pediatricians today are at least aware of the increased involvement of fathers in the care of their children, some need to be reminded that this means speaking to fathers on the telephone and including them in conversations during an examination. Talk to the physician, or anyone else who responds negatively to your involvement, and make it clear that you are one-half of the parenting team and you expect to be treated with consideration and respect.

Some men experience shock the first time they are left alone to care for the baby. While their mates may be able to soothe the infant very quickly, the new fathers often find that nothing they do helps. This causes tension, which leads to more crying. "Why does the baby love only my wife? He goes to sleep when she rocks him, but he doesn't respond to me at all. I guess he just doesn't love me."

"It looks so easy when Pat does it. I just can't seem to communicate with the baby."

Understand that the more contact you have with your child, the more responsive he or she will be to your efforts and attentions. If your mate does all the holding and hugging, the baby gets used to the way she holds him or her. When you're doing the cuddling, the baby senses that someone different is around. Also, the first few times you are alone with the baby, you are apt to be a bit apprehensive and babies are very sensitive to this. The more the baby cries, the more tense you become—one affects the other. When your mate returns home, her calm, easy touch may convey "all's right with the world" and your baby drifts off to sleep leaving you to feel somewhat inadequate and inept. Know that the more relaxed you are, the more your baby will respond by relaxing. The more time you spend caring for your son or daughter, the more relaxed you will be about it! Also, it might be beneficial to take an infant care class together with your mate. Call your local Red Cross or Visiting Nurse Association to ask if a nurse can come to your home to help you learn, or if there is a class you can attend.

If you find yourself feeling increasingly tense while trying to soothe your crying baby (a very common reaction!), do something to break the tension-crying-tension cycle. Take the time to relax: listen to soothing music, put the baby down for a few minutes and do some slow chest breathing. Doing something to help you unwind may result in an easier time with the baby. Many parents find that if they call the pediatrician for advice in dealing with a baby who is experiencing an episode of irritable crying or who is colicky, the crying often subsides while they wait for the physician to return their call. The knowledge that the pediatrician will call helps the parents relax—and very often when they relax, the baby relaxes!

Some men complain that their wives criticize how they hold or dress or handle or change the baby.

"I want to help, but as soon as I go to diaper him, my wife is in there supervising. Does it really matter if I put the thing on backwards or forget to use petroleum jelly? His bottom won't fall off. It really makes me feel like handing her the baby and saying 'Do it yourself!'"

"I promised her some time off every Wednesday evening so she can do whatever she wants to for a few hours. She usually stays home and does some sewing or knitting by herself. That's what she likes to do. But as soon as she hears the baby crying, she goes off the wall! 'Why can't you soothe him?' she complains. 'Why do you let him cry?' Let him cry?! I'm up there doing everything I can think of to get him to *stop* crying, but she's up there too, breathing down my neck when all I'm trying to do is give her a break!"

If you find your efforts to participate in childcare are met with criticism, talk to your mate. Explain that you feel committed to working together to care for your child but when you are "on call" you resent it when she supervises your every move. You might feel that the implication in her response is that you are inept or that you might harm the baby if you don't do things the "right way." If so, tell her that's what you're feeling, but be prepared for the possibility that she might be sensitive and find it difficult to give up some of her control over the baby. Some women derive a good portion of their self-identity from motherhood—especially women who do not return to work outside the home or who have few interests outside the home and family. Everyone needs to feel "in charge" of something and some women find it difficult to relinquish control even temporarily to someone offering them time to rest or pursue other interests—no matter how desperately they want the relief. While it is important to discuss and agree on infant care decisions—such as whether or not to let the baby "cry it out," whether to feed on demand or try to follow a schedule—there are very few *rules* in parenting beyond "love and respond to your baby to the best of your ability." Your mate may need help to realize that what the baby is wearing or whether or not you use petroleum jelly after *every* diaper change is really not terribly important. Reassure her that she is an essential individual in your life and the baby's and although the baby survives her absences very nicely, she really is irreplaceable!

Realize also that feelings of incompetence in the early weeks are very common. No one licenses us for parenthood. We learn how to care for our children by observing others, by reading whatever material is available or attending classes in our community—if they exist. But, mostly we learn by trial and error. Most parents respond to their babies correctly most of the time, but it will take time and mistakes before you feel accomplished as a parent. It is interesting to note that pediatricians, pediatric nurses and other health care professionals who work with children frequently experience feelings of being inept in dealing with their own babies. No matter how much you know about infants it takes several weeks or even several months before you feel "settled in" as parents.

You might worry about what kind of father you will be. Perhaps you want very much for your children to respect and love you and you strive to work out a formula of behavior for child-rearing in order to accomplish this. You'll probably find yourself thinking about your relationship with your own father—how you are alike, how you are different, what aspects of the way you were raised you'd like to duplicate with your own children, what decisions you'll make differently. You may compare your mate and your mother as well. Many men experience a new respect for their parents, or at least an increased understanding of what they went through as parents.

"I realized I knew very little about what I was doing as far as childcare was concerned. The thought struck me: 'Hey, my folks were in their early twenties when I was born. They were kids themselves!' And here I am, thirty-five, probably making a whole bunch of mistakes myself. It was quite a realization!"

Your relationship with your parents and in-laws, as well as other family members, changes once you become a parent. For many individuals parenthood represents the last step into adulthood and some are disappointed at how the baby's grandparents respond to their new role. You may find your mate has complaints about your mother's suggestions, overconcern, or lack of attention, or you may think that your mother feels compelled to unburden herself to you of all her criticisms of your mate. This can be difficult to handle and you may have feelings of mixed loyalties—wanting to be supportive of your mate but at the same time wanting to please your mother.

It may be difficult, but try not to get caught in the middle. You might suggest to your mate that she speak directly to your parents (or other family members) to try to resolve the conflict. You can refuse to hear your mother's complaints—or listen but don't convey them to your mate. If you find you must act as mediator, remember that you are part of a new family unit, created by your baby's birth. Your decisions about how to handle the specific situation you are faced with should be made on the basis of what is best for *your* family—you, your mate and child.

"My parents used a technique my wife and I called 'divide and conquer.' They would ask us individually whether we'd like a particular gift or what we felt about a particular situation. When they had my opinion, for example, they would catch her alone and ask the same question. If she disagreed, my mom would say, 'But Michael said that it would be okay...' It infuriated us until we agreed never to commit ourselves to anything without discussing it. Even issues we know the other's opinions on are responded to with 'I have to discuss it with Jane.' Eventually we hope that they'll catch on and cut it out. But even if they don't, it's not disruptive anymore."

You may find yourself wondering how well you're handling your role: Are you helping enough? Are you meeting your mate's needs? Are you a responsive father? You would probably welcome reassurance from your mate. Again, discuss your feelings!

You may worry that the life-style of the early weeks will never change—that postpartum is what parenthood is all about. Not true! While your life-style does change after a baby is born, the chaos lasts only for as long as it takes the new parents to begin to recognize and deal with the different needs of their baby and as long as it takes the baby to settle into a schedule of sorts. When the baby's needs can be anticipated, other things can also be accomplished. When the tension of not knowing what to do whenever the baby cries passes, the entire atmosphere in the home is more relaxed.

"I wondered when life would return to normal. Then I realized that what we were experiencing and developing was a *new* normal. It was a relief to realize that eventually we'd be able to get out more and do more—that more of our needs would be met too."

You may long for the more carefree days without the responsibility of caring for a family and all that implies. You may associate parenthood with aging and the end of your youth and good times. Certainly, you cannot be "care-free" now that you have more cares. But becoming a father does not automatically cancel out other parts of your life. You can continue your business life, your social life, your hobbies and other interests—albeit on a more limited scale—but you can't be out with your mate every night of the week unless you can afford the babysitting expense and are willing to be away from your new baby that often.

"After the excitement of the birth was all over and Marie came home from the hospital, I got scared and a little depressed. I realized that it was no longer just a fun thing, going to classes and seeing the birth. It was real and this baby was here, ours, forever. And I thought of my father and my image of what a father was: serious, responsible, sitting home after a full day's work reading the paper, watching television. I wasn't like that. I was always going places and doing things with Marie and our friends. I couldn't bear the thought that all that would change now that I was a 'father.' And then it hit me: that person was *my* father. I didn't have to be like that person. My personality did not have to change to fit the title 'father.'"

Until you and your mate have more free time, it can be helpful for you each to identify the one or two pursuits you find are central to your feelings about who you are. Juggling time and responsibilities to ensure that you can at least include these in your lives will help you feel better about having to give up other activities temporarily.

"I love riding my bicycle. I used to ride every morning before work. For me, the feeling of zipping over a hill with the adrenaline flowing and the extra blood pumping through my system was fantastic! The rest of the day was easier to get through. Well, early morning rides are out for now. I'm too exhausted. But Sue and I trade time off on weekends. On Saturday she has the afternoon off to do whatever she wants and I watch the baby. Sundays I have the afternoon free and off I go, pedaling over those hills—feeling light and free. It gives me something for me—something to look forward to and think about. When my son is bigger I'll get a bike seat for him and we'll go off riding together. Won't that be something."

There are things you do give up when you have a baby—some temporarily, many for years—like the quiet Sunday morning breakfasts in bed while reading the newspaper, sleeping late on the weekend, sleeping through an uninterrupted night, making love spontaneously in the afternoon, going to the beach on impulse (even in the winter), spending a day reading a book from cover to cover, watching an entire football game on television (or, for that matter, watching a whole television program on any subject). We're sure you could add many things to this list. Some will be possible again someday, but those that will not will be replaced by the indescribable joy of molding and loving a developing human being, seeing a first smile, feeling a first hug, cheering a first attempt at rolling over, standing up, walking, hearing "dada" and knowing that it means you. The entire world becomes a new experience to discover again through your baby's eyes and is never quite the same as it was before he or she was born. Most couples do survive the postpartum period intact and claim that their lives are richer because they have a baby.

"As the father of a 2½-month-old baby girl, I feel as though I have just begun to live. The moment she took her first breath I felt myself ascend into the heavens. What a fantastic feeling. A life-style made up of love and peace and happiness."

"Changing him, feeding him, calming him when he cries —these should be my biggest worries in life! It's worth it all. I love parenthood."

COUPLE COMMUNICATIONS

One of the most important elements of a successful relationship is the ability of both partners to communicate: to express their beliefs and feelings; to listen to their mate's beliefs and feelings with respect and acceptance, if not always agreement; to discuss and resolve any differences; and to take the way each partner sees things as individuals and to evolve a joint approach to any situation.

By the time couples become parents, most have established techniques of expression and problem resolution that work in their relationship, and therefore technique is not something they find it important to think about. Communication "happens," feelings are aired; problems are resolved. For many couples, these previously established ways of communicating greatly facilitate the adjustment process during the stressful early weeks of parenthood. Others, however, are surprised to discover that expressing their feelings and resolving disputes has suddenly become difficult. In addition, there are some couples who have never been able to communicate, a fact which may or may not have mattered to them until they became parents. Others have had no real issues to test how well they communicate. And couples who have allowed one partner to make all or most of the decisions in their relationship prior to becoming parents may find that this arrangement is challenged in the realignment of roles and responsibilities common to the postpartum period. For many parents, how to communicate effectively may become an issue which in itself must be resolved before other issues can be considered.

When and Where

Unless you have an extremely easy-going baby, conversations with your partner will probably not be as spontaneous as they may have been in the past. While some couples set aside a time each week for serious discussion even before becoming parents, many more realize after their babies are born that reserving a set time each week, or every other week, may be the only way they are guaranteed the opportunity to voice their feelings, share their reactions and resolve any difficulties. If a set time is your only way, if at all possible ask someone else to care for the baby for an hour or two while you get away from the house and talk. Coffee at a local diner, a walk around the block, or any place convenient and comfortable can serve as a setting for discussion. Even breastfeeding mothers can leave the baby for short periods in the early weeks. It can be easier to communicate effectively if someone else is "on call" for the baby's cries. If no one is available to babysit, perhaps your infant will nap in the carriage or chest carrier while you all take a walk. The idea is to be together in an atmosphere conducive to conversation—and to talk.

What you discuss will depend on your own feelings, how easy or difficult you find the adjustment to parenthood, how much time you have had for conversation during the week, etc. It is important for the two of you to have time together to re-establish your bonds as a couple, to ask and answer "How am I doing?" and to think about "How are we doing?" If you are not used to making appointments for discussion, the situation may seem a bit contrived at first, but many couples report that it soon becomes routine. You may feel awkward or find yourselves wondering aloud if the baby is all right instead of discussing your reactions and problems. If you are not used to discussing issues, you may find it difficult to open up to each other. It is important to try to do so.

You might start by discussing how life has changed, what you miss about the life-style you had before the baby was born, what joys the baby has brought to your lives, what frustrations you are experiencing. Simply *voicing* your feelings and reactions—not analyzing, blaming or seeking answers—may be all you both need. On the other hand, you may find there are issues you *must* resolve to continue to feel comfortable about your relationship. Some individuals are afraid to voice their needs for fear of provoking an argument because they confuse being assertive—expressing needs in order to develop strategies to meet them—with being aggressive—provoking a confrontation to resolve an issue. Problems cannot be resolved if they are not discussed. It may be difficult to delay discussing issues when there are strong feelings involved. While it's important to find a way to express anger, frustration and tension when they are being experienced, resolution of the underlying disagreement may have to be delayed until a better time for discussion.

Style vs. Substance
Getting the Feelings Out

You learned a lot about discussions by observing your parents and relatives in conflict as you were growing up. In some families arguments are loud; positions are shouted—the tone suggests a depth of feeling that may or may not be present. For some individuals, yelling helps alleviate anger, frustration and anxiety; they may know of no other way to express their strong feelings. In contrast to this, others react to anger and anxiety by becoming very quiet and withdrawn. Feelings, for these individuals, must be mulled over for a time before they can be expressed, if they are expressed at all. Of course, these are the extremes; there are combinations and variations of style in between. As an adult, you may have adopted the style of your parents and other family members, or perhaps you take the opposite approach, partly in reaction to what you viewed during childhood as an uncomfortable way of dealing with feelings and issues. The way you react to your mate's style of expression may also have roots in your feelings about how your parents expressed themselves. Problems can arise when a partner who needs to "get it all out" is in conflict with a mate who needs to "mull it over." Unless each of you recognizes and respects your different approaches, the *way* positions are expressed may become the issue instead of *what* is actually being said. Discussing your reactions to the *tone* you each employ can help you get beyond an impasse caused by conflicting *styles*.

For example, one partner might say: "I can't stand it when you shout at me. Your yelling reminds me of my father's way of dealing with a situation, which was to shout down his opponents until they gave in."

Or: "I cringe when you shout. I feel battered. It makes me want to withdraw even more."

Another example: "When you withdraw into yourself, I feel like I'm slamming into a brick wall. I can't get through to you, so I scream even louder."

Or: "My father used to end all discussions by withdrawing into himself and actually leaving the room. Once he walked out, there was nothing left to talk about. He wouldn't allow it! I found the frustration overwhelming. When you refuse to discuss something, even though I know we will talk about it later, I feel like I did as a child."

One possible resolution is to let the "shouter" get the feelings out in his or her own way, as long as both partners realize that all that is occurring is an expression of feelings. Once these needs have been met, the actual discussion and resolution of the conflict can occur at another time—after the "withdrawing partner" has a chance to think over the situation.

Another possibility would be for each to learn new ways of approaching conflict and dealing with strong emotions. Anger, frustration and anxiety can dissipate in time, if the evocative situation is resolved. To help this along, when discussion and resolution will be delayed, the suggestions made in the section "Postpartum Blues" may be useful: for example, keeping a diary, talking things out with a friend, etc. Also, strenuous physical activity (running, riding an exercycle, paddleball, tennis, brisk walking, vigorous dancing) can help. (Be sure to get medical okay.) Both the "shouter" and the withdrawing partner can have a physical outlet for their frustrations, as well as time away from each other to identify their feelings and think things out before discussion.

It is also important to realize that stress can change an individual's style. A shouter may become withdrawn, or a withdrawer may shout. This can be confusing to the other partner, who may interpret the change in style as an indication that the dispute is of greater importance than it actually is. It may be wise to point out the change to your partner and ask how he or she feels about the *subject being discussed*. Try to focus on the words used first and the intensity of the presentation last.

Need vs. Position

Individuals discussing and attempting to resolve disagreements are involved in a negotiating situation. Negotiations usually begin with a statement of each party's position on the topic being discussed. For example, you and your mate may disagree on whether a crying baby should be held and soothed all the time or whether it might be more appropriate, under certain circumstances, to let him or her "cry it out." For the purpose of this example, let us say the mother's position in the discussion of this issue is "Babies should be held." And the father's position is "Babies should cry it out." At this stage, the argument is without resolution. One partner feels one way; the other, the opposite. However, underlying the position taken by each is a *need* which may not be in conflict with the need of the other individual. Identifying the need behind the position taken by each partner frequently facilitates reaching a decision or compromise that is satisfactory to both.

One cause of the mother's position might be her inability to cope with the baby's cries. She may, in fact, agree that letting the baby cry it out is an option that should be tried in their particular situation. However, the crying may evoke such strong feelings of anxiety that her position ("Hold a crying baby") is motivated by a need to avoid these strong, uncomfortable feelings. Her mate can help her identify her concern by asking her how she feels when the baby cries, or what aspect of the proposed situation she disagrees with. He could then suggest, for example, that she go out for a while and leave him to deal with the crying.

Another explanation for her position might be that she feels strongly that good mothers don't let babies cry it out. *Her need* is to feel that she is a good mother and that she is doing the best for her child. Her mate might feel that the baby, by crying, is being manipulative. *His need* might be to feel in control of his environment and not allow the baby to "take over." In this case, the mother might ask her mate to discuss why he wants to let the baby cry and what he thinks this will accomplish, and she might share information, from her reading on early childhood development, which supports the position that young infants are not manipulative. On the other hand, he may agree that babies should be held in most instances but believes that this particular situation can be resolved only by letting the baby cry it out, or that this strategy should at least be attempted. If he addresses her need and reassures her that she is a good mother and states that in his opinion, what they are discussing is not inconsistent with good parenting but an attempt at resolving a problem, he will be more successful in changing her position. (It should be noted that we are using the "holding" vs. "cry it out" issue here by way of example only. For a discussion of *our* position on this topic, see "How to Handle a Crying Baby.")

Blueprint for Effective Communication

1. *Begin with the positive. State the issue.*

In any discussion of sensitive issues, it is helpful to begin by mentioning the positive aspects of a situation and then to state the problem. This is especially important when our purpose is to affect a change that may or may not be popular with your mate. Before you bring up what your mate is *not doing* or what you feel could be improved on, mention what he or she is *doing well*. This conveys the message that there is a specific issue in need of resolution, not that the entire relationship is faulty. For example:

"I think you are terrific with the baby; you really seem to have a knack at soothing her when I've about given up. But I really wish you'd share more of the housework."

"I know you are working very hard to care for the baby and our home and I think you are a terrific parent. But I really wish you would let me unwind when I first come home from work."

2. *Acknowledge the other person's need.*

Acknowledging that your mate has a need in the situation will help gain empathy for the need you are expressing. Continuing the examples above:

"I think you are terrific with the baby; you really seem to have a knack at soothing her when I've about given up. But I really wish you'd share more of the housework. *I know you need to rest after a hard day."*

"I know you are working very hard to care for the baby and our home and I think you are a terrific parent, but I really wish you would let me unwind when I first come home from work. *I know you need time to unwind too."*

3. *Use "I Messages" to express your feelings.*

Express your feelings about the situation by using "I Messages"—"I feel" not "You are." A statement of *feelings* is more likely to evoke sympathy than criticisms, which can put your partner on the defensive.

"I think you are terrific with the baby; you really seem to have a knack at soothing her when I've about given up. But I really wish you'd share more of the housework. I know you need to rest after a hard day. *But I feel overwhelmed by all I have to accomplish and angry when you sit down, put your feet up and relax while I'm still working in the kitchen."*

"I know you are working very hard to care for the baby and our home and I think you are a terrific parent. But I really wish you would let me unwind when I first come home from work. I know you need time to unwind too. *But I feel angry and tense when you hand me the baby as I walk through the door. I feel pounced on."*

You can be very graphic in your description of your feelings, if this helps you to express them. For example, "I get so angry I want to scream!" or "I feel like I'll explode if I don't get a break!"

4. *Propose a solution.*

Suggest ways of dealing with the problem but also indicate that you will be open to any solutions your mate may propose.

"I think you are terrific with the baby; you really seem to have a knack at soothing her when I've about given up. But I really wish you'd share more of the housework. I know you need to rest after a hard day. But I feel overwhelmed by all I have to accomplish and angry when you sit down, put your feet up and relax while I'm still working in the kitchen. *I think a possible solution might be for one of us to wash the dishes while the other sweeps the floor and takes out the trash. Then we'll both have time to relax when we're finished.*"

"I know you're working very hard to care for the baby and our home and I think you are a terrific parent. But I really wish you would let me unwind when I first come home from work. I know you need time to unwind too. But I feel angry and tense when you hand me the baby as I walk through the door. I feel pounced on. *I think a possible solution might be for me to relax for a half hour when I first get home and then after dinner I'll take over and give you an hour to rest.*"

5. *Use active listening.*

When responding to your mate, acknowledge the suggestions or needs expressed before you discuss your own. This shows respect and consideration for your mate's needs.

A response to the housework example above might be the following:

"I hear you saying you're tired and resentful at having to do the after-dinner clean-up. I hadn't realized you felt that way. Of course, I'll work with you."

Or, "I understand your feelings. You are tired in the evening and resent my resting while you clean up after dinner. I feel that I put in a hard day at work and should be able to come home and relax. What do you think about using paper plates for the next few weeks so no one has to do dishes? I could bring home take-out dinner several nights a week too."

If feelings are being expressed, acknowledge the feelings in your response, even if you can't propose a solution to a described situation. For example: "I hear you. You're exhausted. You haven't slept in three nights and there is no one to give you a break during the day. I have to work this weekend and there's no money in the budget to hire someone. I feel helpless and frustrated because there is nothing I can do. Your feelings are very real and the situation is very difficult for you."

Referring back to what your partner is saying while discussing your reactions helps him or her get feelings out—a result which in itself can provide relief. Although there may be no solution to the problem, your mate will know that you understand his or her reactions and that you are supportive, and this can help to alleviate stress.

If one partner says something that seems hurtful, be aware that he or she may not realize the effect or implication of the words being used. Let him or her know how you interpret what is being said. This may be helpful in clarifying what is being said and establishing what the real issue is. For example:

New Father: "Whenever I walk into the house, the baby is crying. Every time I pick him up, his diaper needs changing! It's very frustrating!"

New Mother's Response: "You're coming across like you think I'm a bad mother. Is that the issue—that I'm not doing my share?"

New Father: "No. I didn't mean that at all! I just feel frustrated that there is so much to do and not enough time to do it. When I walk into the house planning on helping with dinner and the baby is crying and wet, I don't know which way to turn first!"

6. *Resolve one issue before going on to the next.*

Try not to allow the conversation to go off on tangents. While one issue might remind you of another situation that is also in need of discussion, resolve the first before going to the second, or you might find that your discussion time has ended and nothing has been accomplished. Changing the subject is a diversionary tactic sometimes utilized, consciously or subconsciously, when an individual is uncomfortable with what is being discussed. If the subject is wandering, you or your mate should call attention to the fact by saying, "We've gotten off the topic. Are we finished discussing it, or should we go back to it, resolve it, and then go on to the next?"

On occasion, disagreements may arise that cannot be resolved by any of the means we've discussed. Perhaps you each have strong feelings about the issue. Perhaps you cannot arrive at a compromise that considers both your needs. Perhaps neither of you is willing to accept the other's position under any circumstances. If this occurs, it may be necessary to try to agree on a temporary strategy or solution and bring the subject up again at a later date. Frequently couples who have reached an impasse find that in the period between discussions, one partner gains new insight that helps resolve the problem; or, as so often happens in parenting, the situation changes and the issue no longer exists (the baby is less fussy, sleeps longer, etc.).

If, however, you find that problems continue to build and multiply, that you are consistently unable to resolve disputes, or that you are pulling away from rather than toward each other, consider marital counseling. Explain the situation and ask your pediatrician, obstetrician, family doctor or nurse midwife, clergyman or your local mental health association for a referral to a therapist. Family services agencies (listed under Social Services Organizations in the phone book) offer family counseling, support groups led by professionals, and other services.

AFTER A CESAREAN DELIVERY

The cesarean mother experiences the same physiological changes and many of the procedures and discomforts which any new mother does. This section of the book points out those experiences that particularly affect the cesarean mother. Be sure to refer to the sections "Physiological Changes," "Procedures Involving the Mother" and "Procedures Involving the Baby" for information common to *all* new mothers and babies.

Know that the rate of recuperation after a cesarean—the time it takes, the extent of discomfort experienced—varies from individual to individual and even from one birth experience to another in the same woman. Some women—the minority—feel very little discomfort during their postoperative period. They leave the hospital earlier than usual—perhaps a few days after delivery—and some of these women can resume many of their normal activities within a few weeks.

However, many more cesarean mothers find the immediate postoperative days difficult to handle. They are physically limited and they "hurt." The slightest movement causes discomfort, if not pain. Their physical condition takes away from the joy of the occasion: the birth of the baby.

After the baby, placenta and membranes are removed from the uterus, the doctor examines the uterus to be sure that no pieces of placental tissue have been left inside. Then, the surgical repair begins: the uterine incision, which is almost always horizontal (also referred to as a transverse or low-segment incision) and only sometimes vertical (classical), is sutured with absorbable material. Then, the abdominal wall incision is sewn—layer by layer of muscle and fascial tissue beneath the surface of the skin. These internal sutures are also absorbable.

The external incision may have been vertical (from just below the navel to the pubic hairline) or transverse ("bikini" or Pfannenstiel incision, just above the pubic bone, about six or seven inches across).

To close the external incision, doctors frequently use individually tied-off (interrupted) stitches which are made of nonabsorbable material and, therefore, must later be removed.

If the external incision was transverse, either interrupted stitches or one continuous suture may be used to suture the layer of tissues directly beneath the outer skin layer (subcuticular stitch). The suture material can be either absorbable or not. With this method, there are no exteriorly visible stitches.

Another technique involves the use of surgical clamps or clips to close the external incision instead of—or sometimes in addition to—sutures. Some women find the clamps uncomfortable when they move. Before leaving the hospital, the edges of the skin will have fused together and the clamps or clips are removed. Stitch, clip or clamp removal is usually painless. Sometimes, during the removal of sutures, there is a slight burning sensation.

More recently, doctors have been using surgical steel staples applied with a special staple gun to close the external incision. Between each staple, surgical tape is adhered to the skin to ensure proper fusion of the edges.

The type of suturing and incision depends on the doctor and may vary from mother to mother and even from one delivery to another in the same woman.

After suturing is complete—which takes approximately forty-five minutes—you will be moved to the recovery room or special recovery area. If the hospital does not have an obstetrical recovery room, you may be placed in an unoccupied labor room or directly outside one of the labor rooms, within the labor and delivery area, where you will remain for about two to six hours.

If you have had general anesthesia and were asleep for the delivery, you will be very drowsy during the early recovery period. You may awaken now and then, fall back asleep and may also experience nausea and vomiting as a result of the anesthesia. If, prior to receiving general anesthesia, you had a long, difficult labor, or if you had been given scopolamine (an amnesiac) during labor, when you awake in the recovery room you may find it difficult to believe that your baby has already been born.

You may also have a sore throat. This results from a tube which is usually placed into your mouth and throat while you are under anesthesia to ensure a clear breathing passageway and to prevent fluids from getting into your lungs in case you vomit. Usually, before you leave the operating (or delivery) room, the tube is removed.

Your mouth may be dry—probably due to medication (usually atropine) given prior to the administration of general anesthesia (and sometimes prior to regional anesthesia as a precaution in case general anesthesia might later be necessary) to dry up secretions in the mouth and throat. You may request a lemon-flavored swab, which is usually available to wet your mouth until you are allowed to drink fluids.

If you have had a regional anesthetic, it may have been a spinal or an epidural. If it was a spinal, you will probably be required to lie flat in bed, without lifting your head, for about eight to twelve hours. (Breastfeeding can still be accomplished by rolling onto your side.) It is commonly believed that if you do not follow these instructions, you risk getting "spinal headaches," which can be painful and can last for days. There is some thought to the contrary, however, which indicates that spinal headaches may have nothing to do with the mother's position after delivery but may result from the loss of some spinal fluid at the time of administration of the medication.

If you have had an epidural—which does not involve the spinal fluid—you should not be troubled with headaches.

You may have little or no feeling in your legs because of the regional anesthetic. As it begins to wear off—sometimes beginning about two hours after administration—you may begin to feel sensation in the form of tingling or "pins and needles" in your toes and legs and you may be able to move them a bit. Do not be frightened, however, if sensation returns slowly and then only in parts of your legs at a time, or if numbness remains for several hours. You will probably stay in the recovery room until you can move both your legs. Do not be frightened if the nurse asks you to move your legs and you think you can but somehow cannot. It takes a while, sometimes hours, to regain control of your movements.

As you begin to have feelings in your legs, you will also become aware of discomfort at the site of the incision in your abdomen. Do not wait for it to become extremely painful before asking for medication. Painkillers will have been ordered for you and will be administered by injection; a pill is not used because you are not permitted to take anything by mouth during the early recovery period.

During the hours following delivery, you may be either wide awake or sleepy even if you have had spinal anesthesia. Drowsiness may be a result of a long and difficult labor, the administration of a tranquilizer before the spinal, or a tranquilizer or narcotic after delivery of the baby, while suturing is taking place.

In some cases, after a spinal anesthetic was administered and the baby has been born, to ensure continued relaxation and more complete relief of pain, an additional general anesthetic may be given before the suturing is done.

If the baby's father has been with you during the delivery —a growing trend in more and more hospitals—he may follow you into recovery, where the two of you and the baby—if hospital procedure and the condition of mother and baby allow—can spend some time together. Then, the father is usually invited to follow the baby to the nursery, where he can observe through the nursery window. If the father was not present for the delivery, he usually waits in a waiting room or the lobby to hear the news of the birth from the doctor when surgery is completed, which sometimes takes as long as an hour or so. The new father is then admitted to the recovery room to join you and, ideally, the baby, before he or she is taken to the nursery.

Your blood pressure, pulse, temperature and respiration will be checked often, as will your incision and the amount, consistency and color of your vaginal bleeding. Yes, there *is* vaginal bleeding after a cesarean because the no-longer-necessary blood and uterine lining will be coming out of the cervical opening and through the vaginal canal.

Your uterus will be checked (by palpating your abdomen) to be sure that it is contracting as it should. This may be very painful to you because of the abdominal surgery you had, no matter how gentle the nurse is.

The most you can do to minimize the pain—for the several seconds of its duration—is, first of all, to know that it will take only several seconds, and, secondly, to release your entire body as much as possible with the help of a breathing technique such as the Lamaze slow chest breathing or light panting.

The I.V. which had been set up during labor or prior to surgery will remain with you during the recovery period and for the first twenty-four to forty-eight hours, giving you sugar and water (and sometimes salts). It will be discontinued when you begin to take fluids by mouth. The intravenous solution is also necessary to help minimize postoperative fever by avoiding dehydration.

Through the I.V. you will also be given—during the early recovery period—an oxytocic drug which stimulates contractions of the uterus, thus helping it to become firm and to prevent excessive blood loss.

These contractions may feel rather strong and might even be painful. It will help if you release all your body muscle groups and do a Lamaze breathing technique here again. If the contractions become too painful to handle with breathing and relaxation techniques plus medication, or if they seem to be one continuous pain or contraction, tell the nurse!

If you are awake and wish to breastfeed your baby, be prepared for the resulting uterine contractions to be strong and perhaps painful. Slow chest breathing might be helpful, or your doctor can prescribe a pain reliever that will have the least possible effect on your nursing baby.

Since the breastfeeding experience requires that you be as relaxed as possible, it might be a good idea to attempt breastfeeding in the recovery room while the regional anesthetic is still effective. If you are asked to wait until hours later, when you are in your own room, the regional anesthetic will have worn off and the incision area may be very sore; this may make it difficult for you to enjoy this very special moment. Medication for pain may help, although it *might* make you *and* your baby drowsy. This, of course, depends on the kind and dosage of the medication.

If at all possible, whether you plan to breastfeed or not, ask to have your baby (if this is your desire) while lying in the recovery room, where you are able to hold him or her in your arms. (In the delivery room you may not have been able to hold your child if your arms were strapped down, which is usually the case during a cesarean delivery. Holding your baby as soon as possible after delivery allows you and the baby to establish early bonding. If the father is present, he can hold the baby close to your face for you to look at, kiss and touch with your cheek. (See "The Cesarean Baby.")

Even if the hospital policy does not require twenty-four-hour observation of the baby in a special care unit, you may not be given the baby immediately because the medical staff may need some time—perhaps an hour or several hours—to observe the baby in the nursery to be sure the vital signs and body temperature are stable, even if surgery was *not* due to fetal distress. You may not even be interested in holding the baby—especially if you are exhausted and feeling much discomfort from the surgery. When you do get your baby, you will probably need help in order to find a comfortable way to hold him or her. (See below, "Suggested Positions for Breast- or Bottle-feeding," which are applicable for holding the baby, as well.)

If the baby is not permitted to stay with you in the recovery room or for the next few hours when you're in your postpartum room—either because of routine hospital policy, because the child is in actual need of intensive care, or because his or her body temperature needs regulating—try to arrange for the father to be permitted to make trips between you and the nursery so he can fill you in on the baby's activities, condition and whatever procedures are involved. Later on in your own room, if you do not feel comfortable enough to hold and feed the baby, it might be a good idea to have the father care for the baby at your bedside so you can see and get acquainted with him or her.

The National Institutes of Health (NIH) has recommended that the healthy newborn should not be routinely separated from mother and father following delivery. Each baby's requirement should be judged on an individual basis.

The urinary catheter (thin plastic tube) which had been inserted into your urethra prior to surgery usually remains there until approximately twenty-four hours afterward. This was necessary to empty your bladder duing the surgical procedure and continues to be necessary afterward because the bladder may not regain its normal functioning for a while after surgery and anesthesia.

In order to know that your kidneys are functioning properly, the catheter is connected to a special plastic container which measures your urine output. It will be removed painlessly when you are able to walk to the bathroom yourself, or sooner. Even then, your urine output will most probably continue to be measured, this time by catching your urine in a special pan attached to the inside of the toilet bowl. It will be helpful for you to drink fluids and do your vaginal floor exercises in order to encourage urine output and to control urination. Drinking enough fluids may also have some bearing on when the I.V. can be removed from your arm.

You may begin to feel discomfort, aches, or pain in one or both shoulders. This is believed by some health care professionals to be the postoperative result of air accumulations under the diaphragm.

One of the first and most important things you should do in the recovery room—or as soon as you can after delivery—is the following abdominal tightening exercise, which will help prevent painful gas buildup and begin to restore your abdominal muscle tone.

Hold both your palms, fingers interlaced, firmly over your incision, or hold a pillow firmly against your abdomen with your hands joined together on top of the pillow at the location of the incision. Inhale *slowly* and deeply through your nose and exhale *slowly* through your mouth while you apply pressure on your incision with your hands or pillow. Do this again and increase the amount of pressure slightly. Do this once more, but this time, after you inhale, hold your breath for a count of five and exhale slowly as before, while putting pressure on the incision. Do a set of these, every hour, increasing pressure a little each time, but lessen the pressure if you feel pain.

Supporting your abdomen with your hands (with or without a pillow) is called "splinting" and will be referred to as such in parts of this section. It is important that you "splint" whenever you cough, laugh, move your bowels, stand up, sit down, walk or do anything which strains the abdomen during the early postpartum days.

After the Recovery Room

When you're in your own room in the hospital, a nurse will, from time to time, examine your breasts, incision and your sanitary napkin (to check the amount, color, and consistency of the bloody discharge from your vagina). Your fluid intake and output will be measured. Your blood pressure and temperature will be taken. A low fever is common after surgery and usually does not indicate infection. If it rises above 100 degrees, however, you and your baby will probably be separated.

You will be encouraged to move your legs and to breathe deeply to prevent possible postoperative complications, such as phlebitis or pneumonia.

Belly Binders and Elastic Stockings

Your doctor may prescribe a belly binder—especially if you've had a vertical incision—either in the form of a large bandage wrapped around your abdomen or a wide elastic belt to be worn when you get out of bed and are mobile. When you are resting or asleep, it should be removed. Because the binder gives support to your abdomen and back when you begin to walk, it eases the discomfort. Since your muscles were stretched during pregnancy and have just been cut during surgery, binder enthusiasts insist that *something* must support your abdomen. If, when you stand and walk, nothing is there to support the abdominal wall in its flabby after-delivery state, its own weight, as it hangs loosely and uncontrolled, pulls at the incision. This increases pain at the incision site and may cause you to feel that it will split open.

If you do use the binder while in the hospital, expect, when you go home, to feel very strange and perhaps even uncomfortable when walking and standing without it. You may even experience the sensation that "everything is falling out." To prevent this feeling, before leaving the hospital have someone purchase a loose stretchable panty girdle to take the place of the binder. This will give you some degree of support, which may still be needed during your first few days at home—until your own abdominal muscles can begin to take over. For women who have had the "bikini cut," the binder is not considered as necessary, but some support, such as from a panty girdle, is usually recommended for walking and standing during the early postpartum days.

Some doctors claim that the incision bandage gives firm enough support during the first few days. When the bandage is removed, you might feel you need other means of support simply because it *feels* better. Some physicians and other health care professionals believe that it is not wise to have you rely on artificial support. They believe it is better for you, from the beginning, to learn to use your own abdominal muscles—albeit with the help of your hands (with or without a pillow), applying pressure and support (splinting) when you stand, turn over, cough, etc.

Some health care professionals believe a judicious mixture of both methods would be a good compromise for the best possible outcome. For example, the use of the binder for those with vertical incisions or the loosely fitting elastic panty girdle for those with bikini incisions during the first few days of recuperation in the hospital, and only when getting on and off the bed, standing, and walking. During the rest and sleep periods, the artificial abdominal support may be removed. All the while, abdominal tightening exercises (described later in the section) should be done to rebuild muscular ability for *self*-support. By the time you leave the hospital, you can "graduate" from the binder to part-time wearing of the lightweight panty girdle, or from the girdle to less and less use of it, meanwhile continuing abdominal tightening exercises. Eventually, you should be able to use your *own* muscle power to pull in the abdominal wall.

If your doctor advises you to wear stockings after surgery, to help prevent phlebitis, *wear them, take them home with you,* and continue to wear them for as long as your doctor recommends.

Walking

Within the first twenty-four hours after surgery, you will be encouraged to get off the bed and walk, *with the assistance of a nurse*. Sitting up for some mothers will be hard enough; walking can be quite difficult and painful, but it must be done. The longer you put it off, the harder it will be to take the first step. Walking improves circulation (which is vital to your recuperation) and helps to prevent other postoperative complications. Moving around is nature's way of getting all your body's functions back to normal. After your first bout with a bedpan, you may even welcome the struggle of getting off the bed and walking to the bathroom!

To minimize your discomfort, perhaps you can arrange for your first few walks to take place about forty-five minutes after receiving medication for pain. You might become somewhat dizzy from the medication, so be sure to have help the first few times.

One of the most common fears of cesarean mothers is that the incision will open. Be assured that this is highly unlikely. The fear is usually intensified by the frightening feeling—as you are trying to sit up, get off the bed, and stand—of pulling in the area of the incision. It may reassure you—as it has others—to take a good look at your incision before attempting to get off the bed. Actually seeing it, instead of leaving it to your imagination, may give you more confidence in trusting its durability. Also, remembering that there are layers of tissue beneath the skin which are also sutured, can reassure you of the strength of the repair. Then force yourself to get up and out of bed, keeping in mind that this feeling is normal and that incisions rarely open.

How to Get Out of Bed

To get up from a lying-down position, there are several recommended maneuvers. Let us assume you wish to get off the bed from the righthand side:

A: 1. Lie on your back, knees bent, feet flat on the bed. Inch your body over to the right edge of the bed. Lower your legs so that your entire body is flat on the bed. Then position your body and be ready so that when the upper part of the bed is raised, your buttocks will be where the bed creases or "breaks" and there will be no pressure on your abdomen while the bed pushes you into an upright position.

2. When you are ready, ask the nurse to *slowly* raise the back of the bed all the way up, inch by inch, while you concentrate on keeping your back flat against the bed. Remember to ask for the stepstool to be positioned and ready for you.

3. Ask for the upper half of the right rail to be raised so you can use it for arm support when you are ready to stand.

4. The back of the bed is now supporting your weight and you are already almost sitting straight up. Place your right hand, palm down, on the bed alongside and close to your right buttock, and your left hand on the bed close to your left buttock. Press down with all your might with both hands as though they were crutches, just to learn how to raise your body a bit off the bed. Rest. Do it again, *using your arms, not your abdominal muscles,* and this time, lift your body, inching your hands and body over to the edge of the bed. Rest. Support yourself again with *your arms as crutches,* and then, inch by inch or one leg at a time, or both, get your legs over the side of the bed.

5. Rest. Dangle your feet a while (have your slippers put on) and when you feel ready, brace your arms for support. Your right hand can use the side rail; your left hand can press into the bed or be supported by the nurse. Use your arms as crutches again to lift or slide your bottom off the bed, aiming your feet for the stepstool. (Wearing a binder if you have a vertical incision and wearing a loose elastic panty girdle if you have the bikini cut can make it much easier for you to support

your abdomen for this maneuver; there will be less pulling on your incision.)

6. Once standing, you *must* straighten up and stand tall! It will help if you splint your incision with your hands or pillow as you straighten up.

B: 1. While on your back, inch over to the right edge of the bed. Turn onto your right side, splinting your abdomen, and have the nurse raise the bed back *slowly* to a thirty-five- or forty-five-degree angle. Have someone tie a bedsheet securely to the foot of the bed and hold your end of the bedsheet with your left hand.

2. Using your left hand, pull on the bedsheet (or someone's hand) to help *pull* yourself up to a sitting position *while* you exert pressure with your right arm against the bed to *push* yourself up. As you rise upward, *swing both your legs together, in one movement,* over the side of the bed.

3. Continue as in No. 5 of the previous maneuver.

To get back into bed, use reverse procedures.

Important: You may be extremely reluctant to stand straight up because it may hurt a lot. But it is imperative that you fight the common desire to hunch over and adopt the stance referred to as the "cesarean shuffle." This may impede the healing process and can hurt even more.

Bonnie Donovan advises in her book, *The Cesarean Birth Experience,* ". . . remember to walk like a high-fashion model the first and every time that you walk." Keep that image in mind. Also, keep in mind the image of a thin straight scar which logically results from standing upright. Remember that the more mobile you become and the straighter you stand, the better you will actually feel.

Cesarean mothers and others who have had abdominal surgery advise that it is better for you to *straighten up by yourself, setting your own pace of movement* according to the discomfort that you are feeling at the time. The nurse who may be encouraging, leading, cheering you on to straighten up straighter or move a bit faster, cannot possibly know the extent of the "pulling" or discomfort you may be feeling. Moving faster than you feel you can manage may cause intense pain and you may have to go back to the position where you started and redo the process from the beginning. Therefore, brace yourself on a sturdy object or person, but be sure the person *does not pull you or lead you.* The lead should be taken by you.

Be prepared too for the normal sudden gush of blood from the vagina when you stand up after having been prone for hours. Before standing, wrap the disposable pad from your bed, diaper-style, onto you; it will help catch extra blood which your sanitary napkin may not. (It can be less embarrassing for you if no visitors are present during the first few times you attempt to get out of bed.)

Another possibility is that you may feel faint, weak or dizzy. This is normal for all new mothers and is yet another reason to be sure you have assistance before attempting to get up the first few times.

You may find it easier to walk or stand the first few days out of bed if your slippers have a small, wedge-type heel. Whenever you can, and *if* you can, try pulling in your abdominal muscles whether walking, standing, sitting or lying down.

Showers—not tub baths—are usually permitted within a few days after delivery.

If you received general anesthesia, you will periodically be asked to cough (see "Huffing" under "Exercises After Cesarean Birth") and breathe deeply in order to expel secretions and expand your lungs. Before you cough (or even laugh), try to tighten your abdominal muscles as you hold your hands or pillow firmly against your abdomen for support.

Pain Relief

If you feel pain coming on, ask for medication before the pain becomes unbearable. Do not wait for the nurse to offer it to you simply because four hours have passed since the last dose. You must request it if needed. Be sure to remind your doctor if you are breastfeeding so he or she can prescribe medication that will have the least effect on the baby.

Before leaving the hospital, ask your doctor to give you a prescription for some type of pain medication. Although your need for pain relief has probably decreased considerably, you may still need some mild painkillers now and then after you are home and more active.

Sanitary Belt

The sanitary belt, or the clasp on the belt, may bother your incision. You can try placing an extra pad beneath the belt, directly under the clasp. If this does not help, try using safety pins to attach the napkin directly to your underpants. Or, you can have someone purchase self-adhesive napkins (if the hospital does not have these) which attach directly to your underpants. You can also ask if your hospital has specially designed "cesarean sanitary belts"; some do.

Underwear

It is not wise to wear bikini-style underpants in the early postpartum period, no matter which incision you've had. In either case, irritation of the incision is likely where the elastic band makes contact. Have someone purchase full-cut, waist-high panty briefs for you—*preferably cotton*.

Elimination

After surgery, moving your bowels becomes a major concern. Be sure to eat foods and drink liquids which can best encourage easier bowel movements with minimal straining. When you do have a bowel movement, remember to splint the incision while straining.

For information concerning easier bowel movements, urination and perineal care, see the section "Procedures Involving the Mother."

Healing

Your incision may not bother you at all, or it may feel numb, "pull," or ooze a little. The pulling sensation may be coming from inside the abdomen at the site of the deeper *internal* incision which may be higher than your skin incision.

If your incision becomes itchy as it heals, your doctor may advise applying warm compresses. After it heals, baby oil may help relieve itching. Avoid wearing nylon or rayon underpants during this itchy period and while pubic hair is growing back. Cotton panties will be more comfortable. When you get the urge to scratch your incision, try scratching a different part of your body; you may be surprised at how that can help.

Removing the Sutures

Before you leave the hospital, the outer sutures—if they are the non-absorbable type—will be removed. If one continuous suture was used directly beneath the skin (subcuticular), the doctor will clip one end and pull it out. You might shiver at the *thought*, but this is not considered painful. If anything, there might be a slight burning sensation, depending on the material used. If individual sutures were used, they will be clipped and removed one by one.

If clamps or staples were used, these will be removed about five to eight days after surgery and this procedure should not be painful. If your recuperation is good and you want to leave the hospital early, you can have the sutures, clamps or staples removed in your doctor's office after you come home.

First Foods

Many doctors recommend that your first oral nourishment be clear fluids (water, juices, broth, tea, jello), either warm or at room temperature, followed by a soft diet (yogurt, mashed potatoes, creamed soups, farina, broiled fish), before beginning more solid foods. The rationale is that your gastrointestinal tract needs time to recuperate after surgery before getting back to work on the digestion of solids. Other physicians believe solids should *not* be delayed but given as soon as tolerated to prevent or minimize what others consider inevitable: gas pains. Also, they believe you need the nutrients of a well-balanced diet as soon as you are ready to eat it—after childbirth and surgery.

If your diet is restricted to liquids and you do not believe you are receiving the nutrients you'd like, ask your doctor if you can have supplemental vitamin and mineral tablets to replenish your system after the ordeal of surgery. (After childbirth—without having had surgery—you would need a well-balanced diet for health and energy; after surgery, your need is even greater.) Whatever you eat, stay away from spicy and other gas-producing foods.

Gas Pains

Gas pains after surgery are common, although their intensity varies from mild to extreme. They are believed to be caused by one or all of the following: the unavoidable handling of your intestines and exposure to air during the cesarean (which occurs in any abdominal surgery situation); the temporary stoppage of intestinal activity due to anesthesia and the lack of stimulation of normal intestinal action by your activity and lack of food.

To relieve yourself of gas:

●Be mobile. Get off the bed and walk.

●If you are confined to bed and cannot be mobile, move about in your bed; turn over as often as you can (holding your incision with your hands or pillow).

●Ask for the flexible rectal tube to be inserted into your rectum while you are lying down resting or going to sleep for the night. This is not painful and can be very helpful in allowing gas to escape. (In some cases, a suppository or enema may be advised by the doctor.)

●Lying on your belly, with a pillow beneath your hips, can also help you expel gas.

•Lying on your left side, knees bent, while gently kneading your abdominal wall, encourages the release of gas.

•If the back of your bed is raised, be aware of your tendency to curl up in a ball toward the lower end of the bed after a while. This position may block the escape of intestinal gas. Pull yourself up to a sitting position or flatten the bed and straighten yourself out so you are lying flat on your back or abdomen for a while.

•Drink fluids—warm rather than cold—to get your intestinal system working.

•Avoid cold drinks.

•Avoid carbonated drinks, which tend to produce more gas. Some doctors, however, recommend that you drink some warm ginger ale to encourage burping—another way to rid yourself of gas. If so, sip it slowly through a straw *after* some of the bubbles have subsided.

•Try using slow, deep breathing to relax your entire system and help relieve you of gas.

After a cesarean delivery you may expect to remain in the hospital approximately five to ten days—depending on your rate of recuperation and the routine of your hospital and physician. Remember to ask for a prescription for pain medication to have handy at home if and when you need it.

Just as vaginal delivery mothers have physical restrictions during the first weeks at home, so do cesarean mothers—although extra precautions are usually advised. Avoid lifting, climbing stairs, housework, and all strenuous activity until approved by your doctor. Rest, with your feet up, and sleep as much as necessary. Driving a car is sometimes not recommended because you may feel dizzy and have hot flashes for weeks.

If the lochia (postpartum vaginal bleeding) again becomes profuse after it has tapered off, or if it has a foul odor or seems unusual in any way, discuss it with your doctor or nurse midwife.

Be sure to return to your doctor for your postpartum examination, at which time your breasts, incision and abdominal wall will be checked. You will also be given an internal examination (to check your cervix and size and position of the uterus). If all is well, you will probably be encouraged to resume normal activities, including sexual relations.

Breastfeeding After a Cesarean

There is no reason why you cannot breastfeed your baby just because you've had a cesarean. Every statement made to the effect that it cannot be done, it should be done, or "you'll be so exhausted from the ordeal of surgery that you will not have enough milk" can be countered with a statement to the contrary from a satisfied nursing cesarean mother. As a matter of fact, a feeling commonly expressed by cesarean mothers who breastfeed is that after being inactive, non-participating and out of control of the situation during the delivery process, it meant so much to them to be able to actively participate and feel *in* control, through the act of breastfeeding.

If you are taking medication for pain, some of it may reach the baby through your colostrum or milk and *might* make the infant a bit sleepy. Your doctor or nurse midwife can prescribe medication that has the least possible effect on your baby.

Whether you breastfeed or bottlefeed your baby, it may be difficult for you to sit comfortably while feeding. Because of the I.V. in your arm and the incision in your abdomen, your movements and positions will be very limited.

Suggested Positions for Breast- or Bottlefeeding

1. Sit up with good back support and place the baby in your arm, resting your arm and baby on two thick pillows in your lap. This avoids pressure on your abdomen and strain in your arm, shoulder and back. To burp the baby, lean him or her forward to a sitting position, supporting the baby by cupping the chin in your hand while rubbing the back with your other hand.

2. Lie in bed on your side with a pillow supporting your back and your abdomen. Place the baby on his or her side, on the bed, so he or she can reach your nipple. To burp the baby, roll the baby onto his or her stomach, or place the baby belly

down on your chest, roll onto your back with the baby, and gently rub the baby's back. To turn over to your other side, keep the baby on your chest, holding him or her there as you roll over.

Position for Breastfeeding

You can sit up and hold your baby in the "football hold." For example, using your left arm, hold the back of the baby's head in your open palm, with the body resting along the length of your arm, at your side, and the legs pointing in the direction behind your body. You can have a pillow or two along your left side for added support for your arm and baby. This position avoids any pressure on your abdomen from the weight of the baby. If you are having trouble, ask the nurse to help you get the baby into the football-hold position. To burp the baby, turn the infant onto its stomach across the pillow at your side.

Helpful Hints

●Always keep a small pillow handy for ready aid in splinting (supporting your abdomen with your hands).

●To lie on your side, place pillows between your knees, behind your back, and in front of your stomach for support.

●To turn over, splint your incision while you turn. Do not hold your breath. In fact, try inhaling before you turn, then, as you turn, apply pressure to the incision and exhale slowly.

●Before sneezing, coughing, laughing, defecating—splint your incision. (Do not suppress a cough for fear of opening your incision. Splint the incision, take a few in and out breaths and cough.)

●Wear *cotton* nightgowns instead of nylon or rayon. Cotton does not cling, is absorbent, is cooler, and therefore causes less perspiration—a real help because increased perspiration and "hot flashes" are common during the postpartum period. If you cannot locate suitable cotton nightgowns, use other loose-fitting cotton garments.

•Remember, you have had a baby, but you have also had major surgery. Any new mother, after childbirth, needs rest to recuperate, and any person who has had abdominal surgery is expected to go home to bed and rest! You have had both.

•If, in addition, you had a long, difficult labor prior to the cesarean, you need even more rest. Follow the advice given elsewhere in this book concerning rest and relaxation after having a baby.

•Arrange things at home so that you will not need to climb stairs for the first two weeks. Set up your sleeping area on the same floor where there is a bathroom.

•Help at home after a cesarean delivery is vital to your recuperation. Someone—not you—is needed to prepare meals and clean up afterward, do laundry and food shopping, cleaning, and other household chores. Taking care of the baby and your own rest and health care needs is more than enough for you at this time. The more rested you are during the first two weeks, the better you will be able to resume responsibilities afterward.

•If you do not expect to have someone helping you at home, be sure to inquire in the hospital if a public health nurse or a visiting nurse can come to your home once or twice a week without charge to help you out for a while with baby care.

•If you have nobody living in with you to help, you might want to keep your baby in a bassinet near your bed, along with a supply of diapers, lotions and clothing changes so you will have less walking to do. If you are breastfeeding, all you have to do is lift the baby from the bassinet and bring him or her into bed with you. If you are bottlefeeding, you can ask your mate to prepare and bring the bottle to you so you can remain in bed to feed the baby.

•The more help you *ask for* and *take,* the sooner you will recuperate and be able to resume your normal activities.

•Try always to have someone with you or readily available during the first two weeks. If you are not up to dealing with a crying baby when you're trying to deal with your own abdominal discomfort and exhaustion, it can be a blessing to have your mate, neighbor, friend, mother or relative cuddle the baby for a while.

•Eating a well-balanced diet is essential to *all* new mothers, and even more important to the cesarean mother to aid the healing process.

•Plan to wear loose-fitting clothes for a while. You may be feeling too tender to wear regular slacks or jeans the first few weeks, even if you can fit into them. Zipper-front pants are especially difficult to negotiate.

•Showers are more practical than baths because they are easier to manage than getting in and out of a low tub.

•You might be able to obtain (through rental or purchase) an elevated toilet seat that easily attaches to your regular one. You can use this in the hospital as well as at home. This minimizes the discomfort involved in lowering and raising yourself to and from the level of the ordinary seat, which, after abdominal surgery, becomes a major project.

•When riding in the car, *use* the seatbelt—placing a small pillow between the belt and your belly if your incision is tender.

•Remember that each day you will feel better than the day before.

•If you have older children, you will temporarily be unable to lift or play with them the way you may have before—due to your recent surgery. You will also be spending a lot of time resting in bed. *Use* this time to give your older children the love and attention they need. Ask them to keep you company and read, draw pictures, talk, sing, cuddle, or watch TV together.

•After you have your postpartum examination and receive permission to resume sexual relations, you may be faced with some of the same problems experienced by vaginal-delivery mothers, including lack of or decreased desire, exhaustion, decreased vaginal secretions, embarrassment concerning leaking breasts, stretch marks and flabby abdomen and general physical discomfort. (No discomfort in the perineum, however, because there was no episiotomy!)

•In addition, the cesarean mother (and father) may fear that sexual relations might cause pain at the site of the incision, cause rupture of the scar or in some way interfere with the healing process. If your doctor or nurse midwife has given you the go-ahead after your postpartum checkup, you can be sure that this will not occur.

•Position during sexual relations is sometimes a problem. For some, the man-above position is very uncomfortable. The woman-above position gives more freedom of movement and is more comfortable. For others, the woman-above position is more difficult due to the pull of gravity on the incision, but the man-above position is less stressful (providing his body is not pressed against hers). Much depends on the extent of healing and the physical builds of the partners, etc.

•Body image after childbirth is usually a problem— whether the baby was born vaginally or abdominally. This is often a greater source of difficulty for the cesarean mother, who has to deal not only with flabbiness and stretch marks on her belly, but also itchy pubic hair re-growth and the appearance of the cesarean scar on her abdomen.

The vividness of the stretch marks and scar will fade in time, but somehow, *knowing* this does not help at the moment. What *can* help is dimming or changing the color of your bedroom lights (try a pink bulb!), wearing an attractive shortie nightgown and directing your thoughts far away from your incision and stretch marks!

EXERCISES AFTER CESAREAN BIRTH

There are several exercises that can be done after a cesarean delivery to prevent possible postoperative complications. These exercises involve respiration, circulation and muscle tone. Be sure to get your doctor's permission before beginning any exercise program.

Slow Chest Breathing (Lamaze)

To expand your lungs after inactivity during surgery, inhale a long, deep breath *slowly* through your nose; exhale *slowly* through your mouth, while you try to pull in your abdominal muscles. Let the exhalation take a long time in getting out; try imagining making a candle flame flicker with your slowly exhaled breath for as long as possible. Do three of these ins and outs every fifteen minutes as soon as possible after delivery. (Each group of three should be done at least once an hour.)

Slow Breathing with Abdominal Splinting

To prevent and relieve gas pains and to shorten the recuperation period, the following technique should be started as early as one hour after delivery and should be continued four or five times every hour you are awake and for at least five days. You will find this very uncomfortable the first time you try it, but it becomes easier each time.

Splint your incision with your hands or pillow. Take a deep breath into your chest. Let it all out slowly while applying a little more pressure on the incision. Take another deep chest breath in and hold it for a count of five; let it all out while slightly increasing the pressure. Take a final deep chest breath in and let it out, applying slightly more pressure. The pressure should not result in pain. (Note: If you are able to tighten or pull in your abdominal muscles, *while you breathe out and splint,* do so.)

Not all hospitals are familiar with this exercise technique, so you may be questioned by the nurses as to what you are doing and why. This exercise is becoming a standard recommendation by cesarean childbirth support and education groups.

Huffing (Instead of Coughing)

Postoperative patients are told to cough during the early recuperative period in order to dislodge mucus from the lungs. Coughing as we know it is not usually effective, partially because the postoperative patient is so afraid that her abdomen will hurt that she attempts to please the nurse and gives a few coughlike sounds from the throat while tensing up, thereby increasing internal pressure on the abdomen and pelvic floor muscles. This action is counterproductive because it usually does not bring up mucus and causes unnecessary muscular strain.

To better accomplish this dislodging of mucus with less discomfort and more benefit to the internal organs, a technique referred to as "huffing" is being recommended by cesarean support groups and its use is spreading among post-cesarean mothers.

Before huffing, splint your incision with your hands or a pillow. To huff, pull in your abdominal wall and use your diaphragm to force air from your lungs (all the while helping yourself by holding your incision). Your mouth should be opened wide with your jaw dropped. A huff should be quick (in order to be most effective) and the sound you would be making is that of a loud whispered "ha." (The sound of a cough involves the throat; the sound of a huff does not.) You should huff one or two times every hour until you feel no more mucus present.

If mucus comes up into your mouth, be sure to spit it out into a tissue or cup. Swallowing it only defeats the purpose of huffing and you will have wasted your effort.

Ankle Rotating

For blood circulation and toning of leg muscles, rotate each foot at the ankle in a circle. Rotate from one side to the other and then point the toes downward, bringing them around and finishing a circular motion. Rotate each foot separately or both together in the same or opposite directions.

Foot Flexing and Stretching

This exercise is also for blood circulation and leg muscle toning. Flex your foot slowly at the ankle with toes pointed toward your body; you will feel stretching in your calf muscles. Then point your toes slowly away from you. Do this several times with each foot. You can do one foot at a time or both together in the same or opposite directions.

Single Leg Sliding

To strengthen the abdominal muscles, from a flat-on-your-back position, slide one leg up toward you, bending your knee, until your heel is near your buttocks. Then slowly slide the leg back down to its starting position and press the leg into the bed, holding it for a count of three. (Do not hold your breath.) Do the same with the other leg. Do a minimum of five each leg, every hour, for the first two days at least.

Buttocks

Contract your buttock muscles, holding tightly for a count of four. (Do not hold your breath.) Do five of these contractions every hour for the first two days at least.

Pelvic Floor

Contract your pelvic floor muscles (those you would use to stop the flow of urine) and hold them for a count of three. (Do not hold your breath.) Do five of these contractions every hour for the first two days at least. Eventually, build up to a total of fifty vaginal contractions a day for the rest of your life.

Pelvic Rock

To strengthen abdominal muscles, improve posture, relieve backache and to stimulate intestinal activity, lie flat on your back with no pillow beneath your head, knees bent and feet flat on the floor. Take a slow, deep breath in through your nose, allowing the small of your back to curve away from the floor a bit. Exhale slowly through your mouth as you slowly pull your abdominal muscles in tightly, with the aid of splinting, and let out all your air as you go, while pressing the small of your back as flat as you can against the floor. Then start again, eventually reaching a total of five ins and outs.

Rocking

The use of a rocking chair helps blood circulation, which promotes healing.

After your doctor has given you the okay, you can increase your exercises and other physical activities as you feel ready and as your strength and abilities grow.

THE CESAREAN BABY

The intent of this section is to point out procedures particularly common to the cesarean-delivered baby. For more information concerning procedures involving *all* newborns, we refer you to the section "Procedures Involving the Baby."

Ideally, during a cesarean delivery, a pediatrician is present or nearby and readily available should any problems or complications arise.

In a cesarean, as in a vaginal delivery, the baby may be born head first or breech first. As soon as the head is delivered, mucus will be suctioned out of the nose and mouth to allow a clear passageway for breathing. When the entire body is born and if the umbilical cord is long enough, the obstetrician may hold the baby up high enough for you to see over the screen that covers your chest. If the baby's father is present for the delivery, he will have about the same span of vision from his seat on a stool alongside you. His head will be approximately level with yours and his view of the surgical area will be hampered by your chestscreen.

At first sight, your baby will be wet, perhaps covered with some vernix, and the skin may be bluish. Usually, a bit of blood picked up during the birth process coats part of the skin. (For more details, see "Characteristics of the Newborn.")

After the cord is clamped and cut, the baby will probably be handed to a pediatrician or nurse, who then carries him or her to another area of the delivery room where he or she is further attended to.

The baby will probably be placed in a special unit, which will regulate body temperature, has equipment for sucking out more secretions from the mouth, nose and throat, and has oxygen available in case it is needed. The pediatrician will examine the baby to be sure all vital signs are good and that there are no serious problems. This may take approximately three to five minutes.

After the baby has been examined, suctioned and judged to be out of danger, he or she will be wrapped and may be brought to you while you are still on the delivery table and the obstetrician is tending to your abdomen. If the father is present, *he* can hold and bring the baby to you. If your arms are not free, the baby can be held—by the father or nurse—close to your face for you to look at, kiss and touch with your cheek. If one arm can be freed (which usually can be arranged), perhaps the baby can be placed on your chest for you to hold with your free arm.

After the usual delivery room procedures and, possibly, some time spent with the parents, the cesarean-born infant is—in many cases—routinely whisked away to the nursery for special observation and care and is kept there for an eight- to twenty-four-hour period.

The rationale for this is that cesarean babies tend to have more mucus and respiratory problems than those born vaginally and they therefore need closer observation.

However, if there is no indication of respiratory difficulty and no medical reason for the baby to be kept under special care in the nursery (other than routine observation) *and* if you would like to hold and get to know your baby for a while, express your wishes. Many health care professionals see no reason against this and every reason to encourage early bonding, which can take place in the delivery or recovery room. More and more hospitals today are beginning to relax their previous inflexible rules and are treating each cesarean baby according to the infant's individual condition and birth circumstances, instead of using one ruling for all. The National Institutes of Health Task Force has recommended that the healthy newborn should not be routinely separated from

mother and father following delivery. Each baby's requirements should be judged on an individual basis.

If your baby is kept under special care for observation (not
treatment) he or she will probably be in a warmer (heated crib)
to stabilize the body temperature. If the baby is premature,
weighs under five pounds, or has any respiratory or other
problems, he or she will be in a special enclosed unit which
regulates temperature and provides a sterile atmosphere. In
more and more hospitals today, under certain circumstances,
the new mother can come to the nursery and touch, caress and
sometimes feed her infant through the special openings (port-
holes) in the enclosed unit. The cesarean baby who has been
separated from his or her mother for many hours or several
days needs *extra* cuddling and loving.

Possible Problems of the Cesarean Newborn

Because cesarean babies do not pass through the vaginal
canal, they do not benefit from the "big squeeze" which the
narrow passageway would ordinarily give to the lungs. As a
result, they are born with more fluid in the lungs and may
have more difficulty breathing and clearing the respiratory
passages.

Just as fluids are squeezed out of vaginally delivered
babies' lungs, so gastric substances are squeezed out of their
stomachs. Not having benefited from this pressure cesarean
infants tend to be more "mucusy."

Many premature labors result in cesarean deliveries and
these premature babies tend to develop what is called a "hyaline membrane" in their lungs; this interferes with breathing.
Hyaline membrane disease is often mistakenly thought to be
the result of cesarean birth. The cause seems to be related to
the immaturity of the infant's lungs, *not* to the method of
delivery—and this cannot be helped if labor begins and the
baby is born before being mature enough. Sometimes, however, an attempt is made to stop labor or to speed up fetal lung
maturity by administering certain medications to the mother.
When a cesarean delivery is planned in advance (such as a
repeat cesarean or one necessitated by an inadequate pelvis),
precautions can be taken to prevent the possibility of deliver-

ing a prematurely developed infant. This is done with the aid of amniocentesis or sonography. When fetal maturity is thereby confirmed, a date can more safely be chosen for scheduling the cesarean.

FEELINGS AFTER A CESAREAN

One of the most difficult aspects of a cesarean delivery is coming to terms with the fact afterward. No matter how advanced the technology, no matter how common the procedure, major abdominal surgery *did* occur and the early days of recuperation will most likely be extremely difficult.

If your cesarean was performed under emergency conditions and you were awake at the time the decision was made, you may be able to readily accept the reality of what has happened. If your baby had been in danger and the most feasible way to accomplish a safe delivery was by surgery, you may very likely feel thankful that cesarean delivery was a safe alternative, and feel relief that the danger has passed and joy at the sight of a healthy baby.

One woman reported, "When they said 'fetal distress' and started rushing around and someone tried to calm me by saying 'Everything will be all right,' I knew that everything might not be all right and after the cesarean all I could think was 'Thank goodness the baby's all right.' If they had waited or if this had been a century ago, I would not have my beautiful and healthy baby."

If you had a long, painful labor, you may feel a great sense of relief that it's all over and be grateful for the end of your suffering—thanks to a cesarean delivery. One woman said: "I never thought I could actually welcome the idea of a cesarean, but by the time the doctor decided to go ahead with surgery, I was the happiest woman in the world. I had been in hard labor for many hours and this meant that it would soon be all over."

It is quite possible that you *have* accepted your surgery as a matter of necessity, fully understanding the circumstances surrounding it, and are not upset that it has occurred. Some cesarean mothers do express feelings of being glad labor is over, that they and the baby are healthy—and who cares about the scar as long as everything is all right?

Sometimes, however, negative thoughts and feelings about the experience may be blocked temporarily and can surface the next day, or weeks or months later when a related incident can open the floodgates. A simple statement from a new mother you meet at your childbirth preparation class reunion ("Lamaze is the only way to have a baby!") or a question from another mother at the pediatrician's office ("Did you go natural?") can set you off. After a cesarean delivery, many new mothers do *not* easily accept what happened. In reliving the events in your head you may begin to feel that the hours of labor and discomfort prior to surgery were all in vain. You may begin to resent your doctor for allowing the labor to go on for so long before deciding on the cesarean. Or, if the decision to do it was made early in labor, you might now be questioning the motives and silently accusing the doctor of being "knife happy," "planning all along to do a cesarean," or "in too much of a hurry" to give you "more of a chance to get that baby down" yourself.

No matter what the circumstances were at the moment of decision—whether it was an emergency or not, whether you had been prepared in advance for the possibility of surgery or not—you may now have a very strong need to understand exactly what happened. It may become vital for you to reconstruct the events—one by one—leading up to and culminating in the doctor's decision to operate. No matter how much your doctor may have been able to explain prior to surgery (if you were awake), no matter how well you were able to understand the reasoning at the time, you, the cesarean mother, need to and deserve to hear it all again. You may hear yourself asking question after question, repeating yourself many times to several different people—the doctor, the nurses, your mate, anyone who knows something about your experience— to fit together the missing pieces of your experience. In fact, this is probably even *more* important to you than to a vaginal-delivery mother because you have the additional need to *justify* in your own mind the way your baby was born.

Even after receiving all the information and reassurance you can get, you still may feel disappointment in the way things turned out.

If you had hoped to have a Lamaze or other such prepared delivery, your feelings may range from disappointment and frustration to anger and resentment for not having "given birth." The baby was "taken" from you by a relative stranger: the doctor.

Some cesarean mothers who had counted on a vaginal delivery may feel "abnormal" because they did not have what is considered a "normal" delivery. Thoughts like these are common: "What's wrong with me? Why couldn't I have my baby the *right* way? I'm not a *real* woman. I'm just not made right."

A sense of failure is also common. "I couldn't do it. Not only couldn't I have the Lamaze delivery I planned and practiced for, but I couldn't even have a run-of-the-mill, old-fashioned vaginal delivery, Lamaze or not!"

Another feeling often expressed is that of being "cheated" out of the birth experience because you didn't "push the baby out." If you were asleep for the cesarean, you might feel this even more acutely because your active participation—even as observer—was removed by general anesthesia.

"I'll never know what it *feels* like to give birth, to push a baby out—like other women."

There are other women, to be sure, who would prefer *not* to feel the feelings cesarean mothers miss.

If you had planned to share your birth experience with your mate after having gone together to childbirth preparation classes, practiced the exercises and looked forward to being together for a most important moment in your lives, your disappointments are greater if the father is excluded. You may feel guilty for "letting him down" and preventing him from being present at his child's birth. More self-blame.

Besides feeling badly for your mate, it is likely that you felt as badly or worse about being "alone" for the delivery. One of the most commonly expressed regrets of cesarean mothers is that of being separated from their mates at the most stressful time—going into the operating room. A feeling of abandonment is common. Although an increasing number of hospitals are welcoming fathers to be present in cesarean delivery rooms, many still do not.

"I felt lost, alone, on my own at a time I desperately needed not to be."

"How could they send Gary away when they saw the difference in *me?* I was so calm and in control and able to handle the whole thing. But as soon as the doctor told him he had to go, I panicked! But they didn't care. All they cared about were the rules."

Your disappointment may lead to feelings of resentment. You may even become angry—at the doctor, your childbirth preparation instructor, the baby or even the baby's father—for their parts in the eventual outcome. The doctor, for the decision to operate; your instructor, for not having prepared you for *this;* the baby, for making labor difficult and vaginal delivery impossible; and the baby's father, for starting it all at conception. If you decide it is unreasonable to direct your anger toward others, you may find it more acceptable to become angry with *yourself.* Why not? you may reason. *Somebody's* got to be at fault.

You may find yourself falling into the "if only" syndrome: if only I had been able to hold out longer, if only I had practiced my breathing more, if only I had pushed better, if only I were more relaxed, if only I weren't so uncooperative, I wouldn't have needed a cesarean.

If you are thinking along these lines, it bears some rethinking: can you really blame yourself if your baby was too large for your pelvis, if your pelvis was too small for your baby, if your baby's position made it impossible to be born vaginally, if your cervix refused to dilate enough, etc. etc. etc.? Logically, no. Therefore, try to catch yourself each time as you think self-blaming thoughts and redirect them to what *really* happened. You *do not* have control over the size of your pelvis, a transverse position, a stubborn cervix, etc.

Your feelings from day to day may change drastically. One day you may be so happy that all is well with you and your baby and not care that yours was a cesarean delivery; the next day you might be very upset and angry that this had to happen to you. Strangely conflicting and shifting emotions may plague you from day to day because you are experiencing normal postpartum hormonal changes and you are recuperating from the shock of a major abdominal operation. In addition, it is possible that medication you may be receiving for pain relief might be having a depressing effect on you. You might want to discuss this with your doctor.

If you were asleep for the delivery—especially if you had not planned it that way—it may be very difficult for you, the cesarean mother, to make the connection between the baby handed to you in a neatly wrapped bundle twenty-four hours after birth and the baby that had been within your body before surgery. There was a time lapse, a missing segment which has to be accounted for and adjusted to. Even if you had been awake and the baby was shown to you briefly in the operating room, before being whisked away to the nursery for twenty-four hours, identifying with the baby is sometimes difficult. Mothers who were awake during a cesarean delivery describe feelings of being "removed" from the birth process because of the screen placed on their chests. The purpose of the screen is to block the possibility of infection from entering the sterile field. However, it also blocks the sight and awareness of the abdominal area.

"My head seemed to be a separate part of me—totally removed from the rest of my body. It was almost like being the showgirl who gets cut in half in a magic show. That's how I felt. The part of me that had the baby was so far away that it wasn't real, it couldn't be happening!"

Concern about the baby's welfare is often aggravated by routine nursing procedures:

"After the cord was cut they took the baby to the other side of the room where I couldn't see him at all. Then, without more than a glimpse of him, they had him out of the room and to the nursery."

These feelings point up the need for change in hospital routines to help cesarean mothers "connect" with their babies. Some hospitals have begun to show sensitivity to these needs by examining the newborn within the mother's line of vision if she is awake so she can *see* her new baby as he or she is being examined and suctioned. If no special care is required and if the father is present, he can hold the baby and place the baby close to the mother's face for kissing and cuddling.

One or both of the mother's hands can be freed of restraint so she can touch and fondle her infant. The baby might also be placed on her shoulder.

Because most hospitals routinely place cesarean babies under special care, you might be separated from your baby for twelve to twenty-four hours. This may give you the feeling that your baby belongs to everyone else at the hospital but you. More isolation. More feelings of being different from other mothers who can have and hold their babies. However, more and more hospitals are relaxing their rules about separating mother and baby and deciding procedure according to the baby's condition. And, through mounting pressure, individually and from cesarean support groups, hospitals are beginning to recognize and meet the special needs of cesarean parents.

Many cesarean mothers who breastfeed their babies say that this was the saving grace for them because in no other way did they feel "normal." "At least I could do *something* right."

If you are having difficulty getting started with breastfeeding, get all the help and encouragement you can from other breastfeeding mothers (contact the La Leche League) in order to help you through the first few weeks, which are usually the most difficult. Without such help, you might be tempted to give up before giving it a good enough try and consider it yet another "failure." The postpartum period is shaky enough under ordinary circumstances, and you, more than the vaginal-delivery new mother, need every boost you can get to enhance your self-esteem.

To compound your feelings of inadequacy, you may hear yourself referred to as "the section in Room 211." Resentment has been so strong among today's cesarean mothers because of the routine use of the word *section* that cesarean support groups throughout the country have latched on to the battlecry: "Grapefruits are sectioned; women give birth!" This clearly expresses the sentiments of cesarean mothers and has helped to raise the consciousness of a growing number of childbirth educators who studiously avoid using *section* in classes and speak instead of "cesarean birth," "cesarean baby," or simply "a cesarean." The next step is to raise the consciousness of our medical and nursing school educators so that each new crop of aspiring doctors and nurses will stop referring to cesarean mothers as "sections."

You, the new mother who happened to have your baby by cesarean, are nevertheless a new mother. You have had a baby and need to be treated not just as a surgical patient—which undeniably you are—but also, and very importantly, as the new mother you are. You need to know *and* accept the fact that it really does not matter through which route your baby managed to enter our world (as long as it was the route of necessity). Think back. Did you say to yourself when you discovered you were pregnant, "I am going to have a baby—

vaginally," or simply, "I am going to have a baby"? Try putting the mode of delivery in perspective; it was not your prime reason for conceiving. This thought may help you to come to terms with what happened. It may also help if you look at yourself in terms of a total person: Does the childbirth delivery route in any way affect the person you are? Does it make you less of a woman, mother, lover, friend, neighbor, whatever?

Crying jags and depression may occur more so to you, the cesarean mother, because there are more frustrations. While the vaginal-delivery mother in the next bed is up and around on the first day, your slightest movement—turning over, sitting up, coughing or huffing—takes enormous effort and hurts during the first several days. While she is heartily indulging in all kinds of goodies from her hospital food trays and snacks from visitors, your daily fare three times a day for the first few days (if your doctor is of the soft-foods-after-cesarean school of thought) is gelatin or custard, clear broth and tea.

While she may be retelling her Lamaze birth experience for the umpteenth time, you may be explaining to friends why your cesarean was necessary. While she's packing to leave for home with her new baby, you're still learning how to "splint your incision" and "stand up straight, honey." And on the day you may have bid farewell and good luck to another roommate who has come and gone before you, a flood of tears can easily be triggered at the sight of yet another tray of food with the inevitable gelatin.

If you have other children at home, and your hospital does not permit sibling visitation, you have yet another frustration to contend with: the lack of contact (other than by telephone) with your children for an extended period. This can be difficult for the children to handle because not only will they have to deal with a new baby in their midst, but also they may find it hard to comprehend why their mother had to be away from home and in a hospital which was off-limits to them—with that new baby! Your frustrations resulting from this situation are not helpful to your recuperation. After such an experience many new mothers—cesareans or not—seek out a hospital for the next time which permits sibling visitation, or they join organizations which work to change existing hospital policies.

Since cesarean mothers as a group tend to include a higher

than usual number of women with high-risk tendencies (due to diabetes or other problems), their babies often are placed in special care units. Knowing your baby is being specially cared for and observed adds to the usual concerns many new mothers have about the welfare of their babies. Mixed with your worry about the baby's condition may be a sense of relief that "someone else is taking care of the baby," while you can recuperate and care for yourself. You may begin to feel guilty for thinking of yourself at a time like this, but it is normal to be concerned with your own physical condition and there is no better time for you than now, when the medical staff is relieving you temporarily. As your physical and emotional strength increase, you may be able to arrange to see and touch your baby several times each day even if he or she is in the special care unit.

When you do come home from the hospital, it may be difficult for you to accept your postoperative condition. The physical limitations may increase your feelings of helplessness. You may feel guilty for tiring easily and having to be dependent on others for the care of your baby, your house, your other children and yourself.

"I felt like such a burden! I couldn't bear lying around and letting everyone *do* things for me. It's not my style. But I had no choice. Whenever I tried to do things for myself and I bent too low or moved too quickly or did too much, I'd *have* to stop. That's when I'd cry from frustration."

"I didn't feel like a new mother, I felt like an old woman, an invalid. It took some of the joy away but when I accepted it—the fact that I was recuperating from surgery—I felt myself getting stronger *and* happier each day."

If yours was a vertical incision, you may feel very upset about the scar on your abdomen. You may believe that it is ugly and that you will never again be able to wear a bikini or undress in front of anyone. You may worry that your mate will not be able to adjust to it and might even be turned off by it.

Many people are left with scars on their bodies, not just as a result of childbirth. Each individual must find a way to accept what has happened. You will need to adjust to your new body image, which includes the cesarean scar. This is now a part of you, just like your nose, your ears or any other permanent feature of your body. If *you* accept it as a part of who you are, if *you* walk proudly, wear clothing with assurance and do not try to cover or hide the scar, others will accept it. If *you* exhibit no signs of shame or embarrassment, your cool and confident manner will set people at ease. If *you're* not upset about the scar, if *you* aren't embarrassed or ashamed of it, why should they be upset, embarrassed or ashamed *for* you?

Because you are so aware of your scar, you may assume that it has monumental significance to anyone who sees it. Your concept of its magnitude and visibility may be out of all proportion to reality. Try to see yourself not as a woman *with a scar on her abdomen,* but as *a woman* who happens to have a scar on her abdomen. Where you place the accent in your own head really makes the difference.

Prime sources for emotional support during the early adjustment period are other mothers who have had the cesarean experience. What a relief you will feel when you know that all your fears, discomforts, complaints and crying jags are thoroughly understood and sympathized with because others have had them too. Contact C/SEC (see "Resource Organizations"), a local cesarean support group, your childbirth educator, or a childbirth education group and ask to speak with other cesarean parents on a one-to-one basis or in a support group setting.

Sharing and exchanging feelings between you and your mate is also very important. It usually helps each of you to know what the other is feeling now about the cesarean experience. Such open discussion will also help both of you to know what aspects of your hospital experience you would not want repeated the next time.

Believe how important it is for you, more than for other new mothers, to get lots of rest to aid your recuperation. If you do not rest, if you try to do everything yourself the first week or two at home, you are likely to become extremely exhausted and find yourself frustrated at not being able to get anything done. The blues may result. On the other hand, if you care for yourself during the first weeks, you'll recoup strength to be better able to take on your responsibilities as you become stronger. The more help you ask for and take, the sooner you will be able to do the things you'd like and resume normal activities.

THE CESAREAN FATHER

As the father of a baby about to be born by cesarean, you may feel confident in and reassured by the physician who is about to begin the surgery, relieved that your mate is in good hands and that the best possible medical care is being given to her and your baby. On the other hand, as confident as you may be in the medical staff, you may feel extremely anxious during the time you are waiting for the surgery to be completed— especially if you had been together with your mate earlier in labor and had planned to be with her for the birth of your baby but are now excluded. Totally cut off, you may feel frustrated, isolated and utterly helpless for perhaps an hour and a half. The longer the lack of contact with anyone who knows what's going on, the more your fears may build: What's taking so long, what's wrong, is she all right, is the baby all right, why isn't someone telling me anything? All sorts of frightening images and thoughts may plague you while you wait. And wait. And wait and wait in the lounge, lobby, father's waiting room, hallway or wherever hospital policy designates you will wait. Each time you hear a doctor being paged on the PA system, you might imagine that he or she is being called to the aid of your loved one and baby. Each half hour that passes may further convince you that something must have gone wrong. Hours may pass without any information. When the doctor finally tells you that you have a baby girl or boy, you may find yourself waiting for the rest of the news, almost sure that it can't be good. Not being there to know what is happening can cause your mind to conjure up the most frightening possibilities. Being separated from the mother *and* the new baby, in some cases for hours after delivery, can increase your anxieties. Your initial joy at the news that mother and baby are doing fine can be minimized by separation.

After hearing that all is well and the danger is over, you may discover other feelings rising within you. One may be of anger for being shunted aside, excluded as though you were a complete stranger who has nothing at all to do with the woman involved. You might be thinking, "How dare they do this to me, the father!" Feeling helpless at not being able to offer comfort and then feeling guilty for not being there when she needed you may cause you great unhappiness.

You may also feel great disappointment for not being permitted to witness the birth of your own child. Perhaps after learning in childbirth education classes how to coach your mate through labor and delivery, looking forward to sharing the birth experience and priming for going all the way into the delivery room, it is difficult to accept the shock of being barred from the delivery room door.

You may feel resentment for having been "cheated" out of witnessing the miracle of birth, denied the thrill of being present at such a momentous event. These feelings may be followed by those of guilt for having thought them in the first place: "How could I be so resentful? I should be happy that my wife and baby are okay. So what if I wasn't there? That's not the main thing."

But still there are nagging jealousies of other fathers who are flying high on excitement from being present at the births of their children. Although there are many fathers who have no desire at all to be present during a cesarean delivery, there is a great deal of misunderstanding surrounding the reasons why any father does. Simply stated, a cesarean father has the very same reasons a non-cesarean father has for being present at his baby's birth: he wants to be emotionally supportive to his mate during the stress of the birth process and he wants to share with her the miraculous moment of their child's entrance into the world. He is *not* necessarily interested in, nor is he invited or expected to observe, the surgery. Seated on a stool alongside his mate's head, his visibility can be limited by the same chestscreen which limits hers.

The reasons given by hospital personnel and obstetricians for not permitting fathers into cesarean delivery rooms echo the very same reasons given twenty-five years ago to keep fathers out of vaginal delivery rooms: there's no room for him, he might get in the way, he might faint, he might introduce infection, he might misinterpret procedures and institute a malpractice suit. These objections were overridden as a result of good experience over the years with no fathers getting in the way, fainting, causing infection or suing doctors. Similarly, only time and experience will override the objections to having cesarean fathers present. An oft-repeated supposition by opposing obstetricians is "What if there is an emergency? How do we tell a father to leave and what if he refuses at a moment of life-and-death decision-making?" This supposition was also raised years ago with regard to an emergency situation during a vaginal delivery. Fathers who are welcomed into the delivery room—vaginal or cesarean—are told that they will be expected to leave if an emergency arises. This has not resulted in any problems, as evidenced by the fact that more and more hospitals are opening their cesarean delivery room doors to fathers; several pioneering hospitals have been doing this for over fifteen years with no bad effects on anyone.

A study made by the National Institutes of Health revealed "no evidence of harm to mother, neonate or father. The presence of fathers in the operating room and close contact between mother and neonate appear to improve the post-cesarean behavioral responses of the family." The NIH Task Force went on to recommend that hospitals liberalize their policies regarding fathers (or other support persons) in cesarean delivery rooms. For information on hospital policies regarding cesarean delivery, contact C/SEC, 22 Forest Road, Framingham, Mass. 01701.

REPEAT CESAREAN DELIVERIES VS. VAGINAL BIRTH AFTER CESAREAN (VBAC)

"Once a cesarean, always a cesarean" was for many years the general rule to which most obstetricians adhered. The fear was that if subsequent labors were allowed to progress, uterine rupture might occur at the site of the incision and place the mother and baby in immediate danger. Today, vaginal birth after a cesarean (dubbed VBAC) is considered an appropriate and acceptable alternative in an impressively growing percentage of cases.

It is now realized that if the original cesarean incision was made transversely into the lower portion of the uterine wall (referred to as low segment transverse, low flap or low cervical cesarean), it would be under much less stress during the contractions of subsequent labors and would therefore be less likely to rupture than would a vertical incision (classical) made higher into the uterus—the previously standard technique. Practically all cesareans today are low segment transverse, although a vertical incision is still sometimes necessary in some situations.

The type of skin incision on your abdomen does not necessarily indicate the type of incision made into your uterus. For example, you might have a vertical external scar, while your uterine incision was low transverse, or you might have a transverse skin incision with a vertical uterine incision. Keep in mind also that all references here to incisions as classical/ vertical or low-flap/transverse refer to the *internal uterine incision,* not the external abdominal one. (The terms "Pfannenstiel incision" and "bikini cut" refer to a low transverse *abdominal skin incision,* not the uterine incision.)

In the unlikely event that a low segment incision does rupture in a subsequent labor, there would be less blood loss from that area than from higher in the uterine wall. And according to authorities, there is less chance for such a rupture to have dire results today because of the more widespread availability of sophisticated modern technology—fetal monitoring, anesthesia and obstetrical support services.

Another realization which has come as a welcome surprise to many is that risks to mother and baby are no higher with a VBAC under carefully controlled conditions than with repeat cesarean births. A repeat cesarean, simply by being a surgical procedure, carries its own set of risks to mother and baby. Therefore, today, *routine* repeat cesareans are being questioned. In many instances, a vaginal delivery after a cesarean is considered less of a risk than surgery.

According to a report by the American College of Obstetricians and Gynecologists in January 1985, 50–80% of women with low transverse uterine scars who try for VBACs are successful. These and other reports of successful outcomes of many vaginal births after cesareans have obviously encouraged many more physicians to reevaluate their earlier positions on the subject. The constancy of purpose and the bravery of those women, physicians and nurse midwives who believed VBACs could have a rightful place in today's obstetrics led the way toward major changes. Organizations like C/SEC (Cesareans/Support, Education, Concern), CBAA (Cesarean Birth Association of America) and the National Cesarean Prevention Movement have worked long and hard to encourage these changes.

Many more physicians have become less fearful of what used to be considered not only a highly risky procedure to mother and baby, but to themselves in the form of possible legal action in case something went wrong.

In 1980, the National Institutes of Health recognized VBAC in its Consensus Development Conference Summary: "Data from national and international sources suggest that labor and vaginal delivery after a previous low segment transverse cesarean birth is of low risk to mother and fetus in properly selected cases." The NIH went on to recommend: "In hospitals with appropriate facilities, services and staff for prompt emergency cesarean birth, a proper selection of cases should permit a safe trial of labor and vaginal delivery for women who have had a previous low segment transverse cesarean birth. Informed consent should be obtained before a trial of labor is attempted."

The American College of Obstetricians and Gynecologists Committee on Obstetrics recommended VBAC as a relatively safe choice in certain instances and published a set of guidelines in 1982 and a new set of revised (and more liberal) guidelines in 1985, suggesting criteria to aid doctors in determining VBAC advisability.

If adequate facilities and staff are available and if criteria recommended in the ACOG guidelines are used to further minimize risk, ACOG supports giving a woman the opportunity of trial labor for a VBAC. The use of I.V.s and monitors are considered by most authorities necessary safety precautions for VBAC mothers and babies. Early in VBAC history, it was believed that no sedation or anesthesia could be given for fear of masking early rupture signs. Today, most obstetricians who permit a trial of labor will allow the use of judicious amounts of sedation and even anesthesia when there are no problems and satisfactory progress is being made. Some doctors will even use oxytocin (pitocin) stimulation when they consider it necessary and appropriate.

The ACOG Committee's Guidelines did not recommend VBAC for multiple births or for babies weighing over 4,000 grams (8.8 lbs.). And since the risk of labor has not yet been thoroughly evaluated for women having had more than one prior cesarean birth, women with a vertical uterine scar or with a breech presentation, the committee points out that its guidelines do not apply in these cases.

VBACs, however, are occurring in some such instances. Nancy Cohen, founder of C/SEC and currently Chairperson of the Education Committee of the National Cesarean Prevention Movement, claims that women are having vaginal deliveries after as many as five cesareans, having more than one VBAC after previous cesareans, delivering ten-to-twelve-pound babies vaginally after several cesareans and even VBACing twins and triplets!

Some physicians who are otherwise supportive of VBAC will not agree to a trial labor if the reason for the first cesarean might still be present for the next delivery. They believe such a situation exists, for example, when the size of the mother's pelvis was considered too small for the first baby to be born vaginally, thereby lessening the chance for the next baby to make it through the pelvis safely. Yet, there have been women whose cesareans resulted from such disproportion diagnoses but who went on to have subsequent vaginal deliveries. One explanation given for these successful outcomes is the encouragement of the mother to vary her birthing position, allowing easier fetal descent—indicating that it is not always the size of the baby but the angle of the mother's pelvis and/or position of the baby's head during expulsion which can determine adequate and safe passage.

"Failure to progress," a catch-all phrase which covers any of several possible conditions, has been widely believed in medical circles to imply disproportion between the baby's head and the mother's pelvis. Yet, according to the ACOG Committee on Obstetrics, studies show that up to 70% of women whose cesarean deliveries were based on "failure to progress" were able to accomplish later VBACs.

Even if the reason for the first cesarean is unlikely to exist the second time around (as in the case of fetal distress), there are physicians—plagued by the ever-present fear of uterine rupture—who are still reluctant to allow the mother to go into labor. In such cases, a date for surgery is scheduled in order to deliver the second baby before labor begins. However, care must be taken to be certain that the baby is "at term" and that his or her lungs are mature. This is accomplished by careful reevaluation of the approximate due date, tests of the amniotic fluid via amniocenteses and sonograms (soundwave photo images) prior to the scheduled cesarean date.

Some health care providers advocate waiting for labor to begin before performing a repeat cesarean. One reason given by some is ther belief that even an hour's worth of uterine contractions is advantageous to the baby. Also, following nature's timetable gives a reasonable measure of security that the baby's lungs are mature before birth. In addition, if the doctor finds that rapid progress has been made, he or she might then consent to a trial of labor after all.

It is necessary to point out that there are women who prefer *not* to experience labor and a vaginal birth after a previous cesarean; if they request a repeat cesarean, most obstetricians will comply with their wishes.

A common concern is the number of children a woman can safely have by cesarean and how close they may be spaced. Medical opinions vary on this, but many doctors recommend cesarean deliveries be limited to three and they be at least two years apart. We do continue to hear, however, accounts of women having more than three—as many as seven—cesareans with no apparent deleterious repercussions. For more information on cesareans and VBACs contact, in addition to your physician or nurse midwife: C/SEC, 22 Forest Road, Framingham, Mass. 01701; National Cesarean Prevention Movement, P.O. Box 152, Syracuse, N.Y. 13210; N.I.H., 9000 Rockville Pike, Bethesda, Md. 20205; ACOG, 600 Market Avenue, S.W., Washington, D.C. 20024-2588.

FEELINGS AFTER: THE LOSS OF A BABY, OR THE BIRTH OF A HANDICAPPED OR SEVERELY ILL CHILD

"What did I do to cause this?" is the most common question that parents of babies who are severely ill, handicapped, or do not live ask themselves and their health care providers. No matter what the cause, taking on guilt and punishing yourself for what you may or may not have done to contribute to the baby's condition is not going to change the situation at all. Blaming yourself for having chosen a particular doctor or hospital or other place of delivery which may or may not have led up to the tragic result also serves no purpose. It will only make things worse because your feelings affect the way you function and deal with the problems as well as how you relate to the child.

Another common reaction after the birth of a handicapped child is the thought that there must be something abnormal about you—especially if this was a first child.

"What's wrong with *me* for creating such a child? Something inside of me did this to Lucille. Because of me, her own mother, she will have to live with this for the rest of her life."

When something unfortunate occurs it is natural to want to find a reason for it. An explanation somehow helps to mend our emotional wounds. Being able to place the blame on someone, even ourselves, gives some semblance of satisfaction; it helps to close the door on uncertainty and unanswered questions. But continually living with self-hatred is destructive. It is a waste of energies that can otherwise be put to better use to reconstruct your life and go onward, dealing positively with the situation as it is.

If your baby is ill, you may find you are asked to sign consent for medical tests to facilitate a diagnosis or to determine the severity of the illness. Physicians may also ask for your permission to perform certain procedures and may ask you to consider their recommendations and choose among alternative treatments, all at a time when you are probably in a state of emotional turmoil and perhaps unable to think clearly. Ask the physician if you have the luxury of time to think about a decision—or if you must make it immediately. Even ten minutes to take a deep breath and think might help you come to a better decision. Make sure you clearly understand the information being presented. Frequently, in a crisis situation, thought processes become somewhat muddled and you may not remember the answers to questions you've already asked. If this is the case, ask again. Physicians are usually sensitive to the fact that it may take several explanations before the information "sinks in."

When the initial heightened feelings of anguish subside somewhat, take the time to think again realistically about your baby's condition. You and your mate should discuss the information you have already been given and make a list of any additional questions for the physicians involved. Ask yourselves: What additional information do we need to make any decisions likely to be necessary about the baby's care or about future children? Are we satisfied that our baby is receiving the best possible care and/or should we ask for a second medical opinion? What additional information do we need to help us feel less anxious about the situation? In addition, ask the physician and nurses for suggestions of additional sources of information—books, articles, etc. Discussing these matters and perhaps doing research as a team will enhance your feelings of togetherness, which is very important, especially at this time.

The natural mother-infant and father-infant bonding process by which attachment to the new baby if formed is somewhat interfered with in the case of a severely ill newborn. When the parents know that the infant's life is in danger, they may feel reluctant to become too attached to the baby for fear of hurting too much if the child does not live. So the natural instinct might be to hold back, not ask too many questions, not give of oneself, and minimize visits to the nursery.

"I couldn't look at him too much. I had to brace myself for the possibility that he wasn't going to make it. I couldn't get myself to love him when I felt he was probably going to die anyway and my heart would break."

"She was so tiny and so weak and the doctors prepared me so well that I shouldn't keep my hopes up. 'Don't get too attached to her,' my mother warned, and even though I knew intellectually that this baby needed much *more* love than normal babies, something inside of me kept my feelings back. Kind of self-protection, I guess."

"I didn't want to ask too much, to know too much, because I hurt so much. Then I realized that I was being selfish. I had a responsibility to find out all I could and help in the decision-making. I knew I had to feel that we had given her the best possible shot at making it and if I wasn't involved in making decisions or at least knowing what was happening, I'd have that to deal with in the future as well as whatever happened."

It's important to know that a feeling of detachment may also occur after the birth of a healthy baby if a previous child had lived several weeks or months and then died. The memory of having been attached to that child and loving him/her and then the profound loss felt afterward can prevent an open flow of loving feelings toward the new baby.

Reverses often occur and the infant who was expected to die lives. This unexpected happening can result in extremely mixed emotions. After having adjusted to and thereby in effect "mourned" the baby's death in advance, it may take a while and some concentrated effort to establish the parental-infant bond that had been delayed. To establish this bond there must be enough trust and belief that the child will now, after all, live—and that it is now safe to invest loving feelings without fear of the child's demise.

Seriously ill babies are not given to their mothers during the hospital's scheduled feeding times, nor can they room-in; of necessity, they must be kept and cared for in the nursery. This separation of baby and mother accentuates the mother's feelings of loss and of being different from the other mothers, and her tendency to emotionally detach from her baby. If she shares a room with mothers whose babies room-in with them or are brought in for feedings, her feelings of being different are dramatically reinforced several times each day.

If parents of a sick or premature infant desire to visit the nursery to see and hold their baby, all efforts should be made to encourage and accommodate their desires. A sick baby or one who is in a special care unit because of prematurity or for observation after a cesarean delivery needs more love and attention than usual, simply because he or she *is* isolated. In addition, the mother of such an infant may have a strong need to be needed by the baby. During her pregnancy, the months were spent waiting to become a mother and care for an infant. Suddenly, after all the hoping, waiting, preparations, expectations—the baby is being cared for by others. The mother should be encouraged to come to the nursery. If the baby's condition allows, she can feed, fondle, talk, or sing to the baby while still in the special-care unit. The baby needs mothering as much as the mother may need to give mothering. (Even if the baby has an I.V. or nasal tube, it may be possible to hold him or her. Ask the nurse how best to accomplish this.)

Your baby may need to remain in the hospital for additional care for several days (or longer) after you go home. Such a situation is likely to provoke feelings of emptiness, loss and depression, because of the enormous disappointment at having to go home without the baby. The previously prepared infant furnishings in the house serve to remind you constantly that your baby is not with you.

"The worst time for me was the two weeks I had to leave the baby in the hospital. I visited him every day and spent a lot of time there in the nursery, but when I had to leave and came home and felt the emptiness of the house and every time I passed the bedroom where his crib stood empty, I'd choke up with tears."

"I knew my baby was going to be all right. She just had to stay in the hospital until she gained some more weight. But that didn't make me feel any better when I was at home without her. Everyone told me I should use the time to catch up on things, especially sleep, because when she'd come home I'd need the energy. But who could sleep!"

"The only thing that helped while the baby was in the hospital was keeping busy. My friends and my family kept me constantly involved going places and doing things and being with people so there'd be less time to dwell on not having Matthew at home with us."

If your baby needs special care that cannot be adequately provided in the hospital in which you gave birth, he or she may be transferred to a specialized infant care unit in another medical center. Your being in one hospital while the baby is in another can lead to feelings of depression because you cannot even *see* your baby to reassure yourself that everything is all right. In addition, it may be difficult for you to reconcile your recent labor and delivery experience with the existence of a baby you may only have seen for a few minutes, if at all. It might be best for you to ask to be discharged as soon as possible, so you can visit your baby. Until you can be discharged, however, perhaps you can be given the telephone number of the special-care unit so you can be in touch with those caring for your baby.

If a child has a handicap, some new parents, in addition to any feelings of guilt or self-blame, tend to feel very uncomfortable while with the baby in the presence of others—in the hospital, or weeks later, walking down the street, in the pediatrician's office, in the supermarket, etc.

You might actually feel embarrassed when people—adults or children—look and sometimes even stare and point at your baby. Then you might feel very guilty for having felt embarrassed in the first place. This is a common reaction.

"How *could* I have been embarrassed? What was the terrible shame? Robert couldn't help how he looked and certainly no one wanted him to look that way. And neither he nor I did anything foolish to make it happen, so why should I feel that way? And yet, the wave of shame came over me!"

We all want perfect babies with perfect bodies and minds. Not producing such perfection, we tend to feel that we have failed, that something has gone wrong and it is a reflection on us and our abilities. However, all the guilt, shame, worry, and blame in the world will not change the situation. And although we cannot prevent or stop the feelings we feel, we can decide *not to indulge in self-hurting thoughts*. We can decide not to encourage or prolong them to the point where thinking about what happened is no longer a necessary and natural relief, but instead becomes a negative factor causing more unhappiness in our lives.

The exhaustion of running back and forth to the hospital and the tension of perhaps not knowing the final outcome all take their toll. Some parents find that even when they can let go and relax a bit, they feel guilty.

"One of the worst feelings I had was when Nathan was so seriously ill in the hospital and his living was a matter of touch and go and there I was on the outside, living. And if I would forget for a moment about Nathan and laugh at something funny someone said, I would suffer so much. It was like how could I laugh, how could I have fun and enjoy *anything* while my poor little baby was sick."

"In order to go on, I *had* to have some relief. It took me a while to realize that a change of scenery (away from the hospital and the baby), a change of subject, going to a movie, listening to music, lunching with friends was medicinal!" Also, there is a tendency for the parents to overlook each other's feelings during this period of intense interest in and concern for the baby. Remember that each of you needs love and understanding from the other—especially in cases of long hospitalization of the baby. And your other children need understanding, attention and love as well. They also need help in understanding what is happening.

Many couples in this situation worry about how much information to give their other children. A good guide is to answer their questions, but not to volunteer information beyond what they have asked. If they need more information, they will continue to ask questions. If you are unsure of how to answer their questions, ask your pediatrician for advice.

Occasionally, an infant is stillborn or so severely ill or malformed that the baby lives only a short period after birth or dies some time after. If her infant has died and the mother remains on the same maternity floor of the hospital, exposed to happy mothers, fathers, gift-bearing visitors, and the acute awareness of the baby nursery down the hall, this further accentuates her loss and can be devastating.

"There I was, empty. No baby within me. My breasts filling up with milk for a baby who would never drink; my arms aching for a baby I would never hold; my stitches a constant reminder of a hard labor and the baby who had passed through my birth canal. I had nothing to show for my labor. And every time my roommate held her baby, fed her baby, opened another baby gift or had another congratulatory phone call, I wanted to scream. But I cried and cried. It was cruel, seeing all those babies so soon after mine was taken away."

Accommodations should be made on another floor in such cases, and early release from the hospital should be arranged if at all possible.

If your infant dies, it is important for both grieving parents to be encouraged and allowed to do just that—grieve. There is often no solace in sentiments such as "It was better that way . . . it was meant to be . . ."

Everyone reacts to grief in his or her own way. Allow yourself to cry when you feel like crying; don't worry about the reactions of those around you. If you think that seeing your infant will help you adjust to the reality of his or her death, by all means ask to do so. Whether or not you should see the baby is a subject of controversy. Some people—professional and non-professional—believe that if the infant was malformed, it is better that you not see him or her so you will not be haunted by the memory afterward. Others believe that if you do not see the infant, your imagination can conjure up far worse images than reality imposes, thereby making you suffer more. We believe you should first discuss the baby's appearance with the doctor and then it should be *your* choice —not the hospital personnel's—whether or not you see the baby. And if you want to be moved off the maternity floor, speak up.

Some parents find it comforting to refer to the baby by the name they had chosen during pregnancy. Others prefer not to. Some have a formal burial service, feeling that going through the rituals surrounding death helps to resolve their experience by allowing them to mourn the baby as their infant who died, instead of removing themselves from the entire process by allowing the hospital to make arrangements in which they do not participate. Other people prefer not to be involved. Whatever your desires, it is crucial that you keep in touch with each other's needs and feelings. Men in our society are not encouraged to cry or express their feelings and often believe they have to be "strong" to help their mates. *Not true*. You both will need *to help each other* through this period with as much love and understanding as possible. Communication is also essential at this time so misunderstandings can be avoided. Bereaved parents are under exceptional stress and do not need the additional pressure of friction between themselves. The death of an infant can put a huge strain on a marriage. One partner may be so upset and involved in his or her own grief that the other partner's feelings may not be considered. Feelings of guilt for what happened can lead to blame and, before long, both bereaved parents may find themselves working against each other instead of side by side. Reach out and give comfort to each other. *Both* of you are hurting.

Unfortunately, the medical and nursing staff at the hospital may feel uncomfortable talking to you or dealing with you about the tragedy and you might interpret this to mean they are unfeeling or nonchalant. Or, in their uneasiness, they may say or do something rather inappropriate. A casual remark or the use of a word intended to help you may resound like thunder and hurt you to the quick.

"After my baby died, nobody wanted to talk to me about it. They decided it would be better that way, for me. Even my husband thought he was doing me a favor by telling the nurse not to discuss with me what arrangements they would make for the baby. But I *wanted* to discuss it and I asked the nurse about it and she said not to worry, they'll 'dispose of the child' for me. Dispose! As though she were talking about an old piece of clothing. The thoughtlessness of using that word to a woman whose infant had died!"

Grieving parents are not helped by well-meaning people who avoid the subject and stay away. The expression of sympathy to parents mourning the loss of an infant is vital. Yet people tend to retreat for fear of "not knowing what to say." They don't understand that they need say nothing more than "I don't know what to say. I want to cry with you."

Often, grieving parents feel an extreme sense of isolation and cannot understand why friends and relatives are not calling or visiting. They may assume that no one *cares* to spend some time with them and help them through the grieving process. Yet, *very often they need and want to talk about their tragedy,* but no one introduces the subject for fear of upsetting the couple and bringing on tears. But tears are a necessary part of the grieving process.

If people seem to be avoiding you in your time of need, try to understand that they are probably feeling helpless and do not know how they can console you. It might be necessary for you to make the move and call friends to let them know you *want* their company and *need* to talk. Allowing the tears to fall and the words to spill out can be surprisingly relieving. Simply expressing your feelings and thoughts can be marvelous medicine for your wound.

If there are other children in the family, remember that they also have a need to express their feelings. They too go through a grieving process and need comforting. They need to talk about what happened and be reassured that everything possible was done to help the baby. Keep in mind the possibility that siblings may have felt resentments toward the new baby and may be suffering with the thought that they were responsible for the tragedy, merely by thinking negative thoughts. And they may be terrified at the thought that they could die too.

The more you can get them to verbalize their fears and feelings, the more you can understand and help them through this difficult time.

If your baby was a victim of Sudden Infant Death Syndrome (SIDS)—a usually fatal condition occurring to apparently healthy and thriving babies—the shock of this unexpected death can be devastating. Although self-blame is common, it is useless and invalid, because to date the cause is not known and there is no way to predict this tragic occurrence. For more detailed information, literature, and guidance, we refer you to the National SIDS Foundation, Two Metro Plaza, Suite 205, 8240 Professional Pl., Landover, Md. 20785. 800–221-SIDS.

It is common to experience insomnia and nightmares after losing a baby. This seems to be part of the adjustment period. It may be difficult to work or even to concentrate on anything for any length of time because your mind tends to wander. You may experience a loss of appetite and may need to force yourself to eat small quantities of easily digested foods several times a day instead of the traditional three full meals a day.

It is normal to think you hear your baby crying in another room and then realize the cries were in your head.

You may find it unbearable to be alone for hours in the house where the baby was to have joined your family. Make it a point to have a friend or relative spend time with you each day for the first few weeks until you are better able to adjust to and cope with the reality of the situation. Plan in advance to do something with someone each day. It will do you no good to isolate yourself and dwell on the tragedy. Ask yourself: Will making myself miserable, cutting myself off from the world, and denying myself some pleasure make a difference in what happened?

"After our baby died, I didn't want to go anyplace where I'd have fun because I felt like I was betraying his memory. What kind of mother am I if I could forget so soon? But I learned by going to grieving-parent discussion sessions that I was doing a very common thing—punishing myself and that all my sadness wouldn't help my baby—and it wouldn't make me a better mother, so why be sad? And what about my other children? Don't they count? Shouldn't they get some smiles out of me? It helped me so much to exchange feelings with other parents."

Whatever the tragedy, being in touch with other parents

who have had the same or similar experience—sharing and exchanging your feelings as well as practical advice for day-to-day living—can do wonders for you. Learning how other parents cope, maintain family and social lives, handle the stares, questions and remarks of strangers, friends and relatives and through it all develop an ability to enjoy life—even managing a sense of humor to help them survive the difficult times—may surprise and inspire you.

"It didn't change things. Anthony still had spina bifida (exposed spinal area) and we still don't know if he'll ever walk, but the group has been a blessing. We're with people who understand. It's so supportive, I don't know how we would be managing without those people, who've become our dearest friends."

Ask you doctor, nurse midwife, childbirth educator, hospital, or the March of Dimes to put you in touch with a local self-help group for this purpose. If there is no such group available, you can ask to be put in contact with other parents like yourselves and you can get together informally on your own to discuss mutual feelings and problems. (See also "Resource Organizations.")

POSTPARTUM BLUES

"None of my friends ever told me this could happen so I was ashamed to tell them what I was feeling. I thought they'd think I was terrible to be so depressed when I had such a beautiful, healthy baby. One day I read somewhere that other women went through the same thing and I realized it wasn't only me. It wasn't my fault. And then I started feeling better."

"The main thing that helped me get out of feeling so low and depressed was when I heard on a radio program that some postpartum depression was normal. I had never heard of postpartum depression until then and I thought there was something wrong with me!"

In medical terminology, the word *depression* refers to a

condition requiring medical treatment, which is generally not the case after childbirth. *Depression,* as we use the word and as it is frequently used in everyday language, refers to the common "down" or "blue" feelings many women (and men) experience after having a baby. *The New York Times* has quoted Yale University psychiatrist Dr. Myrna M. Weissman as saying that the postpartum blues occur with such proven regularity "that it is to be considered normal" (Dec. 10, 1976, B12). Postpartum blues can occur after a first or subsequent baby. Fathers as well as mothers experience some degree of the "blues." While it may be difficult to predict who will have a rough adjustment period, there are some indications that certain conditions may predispose a woman to the "blues." These include exhaustion, isolation, lack of emotional and physical support, unusual family pressures, separation of mother and baby (the longer the separation, the greater the blues), inability to reconcile expectation of what life will be like with the reality of the situation after the baby is born, and rigid temperament or lack of flexibility in dealing with situations.

Postpartum blues can be experienced in varying degrees—from vague feelings of sadness to some teary-eyed moments to unexplained crying jags to feeling down for several hours, days or weeks. It is believed that the blues are caused by a combination of psychological, sociological and physiological conditions.

Some degree of tension, anxiety, and general "down" feelings are common to the adjustment period accompanying any new situation or experience. Think back: Was your decision to share your life with your mate accompanied only by joy and expressions of love, or were there some misgivings, doubts, worries? What were your feelings during the early weeks of living together—total happiness or was there some degree of friction? But your commitment to each other and to evolving a life-style together was not made blindly. You knew something about the person you were going to live with and this knowledge was complemented by the feelings that were already established between you before your lives were joined. You also knew something about couples and how people live together from observing your parents, the parents of others and perhaps some of your own friends.

The adjustment period after having a baby is similar in

many ways to the adjustments after marriage or "moving in." New roles are defined. New household tasks are apportioned. But there are many significant differences. Very few couples today start a family truly knowing what they are getting into. Their commitment in this case is often a blind one, based on love for each other, the decision to have a child (for whatever reason), and the faith that they'll be able to "handle it"—"it" never really being fully defined. Of course, there is some information to fall back on and patterns of parenting you are familiar with—how you were raised as a child, what your friends are doing with their children, what your pediatrician advises and what the books say. At least when you had time to adjust to considering each other, you knew something about each other. The adjustment to new parenthood is complicated by the fact that you now both have to consider the feelings and desires of a total stranger who can make his or her preferences known only by crying.

Giving birth also means a shift of the spotlight away from you, the expectant parents, to your baby and then the realization that you will both be responsible for this baby's well-being for years. This is felt most acutely by the mother. The fact that she is no longer pregnant hits quickly; there is no gradual adjustment period. And if either or both of you felt strongly about having a particular planned birth experience and things didn't go as you had anticipated, one or both of you may feel the blues.

If either of you are staying home with the baby after having worked outside the home, new parenthood also means a drastic change of life-style. Today, women in our society are encouraged to attend college and find fulfilling careers. They are then expected to shift gears suddenly and find perfect contentment in the world of motherhood—forget the brain they were encouraged to develop, drop all of their skills and training, because it's time to be a mother. And those who return to the work force may find it overwhelming to juggle everyone's needs: baby's, mate's, other children's and their own, which can lead to the blues.

We are a generation in transition. For the most part, our parents had clear ideas of what was expected of them. Women stayed home and cared for the children and men went to work to earn a living. This is no longer true today. While it's exciting to be part of the evolution of new gender roles brought about in large part by the women's movement, it can be frustrating as well. Few couples today grew up with clear role models of how to combine parenthood, home and career. While it is challenging and rewarding to be establishing new norms and developing new roles as individuals and as couples, many find it surprisingly difficult as well. Some women express the feeling that just once it would be nice to know automatically how to deal with a situation—to have a comfortable role to slip into without having to be concerned with "what's the right thing to do." Many men are unsure of what's expected of them as husbands and fathers. "I know I should help," one father complained, "but how much? Doing what? I don't hear the other guys talking about scrubbing toilets." Men who stay home to rear their children may find that they have less in common with their friends. "The other guys are talking football and promotions and I'm talking diapers and formula! There are few men in my situation and sometimes I really feel isolated. All the other parents in the park are women!"

Most couples today become parents at a later age and are better educated than those of previous generations. Being used to a world with a system of almost immediate rewards for a job well done (A's on report cards, raises, promotions, etc.), with built-in measures of competence (degrees, licenses, job titles), with a clear sense of the "right" and "wrong" way of doing things, it can be difficult to adjust to the realities of new parenthood. This can result in feelings of the blues.

Many couples find they weren't prepared for this part of their lives, yet they're expected to know how to handle it. Our society sets up a rough adjustment period for many individuals.

The baby's behavioral characteristics as well as the personalities of the parents also play a part. Some individuals who need a sense of order, a strict schedule, a feeling of control over their environment may find it difficult to adjust during what many find to be the chaos of the early weeks. If the baby is low-key, easy-going and adaptable, things may go smoothly. If, however, the baby has a rigid, irritable, highly reactive response pattern and in addition needs very little sleep, the parents, unless they are very flexible individuals, may find they are soon worn to a frazzle . . . and feeling the blues.

There are also physiological factors affecting the mother. A good part of the emotional highs and lows she might experience are related to the hormones in her system which have not as yet leveled off. Discomfort and fatigue are strong contributory factors. Occasionally the blues are a symptom of a thyroid dysfunction or a reaction to a medication.

Whether you are the mother or the father, when things do not go as planned or expected, there is surprise, disillusionment and frustration. When these are compounded by the physiological changes the new mother is undergoing, the changes in life-style and the realization of what parenthood really entails, it is easy to see why the joy after childbirth is often accompanied by what we refer to as the blues.

How to Minimize "Down" Feelings

EXPRESSING AND ACCEPTING YOUR FEELINGS—whatever they are—is a major step toward dealing with them and avoiding the blues. Some women (and men) find it helpful to keep a journal for writing out their feelings. You can say anything you want without fear of interruption, contradiction, ridicule or reprisal. Journals do not talk back. Committing yourself to keeping a journal ensures you time for introspection, the opportunity to identify by name the feelings you have, the chance to understand and deal with them most comfortably, and the luxury of getting to know and keeping in touch with yourself.

You can begin your journal during pregnancy and continue it during the hospital stay. At home, choose a time of day or night when you can be completely alone with your thoughts. Evaluate your day in terms of emotions. Write your thoughts in a continuous flow, without stopping to correct spelling or grammar, include your sad and negative thoughts and feelings as well as your happy and positive ones. This is not to be a log of your activities, but a record of your reactions to your activities; to being a parent, your new life-style, your relationships. Include not only the baby's latest achievement but also your reactions to seeing him or her grow and develop.

COMMUNICATE, COMMUNICATE, COMMUNICATE. Your mate can't know what you're feeling unless you tell him or her.

Discuss what you are feeling. *Both* of you! Don't let your feelings—positive or negative—stay bottled up.

HOUSEHOLD CHORES SHOULD BE AVOIDED or kept to the barest minimum for the first month at least. Before doing anything at all, ask yourself, "Does this really *have* to be done? Can't it wait?" Have someone help with household chores so the new mother can recuperate and the new father can get some rest. Exhaustion lowers your defenses.

SLEEP (not just rest) should be gotten whenever possible. Fatigue lowers your ability to cope.

DO NOT OVERCONCERN YOURSELVES WITH PLEASING OTHERS by trying to do things their way or by entertaining them during the postpartum period. Your obligations are first to each other and the new baby.

POSTPONE MOVING YOUR FAMILY TO ANOTHER LOCATION IF AT ALL POSSIBLE, until at least six months after the baby is born. The extra pressures and work involved in having to locate sources of goods and services, and perhaps having to make new friends in a new community, in addition to the usual difficulties encountered during the postpartum period, can be devastating.

SPEND TIME ALONE TOGETHER AS OFTEN AS POSSIBLE— even if it is just to take a long walk and have the opportunity to talk while someone else watches the baby. Re-establish your bond and interest in each other. Let each other know you care and will work together during the rough periods.

MAKE IT A TOP PRIORITY TO FOLLOW YOUR USUAL DRESS- ING/BATHING/HAIR-CARE REGIME. Knowing you look well helps to make you feel well.

EAT A WELL-BALANCED DIET. Be sure you eat foods high in protein and iron. This will help facilitate the new mother's recuperation.

ASK FOR HELP WHEN YOU NEED IT. Don't allow feelings of embarrassment or worry that you are imposing get in the way of the new mother's recuperation. Some individuals find this especially difficult to do—feeling they must be in control of every aspect of their home and environment. It's important to realize that identifying your needs and developing strategies to meet them is a form of being in control.

KEEP UP YOUR SOCIAL CONTACTS THROUGH THE USE OF THE TELEPHONE. This allows you to maintain personal interests, gives you the feeling of being in touch with the outside world instead of being isolated, keeps lines of communication open and affords you outlets for expressing your feelings—all while you are resting at home. If you were working before the baby was born and are now staying home, keep up your business contacts. Keep in touch with co-workers.

CHANGE YOUR ENVIRONMENT by getting out of the house daily, if possible, for brief, non-exhaustive periods, with or without the baby.

DO NOT TAKE ON THE CARE OF ELDERLY OR SICK RELATIVES DURING THIS TIME.

DO NOT BELIEVE THAT TO BE A "GOOD PARENT" you must spend your time constantly with your baby. Everyone needs some relief from responsibility.

PLAN SOMETHING IN ADVANCE TO LOOK FORWARD TO DOING EACH DAY AND DO IT! Shop for the perfect chocolate chip cookie, plan to visit a specific shop or park, write a letter to your loved one, do disco-dancing to a record in your living room, plan a future business project, read a chapter in a book, take up a new hobby, sharpen business skills, take a home study course, etc.

FIND A COUPLE WITH A CHILD APPROXIMATELY YOUR BABY'S AGE. If none of your present friends fit this category, ask your obstetrician, nurse midwife, pediatrician, childbirth educator or La Leche League leader to put you in touch with other parents. Comparing notes with a "buddy" allows you to realize that you are not alone in your feelings. (Also, socializing with other new parents, all of whom have babies in tow, can be fun. All understand the pressures and can be supportive if a baby cries or a parent needs assistance.)

JOIN OR ORGANIZE A SUPPORT GROUP. Exchanging thoughts and feelings with others going through a similar adjustment can be invaluable. (See "Postpartum Support Groups.")

COMPILE A LIST OF THINGS TO DO, IN ADVANCE, FOR DAYS YOU CAN'T GET OUT so that on those days you don't have to wonder what to do with your time.

DEVELOP OTHER-THAN-BABY INTERESTS. Make it a point to do something for yourself *daily* (reading, working on a project, etc.).

TRUST THAT "THIS TOO SHALL PASS." New mothers who have gone through the adjustment period will tell you how difficult it can be to believe *at the time* that the sadness, the fatigue, the chaos, the feeling of helplessness and the feeling that things will never change will *not* last forever. New fathers also need the reassurance that things will settle down in time and that a sense of "normalcy" will return to their lives. The chaos does pass and things will, in all likelihood, get better. So hang in there!

TRY TO PINPOINT EXACTLY WHAT YOU ARE FEELING AND WHY. For example: I am feeling *trapped* because I haven't been out of the house for several days. I am feeling *angry* because everyone pays attention to the baby and ignores me. I am feeling *tense* because the baby's been crying for hours, dinner isn't started, I'm still in my nightgown and my mate just called to say his boss will be here for dinner with a gift for the baby. I'm feeling *overwhelmed* by all the pressures: working, caring for the baby, cleaning the house, etc. I'm feeling *out of control* because I can't manage my life the way I'd like. It is easier to deal with a specific emotion occurring in reaction to a specific situation than it is to handle a nebulous feeling of "the blues" that seem without cause.

VERBALIZE WHAT YOU ARE FEELING. Say it out *loud!* Tell the baby! Call someone with whom you can be open about your feelings without fear of being "laughed off" or "ridiculed." Even if at times you can't pinpoint exactly what you are feeling, saying aloud "I am feeling down," even to yourself, can be a tension reliever.

DEVELOP STRATEGIES TO HELP YOU DEAL WITH THE SITUATION. If you are feeling overwhelmed, evaluate who's doing what around the house. Can tasks be reapportioned? Should outside help be considered? The new parent who is staying at home and feeling trapped can take a walk; forget the housework and get out of the house (with or without the baby as you prefer and your situation allows). In cases where you absolutely cannot get out, such as bad weather or illness, visit with friends by phone, read, write letters, do something new—try a new recipe, *begin* a project, rearrange the furniture (on paper in the early weeks), hire a sitter, enroll in a course, etc.

If you are feeling left out, besides telling your mate what you're feeling, *do* something for yourself! Buy yourself flowers, a new book, tape, recording or software; take yourself out to lunch; change your hairstyle; write yourself a love letter telling yourself how wonderful you are. If you are feeling isolated, take a walk in search of other new parents (shopping centers, parks, libraries and bowling alleys which have nurseries are good prospects). If you cannot get out, scan the telephone directory and compile a list of places where it is possible to meet other parents. Call the obstetrician, nurse midwife, pediatrician or childbirth educator for a list of names to organize a support group.

A new parent who is feeling tense can try taking a mini "vacation"—a break from the tension-producing situation before dealing with it. Sit down, put your feet up and do slow breathing (slow, equal in and out breaths—in through the nose; out through the mouth). Supplying your system with more oxygen works to lift your mood. While you are doing the breathing, consciously release every muscle in your body, beginning with your facial muscles, working your way down your body to your legs and toes. When you are fully released, continue the breathing and try to imagine yourself in a restful situation—on a beach, on a raft, on a grassy hill beneath a beautiful tree, having a picnic—whatever works for you. Try to imagine it so clearly that you are "actually there." What color is the sky? What sounds do you hear? What does the grass, sea, etc. feel like? Smell like? Continue this for fifteen or twenty minutes.

If you are keeping a journal, take the time *now* and make an entry or *start* a journal. You can even write while holding a crying infant if you have to. Getting the feelings out helps!

When the new mother is given the okay, she can try yoga

and deep breathing exercises which supply the system with more oxygen. Try jogging or jumping rope. The increased activity can help your mood and give you energy and a sense of well-being. (Of course, her mate can do these at any time!)

When to Seek Professional Help

The adjustment to having a baby in the house is not an easy one and some new parents find they need professional help to learn to deal with their feelings. If you, the new mother (or new father), consistently feel "out of control," "out of touch," unable to cope—by all means seek help. If the new father observes these signs of depression in his mate, it's important to seek help. In addition, seek help *if*:

●talking out your feelings with friends, relatives or in a support group doesn't help you to resolve them

●you feel that nothing in life is giving you any joy, that life seems to be one big zero—all work and no fun

●you have no interest in caring for yourself or the baby

●you choose to remain in bed and not get dressed every day

●you withdraw and do not want to communicate with anyone

●friends and relatives constantly point out that you are not "yourself"

●you find that minor incidents continuously cause anxiety

●you know that if your feelings persist you will harm either yourself or the baby

●you have difficulty sleeping, lack of appetite, and/or severe constipation without ascertainable physical cause.

Call your obstetrician, pediatrician, nurse midwife or family doctor and make an appointment to discuss what you are feeling. Ask for a referral to a psychiatrist, psychologist or therapist who is familiar with treating these symptoms. If you find that the health care professional you have consulted is not helpful, laughs it off, or tells you these feelings will pass, but you find they don't, *seek help yourself*. Contact your clergyman and ask for a referral. Call your local mental health association. Call your local hospital and ask them to refer you to a staff member. Family services agencies (often listed under Social Services Organizations in the phone book) offer family counseling, support groups led by professionals, and often the services of a homemaker on a temporary basis to aid a family under stress. Contact your childbirth educator, local childbirth education association, or La Leche League chapter for referrals.

POSTPARTUM SUPPORT GROUPS

There is an increasing awareness today of the need new parents have for information about child-rearing and development, and the need for support during the time of transition following the birth of a baby. Support today is available in many forms, ranging from books like this one to informal conversation among friends, to a more formally organized parent discussion group. In our experience, the majority of such groups meet during the day and attract women who are staying home as primary caretaker parents on a permanent basis, or who stay home temporarily while awaiting a return to work outside the home. However, an increasing number of groups are available for men and for couples.

While many more men today feel able to "open up" and express their feelings informally to friends, or in a group situation, many others—as measured by the difficulty many organizations have in attracting fathers to group sessions (even those held in the evening or on weekends)—either do not feel the need, do not find the time, or do not identify these sessions as being consistent with their views of what men should be doing. Men and women who work outside the home often express a desire to join a support group tailored to their particular needs, and although such groups do exist, many of these parents are frustrated by their inability to commit time to a group on a regular basis. Many companies today, recognizing the need of employees for support services, offer group discussions on parenting issues, among others, during lunch breaks or immediately before or after working hours.

New parents adapting to the changes a baby brings need to know that others are treading similar ground. They need to exchange stories, experiences, desires, and worries with others who have been and are exactly where they are. They need to feel "normal."

They need to feel free to bare themselves in an accepting and understanding environment, where they can trust their peers to handle feelings with sympathy and understanding. They need to know that they are not the only parents in the world who experience negative feelings about their offspring and that they are not "bad parents" as a result. New parents need to know they are not alone if their interest in sex has diminished since the arrival of the baby. They need friends. They need reinforcement of themselves as individuals, as couples and as parents.

Often, the new mother is alone after the initial excitement has leveled off, visitors have waned, the helping hands have been withdrawn, and she must settle into her new routine in the unfamiliar baby world—alone with her infant.

Her daily fears and concerns for the baby's health, development and sleep patterns might be in need of expression to someone other than her mate. She may have conflicting feelings about her new role and need someone in the same situation to whom she can talk. She may feel overwhelmed by the amount of time baby care involves. She may need practical advice on how to get through each day more efficiently and how to take time for enjoyment as well as work, work, work. Or, she may simply need the sympathetic ears of other mothers with similar problems and feelings. She may need to compare notes with other mothers to be reassured that her baby is "normal" and that other new mothers have made the same mistakes she has in the learning-to-care-for-baby field. She may need to know that she's not "crazy" for feeling the unexpected feelings she's been experiencing. She may need to have a buddy to call during a difficult day to help break the tension.

If in addition she works outside the home, she may need suggestions on how to juggle time and priorities, reassurance that other mothers in her situation also feel overwhelmed at times by the amount they must get done during the day, and by the occasional feelings of guilt at leaving the baby (and/or at not giving 100% to their job), and help in making plans to deal with the 1001 "crises" that tend to arise during a typical week.

In urban areas, new parents who live in apartment buildings may get to meet other parents and their babies in the laundry room, the elevator or the park. Mutual interests can serve as a natural means of starting an acquaintance leading to friendship. However, parents who live in a suburban area or buildings without many young families often experience strong feelings of isolation. It is such parents—men and women—with no natural access to other new parents, relatives or friends with children, who *must* find such people. How? By starting or joining a parent discussion group.

In many communities, discussion groups are readily available. You can locate such groups by contacting a local chapter of ASPO/Lamaze (1840 Wilson Blvd., Arlington, Va. 22201); I.C.E.A. (International Childbirth Education Association) (P.O. Box 20852, Milwaukee, Wis. 53220); local childbirth educators; your physician, nurse midwife or hospital; a local Y, adult school, church or synagogue, community center, mothers' center, college or day-care center; or any organization you can think of which might have some knowledge of the existence of new parent discussion groups.

Some of these are strictly self-help groups consisting of peers in similar situations. Others are led by professional counselors, therapists or specially trained group leaders. Some are free. Others involve a fee. Discussion groups are not encounter groups and should not be substituted for needed therapeutic counseling.

Groups differ in content and focus as well. Give some thought to what your needs are and find out as much as you can about any sessions you consider attending. Will the group leader present information on child development, infant care, strategy planning? Is he or she qualified to do so? Or will the leader be more of a facilitator, guiding an open discussion? Is the group primarily for breastfeeding mothers? Mothers of newborns? Parents of older infants and children? Can babies attend with their parents? Are infant-care facilities provided? If so, who is the caretaker? In many communities, programs like swim/gym and Mommy-and-Me exercise sessions are also available. These give parents the opportunity to meet and enjoy informal supportive discussions, while involved in an activity with their babies. Your local newspaper may contain advertisements or notices about such groups.

If there are no groups in your area, seriously consider forming a self-help group yourself. This is easier than you might imagine. The ideal times for discussions are several weeks before and soon after you give birth. The first weeks after becoming a parent are the most confusing; having a well-established group to share feelings with is extremely beneficial.

We've found that the most successful groups are comprised of individuals who have similar backgrounds in terms of age and education and live in the same general area. If this is your first child, try to locate other first-time parents or at least try to achieve a fairly even split between first and second timers. Also, your group will be more successful if all members have children who are close in age, perhaps covering a span of six months. This does not mean you should scrap the idea if all potential participants are not your age with children who have the same birthdates. Homogeneity may be the ideal, but if your group comes fairly close to it, it can still be successful.

Some people find it beneficial to form groups consisting of couples. This way, men and women together share their feelings and offer advice to each other. Opening up in a controlled, nonjudgmental atmosphere amidst peers can be an asset to a couple who otherwise might not experience such valuable communication between themselves.

Ask your obstetrician, pediatrician, nurse midwife, childbirth preparation instructor, La Leche League leader, etc. to suggest names of individuals who might be interested in joining your group. When you have a list of ten to fifteen names, start calling. You can begin the conversation with how you received that person's name and number. As you've probably found out through experience, new parents are deluged with calls from photographers, baby furniture manufacturers, and diaper services. Therefore, it's helpful to say, "Hello, my name is _____. I got your name from _____. Please don't hang up! I'm not selling anything." Identify yourself further as a new parent with the need to meet with other new parents to help each other through the early months. Explain that you'd like to form such a self-help group and be sure to state that it is not intended as group therapy or counseling—but as a form of experience sharing. Specify a time and date for the first meeting and extend an invitation to join. Many first-time mothers prefer meetings to be one afternoon every other week for about three hours, with their babies in tow. Groups for couples and for mothers who work outside the home might choose to meet weekends or evenings.

Unless you have facilities for many babies, suggest that all participants bring blankets to spread on the floor for the infants. Ask parents of more than one child to try to arrange for a sitter for their older children because their presence is a distraction and some individuals do not feel comfortable discussing things in front of a child old enough to understand. Hosting the meetings can be on a rotating basis, unless the group agrees to another alternative, such as regularly using one or two of the group members' homes because they are more spacious.

As the initiator, your function at the first meeting is to introduce the idea of experience-sharing in a support group. Tell any experiences you may have had which would illustrate how talking things out can help. Make it clear that the purpose of the group is to provide a forum for talking out feelings without fear of being judged or criticized. Ask each member in the group to introduce himself or herself and talk about what each hopes to gain from the group experience. Share childbirth experiences if you like. Begin to get to know each other. Draw up a set of ground rules for ensuing discussions. (You can use our recommended ground rules as a guide.) Explain the necessity for the group to decide how often it will meet, for how long the group will continue (three months, six months, etc.), when the group will discuss renewing its commitment to continue for the next few months, when, how, and if the group will accept new members, etc. Propose that these be discussed and decided upon at the next meeting. Before the first meeting ends, select a location, group leader and time for the next meeting, as well as two topics to be discussed. One topic could be of a practical nature, such as "how to handle advice" or "travelling with an infant." The other topic could be one relating to emotions, such as feelings about being a parent.

At the next meeting, ground rules can be formally adopted, decisions about how often to meet, etc., can be made and the group members can continue to get to know each other through a discussion of areas of common interest. Each meeting should end with a selection of a location, leader and topics for the following meeting.

All may not be smooth sailing. It has been our experience

that at some point in the early weeks, many groups go through an adjustment process. It may be that side conversations are happening too often during a session and there is a loss of the all-important group interaction. There may be personality conflicts or not everyone in the group may feel comfortable in the leadership role. The important thing is that the group talks out the problem and works to find a solution. Realize also that not everyone who comes to the first meeting will want, or be able, to continue. People do relocate, return to work, take care of sick relatives, etc. We suggest that you try to invite twelve women (or six couples) to the first few meetings, hoping eventually to end up with a group of ten individuals.

The following pages contain the information we distribute at meetings of support groups we have formed. You may want to use them as a guide to forming your own groups. The ground rules, suggested topics for discussion, etc. which your group develops should reflect your personalities, needs and situations.

Some groups meet only for the first few months. Others continue twice a month for several years, helping members to get through the trying periods of coping with their children's behavior patterns. The need usually determines the life of the group. Some groups expand their functions to include the formation of babysitting pools, group purchasing power, infant care and parenting book discussion groups, parent pressure groups, etc. Ideally, your group can be whatever its members want it to be.

Guidelines for Parent Support Groups

PURPOSE

Support groups provide a welcome environment for new parents interested in sharing their joys as well as their problems with others in similar situations. There is a need during the early months of parenting for support, bolstering of self-confidence, and giving and receiving encouragement. There is also a need to know that you are not alone and that others experience similar feelings, fears and doubts.

In addition, there is a need to have fairly open-ended time to talk during which each individual can speak freely without interruption, airing and sharing feelings (negative and positive) without fear of being cut off, attacked, put down, or ridiculed. The aim of the sessions is to encourage the expression of *feelings* on each topic covered, to share helpful advice, comments, and support, in an atmosphere of acceptance. Feelings are neither right nor wrong.

SCHEDULES

The group should agree on how often and where to meet. It is suggested that group meetings be held every two weeks, that group members commit themselves to continuing the group for a six-month period, after which time the commitment can be renewed or terminated, that there should be no more than ten members in a group, that the location of the meetings should be rotated and that the leader of each meeting can be the person in whose home the group meets that day, unless other arrangements are decided upon. The group should decide what its rules are concerning the admission of new members, how many meetings in a row may be missed by a member before that member is considered out of the group, and so forth.

GROUND RULES

1. No judging or put-downs! Disagreement is okay, but not disapproval. ("I don't agree with you. I think it could be handled this way. . ." not "You're wrong. My way is right.")

2. Be helpful, supportive, encouraging. Point out the *good* things of a given situation; then, if you can offer helpful comments or suggestions, do so.

3. *Share* feelings and experiences. ("I tried this and it worked" or "It didn't work.")

4. At the end of each session, the group should choose two topics for the following session so there is time to think about what you might want to say or ask. We suggest that one topic be of a practical nature, the other one relating to emotions.

5. Each person takes a turn at speaking on the topic *without interruption*. The aim is to allow the person speaking to

"get it all out." Questions, suggestions, or sharing of feelings by the others must wait until the individual speaking finishes what he or she wants to say. If this becomes a problem, reasonable time limits may have to be set, preferably in advance. When a member is finished speaking, the interplay between that individual and the group should not be permitted to veer off into private conversations, or go on too long and thereby take time away from others who have not yet had their turn.

6. After everyone has had a turn, the leader asks if anyone has comments or additions to make.

7. Alternate homes for meetings. The leader in whose home the meeting is held provides refreshments (which should be limited to simple beverages, such as juice, coffee and tea, and simple snacks or cookies, so there is minimal preparation and expense involved.) The person hosting should also assume the role of group leader, unless that person chooses not to, in which case another group member can be asked to assume this role. The session leader must see to it that there is no interruption, that the chosen topic is adhered to, that reasonable time limits are upheld, that a new leader is chosen for the next meeting. If there is anyone felt to be attacking, interrupting, or otherwise going against the rules, the leader must gently remind everyone of the group's rules ("We cannot have judgments . . . No attacking . . . If you want to disagree, that's fine, but no disapproval here . . ."). These possibilities should all be discussed and mutually agreed upon at the opening session. Everyone must agree to the rules!

8. If there is a particular problem someone is having, the group can give up part of its prearranged topic time to the new problem. Members can hear the problem and each can take a turn reacting to it, making suggestions, etc. The group might agree to allow the problem question to open the session and then go on to the prearranged topic if there is time.

9. It is also a good idea to prearrange the ending time of the formal part of each session—as well as how long informal socializing will continue afterwards.

10. A list of each member's name, address and phone number should be given to each participant.

11. It should be mutually agreed *in advance* that if one member seems very distressed, disturbed, or so in need of more help than the lay group can give, the group can and should, gently, lovingly, as friends, suggest outside profes-

sional help. The group should explain its inability to help in such situations.

SUGGESTED TOPICS FOR DISCUSSION

These topics are suggestions only, based on the situations we know confront many new parents. You might choose to add or delete topics and/or change their order. A support group is a living entity that grows as its members' needs change. Topics that reflect the needs of the group members should be selected as these needs arise.

1. Finding time for yourself
2. Feelings toward the baby—positive and negative
3. Feelings about parenthood—positive and negative
4. How to handle advice and suggestions from friends, relatives, strangers, mates
5. Relationships with parents, grandparents and other family members
6. Relationships with other children
7. How to get outside help—babysitter, housekeeper, etc.
8. How to involve your mate with the baby
9. How to handle a crying baby
10. Can you spoil a baby?
11. Jealousy of your mate's life-style
12. Sex
13. Finding time to be with your mate
14. Traveling with an infant—where to go and what to bring
15. To childproof the house or to teach the child not to touch
16. Values we want our children to have and how to instill them
17. Fears—about the baby dying, that you can't cope, etc.
18. Finances—inexpensive recipes, money-saving ideas, budgeting, low-cost recreation, vacation ideas, ways to earn money at home, insurance, wills, etc.
19. Time management—time savers, how to organize the day, choosing priorities
20. Ideas for a rainy day
21. Changes in social relationships
22. Working outside the home
23. New gender roles: what gets done by whom and when

OTHER PROJECTS THE GROUP CAN CONSIDER

One of the beautiful things about a support group is that in addition to meeting for the basic discussion session, members can plan whatever activities, functions or projects the group desires.

1. *Reciprocal babysitting*. Members can babysit for each other informally or set up a formal reciprocal babysitting service.

2. *Telephone round robin*. A member wishing to pass along relevant information to the rest of the group (infant supplies on sale, a new child safety law, a drug called off the market), can do so by calling the member whose name follows his or hers on the membership list. That member will in turn call the next on the list and so on until all have been reached. The last member on the list calls the first.

3. *Socializing with members*. Five members (or couples) babysit in one location for all ten children, while the other five go to the theater, out to lunch, to a museum, etc. The next week roles are switched. Those who went out, babysit; those who babysat go out.

4. *Cooperative buying of baby items*. Does everyone need a highchair? A car seat? Try approaching a local merchant and asking for a discount if several or all of your group buy from him or her.

5. *Parties with your mates*. If your group is for women, or men, only, you might wish to get your mates involved on a social level. Agree on a place to meet, share the cost of paper goods and beverages and have a party one evening. Each member can prepare a dish based on a menu coordinated by the host member. Whether or not to include babies can be decided by group discussion and vote.

6. *Meeting with your mates*. Why not get babysitters one evening and have a discussion session with your mates? Agree on a topic in advance, make sure everyone understands the ground rules, and try it.

7. *Book (or movie) discussions*. Agree on a book to be read by a certain date. In addition to (or instead of) the usual discussion of a topic, share your reactions to the book.

8. *Toy/clothing/coupon exchange*. Did you receive a gift that you do not like or cannot use but can't exchange? Is the baby tired of a particular toy? Do you have a discount coupon you can't use but think someone else can? Try swapping with

another group member. A toy swap can be for a limited period of time, perhaps two to three weeks, after which time the baby it is returned to will probably be delighted with the "new" toy.

9. *Demonstrating skills or crafts*. Does anyone in the group have a speciality that can be demonstrated to the whole group: knitting, crocheting, cake decorating, computer programming, using a word processor, etc.? Sharing the skill expands everyone's abilities.

3. Practical Problems and Solutions

BREASTFEEDING

This section is for the woman who had decided to breastfeed. Since there are many excellent books on the subject, we have limited our coverage of this topic to what we believe is essential to help you through the early weeks. We have purposely omitted advice on breastfeeding techniques, manual expression of breast milk, etc., because we believe this material is well presented in other sources. We suggest that you purchase one or more of the books that deal with every aspect of breastfeeding to use as a ready source of reference if questions arise.

Breastfeeding can be one of the most beautiful aspects of motherhood. There is a special quiet joy in knowing that your body nourishes your child and that the close physiological interrelationship between you was not abruptly terminated at birth but will end more gradually, more gently, more naturally. However, in the early weeks of physical and emotional adjustment to new motherhood, the breastfeeding woman especially needs love, support and assistance from her mate and other family members. In addition to recuperating from childbirth, you must learn how to breastfeed—possibly never have observed another nursing mother, possibly under pressure to bottlefeed and perhaps questioning your ability to successfully nurse your child. At the very beginning there are few tangible ways to determine how well you are succeeding. Some mothers say they wish they had ounce markings on their breasts so they would know how much the baby is drinking! If you're lucky, your baby sleeps between feedings and that is one indication he or she is satisfied (so are frequent wet and/or dirty diapers). But not all babies sleep all the time—and if the baby is the wakeful type, you may need reassurance that the crying is not from hunger. Usually, the first visit to the pediatrician brings this reassurance as you find that baby is gaining

weight and growing. Knowing "It's from my milk" brings a
delightful feeling of pride. (You might consider scheduling
this appointment earlier than usual or asking if you might
bring the baby in for a weight check if you are having a rough
time and feel that knowing the baby is gaining weight will
help.) In the early days, your baby must also learn how to
nurse—how to grasp the areola and nipple, how to get the
milk. Only the sucking and rooting (nipple-locating) reflexes
are instinctual.

While you and your baby are learning together, your
breasts are undergoing an adjustment process. The nipples
"toughen" to meet the new demands placed upon them by the
baby's tongue, lips and gums. The milk-producing glands adjust their output to suit the baby's needs and the let-down
reflex establishes itself. As a result of these adaptations, some
women experience temporary physical discomfort.

In the Hospital

It is a good idea to tell your obstetrician or certified nurse
midwife in advance (and to remind him or her during labor
and delivery) that you'd like to breastfeed immediately after
the baby is born or as soon as possible thereafter. Immediate
breastfeeding is good for both you and the baby. The newborn
is welcomed into the world with warm, loving arms and a
healthy start in life from the colostrum he or she gets from
your breasts. Sucking will cause oxytocin to be released,
which will stimulate your uterus to contract, help deliver the
placenta and prevent hemorrhaging. Know, however, that if
you have taken any medication during labor and delivery, including Demerol (a narcotic), the baby's sucking instinct may
be temporarily suppressed or the child may be sleepy. Even if
you have taken no medication, your baby may not be interested in breastfeeding right after being born and may prefer to
sleep or to look around. Ask if you can try again in an hour or
two.

If you require any medication for any reason during your
hospital stay, remind your obstetrician or nurse midwife that
you are breastfeeding so they can, if at all possible, prescribe
something that will not be harmful to the baby. Remember that
most medication you take will pass through your milk to the

baby. In most cases this is not harmful, but it is important to remind hospital personnel that you are breastfeeding before you take any pills, injections or liquids offered. In some hospitals, sleeping pills and painkillers are routinely prescribed for all patients. If you require any medication for any purpose for the duration of breastfeeding, check with your pediatrician, obstetrician, certified nurse midwife or La Leche League Professional Liaison Officer to obtain specific information on any known deleterious effects on the milk supply or harmful effects on the baby. If you must temporarily take a drug that could be harmful and a "safe" drug cannot be substituted, you can hand-express your milk or use a breast pump to keep up your supply, discard the milk, and formula-feed your baby for the time involved, rather than permanently wean the baby.

Guidelines During Your Hospital Stay

Contrary to standard advice given in some hospitals, it is unnecessary to wash your nipples and areola with soap and water before each nursing. Your breasts produce their own natural cleansing substance. Occasional rinsing is fine, but stay away from soap and pads saturated with alcohol. Both are drying. Do wash your hands with soap and water, however, before handling your breasts. Bring a travel alarm clock to the hospital and set it to ring fifteen minutes before the middle of the night feeding (usually 2:00 A.M.). This will give you a chance to go to the bathroom, change your sanitary pad, get washed and be ready when the baby is brought to you.

We recommend you breastfeed the baby at all feedings, if you feel up to it, including those during the middle of the night. This is important to establish your milk supply. This will also lessen the chance of engorgement and can help relieve it if it does occur. Another point to remember is that if the bottle is offered often enough, the baby may prefer getting food from the bottle, because it takes less work to get it. Sucking at your breasts is what stimulates your milk supply. Remember, breastfeeding is a supply-demand process. The baby signals his or her requirements to the breasts by the duration and intensity of sucking. Know, however, that the recommendation to nurse your baby at all feedings has to be balanced against your own needs. If you've had a particularly rough labor and delivery experience, a night or two of uninterrupted sleep before you leave the hospital may go a long way towards speeding your recovery and ensuring a positive breastfeeding experience.

It is not necessary for your baby to be given a bottle of glucose water between feedings. This will cut down on his or her appetite for the next feeding. If the nurses are insistent and want to give your baby some liquid between breastfeedings, you can insist on plain boiled water, although even this is not necessary. (See the section on jaundice in "Characteristics of the Newborn.") Ask your pediatrician to leave instructions that your baby is to have nothing except breast milk and if it would be possible to have the baby brought to you whenever he or she cries (if rooming-in is not available). Another possibility is that the nursing staff might let you come to the nursery when the baby is crying to be fed. Sometimes a doctor's order can cause hospital rules to bend.

Take advantage of rooming-in if it is available and if you feel up to it. With the baby in the small bassinet at your bedside, you can remain in bed resting until your baby awakens, then change the diaper and get back into bed to nurse. Be sure to get your rest whether you have rooming-in or not. Take the phone off its cradle (or ask the telephone operator to hold your calls) and get some sleep whenever possible.

Contrary to what you might be told in the hospital, it is not necessary to limit breastfeeding to a few minutes and then gradually increase the amount of time you nurse the baby on each breast in an attempt to avoid sore nipples. If sore nipples are going to occur, they will do so regardless of any such precautions. In the early days, your milk may not let-down in the first minute or two of a feeding. If you do limit the amount of time at the breast to under five minutes, your baby may not get all the milk available, and if over a period of time a breast is not emptied, you *may* develop a breast infection.

Ignore any nurse or doctor who clucks disapprovingly and tells you your baby looks hungry, or comments on how frequently you feed.

If your baby is brought to you for a feeding and is fast asleep, try not to view this as a personal rejection. Several explanations are possible. He or she may have been fed formula or water in the nursery and isn't hungry. Remind the nurse that you are breastfeeding and ask if the baby has been fed. Make it perfectly clear that you want to feed the baby your way.

Or the baby may have been hungry before a scheduled feeding time, cried, and then fallen asleep.

In either case, don't slap the baby's heels or bottom to force the baby awake; some babies will nurse in their sleep. Try gently stroking the cheek with your nipple. The baby may turn toward it, open his or her mouth and nurse. You might also try unwrapping the baby and laying him or her flat on the back. If these don't work, cuddle and talk to your baby, gently letting your presence be felt. Ask the nurse if you can come to the nursery when your baby awakens and breastfeed him or her then.

If the baby is brought to you awake and crying but refuses to nurse or begins to nurse and drops the nipple, try not to be upset and don't give up. He or she may be frantically hungry. Remember, the baby is learning to get the next meal just as you're learning to give it. Be soothing, gentle and firm, and rock your infant. Try expressing some milk into the baby's mouth and then offer the breast again. Don't let anyone talk you into giving a bottle because "the poor dear is so frantic."

In general, the hospital environment is not conducive to establishing a nursing relationship. Scheduled feedings, constant interruptions during the day and not being in your own familiar surroundings contribute to fatigue and lactation difficulties. Perhaps the best advice we can give is to go home as early as your medical condition and the condition of your baby permit. Try to have help with the housework so you will be free to rest and nurse your baby. If you have no help, let everything else wait. You need to rest and care for your baby.

Many hospitals have nurses who are extremely supportive and will help you and your baby learn to breastfeed. Understand, however, that when a hospital is overcrowded or a nurse has had no personal experience with breastfeeding, she may not have the time or ability to assist you; besides, bottle-feeding may seem easier to her .It would be wise to have Cecilia Worth's book, *Breastfeeding Basics,* with you in the hospital for easy reference. For more extensive information we recommend the La Leche League's *The Womanly Art of Breastfeeding* and Eiger and Olds' *The Complete Book of*

Breastfeeding (see "Bibliography"). If you have any questions or problems, call a La Leche League Leader. She can offer information, suggestions and support. In addition, some hospitals have "lactation consultants" on staff who also may be able to assist you.

If your baby must stay in the hospital for a period of time after you are permitted to go home, try to arrange a visit several times a day to breastfeed. Or, if this is impossible, you may be able to arrange to collect your milk at home and send it to the baby, following the hospital's instructions. Even if neither is possible, you can pump your breasts (ask at the hospital if you can borrow an electric pump or you can purchase a manual pump at a pharmacy) to keep your supply up until the baby comes home.

Whether your hospital experience is positive or negative, we suggest you write a letter to the supervisor of nursing and let him or her know your feelings. This may encourage the department to give the kind of support so much appreciated by breastfeeding women and their families. (For information about breastfeeding after a cesarean delivery, see "After a Cesarean Delivery.")

At Home

GENERAL ADVICE. When you are home from the hospital, get into bed and rest. Don't overwork yourself with entertaining or housecleaning. While this advice is important for all new mothers, it is especially critical for breastfeeding women. The best way to prevent nursing problems is by getting adequate nutrition, plenty of rest and avoiding stress. You can clean the house in a few weeks; pamper yourself now.

It is not necessary for you to eat special foods or avoid others while breastfeeding. Just eat a well-balanced diet and drink plenty of fluids. You may find that your baby nurses less avidly or develops gas after you have eaten large amounts of certain strongly flavored or gassy foods. Your diet is reflected in the flavor and content of your milk, but unless you make a connection between something specific you have eaten and gas or decreased interest from your infant, it is unnecessary to restrict your diet in any way. Exceptions to this are large amounts of caffeine and alcohol. If you are in doubt about what you should be eating or drinking, ask your pediatrician for advice and/or read the section on nutrition in *The Womanly Art of Breastfeeding*.

We believe it is best to ignore schedules and to nurse your baby on demand. He or she knows when it is time to nurse; the clock does not. On the average, most newborns nurse approximately every two hours round the clock. Many mothers express surprise that their babies nurse more frequently at home than they did in the hospital. Know that many babies are sleepy for a few days after birth and that, also, the four-hour hospital feeding schedule is for the convenience of the hospital staff, not babies. We occasionally hear of a baby who is so low-key that he or she almost forgets to ask to be fed—consistently going for long periods between feedings (four–five hours or more) and/or not nursing vigorously. If you suspect your baby is this type, it's a good idea to check with your pediatrician and perhaps a La Leche League Leader to discuss whether to awaken your baby for more frequent feedings—possibly necessary for your baby's health and your continued milk supply.

By the end of the first six weeks, you may observe a schedule developing. Many babies begin to sleep through the night at this point. Remember, the first six weeks are usually the hardest; after that nursing becomes much easier as you and your baby adjust to each other and to breastfeeding. Believe it or not, by the time the baby is three months old, you will be quite adept at breastfeeding.

Knowledge is your best defense against people who think they are doing you a big favor by trying to influence you to stop nursing. People who make negative statements about breastfeeding usually do so with the best of intentions. They may have been convinced of the advantages of bottlefeeding when they had children. When formula was introduced on the market it was presented as the "scientific" way to feed babies, and women of that generation may not understand why some of today's women would prefer something "unscientific" or "primitive." It's also possible that they had a negative nursing experience themselves and want to "spare" you. Being able to answer a critic's statement factually and with confidence will help bring an end to any pressure that may exist. Read books and articles. Attend La Leche meetings or write to La Leche

League International at 9616 Minneapolis Avenue, Franklin Park, Ill. 60131.

Besides relatives and friends, there are some medical professionals who by lack of information or personal preference cannot or do not offer the support and assistance breastfeeding women need. The majority of doctors have had little or no experience with breastfeeding women during their medical training. The courses in medical schools and many medical textbooks may emphasize the different types of formula, but do not discuss how to assist lactation. Their knowledge about breastfeeding is frequently gained through whatever reading they choose to do, their eventual contact with nursing women in their practices and what they hear their colleagues advise breastfeeding mothers. While many doctors have the interest and take the time to become "self-trained," others do not. Due to their lack of information, these physicians may find that when problems arise, the easiest solution, for them, is to offer advice that encourages bottlefeeding. Fortunately, there are a growing number of doctors who strongly believe in the value of breastfeeding, have taken the time and initiative to learn (or at least to locate sources of additional information for the patients) and offer a wealth of knowledge and advice. It is often difficult to tell the difference between doctors who are knowledgeable and supportive and those who by lack of knowledge or interest are not. How can you tell the difference?

•Pediatricians who press parents to accept formula samples whether they are breast- or bottlefeeding because "One day you'll find you need it" are not being helpful. When the "one day" comes, encouragement and support will go a lot further than formula to alleviate the situation.

•Be suspicious of comments such as "I'm totally in favor of breastfeeding, but have found few women who are successful at it" or "Go ahead and try, but it's been my experience that when women tell me they're having problems, I know they want me to tell them to stop" or "You're too nervous to breastfeed." A supportive pediatrician should not predetermine that you will fail before you even get started.

•Except in extremely rare instances, if your doctor suggests that you feed the baby formula after every nursing, you may rightfully suspect that he or she is unsympathetic or poorly informed. Breastfeeding works on the basis of supply and demand. Your breasts will produce enough for the baby if you nurse as frequently as the baby wants. Short intervals between nursing are the baby's way of telling you his or her appetite has increased so your breasts will produce more milk. Filling the child with formula defeats this process. Another sign of a nonsupportive or poorly informed pediatrician is the advice to start feeding the baby cereal when a parent reports that her six-week-old baby wants to nurse very frequently. The fact is that at six weeks most babies have a growth spurt and need to nurse more frequently, which encourages the production of more milk.

•On the other end of the spectrum you may hear: "Your baby is getting too fat. Your milk must be too rich. You'll have to stop breastfeeding and give formula." In general, breastfed babies don't overeat. They take in only what they need at each feeding. As long as the baby is totally nursing— being fed no solids, no formula—he or she most probably will not be overweight.

•Some doctors decide quite arbitrarily that it's time to wean the baby. "You've been nursing long enough," or even more subtly, "You mean you're still nursing!" You should be the sole judge of when it's time to end the breastfeeding relationship with your child unless there is a sound medical reason against it. Some women decide to breastfeed for a certain length of time and no more. Others believe in the value of baby-led weaning and stop nursing when the child indicates he or she no longer has this need. However, if you must temporarily take medication that could be harmful to your child and no other can be substituted, you can pump your milk, discard it, and temporarily formula feed your child in order to keep up your milk supply.

•In most situations, there is no nutritional reason to start solids before your baby is four to six months old. Question the reasoning of any pediatrician who suggests otherwise. Sometimes cereal is started early as a means of getting the baby to sleep through the night, filling the infant up so he or she doesn't awaken. However, this is replacing a complete food —your milk—with one that is incomplete—cereal—and it doesn't always work! The baby will sleep through the night when he or she is ready to. (If your baby is sleeping a six to eight-hour stretch from early evening to the middle of the night—such as 9 P.M. to 2 A.M.—you might try to get him or her to sleep the same number of hours at your convenience.

Before you go to sleep—perhaps at 11 P.M.—try to nurse the baby. Many babies will nurse in their sleep or will awaken briefly to nurse and then sleep six to eight hours from that feeding. If the baby awakens again at 2 A.M. anyway, wait a week or two before trying again.)

If you receive breastfeeding advice from your pediatrician that you are unsure of, call a La Leche League Leader and ask if, through the League, she can contact medical advisory personnel who are knowledgeable about and sympathetic toward breastfeeding and can obtain current information for you.

If you find your pediatrician does not share your views about breastfeeding (or anything else of importance to you), you will have to decide whether or not to continue to use his or her services. You have the right to use the services of any doctor you choose—even after you've had several office visits and have called the doctor for advice. Admittedly this is a difficult decision to make. If you do decide to change doctors, ask a La Leche League Leader if she can recommend several doctors who are knowledgeable about and supportive of nursing. Then you can follow the recommendations we made in the section "Finding a Pediatrician." When you have made the change to a new doctor, we suggest you write to your original pediatrician telling him or her the reason for your decision. We believe that it is important to let the doctor know what your feelings are. Perhaps the doctor is not aware of his or her lack of support or misinformation.

You might decide to continue using a doctor whose knowledge, reputation and supportiveness in other areas compensate for the inconvenience caused by his or her lack of knowledge and support about breastfeeding. Many breastfeeding mothers believe that the only way to educate such doctors is by providing them with a model of a successful breastfeeding mother themselves. If you decide to continue using your present doctor's services, you will have to rely heavily on other sources for support and information. If you disagree with advice your pediatrician may give about breastfeeding, perhaps you can show the doctor the source (preferably more than one) which contradicts what he or she says. Referring to several items in print is stronger than saying, "I read that somewhere."

THE CONSTANT NURSER. A baby who wants to nurse for hours and is otherwise inconsolable can detract from your breastfeeding experience. As much as you may enjoy nursing, at some point if you have a constant nurser, you are likely to be tempted to say, "Enough! I've had it!" You might begin to question if you have enough milk or whether you are starving the baby, and frequently mothers, especially those with sore nipples, find they are beginning to get discouraged. It is highly improbable that your baby will starve. It is more likely that your baby is going through a growth spurt and is nursing frequently to increase the milk supply. Know that as babies grow and develop they signal the breasts to produce more milk to meet their new needs by nursing more frequently for a day or two until supply again meets demand. Then the intervals between feedings lengthen again.

If you are faced with seemingly endless nursing, ask yourself if you've been especially tired or tense. This may affect your let-down reflex and your baby may not be getting all the milk your breasts have to offer. As your nursing experience increases, your let-down reflex will become well-established and nothing will interfere. Until then, try to relax and avoid stress. Put your feet up during each nursing. Listen to relaxing music. Think of a fun time you've had. Drink a glass of milk, juice or even wine. Get more rest. Have you been eating and drinking enough? Some women find they have little or no appetite for a while after giving birth. You have to drink liquids to produce a liquid and you have to be well nourished to maintain your own health and provide nourishment. It is also possible that your baby nurses for a long time simply because he or she enjoys it. Infants are born with a strong sucking instinct.

If you're the mother of a "marathon nurser," you have several options in addition to the ones suggested above. The most obvious, if your nipples are not sore, is to let the child nurse. Curl up in front of a television or read a book to keep your mind occupied. If you have older children, use this opportunity to read stories to them, put puzzles together or play word games with them. Another option might be to offer the baby a pacifier, or to let the baby suck on your little finger—especially if it has been significantly less than one hour since you've fed the baby. Pacifiers should be made of one molded piece to prevent any part from falling off and becoming lodged in the baby's windpipe or throat. The shield should also be large enough so that the entire pacifier cannot become lodged in the throat. Pacifiers should not be overused. Your breasts need the stimulation of the baby's sucking to continue to produce milk.

LEAVING THE BABY. Many women feel they need to leave the baby and get away by themselves or with their mates for a few hours. This is especially true if the baby is very demanding or fussy and the new mother has little time for herself. If you are breastfeeding and need time off, you have several options.

•Leave as soon as you nurse the baby and return before the next anticipated feeding. During the first few weeks these intervals are very short, but they will become more predictable and can extend for several hours.

•Provide a bottle of previously expressed breast milk.

•Provide a bottle of formula (the American Academy of Pediatrics recommends that cow's milk should *not* be offered before the end of the first year of life).

If you only occasionally (once or twice a week on nonconsecutive days) leave the baby with a bottle but breastfeed at all other times, your milk supply should not diminish. (It is important to maintain your fluid intake, however.) You may decide you'd like to skip an early morning nursing this way and count that as part of the total number of missed nursings a week. When your baby begins solids, the sitter can feed these in your absence.

We suggest that you not give any relief bottles during the first two weeks while your milk supply and let-down reflex are becoming established. Thereafter, if you do plan to give an occasional bottle (either of breastmilk or formula), we believe that this should be done regularly, once or twice a week, regardless of whether you leave the baby. (It is wise to have someone other than the mother offer the bottle since babies can be confused by sensing the closeness of the breast but being fed by bottle.) It has been our experience that if not kept familiar with drinking from a bottle, at some point many babies will reject it altogether. If this happens when your baby is older, ask your pediatrician if the baby can be given plain yogurt. If the doctor approves, see if your child will take it before leaving him or her with a sitter.

Physical Problems

ENGORGEMENT. This condition, caused by the filling of the milk ducts, the increased amount of blood in the veins and arteries, and the swelling of breast tissue, is often experienced when the milk comes in. This is partly due to the four-hour feeding schedule imposed by most hospitals. Nature intended that nursing be on a demand basis from birth on; the separation of mother and child practiced by most hospitals is contrary to this intent. You may also find your breasts engorge the first few times the baby skips a feeding during the day or begins to sleep through the night. In this case, your breasts fill up to satisfy the baby according to your infant's original requirements; but if he or she sleeps past the original feeding time, you may be "overfull" for the next nursing. In a few days, supply and demand even out again and the problem disappears. The symptoms of engorgement are hard, often painful, lumpy breasts that may feel hot to the touch. To relieve the discomfort you can massage the breast and manually express some of the milk. A hot shower is also soothing and will help the release of milk. The application of either heat or ice is also helpful. The idea is to make yourself as comfortable as possible while your body adjusts to the baby's needs. Depending on how long you're away, overfilling can also occur if you leave the baby with a sitter who will feed him or her previously expressed breast milk or formula. (If you want to ensure no decrease in your supply, carry a manual breast pump, go into a restroom and empty both breasts. We prefer the type of breast pump that consists of two cylinders—one fitting inside the other—for example, Au Natural or the Marshall Kaneson brand.) Mothers we've spoken with have had very limited success with breast pumps that have a squeeze bulb on one end.

LEAKING. Although the sudden release of milk from the breasts can occur at different times, the reason is always the same: something has triggered your let-down reflex. This can happen while you quietly stand and watch your child sleep, while having sexual relations, or while out for dinner with or without your baby, or when you hear someone else's baby cry. It's also very common in the early weeks for one breast to leak while the baby is nursing on the other breast or for both breasts to leak when you are overfull. Nursing pads worn inside your bra to absorb any leakage are helpful. You can cut up pieces of clean cotton cloth or gauze to fit your bras, wash and reuse them, or you can buy disposable pads at the drugstore. If you use the disposable pads, try to find large, thick round ones without plastic. Plastic traps moisture which can be irritating. If pads without plastic are not available, either wear the plastic side away from your skin or remove this section entirely, as it can be irritating to your nipples. An effective way to stop the leaking is to place the heel of your hand, or even one finger, against the nipple for about a minute or to cross your arms over your breasts. Yes, leaking can be embarrassing—especially if you're out in public and whatever you are wearing suddenly becomes noticeably wet. If you are having this problem and feel self-conscious, carry a sweater, poncho, or shawl you can put on to conceal the wetness until you get home. (A baby in a baby carrier covers it all up!) Be assured that in time you will no longer have this inconvenience.

SORE NIPPLES. Your nipples must toughen to adapt to the new stresses placed upon them. Many women find they have a day or two of soreness which disappears. Sore nipples can also occur when the baby gnaws at the nipple instead of nursing properly. It is important to make sure that at least a portion of the areola, the dark area surrounding the nipple, is in the baby's mouth and that the baby's tongue is between the lip and the breast. (This can be checked by pulling the baby's lower lip down while he or she is nursing.) It is important to raise the baby up to your breast instead of leaning over to feed the baby. A pillow placed in your lap while you rest your elbow on the arm of a chair can help achieve the correct position. Sore nipples can be quite uncomfortable and in severe cases, the nipples may even crack or possibly bleed. While in the privacy of your own home, you can wear an old sweater or blouse with holes cut out for your exposed nipples (open the flaps of your bra). Another possibility is to place tea strainers in your bra cups to allow air to flow around the nipples. Warm air from a blow dryer or cautious exposure to sunlight or the heat from a lightbulb or high-intensity reading lamp can be helpful. Breastfeeding authorities recommend that you do *not* use alcohol, soap, tincture of benzoin, or any similarly drying substance on your nipples. Pure hydrous lanolin may be applied and should not be washed off before the baby nurses. Nursing in different positions each time will eliminate a constant strain on the same area of the nipple. Note: if the condition is due only to sore nipples, the painful sensation should occur only for the first few moments of any feedings, should stop when your milk lets down and should be less noticeable when you begin to nurse on the second side. It is wise to begin feedings on the less sore side or express some milk at the beginning of a feeding to get the milk flowing so it will take less time for your let-down reflex to operate. The discomfort should continue for no more than a few days. *In extreme cases,* your pediatrician may recommend that you use a nipple shield for a few days or during alternate feedings until the problem is resolved. If the entire nursing procedure is painful, if the pain continues for longer than several days, or if the discomfort extends from the nipple area into the breast, check your baby for white patches along the roof of the mouth. This might indicate the presence of an infection called "thrush," which can be cleared up easily. Contact your pediatrician for information. Even if thrush is not present, call your obstetrician.

CLOGGED DUCT AND MASTITIS. Mastitis (breast infection) has several causes. In some cases, bacteria (staphylococcus) enter the breast through a crack in the nipple. They may be present in the baby's mouth or throat and transmitted through the nipple (cracked or otherwise) during a feeding. It is also possible that a milk duct is clogged, preventing the passage of milk, which results in a back-up; or, more commonly, the let-down reflex is temporarily malfunctioning. In either case, if the milk doesn't flow, an environment conducive to the growth of bacteria either already normally present in the breast or transmitted by the baby develops. This causes an infection known as mastitis. A red sore lump on the breast is a symptom of a clogged duct and should be cared for so that mastitis does not develop: Be sure your bra fits properly and is not constricting, because this may have caused the clogged duct; increase the number and duration of nursings, to keep the breasts fairly empty; nursing in different positions and gently massaging the sore area toward the nipple might help. If engorgement, headache, fever and a flulike feeling develop, call your obstetrician. Breastfeeding authorities recommend that you rest in bed, apply heat to the sore breast, increase your fluid intake and continue the increased nursings. Your doctor may prescribe antibiotics and/or analgesics. Be aware that your baby may get diarrhea from the medication or that the taste of the milk may change slightly after four or five days. Although some obstetricians still order weaning in cases of mastitis, breastfeeding authorities insist it is most important that you continue to breastfeed to keep the milk flowing. Even though you have an infection, your milk will not harm the baby, nor will most antibiotics or mild analgesics. *If you abruptly terminate nursing when you have mastitis, a breast abscess is most likely to develop.*

ABSCESS. An abscess is an accumulation of pus that is surrounded by damaged and inflamed tissue and confined to one area. Breast abscesses usually form when mastitis is neglected or improperly treated. In the case of an abscess, depending on its location, your health care provider might tell you to nurse only on the healthy breast. If you must temporarily stop nursing, the abscessed breast should be emptied either manually or with a breast pump to keep the milk flowing. The milk should be discarded. Your doctor may tell you to apply hot compresses to the affected area in the hope that the abscess will open and drain. It is frequently necessary for the doctor to lance the abscess to promote drainage of the pus. When the abscess heals, you can resume nursing on both breasts.

BOTTLEFEEDING

Parents who bottlefeed have several decisions to make, guided by their common sense, their baby's reactions, their budget and their pediatrician's advice. There are different types of formula to choose from, differing not only in chemical composition but also in the amount of preparation necessary. Nipples and bottles differ in size and shape as well as material.

Sterilization

While some pediatricians recommend that the formula be poured into clean bottles, capped with nipples and then sterilized, others believe the water in a dishwasher is hot enough to thoroughly clean bottles before the formula is placed in them and then refrigerated. Some dishwashers have a covered section in the silverware tray especially for nipples. Be sure to thoroughly clean nipples before placing them in this section, because water may not be forced through the nipple holes and clogging can occur. If your dishwasher does not have such a section, you can place the nipples, nipple end up, on the bottom of the silverware tray and place utensils around them, securing them to the tray to prevent their floating around. (Do not place nipples loosely in an uncovered silverware tray or on the glass rack, because they will fly around during the wash cycle and can clog the pump.) Nipples can be sterilized by boiling them for five minutes. Some doctors believe sterilization is unnecessary and that it is sufficient to wash bottles and nipples with special brushes in hot soapy water, followed by thorough rinsing. Interestingly, many pediatricians believe that there is no need to warm formula for a feeding and that it may even be offered cold from the refrigerator. Through trial and error you will discover if your baby has a preference as to the temperature.

Formula

The following is a list of the types of prepared formulas available, starting with the most expensive and ending with the least (as a general rule, the less you need to do to prepare the formula, the more expensive it will be):

FILLED, STERILIZED 4- AND 8-OUNCE BOTTLES. Some come with nipples already in place; others require the addition of nipples. These are good for carrying with you when traveling with the baby, as they require no refrigeration. You also might consider keeping these in the baby's room for middle of the night feedings so you will not need to go to the kitchen to get and possibly heat a refrigerated bottle. These ready-to-use bottles are often too expensive to offer for all feedings.

READY-TO-POUR CANS. These come already prepared in cans and need to be poured into clean or sterilized bottles, depending on your pediatrician's advice.

CONCENTRATE. This is a liquid which must be diluted per package directions.

POWDER. It must be dissolved with water per package directions.

You can also make your own formula following your pediatrician's directions. This is the least expensive method of formula preparation, but it is also the most time-consuming.

Formula must be properly cared for to inhibit the growth of bacteria which can thrive on the sugars present. To avoid spoilage:

•If you use the cans of ready-to-pour formula, wash the top of the can before puncturing it. Pour the entire can into clean bottles, cover them and refrigerate. Warm and use as needed. Never store formula in an open can.

•Do not leave formula in the refrigerator for more than forty-eight hours. We suggest you prepare a day's supply at a time—no more.

•Discard any formula left in a bottle after a feeding. Some saliva (which contains bacteria) may back up through the nipple and multiply in the formula, causing spoilage.

•Check the expiration date of any formula you purchase. Rotate any stock of formula you keep at home so you use cans with the earliest expiration dates first.

•Different formulas have different chemical compositions. Some are cow-milk based, others are made of soybean, and there is even meat-based formula available. Prepared formulas come with and without iron. Iron may cause gastric upset, constipation, or diarrhea in some infants. While some babies seem to do well on whatever formula they drink, some tolerate a specific formula better than others. This can show up if your baby is given one formula in the hospital and you use another at home.

Bottles and Nipples

At present, plastic and glass bottles are available in different sizes and shapes. Glass bottles can be cleaned the most thoroughly, but can break if dropped or thrown. If you use plastic bottles and they begin to smell sour, even after being thoroughly cleaned, discard them and buy new ones. You will need eight bottles and nipples to begin with, bottle and nipple brushes, plus tongs and a sterilizer if your pediatrician so advises. We suggest you buy 8-ounce bottles even though initially your newborn will probably drink from 2–4 ounces a feeding. This saves the expense of buying the 4-ounce size initially and then 8-ounce bottles as a child's appetite increases. (By three months, your baby will probably average 4–8 ounces at a feeding.)

There are several different types of bottles that utilize sterile disposable inserts. The insert is placed in the bottle, formula poured in, and the nipple attached. Some mothers prefer these because the insert collapses as the bottle is emptied, thereby theoretically lessening the chance that the baby will swallow air. However, the air babies swallow is usually air gulped through the mouth as the baby sucks—*NOT* air that comes through the nipple. One medical advisor we consulted prefers the short nipple available because it is closer in design to the mother's nipple and encourages the baby to suck more actively, as nature intended. Others prefer the "Nuk," or "orthodontic" nipple that mimics the shape the breast takes in the baby's mouth, causing the sucking to more closely resemble the mouthing action of breastfeeding. Ask your pediatrician which type he or she recommends.

Nipples can be purchased with either a hole or a cross-cut. If the hole is too large, the baby may gag as the formula rushes into the mouth. If your child has a particularly strong suck, consider buying a nipple without any opening and making either a tiny pin hole or a small cross-cut with a clean, sharp razor so the milk will flow more gradually. If the baby seems distressed during a feeding, check to see if the nipple is clogged, causing fruitless sucking.

Additional Advice

No matter what type of bottle or nipple you select, be sure you can see formula in the neck of the bottle while you are feeding the baby. This helps prevent the ingestion of air which can cause gas. Regardless of the type of bottle and nipple you use, your baby will swallow *some* amount of air. It is therefore important to burp your baby midway through and after every feeding so that any air bubble will come up and not travel through the baby's digestive system and out the other end.

Never prop a bottle! A baby left with a propped bottle may gag on the liquid and choke. Furthermore, studies have shown that all infants need cuddling to develop normally. Breastfeeding mothers *must* hold their infants while they nurse, and it is wise for the bottlefeeding parent to do so as well. Look into your baby's eyes; smile and coo—talk or sing to the baby during a feeding.

Your pediatrician will advise you when and how to gradually begin giving your baby solid foods (usually between four and six months). If you use commercially prepared baby foods, do not feed the baby directly from the jar unless you plan to discard any food left over. The saliva transmitted from the baby's mouth into the jar via the spoon can cause spoilage. Also, know that you can prepare your own baby food using a blender or baby-food grinder—and freeze the food in portion sizes. This is more economical than using prepared baby foods. There are several cookbooks available with recipes for baby foods.

HOW TO HANDLE MIDDLE OF THE NIGHT FEEDINGS

Middle of the night feedings can be accomplished with a minimum of disruption. If you are bottlefeeding, consider using the prepared bottles of formula that come with the nipple already in place. These do not require refrigeration. Keep them in the baby's room so you won't have to stumble around in the dark to locate them. And, if you usually heat the baby's refrigerated formula, during the night this may not be necessary if you use the prepared bottles.

Who should get up to feed the baby? Consider making the decision on the basis of who's the most fatigued. If the new mother is more exhausted, the new father can get up. If he is more exhausted, she can get up. Some couples solve this problem by having the new father (if he works outside the home) take care of the middle of the night feedings on weekends while his mate handles weeknight feedings.

If you are breastfeeding, consider taking the baby into bed with you either by sharing your bed the whole night, or by letting the child join you upon awakening in the middle of the night. Simply attach baby to nipple and go back to sleep. While there is still controversy about this, the La Leche League manual assures readers that it is safe. Tine Thevenin has written a book called *The Family Bed* which discusses the advantages of "co-family" sleeping. When asked what he thought about taking the baby into bed, one pediatrician replied, "I have a wife, three children, and a dog, and sometimes I wake up in the morning and don't know who is licking my face!" Some couples wonder if this causes dependence problems later, if the child will refuse to graduate to a crib or bed or will never sleep through the night. Parents we have spoken with who've tried it said that this does not generally occur—that, eventually, the baby usually does sleep through the night, in his or her own bed. Mothers whose infants sleep with them for the entire night, report that they are less fatigued than other mothers they know because they don't really have to awaken fully to care for their babies.

HOW TO HANDLE A CRYING BABY

It is important to understand that a baby has only one way of communicating his or her needs—by crying. While the tendency of new parents is to assume a crying baby is hungry (especially if breastfeeding), babies also cry because they are cold, tired, lonely, wet, dirty, hot or in pain. We believe that a new baby's cry usually means there's a problem, although admittedly it's often difficult to ascertain what the problem is.

When you hear your baby cry, relax and trust your instincts. What do you *feel* is wrong? Does the baby *sound* like he or she is in pain? Tired? Is it a high-pitched shriek, a sob, a call? Did the baby sound like that the last time he or she was cold or wet? Is the baby turning his or her head from side to side and opening the mouth to suck (indicating hunger)? Babies have different cries to express different needs. As time goes on, you'll learn to know what's wrong almost immediately and how to help. Until then, we'd like to share some baby-soothing strategies with you.

•*If breastfeeding, offer the breast*. Breastfed babies can be hungry as often as every hour at times during the first few weeks. Even if they are not hungry, the additional sucking may be all they need to feel comfortable again. If the baby has been sucking for an extended period of time, consider trying the pacifier. However, if you find that you are nursing at very frequent intervals every day and that you rarely can go two hours or more without nursing, chances are you may be misinterpreting your baby's signal. While the nursing may be satisfying the baby, with some experimenting you will probably find something else that will satisfy him or her as well. Keep in mind that overtiredness and gasiness will frequently cause a baby to nurse for extended periods.

•*If bottlefeeding, follow your pediatrician's advice on how often to offer a bottle*. Bottlefed babies often require additional sucking; if it's not time for a bottle of formula, you can offer some water, or a pacifier. Do not use pacifiers that are made of more than one piece unless the nipple portion is securely attached to the shield. Also beware of pacifiers that are so small they can be swallowed. Some parents prefer not to let a baby become attached to a pacifier because it might not be there when needed; they'd rather help him or her find the thumb instead.

•*Change the diaper*. Some babies are uncomfortable when they are wet or dirty.

•*Burp the baby*. Perhaps a gas bubble is causing discomfort.

•*Feel the baby's face or back of the neck for signs that he or she is too cold or too warm (perspiring)*. Cold hands and feet are not reliable signs that the baby is feeling chilly. These areas usually do feel cold to the touch because of decreased blood circulation there. Also, check to see if the crib is too near a radiator or in a draft.

•*Observe the baby's stomach. Is it distended?* Does the baby pull the knees up to the chest and then bring them down sharply? These can indicate gas pains. Try the following:

—Hold the baby across your lap, with his or her tummy on your knees, and gently rub the back.

—Hold the baby upright with his or her back against your stomach. Place your arm around the waist and exert gentle pressure.

—Hold the baby face up, cradled in one arm, and gently rub the belly.

—Hold the baby upright against your body with his or her head facing and against your shoulder. Gently pat the back, rub it in a circular motion, or rub the back gently *upward* from the waist to the shoulder level and repeat several times.

—Place the baby belly down on a warm (not hot) hot-water bottle. (Test the temperature of the bottle on the inside of your wrist first. Never leave an infant alone this way.)

—When he or she starts to cry in pain, do *not* let the baby "cry it out!" The longer and harder the baby cries, the more air is inhaled, which results in more gas and pain.

—Try holding the baby upright to encourage better digestion

and elimination of gas. You might try a papoose-type infant carrier. (Keeping him or her in an upright position after feedings can also be a good idea, to encourage any air bubbles to float upward and out through the mouth. A mother we know took this suggestion a step further one night. She was exhausted and her daughter seemed to be having gas pains. She placed her in a chest carrier so the baby couldn't slip out of her arms, arranged a pillow and some blankets, and slept upright in a comfortable chair.)

—All babies swallow some air when they feed. Some babies —breast- or bottlefed—are air gulpers. They feed so avidly you can actually see them gulping down their breastmilk or formula and lots of air. In addition to holding the baby upright for about twenty minutes after a feeding, try holding him or her in a semisitting position while feeding, with the head higher than the buttocks. This encourages the air to collect on top of the milk instead of slipping under; it will therefore be easier to expel via the mouth instead of having to travel through the digestive system and out the other end.

—Remember, do not offer more breastmilk or formula if the baby cries *very* soon after a good feeding. The cries may not mean hunger, but discomfort. If so, the more you feed the child, the more discomfort he or she may have.

•*If the crying continues and sounds piercing, strip the baby naked*. Take off everything, including the diaper. Check the body carefully. Possibly a piece of thread from the clothing has wrapped itself around a finger or toe. If you are using cloth diapers, a pin may be open. Look for red marks around the thighs and waist—an indication that the diaper or plastic pants are too tight. Check the diaper area for a rash that might be causing discomfort. As you dress the baby again, make sure the clothing is not constricting.

•*Perhaps the baby is bored*. Try the following:

—Change the baby's position in the crib so the room can be seen from another angle.

—Dangle brightly colored objects over the crib. Some babies like mobiles, and you can make your own of string and household items such as spoons and colored paper. Fisher-Price makes a mobile that turns for ten minutes when wound. (When purchasing a mobile or making one, look at the toy from the baby's angle. Will the baby see more than just a few black lines going around in a circle? Also, be sure to remove the mobile before the baby is old enough to reach and possibly become entangled in it.)

—Turn on the radio and play soft music. (Some babies prefer music with a beat).

—Sing to the baby.

—Make funny sounds. This seems ridiculous but can often be distracting. (If not to the baby, then to you!)

—Put the baby in a chest carrier from which he or she can see the world and feel your closeness as you go about your business, providing a constant change of scenery. The upright position can also aid digestion and/or help bring up another air bubble.

—Get out of the house with the baby. Put him or her in a chest carrier or carriage and take a walk. The change of scenery will do you both some good.

●*If bottlefeeding: are the baby's bowel movements hard?* Have you recently changed the formula?

●*Are you tense? Under pressure? Have you just had an argument?* Babies sometimes cry because they sense you are under stress. Sit down, get your feet up, and tell each part of your body to relax. Try some slow breathing for about fifteen minutes.

●*Does your baby seem very sensitive to stimuli—touch, sound, smell?* Does he or she startle awake every time the phone rings? Do you notice a correlation between the baby's crying spells and strong odors like onions cooking? Some babies need a very quiet, modulated environment. Speak softly, handle the baby gently, and move slowly when caring for this type of baby. Give the baby as much of a feeling of calm, quiet, and softness as possible. Dim lights and soft, smooth-textured baby blankets and clothing can also be helpful. Try to release as much tension as you can from the baby's body by your quiet tone and soothing, lightly massaging touch.

●*Other soothers:*

—Try out one of the mechanically operated infant swings, before purchasing one, to see if it soothes the baby. It can be very helpful during a fussy period, especially during your mealtimes.

—Rock the baby in a rocking chair or carriage or while standing, holding him or her in your arms.

—Buy a recording of sounds taken from an actual fetal environment. Hearing the mother's heartbeat, placental circulation, and the movement of amniotic fluid is frequently soothing, especially if you begin to use such a recording soon after you come home from the hospital, while these sounds are still familiar to the newborn.

—Keep the baby comfortably warm, perhaps with the belly skin-to-skin on yours for a natural source of warmth and comfort.

—Try giving the baby a warm bath. Be sure the room temperature is warm so he or she will be less likely to be chilled when removed from the bath water. (Remember, the umbilicus must be thoroughly healed before giving the baby a tub bath.)

—If the baby's umbilicus has fallen off and healed completely, get undressed, undress the baby, and take the baby with you into a tub of warm water. Skin-to-skin contact and the liquid environment are often soothing.

—Get undressed, undress the baby, and get into bed with the baby. This is especially effective if you are breastfeeding and can nurse the baby under the covers. Again the skin-to-skin contact and warmth often do wonders. (It might be advisable to leave the baby's diaper on!)

—Since many babies like to be swaddled, wrap yours snugly in a light blanket.

—Use the crib bumpers to divide the crib into two halves. Some babies prefer to be in smaller places. Try placing the baby alongside the bumper to give him or her a sense of security.

—If you've been holding him or her for a while, try putting the baby in the crib on his or her side, with the back supported against the side of the crib or a rolled-up blanket, or try putting the baby on his or her stomach. Sometimes, it's comforting to a baby not to be held or handled for awhile. Try changing the position after a few minutes if the baby is still uncomfortable.

—Take the baby for a ride in the car.

There are two schools of thought about what to do if the baby continues to cry and cannot be soothed despite all efforts to meet his or her needs. One school says to let the baby cry it out, in the belief that if you constantly hold and rock your child, he or she will get to like it and demand the attention even when it is not needed. Life, according to this theory, is difficult, and the time to begin learning this is when you're young. A variation on this advice is to let the child cry but to pick the infant up every twenty minutes to let him or her know you're there and then put the baby back because babies shouldn't be "spoiled" and need to learn to be by themselves.

Another group believes that after everything has been tried, *even if cuddling and holding don't help,* a crying baby should be held and cuddled. They believe that no infant should be left to cry simply because "nothing helps anyway." Current thinking on newborn care embraces the "don't let a newborn cry" advice, based on the theory that if early needs are met, the child will have the basic foundations of love and security with which to deal with the rigors of life and co-existence with other human beings. If left to cry for long periods during the first few months, the infant knows only discomfort, frustration, and isolation, which foster negative, not positive, feelings toward the world. Further, today's childcare authorities claim you cannot spoil a young baby. It is interesting to note that in other cultures where babies are carried in back or front packs close to their mothers wherever they may go, infant crying is rarely heard. Warm body contact, the comfort of feeling close to mother—all say to the baby, "There's someone near who's trying to help you. You're not alone."

We're not referring to an older baby, who, for example, is exhausted and refuses to go to sleep, or, when told he or she can't have a cookie, throws a temper tantrum. We believe there comes a time when children have to cry things out, but that time is not in the early weeks when the only way they can communicate a genuine need is through crying—and we include loneliness and boredom as needs. At what age should children be left to "cry it out"? We can't answer that question for you. You know your child and your own feelings. We're only suggesting that the time to teach children that they can't have everything (including your constant attention) is *not* in the early weeks.

We understand that parents feel tension when their baby cries. As parents, we have experienced that tension ourselves and know that, continued over a period of time, it can be overwhelming. If crying is "getting to you," call a friend who has a baby. There's nothing like comparing notes with another new parent. By all means get out of the house for a while if you so desire, either by yourself or with the baby. (Going outdoors often does wonders for a crying infant, and the change of scenery will do wonders for you!) If you go out without the baby, *leave the baby with someone who will hold him or her in your absence*. (If you ever feel so tense that you think you might harm the baby, place the baby in his or her crib, shut the door, and call an organization such as Parents Anonymous. The individual who answers the phone will help you to better deal with the situation and to accept your feelings of frustration, anger, and hostility without taking it out on the baby. All conversations are confidential; no one asks you name.)

When should you call your pediatrician? Again, learn to trust your instincts. If you feel something is wrong, that the crying has continued far too long—call. If you need reassurance that the crying is nothing to worry about—call. It often pays to spend the extra money and have your child examined by a physician before the next scheduled office visit to rule out any physical reason for crying. Even if that examination finds nothing wrong—at least you'll be reassured that the crying is not your fault.

Know that the advice to always respond to a crying baby even if holding doesn't help can be carried to the opposite extreme. Parenthood is not an invitation to martyrdom. When you've been holding and soothing and feeding and comforting a crying baby for hours on end and you've called the pediatrician and maybe even brought the baby into the doctor's office to be checked and you've been assured that there is nothing medically wrong; when it's 3:00 A.M. and you've been up since 5:00 A.M. the previous morning and you can't call a friend or get a sitter and your mate is not available to help for whatever reason—in any situation where you feel you just can't deal with things any longer, it's okay to say that *your* need for a break has to take priority over the baby's need to be held! Put the baby down in a safe place, such as the baby's crib, and take a warm bath or a soothing shower. Play some slow, quiet music on the stereo and use some of the relaxation techniques described in "How to Minimize 'Down' Feelings" in the section "Postpartum Blues."

Some parents become overconcerned with doing the "right" thing all the time—leading them to the brink of exhaustion—sometimes out of a fear that the child might need psychotherapy as an adult because he or she was left to cry several times as an infant. It's important to know that no one family member's needs can come first 100 percent of the time and that the overall quality of the parent-child relationship over time is what's important—not any one or two incidents of letting the baby cry for a while. If feelings of inability to cope continue for prolonged periods, however, it's important to get professional help. (See "Postpartum Blues.") If you have a difficult baby, it may be wise to get household help on a part- or full-time basis temporarily.

Colicky Baby

Your baby will probably be called "colicky" if he or she cries a lot—several hours each day. Colic is the name given to the condition a baby is in when he or she *appears* to have gas or some other disturbance in the intestinal tract resulting in crying out. It seems that the baby is hurting because cries are loud, often changing to screams; the face becomes red, and the baby usually pulls the legs up toward the body in apparent pain. Inexplicably, many babies' colic attacks seem to occur at about the same time each day—usually late afternoon or early evening. Some attacks are less predictable and sporadic. No one has come up with a conclusive explanation or reason for colic, and some pediatricians claim it has become a catch-all term for unexplained periodic crying in a young infant.

If your baby is "colicky," it is important that you and your mate acknowledge and accept the fact that you are going through a *very* difficult period that will probably last several months. If your baby's colic attacks are predictable, try to plan them into your day. This way they are an expected occurrence, not a disappointing surprise. Try to analyze when they occur and how long they last. Ask yourselves what you would be accomplishing during that time slot and rearrange your priorities if necessary. For example, if colic attacks usually occur in the late afternoon around the time you would be preparing dinner, plan on cooking earlier in the day. Then when the baby needs attention, dinner is ready to be warmed up, and you are free to attend to your child.

Discuss the situation with your mate and together try to

resolve any problems you are currently facing because of the stress you are experiencing. Also, try to anticipate problems that are likely to arise over the next few months as the colic continues. What can you each do to alleviate the situation? What needs do you each have that will have to be temporarily deferred? What needs do you each have that cannot be deferred, and what strategies can you develop to meet them? Focus specifically on sleep needs and "time off"—time to stay away from the baby—in addition to any others you may identify. Remember, you cannot meet someone else's needs all the time if none of your own needs are being met.

●Get away from the crying whenever possible by asking someone to stay with the baby (your mate, a relative, a friend, or a sitter). Go to a movie, a store, a lecture—anything that will take your mind away from the crying baby.

●Get as much sleep as possible, so you can better cope with the crying. Hire a sitter if you must or ask someone to stay with the baby while you go to a friend's house to sleep or have a sitter take the baby for a walk in the carriage while you sleep at home! It's worth it.

●It is important for you and your mate to realize that you're both in this together and that *it's not your fault!!!* Blaming each other for not being able to soothe the baby is not only futile but destructive. It further aggravates the situation. Be aware that each of you—baby, father, and mother—needs comforting, understanding, and support at this time!

●Proponents of infant massage claim their techniques are foolproof ways to soothe a colicky baby. Read Vimala Schneider's book *Infant Massage* or locate a class in your community. Two organizations that offer information about infant massage are Special Delivery/Special Handling (147-32 15 Drive, Whitestone, N.Y. 11357) and the International Association of Infant Massage Instructors (National Stress and Health Ctr., N.T. Enloe Memorial Hospital, W. 5th Ave., Esplanade, Chico, Calif. 95926).

For an interesting discussion of colic, its possible causes, and suggestions on how to cope, read Dr. Marc Weissbluth's *Crybabies, Coping With Colic,* Berkley Publishing, 1985.

BODY IMAGE—EXERCISE AND DIET

Your body image is important during the postpartum period. If you have negative feelings about your body and how you look in clothes (and how you look *out* of clothes!) it will be difficult for you to feel good about yourself in your daily life. You might avoid getting dressed all day because nothing fits right. Lounging in a nightgown and robe tends to make you feel more down, draggy, lifeless, purposeless—depressed.

You might find yourself avoiding visiting people, going out for dinner, or having friends in because you don't like the way you look or don't want to be seen. This encourages being cut off from friends, from socializing and from necessary changes in your environment—leading to isolation and depression. You may avoid being intimate and cuddly with your mate because you feel unattractive or unappealing. This can lead to misunderstanding, coolness and estrangement between you.

If you feel good about how you look and how you fit into clothing, you will feel good about your entire self, and your outlook toward your baby, your mate and your life in general will be better.

To help you feel good about yourself while in the process of reaching your desired shape and weight, there are some things you can do. For starters, when planning what to wear the day you leave the hospital, be sure it's a loose-fitting dress or overblouse with a pair of pants you may have been comfortable wearing in your early months of pregnancy or a pair of maternity pants. Most new mothers cannot fit into their pre-maternity clothes for the first few weeks after delivery. (If you can, consider yourself lucky.) Attempting to squeeze into your still-too-tight clothes can be depressing. However, it might be a good idea to try them on once a week to observe your progress in losing your postpartum flabbiness and to encourage yourself to continue your diet and exercise program.

While you keep your eventual goal in sight and work toward it, make the most of what you are today, now! In other words, don't put off buying yourself a new item of clothing "until I lose all that weight" or "until I'm back to normal." This can lead to being more upset each time you see yourself in clothing either too tight or too loose (maternity outfits). You will not feel good about yourself and may tend not to go places for fear of being seen because you "haven't got a thing to wear that fits." Change that mind set and buy yourself one or two items (or outfits) that *do* fit well, even though you are not yet at your desired size! Having something new in your wardrobe can be a marvelous lift and having something that *fits* can add to your pleasure. It also can add to your motivation to go on with your weight reduction plan! (See the section starting on page 270, "Better Your Physical Self-Image.")

Eating Habits

Do *not* make the mistake of going on a crash diet in an attempt to lose weight fast! Just because you've had your baby and the pregnancy is over does not mean your nutritional needs should be thrown to the winds. Although you are no longer responsible for the nutrients going to your baby via your diet habits (unless you are breastfeeding), you are still responsible for your own nutrition!

It is also important for you to remain on a well-balanced high-energy diet after you've had your baby, because you will need all the energy you can get! If you are eating the proper food and a balanced diet, your energy level will be high and you will be more likely to feel able to cope with the work involved in caring for a new baby and the rest of the family, as well as your own needs. If your energy level is low, childcare may be too much for you to handle and you might find yourself feeling weak, tired, exhausted and generally down. Not eating correctly, coupled with not sleeping enough (a by-product of new parenthood), can lower your resistance to illness, as well as cause tension and frustration.

If you are feeling weak, exhausted or have heart palpitations, it may be due to a deficiency of iron, folic acid and/or certain vitamins. New mothers are often advised to continue taking their pre-pregnant vitamins and iron supplements for the first six weeks postpartum. Some health care providers recommend that breastfeeding mothers take calcium and iron supplements for as long as they are nursing. Even non-breast-feeding mothers are advised by some professionals to take iron and calcium for two to six months—either as part of a daily all-purpose vitamin or in separate pills.

Diet

Be aware of everything you consume each day. Your diet should include some of each of the four basic food groups:

MILK OR MILK PRODUCTS: Skim, whole or evaporated milk; cheeses, creams, yogurt.

PROTEINS: Meat, fish, poultry, eggs, beans, nuts, peanut butter, peas.

FRUITS AND VEGETABLES: Dark green and yellow vegetables rich in vitamin A (carrots, spinach, squash, broccoli, sweet potato, cantaloupe, apricots) and those rich in vitamin C (oranges, grapefruits, cantaloupe, strawberries, broccoli, green and red peppers).

BREAD AND CEREALS: Whole-grain breads and cereals (the value of white breads and refined cereals is highly questionable), rice, potatoes, corn.

General Hints Concerning Your Postpartum Eating Habits

Include protein in *every* meal.

Be sure you have plenty of fruits, vegetables and other high-fiber foods in your daily diet to help prevent constipation—a common complaint during the early months.

Every time you feel like snacking, reach for something nutritious, such as a carrot, celery, yogurt, nuts, dried fruits, cheese cubes, pineapple chunks, cucumber sticks, a hard-boiled egg, or green pepper wedges. Avoid cookies, donuts, pies, cakes, candies. It is helpful to have *only nutritious snacks readily available* for the anxious snacker, so the tendency to reach for the always handy cookie jar is minimized. Have a snack bowl filled with non-junk snacks and in full view inside your refrigerator!

Be aware of everything you eat. Aim for foods representing high protein. Avoid foods representing sugars and high calorie counts (consult a calorie counting chart or booklet).

Be aware that alcoholic beverages such as cocktails, wines and beers are high in calories.

Eat from each of the four basic food groups each day.

For your general well-being, avoid unnecessary salt. Although still controversial, salt is considered by many in the health field to be a contributory cause of high blood pressure, a prime factor related to heart attacks.

Stay away from saturated fats whenever possible. These can be easily observed when they harden at room temperature or in the refrigerator, such as on meats, in gravies and in sauces. Remove such fats from your meats; remove hardened fats from the tops of gravies and sauces after they've cooled.

Many nutritionists believe polyunsaturated fats are better for you. These are liquid vegetable oils (which do not harden) such as corn, sunflower seed, safflower, or soybean.

Drink lots of fluids—three to four quarts a day. This quantity can include water, juices, soups, milk, coffee and tea. Do not overdose on coffee and tea—caffeine is not good for you.

Losing Weight
Without Losing Health and Energy

If you want to lose weight and will be cutting down on your food intake, be sure to get your basic nutrients from the four food groups. You can lose weight while not losing your health and energy by cutting down on high carbohydrate and sugar intake—high calorie foods.

Decide to eliminate sugar from your diet. That means no sugar in your coffee, tea or on grapefruit. Do not eat canned desserts, puddings, cakes, pies, cookies—all high in sugar content. Do not drink wine, cocktails or beer—also high in calories.

Prepare an assortment of readily available nutritious snacks. Every time you find yourself reaching for a sugary, high calorie snack, force yourself to think of its harmful effects on you. Imagine, for example, it piling more flab onto you. Think of it negatively as a poison to your system.

Set yourself reasonable short-term goals of perhaps five pounds weight loss and reward yourself each time you lose another five pounds! *But* your reward must never be made of calories! What other rewards are there? How about a show, a new movie, a new blouse, a new haircut or a gift you'd like to buy for yourself?

Stay away from pills to help you lose weight. Most of these are amphetamines, otherwise known as "speed," which is addictive. They can also have serious side effects on your emotions and blood pressure. Besides, many people who have tried such pills for dieting have gained back unwanted weight when they stopped taking the pills.

Stay away from fad diets which stress one category of food but eliminate others which are necessary for your good health.

Remember that how and what you eat becomes a habit. The way you have been eating until now has been a habit and if you want to develop new and better eating patterns, you will need to stick to the new rules you set for yourself for a while until they too become a habit—and you will be surprised to discover how your habits and tastes will change. At first it will be difficult to adjust, for example, to no sugar in your foods, no cakes or fancy desserts. But after a while, you can become so accustomed to this way of eating that sugar-laden pastries, desserts or drinks can actually become distasteful to you. A new and better habit will then have been established.

Good Grooming Habits

Do not stop good grooming habits just because you're at home more than you were before and see less people. Get out of your nightgown and put on regular clothing each day, whether or not you plan to leave the house. Wear something different each day—even if it's a different pair of jeans than the day before with a different top. Comb your hair and use whatever makeup or skin conditioner you would use if you expected company. In fact, assume that someone will be ringing your doorbell and visiting each day. This can give you more incentive to look your best. Looking your best is important to *you*. The better you know you look, the better you will feel—physically and emotionally.

Better
Your Physical Self-Image

Get a new hair style.

Buy a new shade of lipstick.

Try out a new technique of applying eye makeup.

Manicure your fingernails and give yourself a pedicure.

Treat yourself to a new sweater or blouse in a style you do not ordinarily choose.

Plan a daily fifteen–twenty-minute exercise session aimed at reducing the flab of your abdomen and toning up your entire body. (It is important to check with your doctor before beginning an exercise regimen.)

After receiving the okay of your health care provider, plan to jog three times a week, preferably with a friend, neighbor or mate for company, because the togetherness will keep you more committed to the routine. Or, if you'd prefer, ride an exercycle, swim at a local Y or even take brisk walks.

Fill the house with beautiful music while you soak in a bubble bath for twenty minutes.

Get a free makeup demonstration.

Treat yourself to a body massage and sauna or steam bath.

Treat yourself to an ultra-feminine piece of lingerie—nightgown, underpants, bra.

Treat yourself to a facial—or anything that makes you feel good!!!

Aims of Postpartum Exercises

Assuming there is no medical reason against it, a mild exercise program especially designed for your postpartum recuperation period should be started as soon after delivery as possible—in combination with your new dietary habits.

Elizabeth Noble, R.P.T., in her popular and highly regarded book, *Essential Exercises for the Childbearing Year*, states: "Exercises after delivery should begin as soon as possible . . . certainly within twenty-four hours. Muscle work involved in immediate postpartum exercises is not strenuous or in any way potentially harmful."

According to Ms. Noble, the longer you postpone the restoration of muscle tone, the more muscle atrophy and tissue degeneration will take place.

Health care professionals generally agree that postpartum exercises should be done:

●To restore muscle tone in the vaginal canal for more satisfying sexual relations

●To encourage urinary control

●To give vital pelvic floor support to the bladder and uterus

●To restore muscle tone in the abdominal wall and decrease flabbiness

●To encourage correct posture and pelvic tilt, which prevents and helps correct back problems

●To encourage healing of the episiotomy site and hemorrhoids

●To encourage blood circulation in the legs, thereby preventing possible blood clots

●To maintain general good health and well-being through better muscle tone and blood circulation through the entire system.

Before Beginning Postpartum Exercises

If you have had a cesarean delivery refer to the section covering special exercises for you!

Do not attempt any exercise program without first checking with your doctor or nurse midwife to be sure there are no medical contraindications.

Mild abdominal and pelvic floor tightening exercises are beneficial—not at all harmful. Some health care practitioners advise new mothers to begin these exercises right after delivery; others recommend waiting a few days or weeks. Many women are surprised at results achieved in a matter of days or a few weeks. The exercises described herein are specifically designed to be done during the immediate postpartum period —the first days and weeks. Before graduating to more strenuous exercises, be sure to check with your health care provider.

Before and after each group of exercises, take one or two deep inhalations and exhalations. Before rising from a prone position, stretch, inhale deeply and exhale.

Build up your strength and muscular abilities gradually. Do not try to do too much too soon. Do not overdo any exercise. Stop and rest when you are tired, out of breath, dizzy or your muscles tremble. It is less tiring and more beneficial to do a few exercises, several times a day, than to do all of them in a single long session once or twice a day.

Although there seems to be a natural tendency to hold one's breath while contracting muscles and doing exercises, it is best not to. Holding your breath may cause you to exert unnecessary additional pressure, resulting in a strain on the abdominal wall or pelvic floor.

Do not attempt double-leg-raising exercises. These put undue strain on your back and—contrary to popular belief— do little or nothing to strengthen your abdominal muscles.

Be aware of the curve in your back when you stand, walk, sit or lie down so that you do not increase the curvature, adding strain to your back.

Do not do any gymnastics or other exercises which accentuate the hollow in your back!

Mild Exercises

To prevent the possibility of blood clots and to aid blood circulation in the legs, two mild but excellent exercises— especially important while you're confined to bed or if you've had general anesthesia—are *ankle rotating* and *foot flexing and stretching*.

ANKLE ROTATING. While sitting or lying down, rotate each foot at the ankle in a circle. Rotate from one side to the other and then point the toes downward; then bring them around, finishing a circular motion. Rotate each foot separately or both together in the same or opposite direction.

FOOT FLEXING AND STRETCHING. While sitting or lying down, flex your foot slowly at the ankle with toes pointed toward your body; you will feel stretching in your calf muscles. Then point your toes slowly away from you. Do this several times with each foot. You can do one foot at a time or both together in the same or opposite direction.

Other mild exercises include *abdominal tightening, pelvic rock, single-leg sliding, single-leg raising* and *buttock contractions*.

ABDOMINAL TIGHTENING. To restore muscle tone and remove flabbiness, as soon as you can think of it each day, while standing or sitting, pull your abdominal muscles in and hold them tightly for approximately five seconds while you continue to breathe naturally. (Do not hold your breath.) As you become more proficient, increase the holding time to ten seconds. This simple exercise is remarkably effective.

Variation: Breathe in *slowly* through your nose, allowing your abdominal wall to rise; then exhale *slowly* through your mouth, as you *slowly* pull your abdominal muscles in tightly, letting out all your air. Then start again, doing a total of five ins and outs.

PELVIC ROCK (OR TILT). This exercise is designed to strengthen abdominal muscles, improve posture and relieve backache.

•*On all fours:* On your knees, palms of your hands on the floor, head slightly raised, take a slow, deep breath in through your nose, allowing your abdomen to fill with air. (Do not allow your back to sag unnecessarily low, belly drooping to the floor.) Exhale slowly through your mouth while you pull your abdominal muscles tightly in, lower your head, *and* curve your back like a cat (C-shape). The more you contract your abdominal muscles, the more air you will feel coming out of your lungs and the more you should be rounding your back. Then start again, doing a total of five ins and outs.

•*On your back:* Lying flat on your back, no pillow beneath your head, with your knees bent and feet flat on the floor, take a slow, deep breath in through your nose, allowing your abdominal wall to rise and the small of your back to curve away from the floor slightly. Exhale slowly through your mouth, as you slowly pull your abdominal muscles in tightly, letting out all your air, *and* press the small of your back as flat as you can against the floor. Then start again, doing a total of five ins and outs.

SINGLE-LEG SLIDING. To strengthen abdominal muscles, lie flat on your back, with knees bent and feet flat on the floor. Keep the left knee bent while you draw your right knee up toward your chest, breathing in slowly through your nose. Slowly return the leg to your starting position and continue slowly sliding it down to the floor into a straightened position while breathing out slowly through your mouth. While you are sliding your leg downward, press the small of your back against the floor. Then slide the right leg back to your starting position and repeat with the other leg. This exercise helps remove lower backaches and improve posture and swayback.

SINGLE-LEG RAISING. For abdominal and leg muscle toning and blood circulation, lie flat on your back with knees bent and feet flat on the floor. Keep the left knee bent while you draw your right knee up toward your chest—inhaling slowly through your nose—and continuing raising your leg with your toes pointed toward the ceiling. Then flex the foot with toes pointed toward you, lower the leg slowly in that extended position to a flat-on-floor (leg extended straight ahead) position—while exhaling slowly through your mouth. Then, inhaling through your nose, slide the leg back to your starting position—knee bent, foot flat on the floor. Exhale. Repeat with the other leg.

BUTTOCK CONTRACTIONS. Contract your buttock muscles, holding tightly for a count of four. (Do not hold your breath.) Do five of these contractions every two hours for the first several days.

The Importance of Pelvic Floor Tightening Exercises

Contracting and releasing the pelvic floor muscles has come to be known as the Kegel exercise, named after Arnold Kegel, a professor of obstetrics and gynecology at the University of California in Los Angeles. Professor Kegel did extensive research and studies of the benefits of these contractions and today they are considered by childbirth educators to be essential to all women, whether or not they have borne children (cesarean or vaginally) or intend to, and no matter what their age. Contrary to common belief, pelvic floor muscle laxity is not always associated with childbirth and can be caused by other factors, including the aging process, hormonal decreases, a woman's particular physiology, an injury or disease or simply an unawareness of the existence and therefore disuse of these muscles.

After the intense pressure exerted on the pelvic floor by the birth of a baby, however, these muscles need particular attention in order for them to properly support the bladder and uterus thereafter. Allowing these muscles to remain stretched and loose is courting the possibility of later physiological (and resultant emotional) problems, including: loss of control of urination, which may begin as a slight leakage whenever you cough, sneeze, laugh, lift something, or run, and can progress, if unchecked, to not being able to get to the bathroom on time; prolapse (dropping) of the uterus so that it extends deep down in the vaginal canal (in extreme cases, the cervix can be seen or felt at the vaginal opening); little or no feelings for you or your partner during intercourse because the vaginal walls are slack; not being able to keep a tampon within the vagina if the walls are extremely slack; general discomfort in the pelvic area, such as achiness, pressure, heaviness, and the feeling that "everything is going to drop out."

If the Kegel exercises are not done postpartum (and continued *forever!*) the weakness of the pelvic floor may become worse with each subsequent pregnancy and rehabilitation of the muscles takes longer and involves more effort. Doing these exercises as part of your daily routine—like brushing your teeth and combing your hair—can help alleviate the milder problems and prevent them from progressing further. Once such deleterious progression has been allowed to happen, the situation may be beyond the aid of exercises and may require surgery.

More immediate reasons for doing these exercises *as soon after delivery as possible* are to encourage urination and increase blood circulation to the perineal area, thereby promoting healing of the episiotomy site and aiding the relief of hemorrhoidal pain.

The pelvic floor muscles are those you would use in order to stop the flow of urine, grasp a penis during intercourse, or hold back a bowel movement. Since the anal sphincter is usually the strongest of these muscles, it needs very little attention; the other two areas are usually stressed when the Kegel exercises are taught in childbirth preparation classes.

PELVIC FLOOR EXERCISE. Whether or not you've had prior instruction in how to do the Kegel exercises, as soon as you can after delivery (in the recovery room or hours later in your room) you can try to tighten your vaginal floor muscles as though to stop the flow of urine. After being stretched during delivery or possibly as a result of regional or local anesthesia, you may not have much control or even feeling in the pelvic floor area. Try tightening these muscles anyway! They may feel very weak and slack and you may want to give up in despair, but don't! Try to contract the muscles and hold them —no matter how little you can tighten them at the time (your strength will grow)—for about two or three seconds and then release. Rest a few seconds and try again. Do about three of these contractions. Rest for about fifteen minutes and try another session: tighten your vaginal muscles as much as you can, hold for about two or three seconds (without holding your breath), release for about two seconds, and tighten again. As you become more proficient, you will be able to increase the holding to five seconds and you will advance to a capability of five of these five-second contractions in a row. As you become more aware of these muscles, try to concentrate on pulling them *in and upward* for greater pelvic floor support. It might help if you placed one hand at the level of your pubic bone (for a point of reference) and concentrated on pulling in your vaginal muscles, tightening from the opening of the vagina, pulling in and up, continuing tightening higher up and aiming toward where your hand is. It might also help to think of pulling your vaginal muscles upward as though they were an elevator, beginning at the ground floor (where they are loose, slack at the vaginal opening) and tightening your muscles as the elevator rises to the level of the first, second, third, fourth and fifth floors. Then, control the loosening of your muscles as you imagine the elevator descending from the fifth down to the ground floor—totally released.

These contractions should be done every day—not just postpartum, but as part of your daily routine, *forever!* If you do only five contractions at a time, holding each for a count of five—you can eventually master ten of these sessions a day. You will then total fifty contractions which is the minimum recommended. (Some women routinely do one hundred a day!)

It would also be wise to remember that every time you feel a sneeze coming on, or cough, or expect to lift something—or perform any such activity that puts pressure on your pelvic floor—you should be consciously aware of what is happening and pull the floor muscles in and up. This prevents unnecessary stress and downward pulling on your muscles. Also, use the opportunity after every bowel movement and urination to pull your vaginal muscles in and up tightly, holding for five seconds and then releasing.

POINTS TO REMEMBER REGARDING PELVIC FLOOR EXERCISES:

•Lie on your back or your belly to do the Kegel exercises. Most women find lying on their bellies more comfortable if they have had stitches in the perineum.

•It is best to practice Kegels with your legs apart, not together. Closed legs may encourage the tendency to contract only at the vaginal opening, ignoring the higher-up musculature. Also, it encourages confusion with the muscles in the thighs and groin.

•It is not necessary to hold each contraction longer than five seconds; over-long tightening can tire the muscles. It is better to do brief contract-release actions more frequently, than prolonged contractions less often.

•Do not hold your breath while contracting. This increases the tendency to bear downward, instead of pulling your muscles in and upward.

•Be aware of the difference between your *abdominal* muscles and your *pelvic floor muscles*. You can tighten them both at the same time, but if you are not aware of the difference, you might *believe* you are contracting your pelvic muscles while in reality you are using only your abdominals.

•Be aware of the difference between tightening your inner thigh muscles and your vaginal-perineal muscles. You can press you thighs together very well, but this does not necessarily mean that your pelvic floor muscles are contracted.

•Keep in mind the *necessity* for these exercises—to give better support for the internal organs, helping to prevent and control sagging and related problems.

After your postpartum check-up, if you'd like to check your pelvic muscle abilities, you can try to stop the flow of urine midstream several times. (It is unfair to expect yourself to do this upon arising in the morning, when your bladder is extremely full!) The better your control, the stronger your muscle tone. You can also test your abilities by inserting one or two fingers into the vagina and then practice tightening and pulling your muscles in and upward for a few seconds (one to five) each contraction. You might prefer to practice during lovemaking with the penis in the vagina and having your partner's feedback to help you increase your muscle tightening ability. He can sometimes tell better than you when your contractions are tight, weak, improving, or not progressing.

We believe the importance of doing the Kegel exercises is not emphasized enough. Further, there is a certain amount of false security resulting from some obstetricians' practice of placing an extra suture or two at the vaginal opening when repairing the episiotomy—popularly (and chauvinistically!) referred to as the "daddy stitch" or the "husband's knot." The implication is that this will make for a better "fit" for the penis while in the vaginal canal and the further implication is that this improvement is for the man's benefit, not the new mother's.

In reality, this may produce extra tightness at the *opening* of the vagina, but not necessarily along its inner walls. Be aware that the artificial tightening by suture does nothing for the muscle tone of the pelvic floor, just as the artificial support of a girdle does nothing for the abdominal muscles. So, even if your obstetrician has used an extra few sutures, do not relax—either physically or mentally. Contract those muscles!

Posture

When you begin to walk after giving birth, your center of gravity will be different than it was when you were carrying your baby within you. Your way of standing and walking while pregnant may have caused you to develop the habit of allowing your abdomen to fall forward with the weight of the baby while pulling at and causing your back to curve. As soon as possible after the birth, you should make every effort to stand straight—not hunched forward, afraid to pull at your episiotomy stitches, and not leaning backward with your abdomen protruding as during pregnancy—two common postpartum stances. When you stand, you should consciously pull in your abdominal muscles, straightening and flattening your back—and contract your pelvic floor muscles. This serves not only to keep the muscles in tone but to tilt the pelvis back to its correct prepregnant position.

When you sit, be sure to sit straight—not slumped—and with the small of your back pressed firmly against the back of the chair, your abdominal muscles pulled in. Sitting with your back in the S-curve, belly hanging forward—the swayback position—is just as bad as standing this way.

TIPS ON POSTURE:

●Never bend over from the waist without bending your knees.

●Never arch your back (abdomen forward with S-curved back and buttocks extended). Always sit and stand with your tummy pulled in, bottom pushed forward and the small of your back uncurved. When lying in bed, be careful not to fall into the swayback position.

●When you carry packages, a baby, or a heavy object, be aware of the level at which you hold them. Carry them high, not low, and close to your chest, not away from it. This reduces strain on your back.

●Do not twist your body to pick up a child or an object. Line the front of your body up facing whatever you will be lifting.

Walking

Walking is a valuable exercise. It burns up calories and improves muscle tone and blood circulation. As your strength increases, be sure to do some walking each day. Walk whenever possible instead of riding in a car. If you must drive somewhere, purposely park your car a block or two away from your destination—forcing yourself to walk.

Do not attempt jogging until after your postpartum examination and the approval of your health-care provider.

Artificial Supports

Girdles and corsets are not usually recommended because of the tendency to let them do your abdominal work for you. Instead of allowing your abdomen to be supported this way, you should be pulling in your abdominal muscles with your own power.

Well-constructed uplifting bras are recommended because your breasts, unlike your abdomen, do not have their own means of support. (The pectoral muscles which lie beneath the breasts can be developed to lift the breasts somewhat, but cannot adequately support the weight of postpartum breasts.)

Elastic stockings are sometimes recommended by physicians and offer support, comfort and aid for varicose veins. It is advised that they be put on before you get out of bed in the morning, while your legs are elevated and before swelling occurs from standing. Do not wear tight garters or knee socks with tight elastic bands. They constrict blood vessels and interfere with blood circulation.

Making the Most of Routine Activities

Be aware of your body's needs in your daily life, not just during specified exercise periods. Use your routine physical activities to advantage:

●Whenever you think of it, pull in your tummy and straighten your back while standing or sitting (do not hold your breath). Possibilities: while brushing your teeth, waiting for a bus, waiting in line at the supermarket.

●When you think of it, contract your pelvic floor muscles several times and hold them for five seconds each contraction (do not hold your breath). Possibilities: while making a salad, stirring soup, talking on the telephone, in your car at a red light, during sexual relations.

●While seated or lying in bed, rotate your ankles and point and flex your feet several times. Do this each time you put on your pantyhose, socks, or shoes, while one leg rests on the other, while watching television, reading, talking on the phone, sitting in a doctor's waiting room, in a movie theater.

●After sitting in one position for a while, reading, feeding a baby, carrying packages, etc., rotate your shoulders several times.

●Use every opportunity available to pick up something from the floor, as a chance to squat with knees pointed upward, thereby stretching your thigh muscles. And as you squat, contract your pelvic floor muscles!

●Use every opportunity after urination and defecation to tighten and pull up your pelvic floor muscles. Even while urinating, try to stop the flow of urine by tightening your muscles. The less leakage of urine, the stronger your muscle tone.

Rest and Relaxation

The need for *rest* and *relaxation* should be recognized as much as the need for exercise. Your body must recover from the exertion of labor and delivery. You also need rest in order to physically handle your new responsibilities and adjust to the changes in your sleeping habits. By physically releasing tense muscle groups, you will accomplish mental relaxation as well —an important aid to prevent or relieve some degree of blues or depression.

●Take a nap whenever you feel tired, sleeping on your belly as much as possible.

●Sit with your feet up while holding or feeding the baby, talking on the phone, reading, sewing or whatever. If you don't feel sleepy, at least lie in bed to rest for half an hour, twice a day.

●While sitting or lying down, close your eyes and do slow, relaxed breathing: Inhale through the nose, *slowly,* exhale (all the way out) through the mouth, *slowly.* When you'd like to get up, take a deep breath in and out, then breathe in deeply and *stretch* every part of you, letting air out as you relax— and then rise.

Sleeping and Resting Position

Lie on your side with one or both knees drawn up toward your chest—just enough to help your back remain straight, not hollowed-out or swayback. If you choose to sleep on your stomach, be sure your back is not in the swayback curve. You can prevent this by placing a pillow beneath your hips and using a thin pillow (or none at all) for your head. This helps straighten your back and reduces pulling on the ligaments. Lying on your stomach is usually the most comfortable if you have had sutures for an episiotomy.

If you choose to sleep on your back, try to keep one leg bent at the knee, resting it on your other leg, which can be comfortably stretched lengthwise. By flexing one leg at the knee, you will be helping the small of your back to remain straight and in contact with the bed, preventing the swayback position.

Breathing Techniques

The following are useful for postpartum discomfort, relaxation and pain relief:

SLOW CHEST BREATHING:
Inhale *slowly* through your nose to a count of four or five.
Exhale *slowly* through your slightly opened lips to a count of four or five.

LIGHT SLOW SHALLOW BREATHING:
Inhale and exhale (equal in and out short breaths), softly, slowly, superficially, high up in your throat. Be sure you are getting enough oxygen with your in-breath.

If you prefer, inhale and exhale with your nose. Whichever you choose, keep it *light, soft-sounding*, without expending unnecessary energy and keep it high up in your throat.

SEX

The addition of a baby to a couple's life affects *all* aspects of their relationship and therefore affects how and when they relate to each other sexually.

Possible Deterrents to Sexual Relations and Dealing with the Problems

EXHAUSTION, IRRITABILITY. It might be necessary to forgo lovemaking until more sleep has been obtained and there are more positive than negative feelings as a result.

FEAR THAT THE BABY MAY AWAKEN AND WITNESS YOUR LOVEMAKING. Plan to make love in another room, or put the sleeping baby in another room.

FEAR OF PAIN AT THE EPISIOTOMY SITE. Episiotomy soreness or pain may linger as long as approximately four to six weeks. Use a surgical jelly (such as KY) on the perineum and at the vaginal opening to help the area be more supple. Remember to continue doing your Kegel (pelvic floor) exercises daily, to encourage healing. The woman-above position may be more comfortable and gives more control of movement, thus minimizing discomfort. If the woman-below position is desired, try placing a pillow beneath your hips; this raises the pelvic area to an angle which may alleviate discomfort.

LITTLE OR NO VAGINAL SECRETIONS, CAUSING PAINFUL ATTEMPTS AT INTERCOURSE. Use surgical jelly (such as KY) or other lubrication at the vaginal opening and on the penis—not just at the time of insertion, but during foreplay. Use gentle, tender touches, loving words. Perhaps you can have a drink before making love; it can relax *both* of you. Do not force relations if they continue to be painful after all remedies are tried. Agree between you to forget about it for a while and then try again. Meanwhile, be sure to continue your Kegel exercises daily to encourage healing of the episiotomy site and hemorrhoids. These will also help you be aware of tension in your vaginal area when attempting intercourse and you will be better able to achieve muscle relaxation for easier entry.

EMBARRASSMENT AND INABILITY TO FANTASIZE DUE TO BODY IMAGE (TUMMY STILL FLABBY, NO WAISTLINE, LEAKING BREASTS). Use soft lights; perhaps a special pink or blue bulb in your bedtable lamp can add atmosphere, intimacy and allure. Instead of being nude, wear a shortie nightgown (with or without your bra and gauze nipple pads). The nightgown will hide the flabbiness while giving the feeling of femininity and attractiveness. It may also be a turn-on to your partner.

DISCOMFORT DUE TO FULL, HEAVY, TENDER AND SORE BREASTS. If you feel more comfortable, wear your uplifting bra with gauze nipple pads. You might also try expressing some milk manually while taking a hot shower to relieve some of the fullness.

BLOODY VAGINAL DISCHARGE. If you have and can conquer negative feelings about intercourse during vaginal discharge, simply take a shower (washing thoroughly) and place some rubber sheeting on the bed with several towels on top. If you cannot accept intercourse while still bleeding or discharging, put it off. Perhaps cuddling and other forms of love play can be used to release sexual tension (massage, mutual masturbation, oral techniques).

DISHARMONY IN THE HOUSEHOLD. Work toward keeping the home environment as calm and peaceful as possible. Recall together your loving relationship and work to keep the bond you both had. Plan time together—alone. Plan a romantic dinner, some drinks perhaps, and dancing in your own home right before making love to set the mood.

FEELINGS OF NEGLECT, BEING OVERBURDENED, NOT BEING UNDERSTOOD, DEPRESSION. Share your feelings with each other. Give mutual understanding, comfort, help and respect. Show your concern, interest and love for each other. *Stress the positives;* delete the negatives.

CONFLICTING FEELINGS REGARDING BREASTFEEDING, GIVING BIRTH, AND SEXUAL INTIMACY. Know that it is normal for breastfeeding to stir sexual feelings in a woman. Give yourself time to adjust to and accept your body's multi-roles; birth-giving, milk-giving and sexual gratification.

CONCERN OVER NEW MOTHER'S NOT ACHIEVING ORGASM FOR A WHILE. Know that for several months after birth—sometimes as long as a year—orgasm may not be achieved. This is normal and although the cause is unknown, it probably has some relationship to hormonal changes.

CONTRACEPTION

When sexual relations are to be resumed, it is vital to have freedom from fear of an unwanted pregnancy. Your health care professional can assist you in deciding the best contraceptive for your particular needs. There are several factors you may wish to consider.

SAFETY. The benefits of any contraceptive technique should be weighed against the possible health risks.

EFFECTIVENESS. You should be aware of the varying degrees of effectiveness among contraceptives and who is making the claims. Information may be biased, depending upon its sources (for example, drug manufacturers). Also, and very important, the degree of effectiveness depends upon the regular and proper use of a particular method. When a contraceptive is hailed as "effective," such evaluation is based on perfect conditions wherein each method is used correctly and consistently. The most effective contraceptive is useless if used improperly. The "best" contraceptive for *you* may be the one rated lowest in effectiveness; your success with it will result from your adherence to its proper use.

COMFORT, CONVENIENCE AND PERSONAL PREFERENCE. A contraceptive should be physically comfortable as well as easily adaptable to your particular life-style and habits.

EFFECT ON SEXUAL RELATIONSHIP. If the use of a particular contraceptive technique disturbs or diminishes the joy of the sex act for either partner, another method—or alternating methods to please both partners—should be considered.

COST. Contraceptives are much less expensive than the medical cost of a pregnancy. However, some contraceptives are less expensive than others and you might think it necessary to consider cost when making your decision.

Oral Contraceptives

Introduced in 1960, birth control pills are made of artificially manufactured hormones which prevent conception by creating conditions within a woman's body similar to those present during actual pregnancy. Since ovulation does not occur during pregnancy, it therefore will not occur if a woman takes her prescribed dosage of pills. Furthermore, oral contraceptives change the nature of cervical mucus and the lining of the uterus, providing additional security against conception.

It has been found that much lower doses of hormones than those prescribed when the pill was first introduced are adequate to prevent conception. The pills prescribed today have a lower incidence of the side effects and risks that have been associated with taking hormones, especially estrogen. And contrary to earlier beliefs, some authorities claim that there seems to be no association between the contraceptive pills currently on the market and breast cancer. However, the package insert on one brand of pills on the market does report one study which suggested an increase in breast cancer in women who already have benign breast disease (for example, cysts) or have used oral contraceptives for two to four years.

There are different types of oral contraceptives: combination pills which contain both estrogen and progestin in each pill; triphasic and biphasic pills (introduced in 1984) which have different amounts of estrogen and progestin in each *grouping* of pills (more closely imitating the actual hormonal pattern of the menstrual cycle); and mini pills which only contain progestin. The mini pill is usually prescribed for women who cannot tolerate estrogen or when the use of estrogen is otherwise contraindicated. Although the lack of estrogen greatly reduces serious risks, there are problems associated with use of the mini pill which are discussed below under "Disadvantages."

It is important to know that different brands have varying strengths and that the quality of the hormones can vary. Also the higher the estrogen content, the greater the risk of blood clotting and other serious side effects. Studies of the dangers and effectiveness of the original high-estrogen pills have revealed that a maximum of 20–30 micrograms of estrogen are all that is necessary to inhibit ovulation, although several brands of contraceptive pills contain a higher dosage.

If a dose higher than 20–30 micrograms of estrogen has been prescribed for you, ask your physician if you have a particular condition requiring it. Your doctor may not want to upset or exaggerate the natural estrogen and progesterone balances in your body which may have some bearing on the type of pill prescribed for you. However, you have the right to question why he or she chose a particular type and to know *all* the issues involved, plus *all* the risks. If using one brand results in undesirable side effects, a different brand more suitable to your body chemistry can be prescribed.

Before prescribing the pill, your doctor or nurse midwife should examine your internal pelvic organs and breasts, take your blood pressure, test your urine and blood and take a Pap smear. You should be asked about your medical history and that of your family to discover possible tendencies toward breast cancer, blood clots, poor blood circulation, migraines, diabetes, etc., which could contraindicate pill usage. You should be questioned about high blood pressure, liver disease, diabetes, irregular periods, previous pregnancies, abortions, miscarriages, or complications of pregnancy, such as varicose veins and toxemia. Your doctor or nurse midwife should also know about your menstrual cycles, how long they last, how heavy the flow, and if you experience fluid retention, swelling and tenderness of the breasts, cramps and mood changes during your menstrual cycles.

Your doctor or nurse midwife should know about any other medications you may be taking because many of them lower the effectiveness of the pill. You should be checked every six months to a year while taking the pill to be sure that no condition has develop which would indicate the need to discontinue its use.

(Note: Nurse practitioners and nurse midwives can prescribe contraceptive pills under standing orders of the physician in charge.)

Some women use an additional means of protection during the first month of using oral contraception to be sure the hormones have enough time to establish the necessary anti-ovulation environment.

Before trying to conceive again, you will probably be advised to use other means of contraception for two or three months after stopping the pill—while the pill's hormones are still in your system.

If you take the pill within six months after delivery, there is a slightly increased chance of abnormal blood clotting. If you are breastfeeding, you will probably be advised not to take the pill because the drugs in oral contraceptives are known to appear in the milk and affect its quantity and quality; also, the long-term effect on infants from exposure to hormones is unknown. Some doctors, however, will prescribe the no-estrogen mini pill since they believe progesterone does not affect lactation as the other pills do. However, other doctors believe that any hormones must be considered suspect—in relation to the baby's welfare. La Leche League, in its booklet, *Breastfeeding: Drugs in Human Milk* claims that progesterone decreases the total amount of fat and protein in the mother's milk and *may* affect infant growth. This booklet, co-authored by Gregory J. White, M.D., and Mary White, is a reprint of an article originally published in *Veterinary & Human Toxicology*, Volume 26, supplement 1, 1984.

ADVANTAGES:

●If used according to instructions, the pill is considered the most effective means of contraception—other than sterilization or abstinence. According to Planned Parenthood, effectiveness for average-careful users is 98%; for super-careful users: 99.5%.

●There is no interruption of love play to apply contraceptive materials.

●Your menstrual periods will be predictable every twenty-eight days.

●You will probably have a shorter and lighter menstrual flow.

●You will probably have fewer or no menstrual cramps and pre-menstrual tension.

●There is less chance of toxic shock syndrome and thyroid problems.

●You are protected from certain types of benign breast disease and ovarian cysts, ectopic pregnancy (except if using the mini pill) and iron-deficiency anemia.

●Women on the pill for at least one year have half the average risk of developing cancer of the ovary and of the endometrium (lining of the uterus). Although no connection between the pill and cancer of the cervix is evident, doctors are being cautious and advise regular Pap tests.

●Women using the pill have half the chance of developing Pelvic Inflammatory Disease (PID)—in the genital tract—a bacterial infection that affects approximately 850,000 women annually and can result in infertility and even, in rare cases, death.

●Women with acne usually discover that estrogen-dominant pills improve their complexion.

DISADVANTAGES:

(Please note: Many of the risks previously associated with taking the pill came to light as a result of studies of older women using the higher dose estrogen pills. Today's low dose estrogen and non-estrogen mini pills are considered by many authorities to carry smaller risk of serious complications. However, much of the information in this chapter should be considered to apply to *all* contraceptive pills, since it has not yet been fully established and accepted that the mini pill has fewer serious side effects than the others.)

●You are risking major health hazards as well as other possible side effects: blood clotting (sometimes resulting in the loss of a limb or of sight, paralysis or death), heart attack, stroke (caused by loss of blood circulation to the brain by clots or hemorrhaging in the brain, which can result in possible paralysis of all or part of the body, or death), rise in blood pressure, aggravation of an existing cancerous condition, growth of polyps (non-malignant tumors) in the lining of the uterus, headaches (migraine or other), increased susceptibility to venereal disease (in the lower genital tract), bladder and vaginal infections, changes in skin pigmentation, gum inflammation, fluid retention, weight gain, nausea, fatigue, breast tenderness, breakthrough bleeding and acne (if taking a progesterone-dominant pill), missing a menstrual period or two, increased growth of body hair, increased risk of having gallbladder disease requiring surgery, decreased vaginal secretions, increased or decreased sexual desire. (The newer triphasic and biphasic pills are designed to reduce these symptoms.)

●You must maintain periodic gynecological checkups to provide early detection of possible serious complications.

●You must remember to take a pill every day, whether or not intercourse has taken place or is planned. If you stay away from home overnight or longer, you must prepare a supply of pills to take with you.

●If you forget to take the pill when you should, you risk becoming pregnant that month. It is then advised that you use another means of contraception in addition to the pill as an extra precaution until your next menstrual period.

●After you stop taking the pill altogether, it may take several months before your natural menstrual cycle returns.

●If you conceive while on the pill, there is a chance that the baby will develop congenital heart disease or other abnormalities which may result in miscarriage.

●If you take the pill within six weeks after delivery, there is a slightly increased chance of abnormal blood clotting.

●The pill is ineffective when taken with certain other medications and in patients who have had lower bowel surgery. Be sure to discuss these possibilities with your doctor or nurse midwife.

●If you become ill with vomiting, diarrhea or high fever, the pill may not be fully absorbed and therefore not be effective! It is best in such cases to use an *additional* form of contraception for the rest of the cycle.

●If you are over thirty-five, there is a higher risk of serious side effects if you take the pill.

●If you are on the pill, you should not smoke—or you risk cardiac and circulatory complications. If you are over thirty and are a heavy cigarette smoker, in addition to taking the pill, you are at even higher risk.

●If you need surgery, you must not take the pill for four weeks prior and four weeks afterward—because of the pill's tendency to affect blood circulation, blood pressure and clotting.

●There are many conditions and family tendencies which contraindicate the use of the pill.

●With the newer lose dose estrogen pills and no-estrogen mini pills, there might be menstrual irregularities such as spotting, breakthrough bleeding, irregular menstrual or no menstrual periods—all of which conditions should be reported to your health care professional. Such irregularities are more common with mini pills than with combined pills, but cycles usually become regular in time.

●Other undesirable side effects related to the mini pill are a higher incidence of ectopic pregnancy, depression, fatigue, decreased sexual desire and increased appetite. Also, the mini pill is less effective than the others—approximately 97% effective, compared to approximately 99% for the combination pills.

SYMPTOMS OF SERIOUS PROBLEMS	POSSIBLE CAUSE
Abdominal pain, severe	Gall bladder disease or inflammatory bowel disease
Chest pain, severe and/or shortness of breath	Blood clot
Headache, severe; dizziness, faintness	Stroke or high blood pressure
Eye problems (blurred vision, flashing lights, blindness)	Stroke or high blood pressure
Severe pain in leg, calf, thigh	Blood clot
Severe depression	Fluid retention or vitamin B deficiency
Speech disturbances	Prior to stroke
Yellowing of skin	Gall bladder disease; hepatitis
Muscle weakness or numbness	Prior to stroke

If any of these symptoms exist, do not wait! Stop taking the pill and contact a doctor immediately! Tell him or her what pills you've been taking and describe the symptoms.

To help you remember the major symptoms, the following ACHES list is a helpful device:

A—Abdominal pain, severe
C—Chest pain and/or shortness of breath
H—Headaches, severe
E—Eye problems
S—Severe leg, calf or thigh pain.

Morning-After Pill

This is so named because it is used *after* unprotected intercourse has taken place. Due to its extremely potent nature, it should only be used as an emergency measure (such as after rape) and should not be substituted for a regular contraceptive method.

The pills contain diethylstilbestrol (known as DES), an artificial estrogen which acts quickly and effectively on the lining of the uterus to *prevent implantation*. DES causes extreme nausea and vomiting. If you must take this, your doctor may prescribe a companion drug to control the vomiting so you will not expel the pill.

In the 1940s and 1950s many doctors prescribed DES to women who had tendencies toward miscarriages, in the belief that the drug would prevent future occurrences. After over ten years of being prescribed, it was discovered that DES did nothing at all to prevent miscarriages. It did, however, have an effect on many of the daughters born to women who had taken DES during their pregnancies: it caused vaginal adenosis and, in some cases, cancer.

Women who were born in the 1940s and 1950s should check with their mothers and/or their mothers' doctors to determine whether DES was taken during their pregnancies. If so, DES daughters should be sure to notify their own doctors and have special vaginal examinations every six months in order to detect early *pre*-cancerous conditions.

You should be aware that if you take DES as a morning-after pill, and it does not work to prevent pregnancy, there is the possibility that a daughter born of that pregnancy may eventually develop vaginal cancer. There is also a possibility that a DES son might develop some form of genital disorder, although this has not yet been proven.

IUD (Intrauterine device)

The IUD is a device which is inserted into the uterus through your vagina and cervical canal by a specially trained person. It prevents implantation of a fertilized egg into the lining of the uterus. Nobody is quite sure just why this happens, although there are several theories.

An IUD is considered less effective than the contraceptive pill. It is rated by Planned Parenthood for average-careful users to be 96% effective and for super-careful users (those using a backup method), 98.5%. There have been cases of IUDs being expelled without the woman's knowledge and of pregnancies occurring with the IUD in place. (Many women use spermicidal foam as an additional means of protection when using an IUD.)

Several types of IUDs have been available in the U.S.:

PROGESTASERT. Based on the principle that progesterone inhibits implantation of a fertilized egg, this device emits the hormone in small quantities over a period of time until it is depleted, usually one year.

LIPPES LOOP. This is made of plastic and has been considered safe and effective when used by a woman who has had at least one child. (A uterus that has not been stretched by pregnancy tends to reject the Lippes Loop.) The larger the size Loop possible to use in a woman's uterus, the less chance for pregnancy to occur. Small ones have been used in women who have never been pregnant. The Loop can remain in place for years until you want it removed to allow pregnancy to occur.

COPPER T (also known as TATUM T) AND COPPER 7. These are considered effective with little likelihood of expulsion and have been recommended for women who have never had children, although others have used them. They are made of plastic wound with fine copper wire. Copper has traditionally been credited with preventing conception, although no one knows exactly how. Tests have shown that the copper is eliminated from the body in normal uterine secretions, although some of it is undoubtedly dissolved into the blood stream. The Copper

T and Copper 7 cause less bleeding, less infection, less pain and are as effective as the Loop. The devices begin to lose some of their effectiveness after three years and should therefore be removed at that time.

(NOTE: As of this writing, February 1986, the Lippes Loop, Copper T and Copper 7 are no longer being manufactured. They have been voluntarily removed from the market in the U.S. by their manufacturers who claimed that because of the increasing costs of product liability insurance and the number of what they considered to be unwarranted lawsuits, it was economically unfeasible for them to continue production. G. D. Searle and Company [manufacturers of the Copper 7 and Copper T], The Food and Drug Administration and the National Medical Committee of Planned Parenthood Federation of America claim that women who are using these devices need not have them removed simply because the company stopped selling them. They can continue using them [unless individual problems exist—to be determined by the health care provider] until the recommended time limit when they are known to lose some of their effectiveness and would ordinarily have to be removed anyway.

At this writing, the only IUD still being manufactured and available in the U.S. is Progestasert. The Lippes Loop, although no longer being manufactured, is still available in short supply. The Copper T and Copper 7 are no longer available for use. The Dalkon Shield and the Majzlin Spring were taken off the market in 1974 and women with these devices are advised to seek professional care for immediate removal!)

IMPORTANT POINTS: An IUD is usually not inserted until your six-week checkup because it may be rejected by your uterus before then. Some health care providers prefer to wait until your second menstrual cycle begins, when your uterus will have returned to its normal state and therefore the IUD is less likely to be expelled. Also, if you are menstruating it is highly unlikely that a new pregnancy exists at the time of IUD insertion.

Before getting an IUD, you should have a complete internal examination. A breast examination, VD test and Pap smear should also be done. If you have a vaginal infection, an IUD can make it difficult or even impossible to cure and will probably make it worse. Furthermore, during the insertion of the IUD, any existing vaginal infection can be carried into the uterus. The doctor must also be certain that you are not pregnant because insertion of the IUD will almost always cause a miscarriage. In cases where miscarriage does not occur, the IUD can cause severe infection and complications. There is concern, based on a study reported in *Obstetrics & Gynecology,* that an IUD inserted during the period of time a woman is breastfeeding is over ten times more likely to perforate the uterus than an IUD inserted after nursing has ended.

Women under twenty-five years old who have not had children and who have multiple sex partners have a higher risk of pelvic infection with an IUD; IUD removal is recommended.

Women susceptible to pelvic infection are more prone to it when using an IUD. Pelvic infection in some IUD users may result in future inability to conceive. Pelvic infection can be caused by the IUD strings protruding from the cervix into the vagina, thereby inviting infection to travel up the strings and into the uterus. This is more likely to occur if the string is composed of several strands (polyfilaments) than if it is made of one (monofilament). IUDs without strings that protrude into the vagina result in a lower incidence of infection but are more difficult to remove and cannot be checked periodically by the woman to be sure it has not been expelled.

You *cannot* use an IUD if you have an unusually small uterus, extremely heavy menstrual flow and/or cramps, VD, a vaginal or uterine infection, pelvic inflammation or previous ectopic pregnancy!

Your IUD should be inserted by a specially trained person who has had experience with such devices. This is usually a physician, certified nurse midwife or certified nurse practitioner.

You should know what kind of IUD you have and when it was inserted. If future findings result in the banning of a particular type of IUD from the market, you would need to know if yours must be removed.

After an IUD has been inserted, *do not leave the examining room until you learn how to feel for the plastic strings from the IUD which protrude through your cervix*. This way you will know how to check periodically to be sure the device has not been expelled without your knowledge. It is wise to check every week, after each menstrual period and every time you have abdominal cramps. It might be easier for you to find the strings while you are in a squatting position or by bearing down while sitting on the toilet. If you cannot locate the strings, try again the next day (your uterus may simply have tipped backward temporarily) and if you still cannot find the strings in a few days or if you can feel the IUD itself, contact your doctor immediately.

It is often recommended that you use an additional means of birth control in the mid-cycle for the first three to six months after an IUD was inserted until your system becomes used to its presence and it is less likely to be expelled or fail to prevent pregnancy.

Call your doctor or nurse midwife immediately if you develop severe cramps, fever, pelvic pain or tenderness, foul-smelling vaginal discharge or unusual vaginal bleeding. (It is common to have a heavier-than-usual menstrual flow while the IUD is in place.) These symptoms may be signs of serious infection which can scar reproductive organs, making it difficult to conceive later on. If untreated, such infection can lead to sterility, the necessity for a hysterectomy (removal of the uterus) or even death. Also, call your doctor or nurse midwife if you miss a menstrual period. Since there is the possibility of ectopic (tubal) pregnancy with an IUD, your health care provider should be alerted.

Never try to remove an IUD by yourself or have anyone other than a specialist remove it. You risk permanently damaging your cervix or perforating your uterus, possibly resulting in an emergency hysterectomy or even death!

If you become pregnant while the IUD is in place, you will be advised to have the device removed, which *may* result in miscarriage. However, if the IUD is left in place, there is a *stronger chance that miscarriage will occur anyway.* If the pregnancy should continue with the IUD in place, complications can occur—including infection and premature labor—although there *is* a chance that the baby will be born at full term and unharmed. However, if you want to give the pregnancy a chance to continue, without risk of serious infection which can result in death, authorities strongly advise that the IUD should definitely be removed!

ADVANTAGES:
- The IUD is high on the list of effective contraceptives.
- Spontaneous sexual relations can be enjoyed without hav-

ing to interrupt foreplay by applying contraceptives (unless you are using additional means of contraception for more thorough protection).

•The IUD is cost-free after the initial cost of the device and its insertion (and until eventually you pay the fee to have it removed when desired).

•The IUD can remain in place in your uterus for years until you want it removed to allow pregnancy to occur, except if yours is a copper device—for three years, at which time it begins to lose its effectiveness—or progesterone device—one year.

DISADVANTAGES:

•Insertion may be painful and may cause lightheadedness or even fainting spells during and soon after insertion. A woman whose uterus has not been stretched by pregnancy usually experiences the most discomfort. Sometimes, a local anesthetic (cervical block) is needed for insertion and painkillers or tranquilizers are required for relief of cramps afterward.

•Side effects include a heavier and prolonged menstrual flow, menstrual cramps, spotting or bleeding between periods during the first few months.

•Possibility of serious pelvic infection which can affect future conception and can lead, if untreated, to sterility, a hysterectomy or even death. IUD users have three to nine times more pelvic infections than nonusers. If you have more than one sexual partner, the risk goes up.

•A higher rate of ectopic (tubal) pregnancy than with other methods of contraception.

•Possibility of expelling the device. This is rare (one to nine cases out of every 1,000 insertions) and is not necessarily serious, although repairing the perforation might involve surgery.

•You might need iron supplements due to loss of blood (copper IUDs seem to cause less blood loss than other types).

•If you are anemic, the heavy menstrual bleeding resulting from an IUD can be serious.

•You must be sure to have a red blood cell count and sedimentation rate taken every year.

•You must have the IUD removed by a trained health care provider if you want to become pregnant.

●If you have never had a baby, the IUD can be painful because it is large for your previously unstretched uterus. This may result in cramping, backache or even expulsion of the device.

●You should check the strings every week and after each period and abdominal cramps to be sure the IUD has not fallen out.

●An IUD is not usually inserted until at least six weeks postpartum—sometimes three months.

Diaphragm with Spermicidal Jelly or Cream

The diaphragm is made of soft rubber in the shape of a miniature bowl with a flexible metal spring rim. When fitted and inserted properly, it should fit snugly over the opening of the cervix, held in place by the pubic bone in front and the vaginal wall behind. The diaphragm may be approximately two to four inches in diameter. Before insertion, spermicidal jelly or cream must be placed inside the diaphragm "bowl" and a little applied around the *inside* of the rim to kill any sperm attempting to get beyond the diaphragm. (Too much cream or jelly on the rim may cause slipping of the diaphragm.)

The diaphragm works in two ways: it blocks the entrance to the uterus and it presses the spermicidal cream or jelly within its cup against the cervical opening, thus killing any sperm which may have gotten past the blockade.

In order to be most effective, the diaphragm must be properly fitted, it must be used with contraceptive jelly or cream, it must be kept in place for at least six hours after intercourse, additional jelly or cream should be applied to the outside of the still-in-place diaphragm prior to each new act of intercourse that follows and no douching should be done for at least six hours afterward.

To obtain a diaphragm, you must be examined by a physician or other trained health care provider who will measure you for the correct size. Usually, after having a baby—whether it was a cesarean or a vaginal delivery—your diaphragm size changes, so *do not* use the one that you used before your pregnancy! You will probably not be fitted until your six-week postpartum check-up and in some cases perhaps not until three months after having your baby, because there may still be swelling in the pelvic area.

After being measured and fitted, time should be arranged for you to be alone in the practitioner's examining room to permit you to practice inserting and removing the diaphragm. The practitioner should be called in to check if it has been placed properly. Before you remove it, study how it feels to your fingers and where it is placed when it is inserted properly. Your practitioner can either sell you a diaphragm or give you a prescription for the size you need. If it is well cared for, a diaphragm can last several years. After the initial cost of the diaphragm and the medical examination, the expense is only for spermicidal jelly or cream.

ADVANTAGES:

●When properly used, this is a considerably effective means of birth control. It is rated by Planned Parenthood for average-careful users to be 90% effective and for super-careful users, 98%.

●There is no known or suspected health hazard connected with the use of the diaphragm and spermicidal jelly or cream, although there are rare mild allergic reactions.

●Women using barrier methods such as the diaphragm have half the chance of developing pelvic inflammatory disease (PID), a bacterial infection that affects approximately 850,000 U.S. women annually and can lead to infertility and even, in rare cases, death.

●Using the diaphragm may help protect you against sexually transmitted diseases.

●Continuing use of the diaphragm may help prevent cervical dysplasias, which can lead to cancer of the cervix.

There is less risk of ectopic (tubal) pregnancy in women who use barrier methods of contraception. There is speculation that ectopic pregnancies are often related to pelvic infections—which are more likely to occur in women not using barrier methods.

DISADVANTAGES:

●A diaphragm will usually not be fitted until at least six

weeks postpartum and sometimes as long as three months.

●You must be sure to insert the diaphragm with jelly or cream *before* having intercourse.

●You must have it with you whenever you need it. You must be sure to have an adequate supply of spermicidal jelly or cream.

●You must be sure to use additional jelly or cream (added to the outside of the diaphragm without removing it!) if intercourse is to be repeated—even if it is less than an hour after the last application of jelly or cream.

●You must leave the diaphragm in place for at least six hours after intercourse has taken place.

●The leaking of cream or jelly from the vagina after intercourse can be annoying. You may need to use a tampon or sanitary napkin.

●You may need a different size diaphragm if you gain or lose fifteen pounds or more, as well as after each pregnancy or miscarriage occurring after the third month.

●Some women are allergic to rubber and must use a plastic diaphragm. There may be an irritation reaction to the spermicidal jelly or cream by the woman or her partner.

●Even when the diaphragm is properly used, pregnancy can occur—although rarely. Because the vagina expands during intercourse, the diaphragm may be somewhat dislodged. Also, there is some suspicion that slipping of the diaphragm can occur in long sessions of intercourse with frequent insertions of the penis, in woman-above positions, and if too much spermicidal cream or jelly is placed on the rim of the diaphragm.

Cervical Cap

The cervical cap, similar to the diaphragm in its barrier-type function, is a thimble-shaped bowl, usually made of lucite, a clear rigid plastic which fits snugly over the cervix and is held in place by suction.

At this writing, the cervical cap has not been approved by the U.S. Food and Drug Administration. However, it is being used under research circumstances in several health facilities. Women taking part in such research should be fully informed, in writing, of the risks as well as benefits of cervical cap use. However, it should be understood that such risks and benefits are not fully known at this time.

The cervical cap must be fitted by your health care practitioner and can be inserted and removed by that person, twice each month—in conjunction with your menstrual cycle—or you (or your partner) can be instructed to insert and remove it yourself. It *must,* however, be left in place at least six to eight hours after intercourse. If the currently available cap is left in place more than twenty-four hours, it is recommended that spermicidal jelly be applied before each new act of intercourse.

There is some concern that leaving the cap in place for an extended period of time *might* cause pelvic inflammatory disease, cervicitis or vaginitis. Also, the cap *might* cause cervical and vaginal ulceration from the pressure of the cap on cervical tissue. However, there is a new cap being tested which is custom-fitted to the cervix (as dentists do with a tooth cap) so there is no pressure on underlying tissues and there is a one-way valve allowing menstrual and other uterine discharge to pass through. This way, the cap can be left in place for longer periods of time. This type of cap is designed not to be used with spermicides and is made of a rubberlike material.

ADVANTAGES:

• The cervical cap can be self-inserted and removed, although it is somewhat more difficult to maneuver than the diaphragm.

• Preliminary research indicates that it is about as effective as the diaphragm and is less likely to be dislodged during intercourse.

• It is not felt by the male during intercourse.

DISADVANTAGES:

• Self-insertion and removal are difficult because the cap must cover the cervix, which is high up in the vaginal canal.

• It must be left in place six to eight hours following intercourse and if left in place longer than twenty-four hours, you must reapply spermicidal jelly or cream before each act of intercourse.

• As of this writing, the cervical cap is still being studied for as yet unknown side effects and therefore has not been FDA approved.

Vaginal Spermicides

These are available in aerosol foam, cream or jelly forms and are specifically designed to be used without a diaphragm or other contraceptive device. When placed high up in the vagina, by a special applicator, spermicides work in two ways: they form a barrier over the cervix, blocking sperm from entering the uterus, and they kill sperm on contact. These are rated by Planned Parenthood for average-careful users to be 85% effective and for super-careful users, 95%-98%.

Aerosol foam is a white aerated substance much like shaving cream in color and texture. It is available in a can or bottle-type dispenser with a plunger-type plastic applicator. It is not as effective as a condom or a diaphragm used with cream or jelly. However, foam *is* more effective than cream or jelly used alone, because of its ability to spread more evenly throughout the vagina. (Note: The creams and jellies made to be used with a diaphragm are not to be used alone because they are less potent.) If you use foam without any other protection, be sure to insert two applicators-full, as close to the time of intercourse as possible. Many women use foam as an additional means of protection during the first month of using birth control pills, when using an IUD, or when their partners use condoms.

ADVANTAGES:
- Spermicides are easily available without a prescription and can be applied easily.
- They are not expensive.
- They *may* be helpful against VD.
- Some spermicidal agents are mildly lubricating, which is highly desirable in some cases.
- Continuing use *may* help prevent development of cervical cancer.
- Spermicides provide good backup protection when using other forms of contraception.

DISADVANTAGES:
- Protection lasts about thirty minutes.
- Foam is not effective enough to be totally depended upon.

●Application of foam, jelly or cream interrupts lovemaking (unless the couple includes it in foreplay).

●Creams and jellies are less effective than foam and they tend to leak from the vagina more than foam after intercourse.

●You must not douche for at least six hours after intercourse or you risk interference with the action of the spermicide.

●The additional lubrication from these preparations may be a disadvantage in lovemaking for some couples.

●You must always have an extra supply available for when you need it. (Some bottles and cans do not show when nearly empty.)

●You *must*—no matter how soon after the last application —apply more foam, jelly or cream every time you have intercourse.

●You must have your applicator and supply with you in case you need it while away from home.

●Spermicidal agents may irritate either partner. The stronger and more effective the spermicidal agent, the more irritating it may be. During the early postpartum period, you may find you will be more prone to vaginal irritation.

●Spermicidal agents can make oral sex unpleasant because their taste is usually not palatable. (Note: Spermicidal agents containing mercury and/or boric acid can be harmful if swallowed and have been suspect in posing other possible risks. Therefore, these are no longer on the market. If you have access to such preparations, it is recommended that you discard them.)

Vaginal Tablets and Suppositories

A tablet or suppository is inserted into the vagina prior to intercourse. Body heat will cause it to dissolve and the spermicidal content is intended to kill sperm cells. However, these agents are less effective than creams or jellies and much less effective than foam because the spermicide does not spread evenly throughout the vagina.

Condom

The condom is a very thin sheath of rubber or processed lambskin which is pulled over an erect penis just before intercourse. (A lubricant—*never* petroleum jelly—can be used on the condom after it is in place to prevent tearing and for easier entry into the vagina.) The tip of the condom catches the seminal fluid and prevents sperm from entering the vagina. If used with care and in combination with spermicidal foam in the vagina, this can be an effective means of birth control. Planned Parenthood rates the condom's effectiveness for average-careful users to be 90% and for super-careful users, 98%.

Condoms cannot be kept in a wallet, pocket or warm place for very long or they will deteriorate. If there is an accidental spillage of seminal fluid into or near the vagina, use spermicidal foam, cream or jelly *immediately* to kill as many sperm cells as possible. (Keep a supply readily available for such emergencies.)

There are condoms now available with a spermicidal agent added to the lubricant inside. Within one minute after ejaculation, most of the sperm are thereby destroyed. Spermicide on the outside of the condom may provide additional protection if the condom breaks. If such condoms are used, the woman need not use spermicidal foam as a backup in case a condom breaks.

ADVANTAGES:
- Easily available without prescription, inexpensive and easy to apply.
- No known or suspected health hazard.
- It protects against VD and other infections.
- For men who tend to ejaculate quickly, a condom can help decrease stimulation and prolong intercourse.
- It is a good backup to other methods.
- Use of the new spermicidal condom minimizes or eliminates the need for the woman to use foam.

DISADVANTAGES:
- Putting it on interrupts spontaneity (unless done as part of foreplay).

●The woman is dependent upon her partner to provide protection.

●A condom might be defective. It may have deteriorated from nonuse or extreme temperature conditions.

●It must be put on before any contact is made between the penis and vaginal area—because even the first few drops of discharge from the penis can contain enough sperm for pregnancy to occur.

●It must be removed very carefully so as not to let seminal fluid escape in or near the vagina.

●The condom minimizes sensation for the man. It minimizes lubrication for intercourse, usually requiring additional lubrication to prevent vaginal irritation. (Never use petroleum jelly; there are pre-lubricated condoms available, but they tend to slip off easily.)

Disposable Vaginal Sponge

One of the newest methods of contraception, the disposable vaginal sponge first appeared on the market in 1983. Available over-the-counter for about $1.00, it is a circular chunk of soft white polyurethane foam, with a depression in the center where it fits over the cervix. At the outside edge, it is about one-half inch thick; its diameter is about two inches.

The sponge contains nonoxynol-9, the most commonly used spermicidal agent worldwide for over twenty years. The spermicide is released when the sponge is moistened in water. Then, the dampened sponge is folded in half to insert it into the vagina where it unfolds. The spermicide is continually released as a result of vaginal muscle contractions and the thrusting of the penis during intercourse.

The sponge acts as a barrier to sperm. Even if it is not placed directly over the cervix, its porous character absorbs semen and its spermicide provides additional protection by inactivating sperm.

It can be left in place for twenty-four hours (no longer!), no matter how many times you have intercourse during that period of time. It must, however, be left in the vagina for six hours after the last act of intercourse—so be sure that the last act of intercourse is no later than eighteen hours after insertion of the sponge!

The sponge is removed by pulling on the flat braided polyester loop attached to its rim. If you cannot remove it yourself or if a piece of the sponge breaks off and might have remained inside, professional help should be sought promptly. Signs of possible incomplete removal are: genital itching or irritation, persistent unpleasant odor or unusual vaginal discharge.

Important: To minimize risk of TSS (toxic shock syndrome—a very serious infection which, if undiagnosed and untreated, can result in death), you must not leave the sponge in place longer than twenty-four hours, and you should never use it during menstruation, right after childbirth or if you have a vaginal infection.

Although each sponge costs only about $1.00 at this writing, because the sponge should not be reused, overall expense depends upon the frequency of intercourse; estimate $1.00 for each day you plan to have intercourse.

ADVANTAGES:

●It is easily available without prescription and is easy to insert.

●It does not have to fit to size and does not require the expertise of a professional to insert.

●It can be inserted in advance of intercourse—when and if convenient.

●If used in combination with the condom, there is less possibility of conception. Planned Parenthood rates the sponge as it does other spermicidal-agent contraception: average-careful users get 85% effectiveness; super-careful users, 95%-98%. Using combined methods, there is 99% effectiveness in even average-careful couples (see FDA estimates below, under "Disadvantages").

●It provides additional lubrication.

●Continued use (because of the barrier action) *may* help prevent development of cervical cancer.

●It provides good backup protection when using other forms of contraception.

●You can have additional acts of intercourse without the need for additional protection during its limited twenty-four hour stay in the vagina—although it must be left in the vagina for six hours after the last act of intercourse!

●The spermicidal agent within the sponge does not leak from the vagina as do jellies, creams and suppositories, thereby minimizing messiness and/or overlubrication.

●Some studies suggest that nonoxynol-9 might provide some protection against gonorrhea and possibly certain other sexually transmitted diseases.

DISADVANTAGES:

●Sponge users may be at increased risk of TSS and therefore are advised to minimize this risk by never using the sponge during a menstrual period, right after childbirth or if a vaginal infection is present.

●Reliable effectiveness rates, based on actual use, are not yet available, since the sponge is so new on the market. However, the Food and Drug Administration estimated in 1984 that if the sponge were to be used exactly according to instructions, effectiveness can be 89%–91%. This is considered low compared to other methods.

●There are no data, as of this writing, on long-term possible adverse effects of the chemicals on humans.

●Some users experience irritation related to the chemicals in the sponge.

●The sponge must be moistened with about two tablespoons of water to activate the spermicidal agent and help toward easier insertion. If water is not available at the required time, the sponge cannot be used.

●Some women whose fingers cannot easily reach the sponge for removal, find this method too troublesome.

●The sponge *may* be difficult to remove or a piece *may* break off, necessitating the assistance of a medical professional.

Rhythm Method

This involves predicting fertile and nonfertile days in each menstrual cycle according to the time of ovulation and the life span of the egg and sperm cells. There seem to be approximately seventy-two hours each month when pregnancy can occur. A woman using the rhythm method refrains from having intercourse during those days—and several other days before and after as an extra safety measure.

Using this "calendar" method is not an accurate means of determining fertile days; it is simply an estimate. Although ovulation usually does occur at approximately the same time each month for many women, there is the chance that it might occur at any time before or after. If you have a strictly regular menstrual cycle which *never* varies, you have a better chance of using the rhythm method—but you are still taking a chance.

The Basal Body Temperature Method

This method is used to calculate "safe" and fertile periods. It is based on the fact that before ovulation, a woman's body temperature drops slightly and then rises considerably twenty-four to seventy-two hours afterward. By keeping a chart of her body temperature highs and lows for a few months, a woman can determine her periods of ovulation—provided that her body temperature is not affected by illness, irregular sleeping habits and other possible factors.

A special basal temperature thermometer is necessary for accurate readings. You must follow directions carefully for most effective evaluation of "safe" periods. This method, if used carefully, may be the most effective way to practice the rhythm method.

The Billings Method

Just before ovulation occurs, cervical secretions become egg-white or clear—compared to the yellowish mucus usually present at other times of the month. Learning to recognize the differences in mucus discharge can aid in determining fertile and "safe" days. Effectiveness of this method is better if "safe" days are limited to those known to occur *after* ovulation. Also, if you have an infection which can affect your cervical mucus, you may not be able to recognize the change.

ADVANTAGES OF RHYTHM, TEMPERATURE AND BILLINGS METHODS:
●These fertility awareness methods are accepted means of birth control for most, if not all, religious groups.

•There is no interruption of love play to apply contraceptives.

•There is no cost beyond recordkeeping papers or special thermometer.

•There is no known health hazard to the mother.

DISADVANTAGES:

•This is not a reliable means of birth control because ovulation can occor off schedule (such as if you run a fever) or sperm may remain in the cervix longer than expected.

•Since there are specified "safe days" for having intercourse, the spontaneity of sexual relations is affected.

•You must keep records for several months before you can start relying on this method for protection.

Douching

This is an *ineffective* method. By the very act of flushing out the seminal fluid from the vagina after intercourse, you may actually be spraying some upward into the cervical canal!

Withdrawal

Withdrawing the penis during intercourse prior to ejaculation is not an effective means of birth control. First of all, there is a chance that the pre-ejaculatory fluid—even a few drops—may contain enough sperm to cause pregnancy. Secondly, even if pregnancy does not occur this way, *any* seminal fluid released from the penis and in contact with the vaginal lips can result in pregnancy.

Withdrawal takes away much of the joy of sexual intercourse for both partners. Both are concentrating on withdrawing "in time" instead of relaxing and enjoying themselves. If used habitually over a long period of time, this method can lead to premature ejaculation.

Female Sterilization

This is a surgical procedure and a permanent form of birth control. Since it is most probably irreversible, sterilization should be used only when it is absolutely certain that no more children are desired.

Sterilization usually refers to the process by which an egg and sperm are prevented from meeting in the Fallopian tubes. This can be done by electro-surgical methods, by applying clips or bands to the tubes or by cutting away a portion of each tube and tying the ends. In order to accomplish sterilization, an incision must be made into either the abdominal or vaginal wall. The following are the methods used:

LAPAROSCOPY: A narrow tubular instrument called a laparoscope, equipped with a light and a telescope, is inserted into the abdominal cavity through a tiny incision just below the navel, where the abdominal wall is the thinnest. The abdominal cavity is filled with carbon dioxide gas through the same opening, to distend the abdomen for better visibility of the pelvic organs. Through the laparoscope (or in some instances, a second—even smaller—incision made at the pubic hairline), another instrument is inserted in order to cut, clip, bind or cauterize the tubes. General anesthesia and a hospital stay is generally necessary. If the doctor cannot gain complete visibility and access to the tubes, the laparoscope incision must be closed and a mini laparotomy is then performed.

MINI LAPAROTOMY: This is a small one-to-two inch transverse abdominal incision made at the pubic hairline through which the doctor can more easily see the tubes and reach them with the sterilizing instrument. If such a small incision is not large enough to allow good visualization of the area, a larger incision—laparotomy—can be made. Carbon dioxide is not necessary to distend the abdomen for mini laparotomy or laparotomy.

Many doctors continue to recommend the use of general anesthesia for mini laparotomy because they believe the procedure can be extremely uncomfortable, if not painful, if performed under local anesthesia. Other doctors claim mini laparotomy can be accomplished under local anesthesia on an outpatient basis—to the satisfaction of the woman.

VAGINAL PROCEDURE: Some physicians prefer to reach the tubes through an incision in the vaginal wall, if this is feasible. This usually requires general anesthesia and a hospital stay. However, if the tubes are not accessible through this route, the vaginal incision would then have to be closed and the procedure done by mini laparotomy. Also, the vaginal route presents an increased incidence of post-operative infection compared with mini laparotomy or laparoscopy.

Sterilization can be done while you are still in the hospital after having your baby. Many women do not choose to have it performed at this time because it seems too final a step to take immediately after having given birth to a newborn whose condition may not always be stable. Others prefer to have it done while still in the hospital because it is more convenient and costs less than if they had to return another time.

ADVANTAGES:
●Sterilization provides permanent free-from-worry birth control.
●There are no known or suspected long-term health hazards.

DISADVANTAGES:
●It is costly and may require a hospital stay.
●There are some risks from anesthesia and other complications, as in any surgical procedure.
●In women with previous psychological problems or those with inadequate counselling, there *may* be psychological reactions which may affect the woman's sexuality.
●The procedure should be considered irreversible.

Male Sterilization

This is called a "vasectomy" and is usually done in the doctor's office or in a special clinic. Using a local anesthetic, the doctor, through an incision in the scrotal skin, removes a piece from each vas deferens (the tubes which carry sperm from the testicles to the penis) and ties off the ends. The procedure takes about thirty minutes.

A vasectomy does not affect ejaculation. Sperm is only a small part of the seminal fluid. Sexual hormones and sperm continue to be produced. The only difference that vasectomy makes is that sperm is prevented from reaching the penis and being expelled with ejaculate. Sexual drive is not affected—unless there are contributing emotional factors.

ADVANTAGES:

●Vasectomy is less expensive than female sterilization because it is a simpler and faster procedure.

●There is no hospitalization.

●There are no known or suspected health hazards.

DISADVANTAGES:

●There may be psychological reactions to the procedure which can affect the man's sexuality.

●It should be considered irreversible.

●The man does not immediately become sterile after surgery; it may take as many as fifteen ejaculations post-vasectomy. Therefore, other means of contraception should be used during that time.

●In 2–4% of cases, there are minor complications, including infection, hematoma (blood clot), granuloma (inflammatory reaction to sutures or sperm which are absorbed by the body), swelling and tenderness near the testes.

Abortion

Unfortunately, some people rely on abortion as a means of birth control. Abortion is the termination of pregnancy by removing the fetus and placenta from the uterus. It is considered unwise to use repeated abortions as a means of birth control because after several abortions there may be a higher risk of miscarriage during a future wanted pregnancy.

Warnings

•Never rely on breastfeeding as a means of contraception. Although ovulation *may* be inhibited by breastfeeding, it also may not!

•Never use the same diaphragm which was used before your last pregnancy, until your health care provider examines you and prescribes the correct size needed. For adequate protection, you may need a different size after each pregnancy and after a gain or loss of fifteen pounds.

•Never take *anyone else's* birth control pills. The hormone content was prescribed for *her!* *Your* system may require different dosages or the pill may be life-threatening to *you!*

•Never lie to your health care provider about previous or current physical conditions or family medical history and tendencies in order to have the pill prescribed for you. You may be flirting with serious illness and death.

•Never try to insert anything into your cervical canal to induce abortion. You are risking serious illness and death.

You will probably be advised by your health care practitioner that you should not resume sexual relations until after your postpartum checkup—usually six weeks after delivery, although some practitioners will approve intercourse after a two-week checkup.

Because the fitting of a diaphragm or insertion of an IUD is usually postponed until several weeks after the delivery, because spermicidal agents may cause irritation, because the rhythm method is unreliable during the early postpartum period, because the pill should not be used while breastfeeding, and because sterilization is too final a procedure for young parents, you may have only one choice in the early postpartum weeks: the condom.

New Methods

New advances in contraceptive technology which are awaiting FDA approval at the time of this writing include the following:

DEPO-PROVERA: Given by injection (intramuscularly) to the woman, every three to four months, is considered to be as effective as the pill, with less side effects.

SUBDERMAL IMPLANTS: Long-acting progesterone which is implanted under the skin of the woman's foream under local anesthesia. This will provide contraception for five to six years and is considered as effective as the pill with fewer side effects and can be removed if conception is desired.

FOR FURTHER INFORMATION ABOUT BIRTH CONTROL:
Planned Parenthood, National Office, 810 7th Avenue, New York, N.Y. 10019.
Zero Population Growth, Los Altos, Calif. 94022.
Association for Voluntary Sterilization, 122 E. 42nd Street, New York, N.Y. 10068.

USE OF TIME

A common problem faced by new mothers is the use of time —the spacing of baby care, household and shopping chores, socializing, entertainment, or whatever possibilities your days may present once you are ready to become more active. You may find it difficult to adjust to and work within what seems to be a huge expanse of each day—without chunks of time specifically apportioned to particular tasks or projects as you might have had in previous working situations. Without a schedule or prescribed tried-and-true work plans to guide you, and no adults around to share the workload or even complaints about the work, you may find the days difficult to get through. When you have an entire day in which to accomplish various things, it is often difficult to decide when to do what and whether or not it really needs to be decided upon in the first place. "Why does planning matter," you may ask yourself, "if your work never gets done anyway?" "But how can that be?" an expectant mother naively asks. "How can there not be enough time?" Many a new mother will attest to the reality that there is not enough time!

Some women find it helpful to apportion a limited and specific time each day for chores, a time for getting out of the house with the baby, a time for reading or socializing with other adults, or whatever it is you discover you need each day, in addition to the routine infant care, to make a well-balanced work-and-pleasure-filled stretch of time.

Other women find it helpful to make a list of what chores must get done in order of importance (make dinner, fold laundry, wash floors, etc.) The first time the baby falls asleep, they start at the top of the list and work their way down, leaving out whatever they don't get accomplished by a predetermined time of day (early afternoon for example), after which they go out with the baby, no matter what!

Some mothers complain, "How can I set aside a specific time for chores or getting out of the house when the baby has no specific time for crying? I may have to hold him during my 'chore time' or 'reading time.'"

If you are the type who needs a specific hour-by-hour schedule, perhaps you can plan your chores to coincide with your child's fussy time and take him or her with you from room to room as you work. Some chores can be done while the baby is happily strapped to your back or chest, papoose-style (ironing, mending, cooking, laundry, bill-paying). Keeping the baby with you and close to you may be soothing in itself (as well as more interesting to the baby than lying unoccupied and alone in a crib) and may afford you the time to accomplish what you'd like.

No matter how you prefer to "order" your day, no matter what happens, stick to your plan to get out of the house daily, weather permitting. Taking a crying or fussy baby out of the house for a ride in the carriage, baby carrier, or car is often the best way to make you both happy. The change of environment and activity and exposure to other people can be stimulating to both of you. And you will have a better feeling at the end of the day having had your break. (See also "Winter Survival Strategies.")

FINDING OUTLETS

Many new mothers who do not return to work outside the home after the birth of their babies complain that, aside from their roles in the family, "there's nothing for me"—no outlets for their talents and creativity. If you feel this way, we suggest that you get involved. There are many groups and causes that need good organizers and volunteer workers. Book discussion groups, adult education classes, theater groups, college courses, new mothers' support groups can be located or organized. Some groups have no objections to babies sitting in on discussions; others even provide babysitters during meetings. Although some groups do solicit members through the mail or telephone campaigns, it might be necessary for you to seek out a group you would be interested in joining. Some suggestions on outlets you might consider:

●Become involved in local community projects designed to solve some problems. Join civic organizations that already exist or work to establish one yourself. Find a problem in the community and seek ways to solve it. Does a particular corner need a stoplight? Is an empty lot a health or safety hazard? Is a needed school or hospital slated for closure? Locate the individual governmental organization responsible and work to have these situations corrected.

●Become a consumer advocate. Join one of the groups fighting for consumer rights, fair labeling, etc. Interested in curtailing environmental health hazards? Want to make hospital emergency room services better? Keep energy costs down? Improve the general welfare of humankind? Join or start a campaign! It can be exciting, invigorating and satisfying.

●Join a local organization or branch of a national group whose concerns you share. This might include charitable organizations such as March of Dimes, Cancer Care or the American Red Cross. You might be interested in a local chapter of the National Organization for Women (N.O.W.) or a group working for family-centered maternity care, such as the American Society for Psychoprophylaxis in Obstetrics (ASPO/Lamaze) or the International Childbirth Education Association (I.C.E.A.). You might even get involved in a local branch of a political party and/or work for the election of a candidate to political office. Telephoning and typing can often be done from your own home. You may enjoy meeting people while circulating petitions or soliciting funds.

●If you are interested in developing your talents in a particular field but can't as yet earn money at it, use the bits and pieces of free time you have now to gain experience and expertise, which later can be used to obtain a paying position, should you be interested. For example, offer your services to a local organization to do free art work for flyers, posters or other advertising. Perhaps they'd like a logo or design that represents their goals and organization. Coordinate speakers, agendas, programs for an organization. Run a membership drive or a fund-raising campaign. Develop such public relations abilities for your own benefit while you increase an organization's publicity and funds. Offer to write press releases, invitations to meetings, letters of thanks for joining the organization, letters requesting volunteer help for the group, letters to prominent people notifying them of the organization's existence, accomplishments and aims. Offer to do public speaking for the organization if you'd like to develop your skills in that realm. If you have other skills in bookkeeping, accounting, law, record keeping, research, book reviewing, offer them. You and the organization of your choice will gain.

●Your local school district might need adults to tutor students who are having difficulty with their subjects. This often can be done in your home.

●Consider doing volunteer work, or if you have a musical or other talent, entertain patients in a local hospital or nursing home. Read to blind patients and/or take them for walks.

●If your local library has no Read-Aloud program for children, consider volunteering to start one. This involves reading stories or poems to a group of children for an hour, usually in the morning.

●If you love animals, volunteer your services to a pet adoption agency or veterinary hospital.

●Join a club through your church or synagogue.

●Join a bowling league, exercise program, dance class, adult education program. Take a course in yoga, painting, sculpting, ceramics, great books, word processing, etc.

●If you have a particular talent in cake decorating, bread baking, computer programming, writing, dance, guitar, piano, or a foreign language, ask what the requirements are for teaching a class at a local adult education center.

●You might give art lessons in your home—to adults, teenagers, or younger children. Choose your medium: pastels, oils, acrylics, charcoal, pen and ink. You could give guitar or piano lessons—or lessons in knitting, crocheting—practically anything. You can bake cakes for special occasions and sell them from your home too. You can hire a sitter to care for your baby while you are at home and classes are in session.

●Try to locate a Big Brother or Big Sister program in your community. These organizations pair an adult with a youngster in need of warmth and companionship. You would be involved with taking the youngster to local community attractions and being available for discussions and sharing.

●You can volunteer to read textbooks to blind students at a local school or perhaps to record books on cassette tapes for the blind.

WINTER SURVIVAL STRATEGIES: HOW TO COPE

For those of us who live in areas that receive a fair amount of snow, or whose climate gets extremely cold, giving birth during the winter months brings a special series of problems. Some new mothers, asked to detail their main concern about getting through inclement weather with a new baby, responded:

"Being stuck in all the time. Getting out during the day has been my salvation. I'm concerned the walls might start closing in."

"I'm afraid the baby will be sick more often."

"How to amuse myself and the baby for prolonged periods of time."

"Running out of diapers and formula in the middle of a snowstorm."

"How can I tell how to dress the baby?"

With some planning and ingenuity, even the severest of winters can be managed.

By the time your baby is a few weeks old, your pediatrician will probably have no objection to your taking the baby out in all but the harshest weather, as long as he or she is properly dressed and in good health. Rule of thumb: If you are comfortable going out on a particular day, the chances are the baby will be too. It's a good idea to dress the baby in layers so that when you arrive at your destination, or even en route, be it the supermarket, a neighbor's home or a museum, you can remove as many layers as necessary without getting the baby undressed entirely. Keep in mind that pediatricians frequently see cases of heat rash during the winter caused by *over*dressing. Ask yourself if you would feel comfortable dressed the way you've prepared the baby and adjust the baby's clothing accordingly. It may not be necessary or even desirable to use a bulky snowsuit as the top layer. If you are walking, one solution might be to dress the baby in several stretchsuits and/or blanket sleepers, depending on the temperature, and to place him or her in a chest carrier under your coat or poncho. Another solution is to pin a blanket over the chest carrier, attaching a corner of the blanket to the shoulders of your coat and tucking the bottom under the carrier to create a "pouch." Make sure the top drapes loosely enough to allow the air to circulate. The air pocket created with either of the above will provide additional warmth. If you're taking public transportation, your coat can be unbuttoned or blanket removed if the bus or train is heated. Wear sturdy shoes or boots and remember that your balance will be affected by the weight of the baby. Practice "gearing up" and walking around the house several times before venturing out in slippery weather.

You can possibly purchase a "wind guard" for the baby's stroller or carriage if it does not come equipped with one. A blanket draped over the bottom front of the stroller will provide additional protection against wind, but be aware that it is important to leave an opening for air circulation.

It also may be difficult, if not impossible, to push a stroller or carriage in the ice and snow. Therefore, give careful thought to whether or not you'd be better off walking with the baby in a chest carrier (you need your arms free to help balance), taking public transportation, or driving.

Winter is usually a time when there's more illness in the community. Try to avoid crowds if possible. If you must do last-minute holiday shopping and have to bring the baby along, try to minimize the baby's exposure by not allowing people to coo and possibly cough in the baby's face. Babies in chest carriers usually don't attract the same amount of direct contact that a baby in a stroller or a carriage seems to invite. You can always stop someone about to swoop down and thrust her face in the carriage to "see" the baby by saying, "Shhh— she's sleeping and if she's disturbed I won't be able to finish shopping." Be assertive!

While getting out as often as possible is certainly desirable, it is ludicrous to *have* to make a trip to the supermarket for one or two items when the weather is bad. (At other times it might be a diversion!) Buy several of each of your most frequently used items so you're less likely to run out of supplies before your next trip to the stores.

If you find the weather is extremely harsh for days and it seems there will never be a break, the walls may begin to feel like they're closing in. One mother called this "cabin fever," recalling the days of the pioneers who were snowed in their log cabins for days—without telephone or television! It's hard enough to care for a baby under any circumstance. Add to that the inability to get out of the house and take a break, either with or without the baby, and you may begin to feel tense and under stress. If these feelings of being trapped are really getting more difficult for you to handle, read "How to Minimize 'Down' Feelings" in the section "Postpartum Blues."

In addition, focusing on future events and on things *outside* the home can help by taking your mind off the fact that you're stuck in. A fringe benefit is that, when the weather finally clears, tasks you might have put off will be completed, allowing you more time to enjoy the better weather.

• Plan an upcoming vacation and send for travel brochures; make lists of what to bring along; compare prices of different accommodations, facilities, etc.

• Address and stamp birthday and anniversary cards for forthcoming months.

• Plan a party or family gathering: Prepare a guest list, address invitations, plan menus, shopping lists, etc. If feasible, begin to cook for the event and freeze your creations.

●Cooking ahead is a good idea at any time. If you have freezer space, filling it once again with prepared meals will help take the pressure off on days you have no time to cook.

●Read the earlier section in this book on "Use of Time." What hints can you come up with to better organize your time?

●Make a list of places you'll visit once the weather improves. Phone ahead and check the facilities available at restaurants, museums, shopping centers, etc. Keep your list and notations for ready reference in the future.

●Read the section "Finding Outlets." Which activities appeal to you? Begin to develop a plan for what you might pursue once you're able to travel around more. What information will you need to get started? When and how can you get that information? What materials are needed? Who should be contacted?

●Read that book you thought you'd never get to; catch up on letter writing.

●*SmartToys* by Kent G. Burtt and Karen Kalkstein has ideas for making your own developmentally appropriate toys for the baby. Read the chapter on the phase your baby will be going through next and make some of the toys suggested in the book.

●Make gifts for forthcoming holidays, birthdays, etc.

To help keep the baby amused:

●For an older infant, divide the baby's toys in half and put some away. In a week reintroduce the ones you've hidden. The baby will think they're new.

●Hold your baby and dance to music. Your baby will probably enjoy the closeness of your body, the movement and rhythm as well as your smile!

●Hold your baby in front of a mirror. Babies are frequently fascinated by their own reflections.

●Young infants like to look at black and white geometric patterns. Create some with cardboard and a black felt-tip marker pen.

●Bring your baby with you while you do your chores. Place the baby in a chest carrier or infant seat (on the floor— not on a chair or table). Talk to the baby as you work.

•Tape record the baby's coos and gurgles and play them back for him or her.

In the last analysis, realize that winter does end—eventually!

THE WORKING MOTHER

Feelings About Working Outside the Home

Many mothers express mixed feelings about their working outside the home. Some are concerned about whether a paid sitter could care for their child as well as they could and whether the baby would become more attached to the caretaker than to them. Some feel guilty about leaving—especially during the first few weeks—and worry that the baby will miss them or be psychologically affected by their absence. They especially worry while working on days the child is sick or when they call home and hear the baby crying. Some women who had not planned on working but found their financial situation required it are unhappy about the situation.

"I resent having to leave my brand-new baby and go to work, but what can I do? John lost his job and hasn't been able to find another one. Unemployment insurance just doesn't cover expenses. It tears me apart to leave every morning, but I have no choice."

Some women find the juggling of priorities and the time involved with caring for their babies, doing well at work, maintaining the house, etc. is more than they can handle.

"The pressure has just become too much to deal with," one mother said. "I found I was exhausted and tense all the time —not enjoying the baby, my job, my husband, anything. We'll be strapped financially for a while, but if I can't work out a part-time arrangement, I'm staying home. It just isn't worth it."

On the other hand, many women express feelings of relief to be with adults all day instead of being home with a baby. Others feel that having the extra money to afford vacations and occasional meals out makes working worthwhile. Some women who are career-oriented and who have good support systems (spouses who take on a fair portion of the baby and house care, paid help in the house, etc.) are pleased to find they can combine their careers with raising a child. Many women express the feeling that they enjoy their babies more because they aren't with them all day. When they come home from work they look forward to caring for and being with their infants.

"I worried that the baby wouldn't recognize me and would prefer the babysitter. This hasn't happened. I have missed out on things—like Philip's first steps and the first time he drank from a cup—but I think it's been worth it. I couldn't handle staying home anymore, and working gives me something for *me*. I think I'm a better mother because of it all."

The Many Ways of Working

Today's women often have a choice not only of what type of job to seek, but also what their hours will be. While many women work full-time from nine to five, others are discovering firms with a system of flexible working hours ("flextime"), enabling them to begin work at their convenience, between seven and ten, for example, and to leave eight hours later. Some firms have instituted four-day weeks, whereby the total number of working hours is divided among four days instead of five, giving employees longer work days, but shorter work weeks. Unique part-time arrangements are sometimes possible. Some women are sharing full-time jobs with others—splitting the weekly work load with a friend or relative by having each work a half-day or alternating days home and on the job. This arrangement calls for two individuals who can openly communicate and make joint decisions. Job sharing need not be limited to friends or even certain professions. We know of a husband and wife, who are both doctors, sharing a practice in this manner. We have also heard of teachers, secretaries, professionals as well as nonprofessionals, successfully involved in job-sharing arrangements. Part-time jobs generally do not pay as well or have the same interest level as full-time jobs. Job sharing allows two individuals to have the advantages of a full-time job while working part-time.

Some women prefer to work from their homes: typing, editing, writing, accounting, babysitting, practicing law, sewing, painting, sculpting, tutoring, etc.

Childcare

The major problem that has to be resolved before going to work either full- or part-time is arranging for adequate care for your baby. Facilities are usually not available at most places of employment, but there are exceptions. Employers are sometimes willing to allow some employees to bring their infants with them. We know of one college professor who held office hours and did research while her son held court in a bassinet next to her desk. An administrative assistant deemed irreplaceable by her company was encouraged to bring her baby with her. Her company even provided a small refrigerator and hot plate to accommodate feeding supplies and relinquished a few shelves in a supply closet for diapers, ointment, etc. One of the authors of this book worked part-time for an obstetrician while her infant son played on the floor near her desk. Accommodating to a working mother (or father) and infant need not interfere with the performance of the employee or disturb other individuals. If you are not lucky enough to find such an employer, or if you have no desire to bring your baby with you, you will have to make other arrangements.

Some women find friends or relatives willing to care for the baby. If you are working part-time, it is often possible to share babysitting duties with another working mother: you babysit while she works; she babysits while you work. Try to locate a babysitting co-op in your area, or organize one, if this is feasible. Other women seek out day-care centers or homes or hire a sitter to come to their homes (generally the most expensive arrangement). Very few day-care centers accept infants and those that do usually require that the baby be at least two to six months old.

A family day-care home is run by a mother in her own home. All states require that these be licensed and homes must meet certain health and safety standards. Some states require that the day-care mother attend specialized workshops. However, there is generally no requirement that mothers running day-care homes have even a high school diploma. Licensing does not guarantee that the home provides programs to stimulate the intellectual development of the children. Also, state licensing agencies do not always have the funds or manpower to inspect frequently; therefore, licensed homes may fall below standards and not lose their licensing for some time. Licensed homes generally accommodate no more than five children, including the owner's children, under six years of age. If you are considering this type of arrangement, obtain copies of state licensing standards and then decide if these meet your needs. When you visit a home, check to see that these standards are still being adhered to. Some family day-care homes are sponsored by organizations that oversee the facilities and types of programs offered. Check with sponsoring organizations to learn what their standards are and how strictly they are enforced. In some areas, unlicensed and unsponsored homes do exist—either because state laws are being ignored, because the state does not have the resources to enforce the licensing requirement or because the arrangement is an informal one between family members, friends or neighbors. You will have to apply your own standards to deciding whether or not to use an unlicensed facility. No matter how good the facility, remember that statistics show that children in day-care centers or homes have an increased rate of illness for the first six months they are in day-care.

As a result of well-publicized scandals involving child sexual abuse in California and New York, Congress appropriated an additional $25 million, added to the Social Securities block grant, in part, as an incentive to the states to pass laws requiring a nationwide criminal records check (fingerprinting) for the operators, staff and employees (or prospective operators, staff and employees) of childcare facilities. The definition of what constitutes a "childcare facility" was left to the states, and at the time of this writing, not all states had passed such regulations. For information on whether your state requires a criminal records check and for a copy of licensing standards, contact the Department of Social Services to locate the Department of Licensing and Enforcement (sometimes called the Department of Licensing and Monitoring). Also, write for a copy of a booklet called "Child Sexual Abuse Prevention Tips for Parents," National Center on Child Abuse and Neglect, P.O. Box 1182, Washington, D.C. 20013.

To locate infant care facilities in your area, contact friends, your baby nurse, your obstetrician, pediatrician, childbirth educator, La Leche League leader, religious or civic organization, local planning board or council, the Department of Social Services, city or state Bureau of Child Health and Welfare, or a local Head Start program. Many companies today offer assistance to their employees in locating childcare facilities for their children. A local library or community newspaper might have a listing of facilities available. Local colleges and hospitals sometimes have day-care centers that will accept children from the community in addition to the children of their employees.

There are important questions to consider before formalizing any arrangements. First, it is important to consider whether the caretaker shares your views on child-rearing and discipline. Are infants left to "cry it out" or are they held? Are they fed on demand or schedule? What are the policies regarding feeding solids, snacks, toilet training (for older children), television, etc.? What facilities will be available to encourage the baby's emotional/intellectual development as well as physical needs? How well qualified is the caretaker to handle any emergency that might come up? Can the caretaker provide an intellectually stimulating, emotionally warm environment for your child? What previous experience does he or she have in caring for infants? Has he or she had a recent physical examination? If you are considering a day-care home or center, ask how many other children are enrolled. What is the ratio of children to staff? Do facilities seem large enough for the number of children? Can they play outside on nice days? What toys are available for them? Are diapers changed on schedule or demand? Has the safety of older children as well as infants been considered (electrical outlets covered, small breakable items placed out of reach or put away, etc.)? Are there different types of activities for the different age groups represented? What facilities are available for a child who becomes ill during the day? If there are older children present, do they seem to be enjoying themselves and do they look comfortable in their surroundings? Does there seem to be total chaos in the facility or do you get the feeling that some kind of control is being exercised by the adults present? Do the children appear comfortable with the caretaker?

Be concerned about facilities for older children even though you have an infant because, ideally, any arrangement should be able to continue for several years. Infants become attached to the person giving primary care and react negatively to changes. In light of this fact, try to ascertain what the staff turnover is at any day-care center you are considering. The fact that the baby/staff ratio is good when you enroll your child doesn't mean it will remain that way.

"I work in a hospital that has on-site day care. I arrived at work with my baby one day to find that the day-care staff hadn't all reported in. There were twelve children under the age of two being cared for by one adult. I took my baby with me and went to see my supervisor, because I felt that the situation just wasn't safe. I was allowed to keep my baby with me until more people arrived and my complaint to the management resulted in the hiring of more personnel. My advice to parents in a similar situation is to be assertive! If management values our work and our demands are reasonable, they will be met."

Even after you settle your baby into a day-care situation, it is important to check in every once in awhile to ensure that things are going well. Some centers go out of their way to communicate with parents via bulletin boards, notebooks, etc. to share the details of the child's experiences at home and his or her day at the center. Some even offer evening workshops, lectures or staff/parent conferences as well.

If you are hiring a sitter to work in your home, discuss exactly the person's duties. Will she/he also be doing light housekeeping? Cooking? Laundry? What should take priority if the baby is crying—the baby or the housework? What facilities will the person be permitted to use—stereo, television, telephone, etc.? May his or her friends visit? What are your views on smoking, drinking, etc.? Can the person supply recent references? If the person formerly worked outside the home, will she/he give you the name and address of previous employers? If the person has no previous employment history, can personal references be supplied? *Check all references*. Call the individuals listed and ask if they were satisfied with the person, what they liked and disliked about the individual and why he/she left their employ. If you are considering an individual whose previous employment history shows a pattern of job hopping, seriously consider finding someone else.

Whatever your plans regarding care for your child, it's important to formalize them well in advance of the date you will return to work. Perhaps the baby can start at day care gradually, increasing his or her stay to the total time eventually needed. It's a good idea to hire a sitter several weeks early so you can each get to know the other and straighten out any of the misunderstanding that can occur relative to what his or her duties are and how the baby should be cared for. This will give you time to terminate the arrangement and seek another sitter if it's obvious that things aren't going to work out. Also, as we suggested in the section "Should Both Parents Work Outside the Home," have contingency plans in case of emergency, such as when the sitter doesn't arrive, the child is sick and can't go to day care, there's a snow storm and public transportation is not available, or the car breaks down.

Finances/Legalities

SOCIAL SECURITY. If you are paying a cook, housekeeper, governess, maid, cleaning person, babysitter, etc., more than $50 per quarter (three months), you are required to file I.R.S. Form 942 (Employer's Quarterly Tax Return for Household Employees) and to pay Social Security for that individual. You must contact an Internal Revenue Service Office to obtain an employer identification number and further information.

WORKMAN'S COMPENSATION. Some states require by law that all employees working a specified number of hours or earning over a specified minimum amount of money be covered by a Workman's Compensation Policy. In some states, this coverage, by law, is included in all homeowner's insurance policies. In states that require Workman's Compensation coverage, any employee who is required to be covered is, if injured on the job, entitled to recover damages, including medical expenses and a percentage of his or her wages, *regardless of who was at fault* in causing the accident. The amount a "covered" employee is entitled to recover is fixed by the State Compensation Board and, in the case of a permanent injury (loss of an eye, finger, etc.), may involve considerable sums of money. If you plan to hire a babysitter and/or housekeeper to work in your home, we strongly urge you to contact your state's Department of Workman's Compensation to see if you live in a "compensation state." If you do, you should check to see if this coverage is automatically included in your homeowner's insurance policy. If it is not, you should purchase a compensation policy through your insurance company or state fund to cover any possible liability in case of an accident. If you do not purchase such a policy and your legally protected babysitter is injured on the job, you will be required to pay the specified amounts from your own funds and possibly a penalty for violating the law. In states that do not require workman's compensation, an employee would have to prove in court that his or her employer was negligent. If so proven, a jury would award damages. Even if you are not by law required to purchase a compensation policy, we strongly urge you to consider buying one.

LIABILITY INSURANCE. This covers payments for damages any individual may sustain on your premises due to your negligence. While homeowners usually carry this type of insurance, apartment dwellers usually do not. Liability insurance does not replace compensation insurance.

INCOME TAX CREDIT. If you are hiring someone other than a close relative to care for your child to enable you to work, you are probably entitled to claim a portion of this expense as an income tax credit. This differs from a deduction in that you subtract the amount you are entitled to claim from the actual income tax you owe the federal government. For more information about this tax credit, see I.R.S. form 2441 (Credit for Child and Dependent Care Expenses) and obtain Publication 503 (Childcare and Disabled Dependent Care) from any I.R.S. office, or call or write to the nearest I.R.S. office. These addresses are listed in the income tax package mailed to you by the federal government, or in the phone book.

Breastfeeding

It is often possible to breastfeed your child even though you are working full-time. It will take some determination on your part, but it certainly can be done.

●Wait as long as you possibly can before beginning full-time work. This will allow your milk supply and let-down reflex to become established.

●Nurse the baby before you leave in the morning, again as soon as you get home, and then for all other feedings during the evening and night.

●It might be possible to arrange to have your sitter bring the baby to you to be nursed during your lunch hour or coffee break. If this is not possible and if refrigeration facilities are available at work, express your milk into a sterile container and store it. This can be given to the baby the next day instead of formula. Breast milk *must* be kept cold. While traveling home, carry it in a small styrofoam ice chest filled with ice, a plastic bag filled with ice cubes, or even a thermos bottle that has been washed with hot soapy water and rinsed thoroughly. You can express your milk directly into the thermos and place the thermos in the refrigerator at work. When you arrive home, refrigerate the container.

●On weekends or vacations, you can either continue to follow your weekday schedule of nursings and bottlefeedings (nurse the baby at the time you would be expressing your milk at work) or breastfeed exclusively. Realize that if you nurse exclusively on weekends, your milk supply will increase by Monday.

●When your baby begins to eat solid foods, have the sitter feed the solids during your absence. Continue to nurse the baby in the morning and when at home.

●Keep a supply of nursing pads at work in case you have a problem with leaking.

Strategies for Mothers Working Outside the Home

All mothers are working women. Realize that caring for a baby and a home is a full-time job in itself. If, in addition, you are working outside the home, full or part-time, something's got to give! You will probably find it's impossible to do everything—have an immaculate home; be a loving, attentive mate; serve gourmet meals; do well on the job; spend time with the baby; keep up an enjoyable social life. Expecting to be a superwomen will most probably lead to disappointment at the least, so we suggest you don't even try!

Resolve to spend a good portion of your "at home" time with the baby. "The first thing I do when I get home from work is play. I need the baby as much as she needs me. It really helps me unwind. We eat a lot of omelettes for dinner."

If you and your mate arrive home at the same time, you might agree that one of you plays with the baby while the other prepares dinner. Alternate nights in each role and switch roles for cleanup.

If you don't have hired help in the house, you and your mate should make a list of household tasks. Think about each item and ask yourself if it is essential or can it be done less frequently than usual. Simplify tasks. The kitchen floor may have to be washed, but does it need to be polished? Your favorite dry cleaner may be at the end of town, but you or your mate may pass another one on the way to or from work. Consider switching. Apportion tasks between you and resolve to meet two or three weeks later to reevaluate the situation and perhaps reapportion tasks.

Cook in advance. While one of you spends time with the baby on a weekend, perhaps the other can prepare dinners for the week.

Food shopping as a family can afford time together and facilitate completing this task as quickly as possible.

THE SINGLE MOTHER

Single parenthood is on the rise for many reasons. Divorce is easier to obtain. It is now possible for an individual who is not married to adopt a child. Some women are choosing to become pregnant and give birth knowing they will have no further relationship with the baby's father.

"I chose to become pregnant knowing that I would have to raise my baby alone. I selected her father because I felt he would provide good genes. We really have had no relationship since my pregnancy was confirmed. In fact, I think he's mad I didn't have an abortion. I just decided it was time to have a child."

"I didn't plan on becoming pregnant, but when I did I decided that I really didn't want to have an abortion. I wanted this child. The knowledge that I consciously chose to have the baby has helped me over some dark moments. Like when my roommate in the hospital asked me when my husband was coming to see the baby, I had the strength to look her straight in the eye and say, 'I am not married.'"

The postpartum period is a time of stress. A study done by the University of California at Berkeley (cited in The *New York Times,* Jan. 7, 1978, Family/Style, p. 10) concluded that "The time of arrival of a first-born child constitutes a major and often insurmountable trauma for its parents."

"It wasn't supposed to be like this," one mother said. "We chose to have this baby; we were close during my pregnancy and then my husband just couldn't handle the stress of having an infant in the house and he left. Now I'm fighting for child support money. I have to take him to court. I have no money. I have to go to work and there are no day-care facilities near my home until the baby is two and a half years old. The isolation is tremendous. I am doing the best job I can as a mother because it's not the baby's fault and I love him . . ."

If you are a single mother by choice because you knowingly sought to become pregnant or decided not to terminate an unplanned pregnancy, the baby's father may be legally obliged to help with financial support if you can legally establish paternity. This is often easier to establish if the father has in any way acknowledged paternity, for instance, a written acknowledgement in a letter, signing a form, or agreeing in writing to have his name appear on the baby's birth certificate. If the father does not readily acknowledge paternity, however, and freely contribute his support, you can contact a private attorney or an attorney of the Legal Aid Society to seek advice. In some states you don't need the assistance of an attorney to establish paternity. You may be able to go to court yourself, or the state agency that administers child support enforcement may be able to assist you. If you are receiving public assistance, the social service agency that administers public assistance will assist you in establishing paternity and obtaining any funds to which you may be entitled. Also, regardless of your marital status, be aware that legislation mandating that the states improve child support enforcement services was passed in the summer of 1984. For information on the Child Support Enforcement Amendments of 1984 and how it might pertain to your situation (including the location of state and regional enforcement offices) send a postcard requesting The Handbook on Child Support Enforcement to Dept. 43, Consumer Information Center, Pueblo, Colo. 81009.

Whether you are a single mother by choice or circumstance, many problems you face are the same. However, an individual who becomes a single mother by choice has the advantage of seeking out support groups and beginning to make financial arrangements before the baby's arrival. A mother who becomes single after the baby's birth—due to separation, divorce, or the death of a mate—does not have this chance to prepare.

"I found that the stress of the sudden separation took a lot out of me physically. I couldn't sleep. I found I needed more nourishment than usual and took vitamins and protein supplements to keep my body going. Exercise helped. Every evening I did exercises until I was so exhausted I had to sleep."

"Men get off easily. When my husband left, I had to deal with the house, the lawn, the bills, and the children. My head was in such a turmoil I found it difficult to tolerate the children. I think the tendency is to take things out on the children, but it's not their fault. It's hard to keep things in their proper perspective when your whole world is crumbling."

"I felt like I had to get away from the children for a while. Even though I was the one who initiated the separation, I felt I needed a few days away from the children to get my head together after I finally left."

Most single mothers we spoke with mentioned the tremendous isolation they were experiencing. Some had been established in their community and had friends they thought they could rely on and found that, when their marital status changed, or when people began to realize they were about to have a baby out of wedlock, they suddenly became social outcasts. Others found their family and friends were supportive.

"People act differently toward you, like there's something wrong with you. It wasn't my fault my husband left. I went to a party with people I had known for years and one couple completely ignored me. When I went over and asked if they recognized me, they said they did and then turned away."

"My family turned their backs on me, hoping to drive me back to my husband, or because they just didn't want to get involved. They didn't realize how much I needed their support."

"I'm lucky. I live in an apartment building where people pretty much keep to themselves and no one seems to care that I have a baby and no husband. But I know if I lived in my old neighborhood, I would be entirely ostracized! My friends have been wonderful."

"My family was thrilled about my decision to have a baby. My brother had some difficulty accepting the fact that I had no intention of getting married, but on the whole, I've been pretty lucky."

Even if you have friends or relatives who stand by your decision to have a child or support you emotionally during the crisis of your separation, you may find it's difficult to meet people because you must rely on others to care for your baby when you go out.

"I spend ninety-nine percent of my time with my son. I crave adult companionship or even the freedom to go to a movie. But I have no money to hire a sitter and no family close by to help out."

"I hate having to rely on others to help me out when I want 'time off.'"

"I feel like a machine at times—a twenty-five-hour-a-day-mother with no relief."

Loneliness is common—especially in women living alone with their children.

"I'm especially sad at times when I'm absolutely exhausted and have no one to turn to, hand the baby to, and sleep for a while—3:00 A.M. can be awfully lonely."

"The impact of what I'm going through hits me suddenly when I realize that I am alone and must make all decisions for my own welfare and the welfare of my baby by myself."

"Although I have had good family support, I still feel alone, stranded, isolated. Maybe this is because I am alone . . . a single parent with no one to share the 'firsts.'"

If at all possible, you might consider living with another person—perhaps another single mother to help remove the loneliness and provide adult companionship.

Finances are often a problem. A single mother usually has to rely on others for financial support, locate adequate day-care facilities, and return to work or accept public assistance. Day-care is frequently difficult to locate for a young infant and some women don't want to leave their babies to go to work.

"I would love to work, but there are no day-care facilities in my area until the baby is six months old. I'm forced to accept public assistance, and I hate it!"

"I went from financial security to nothing. My family wouldn't help. I had no place to live. When I went to the social services office to apply for public assistance, I literally had no money in my pocket."

"I would rather accept public assistance and spend these first years raising my child. I can go to work later. My baby needs me now. Meanwhile we won't starve and that's all I care about."

"I wish that public officials would acknowledge that my situation is becoming more common—there are more single parents around—and that adequate facilities would be available to meet our needs. I strongly urge all single mothers to take advantage of programs available and work for improvements in the day-care situation. Day-care is generally unavailable for young babies, is too expensive, or has a salary cut-off. If I get a raise this summer, I'll no longer qualify and I'm barely making ends meet now!"

If you need financial assistance, go to the nearest Department of Social Services office for help. Get there early in the morning because there are usually long waiting lines. Be prepared to be assertive and persistent. One former Social Services caseworker we spoke to advised that you, "beat on the desk, yell, scream and cry if you get an unsympathetic individual." State your needs and then restate them if necessary and restate them again and again until you get the help you need. If you are in dire need, without funds and without a place to live, they may give you emergency funds immediately, but be persistent. If you qualify, you are legally entitled to receive public assistance. Don't feel you are imposing on people for applying for what is legally yours. If you receive public assistance, the Department of Social Services will automatically make sure you receive food stamps and Medicaid. If you do not qualify for public assistance, you may be entitled to food stamps and Medicaid anyway. Ask someone at the Department of Social Services where to go to apply if they neglect to give you this information. If you're denied public assistance, food stamps and/or Medicaid, you have the right to a "fair hearing," which is a state review of your case. If you are receiving public assistance and are entitled to support from the child's father, the Department of Social Services will summon him to court for you at no charge to you to collect funds to which you may be entitled, provided that the father can be located. However, if he is not living in your state, you may not be able to obtain funds from him.

We believe it is essential that you meet people who are in your situation, with whom you can exchange experiences and suggestions and talk about your feelings. It is important to realize that you are not alone and that others share your problems and concerns. Single parent groups can be located through a local YM/YWCA or YM/YWHA, and quite often these include programs for the children of single parents. Call the community service society or association in your area and ask if they have programs for single parents. A local family service agency (often listed under Social Service Organizations in the phone book) may have support groups for single parents. Parents Without Partners is an organization formed expressly to meet the needs of single parents. P.W.P. sponsors programs for parents and outings for parents and children and they publish a magazine called *The Single Parent* devoted to the needs and problems of individuals in your situation. If there is no chapter in your area, or if you wish more information, you can write to their national office: Parents Without Partners, International, 7910 Woodmont Ave., Bethesda, Md. 20814. Women's centers, the National Organization for Women, or a local mothers' center all may provide the type of support you are looking for. Breastfeeding women have found a great deal of help and support through the La Leche League.

"Spending time with women who think the way I do, regardless of their marital status, made me feel beautiful. Being able to give help to others reaffirmed my own sense of self-worth. La Leche League emphasizes the value of spending time with your baby. I was spending lots of time with my infant, not only by choice, but out of necessity. The League mothers got me to relax in my mothering. I felt a bond with them. They put me at ease and made me feel at home."

"Just knowing there are others out there who have no one to help them at 2 in the morning when the baby is screaming is a comfort. Knowing I have a meeting to look forward to where I can cry with people who understand helps me get through the rough times."

"It helps to be able to say to someone, 'I feel like I'm at the end of my rope!'"

If no support groups are available in your area, organize one yourself. When you contact your obstetrician or whomever to ask for names, tell him or her you are specifically interested in meeting with other single parents. In addition to discussing common problems, you might even consider forming a baby-sitting co-op. (See "How to Start a Reciprocal Babysitting Service" in the following section.)

BABYSITTERS

There is no "right age" at which to begin leaving your child with a babysitter on an occasional or regular basis. It depends on your feelings and needs and those of your baby. Some women find they need to get out without the baby occasionally or frequently from the early weeks onward—others find they do not have this need. Some couples appreciate being able to leave the baby with someone in whom they have confidence and go out. Others are content to take the baby with them and/or stay at home. And some parents think it is a good idea to leave the baby with a sitter now and then so the baby will not be totally dependent on being with them.

It's important that any babysitter share your philosophy of childcare: Should a baby be fed on demand or on a schedule? Cry it out or be held? Be given a pacifier? Before you hire a sitter, even on an occasional basis, discuss these questions with him or her. If you are interviewing an individual recommended by someone other than a close personal friend, ask for the names and phone numbers of other people the person has worked for. Call and ask them if they were satisfied with the sitter's services. Also ask if there was anything they did not like about the sitter. Ask the prospective sitter for a list of days and hours he or she is generally available for babysitting and what the hourly charge is. Ask how much experience the person has had caring for infants of your baby's age—perhaps he or she has helped care for younger siblings.

For a new baby, we recommend you locate a person familiar with handling newborns. A teenaged sitter may not be right for your baby at this stage of life. You might contact a local nursing school and ask if there are any students experienced in infant care who might be interested in babysitting. Through a nursing agency you might locate a licensed practical nurse who specializes in infant care. If so, be prepared for her fee to be higher than a nonprofessional's. If you have a relative or friend in whom you have confidence and who is willing to help you out, this too might be a good idea. Your baby nurse may be willing to babysit or may know someone who is qualified, or you can ask your pediatrician's nurse or lab technician if they babysit or know someone who does. Perhaps you can post a notice in your doctor's waiting room requesting that anyone interested in babysitting call you. Try to locate a few reliable babysitters so you'll have several people to choose from when you want to go out.

No matter what the age of your baby, it's important to leave instructions for any sitter you hire. What will the baby most likely want the next time he or she awakens? Where are diaper and feeding supplies kept? How should a bottle be prepared? Where are flashlights and candles kept in case of power failure? If you have fire or smoke detectors, alert the sitter to their presence and instruct her or him not to investigate if one goes off, but to take the baby, leave the house, and contact the fire department from outside. Does your house have burglar alarms? Alert the sitter to their presence and how they operate. If the sitter must leave the house with the baby in an emergency and does not live close by, to which neighbor should he or she go while trying to reach you? If at all possible, leave instructions on how to reach you—the name and phone number of the people you're visiting, restaurant, theater, store, etc. Also, leave the name and phone number of a friend or relative who will be home while you are out, as well as your pediatrician's name and phone number. Make sure the sitter knows where your essential phone number list is posted. Put all instructions in writing so they will not be forgotten at a crucial moment.

On a separate piece of paper, write the baby's name and birth date, the name and phone number of your pediatrician, what immunizations the baby has had and where you can be reached. List any allergies your baby may have and any medications you or your mate might be allergic to. Instruct the sitter to bring this if he or she takes the baby to the hospital in an emergency.

Tell the sitter what you expect regarding the use of the telephone, stereo, television, radio, etc., what snacks you've left and whether you mind if a friend keeps him or her company. Also, let the sitter know at approximately what time you expect to return home. Instruct the person to open the door to no one, no matter who they say they are or how insistent they become! Leave a pencil and paper for phone messages and call home at least once during the time you are away to ask how things are going.

It's a good idea to have the sitter "meet" your baby before he or she is left in the sitter's care for the first time. It will give you an opportunity to demonstrate how you hold, feed and play with the baby. You might even consider hiring the sitter to care for the baby for an hour or two while you're home doing household chores, letter writing, or whatever. This will allow you to gain confidence in that person's abilities, allow him or her to get to know your child and to ask any questions that may arise, and also may help ease any anxiety you have about leaving the baby. The first time you go out, plan to be away for a brief period—such as an hour or two to sleep or to visit a friend—and come back before the time you're expected. Evaluate the situation upon your return. Does everything seem under control? Has the baby obviously been screaming for some time? If there are minor problems—unchanged diaper, items out of place—discuss them with the sitter and try again; but if the person obviously is not caring for your child as you would like, find someone else.

You might consider setting up a reciprocal babysitting arrangement with another mother for daytime hours. This would remove the cost of babysitters. One afternoon each week, for example, you can offer to care for a friend's baby and she would care for your baby on another afternoon. This, of course, is only feasible if both mothers feel confident enough to handle two infants. It might be easier for you if both babies are close in age, or, depending on your preferences, if they are a few years apart. This takes trial and error until you find the right match for you. Any reciprocal babysitting agreement should be entered into with the understanding that either "partner" can terminate the arrangement without hard feelings for any reason whatsoever.

For an evening arrangement, you and your mate can care for your friend's baby in your own home for several hours and have this reciprocated on another night. If there is more than one child in both families, an evening arrangement would involve your sitting in your friend's home and caring for her children while your mate stays home with yours. When you and your mate want to go out, you reverse the arrangement.

You might discover a babysitting co-op in your neighborhood involving several new mothers or you might start one yourself. Members can be solicited through your obstetrician, nurse midwife, pediatrician or childbirth educator. You might even consider setting up a new mother's support group to discuss common feelings and problems in addition to your babysitting arrangement. (See "Postpartum Support Groups.")

How to Start a
Reciprocal Babysitting Service

A reciprocal babysitting service has the advantage of providing reliable babysitters to all participants. It is cost-free. No one need feel tied down and no one need feel he or she is imposing by asking someone to babysit. Of course, the "rules" listed below can be changed to adapt them to the needs of your group. They're just guidelines to help you get started. The group should have several meetings to enable all members to get to meet and gain confidence in one another.

1. The job of bookkeeper is rotated monthly.
2. A list of who is generally available at what times is drawn up and given to each member. This is not a commitment to babysit during those hours, just a useful guide. Also included should be the names of any children in the family and any allergies they might have or special instructions for caregivers (some groups use a separate sheet of children's names for this purpose). Pediatricians' names and phone numbers should be included.
3. It is the responsibility of the person who needs a sitter to call someone on the list at least twenty-four hours in advance. Forty-eight hours would be appreciated. Of course, in an emergency, this rule could be waived.
4. Points are earned and spent as follows:
    a) 1 point is earned for every ½ hour you sit for someone else (or fraction thereof)
    b) 1 point is spent for every ½ hour someone sits for you (or fraction thereof)
5. Points are owed *to the group as a whole*, not just the person who sat for you.
6. Double points are spent/earned for sitting after 5:00 P.M.
7. Two extra points are spent/earned for sitting that includes giving a meal. The group determines who provides the meal, whether the sitter must provide the food or whether the baby "brown bags it."
8. Sitting will be done in the sitter's home.
9. It is the sitter's responsibility to notify the bookkeeper of the number of points spent/earned.

10. Examples of the bookkeeping:

   a) Alice watches Mary's child for two hours.
      Alice = +4;   Mary = −4

   b) Then: Sally watches Alice's child for one hour, while Mary watches Sue's child for one hour.
      Mary = −2; Sue = −2; Alice = +2; Sally = +2

All points earned/spent are simply added/subtracted from current totals. It is advisable to agree on the maximum number of points a person may accumulate before spending some and, also, the maximum number of points a person may spend before beginning to sit for others. We suggest 10 in either case.

TRAVELING WITH AN INFANT

Going out with a baby can resemble moving day at the circus. The new mother and father can be so loaded down with things that seem essential that going hardly seems worth the effort. Understandably, most new parents overpack for the first few excursions with their newborns. They worry that they'll run out of something important (such as diapers) at a critical moment. One new mother told us that the first time she brought her baby with her to an evening meeting, she packed twelve diapers, three stretch suits, four bottles, as well as other assorted paraphernalia that filled two diaper bags, and, in addition, brought an infant seat, a chest carrier and a carriage — all to a meeting that lasted only two hours! A bit of advance thought about where you are going, how long you'll be gone, how you plan to get there, what facilities will be available once you arrive, and what your baby usually needs during the period you'll be away will do a lot to help ease any anxieties you may have about what to bring.

The following is a list of items that are helpful and/or necessary for traveling. What you choose to purchase will depend on your budget and your life-style. Note: it is often possible to obtain these things at garage, yard, or tag sales or from other mothers who no longer need them. If you obtain any item secondhand, be sure it is in good condition. Also, be aware that there are publications such as *Consumer Reports* (published by Consumers Union, a nonprofit organization) that periodically rate these items, by brand name, as to convenience and durability, and give information about current governmental and safety standards. Be sure that any equipment you buy conforms to *current* safety standards. This is especially important if you buy or receive anything secondhand. Manufacturers frequently make changes in their products and it is important to know the model of the item you are considering, to enable you to use any rating guide.

CAR SEAT. No infant should travel in a car unless properly restrained in a well-constructed car seat that has been secured as per the manufacturer's instructions. In many states, this is now the law and some hospitals will not release an infant unless he or she will ride home in a car seat. Be sure that the car seat you purchase is designed to protect your child in a crash. Studies done by Consumers Union and reported in their March 1975 and June 1977 issues of *Consumer Reports* point up the danger to a child who is riding on a lap, secured only by loving arms:

> The forces generated in a crash may in effect multiply the child's weight 10 or 20 times; the child thus tends to fly out of the adult's arms and slam into the dashboard or windshield. If the adult is unbelted (not wearing a seat belt), so much the worse. The adult's weight, also multiplied 10 or 20 times, crushes the child.

A car bed is not considered safe in an accident, nor is it safe to strap the infant in the car with the adult lap belt. Don't use the excuse that you're a good driver and won't have an accident. Accidents can happen to anyone. For information about current safety standards, contact the National Highway Traffic Safety Commission at 1-800-424-9393.

BABY CARRIER. This is perhaps the most useful of all items you can purchase for the very young infant. Several different styles are available—some with a hard back support for the baby, others made of soft fabric; all enable you to carry the baby, leaving your hands free. Not only is this convenient for the parents, but quite often the vibration of the mother's heart-beat and her warm closeness lull a baby to sleep. Consider using this for shopping trips, bus rides, etc., and also, for around the house when the baby is fretful and you want to get some work done. Many parents find that they can continue to comfortably carry their baby in a chest carrier as he or she gets older. During two days at Disneyland with her family, the 13-month-old daughter of one of this book's authors spent a very contented 27 hours in the carrier—smiling at people and napping at will.

DIAPER BAG. We prefer the large shoulder-bag type with compartments. Several are now available that have a plastic-covered "flap" that unsnaps to form a changing pad. Buy one that is big enough to carry your wallet and other personal items you would usually take in a separate handbag. (You can also use an old pair of jeans to make a diaper bag. Cut the legs off below the back pockets and sew a seam to close the leg holes. Sew a seam across the top to close the waist area—the zipper will serve to open and close the bag. Take one of the legs and fashion a strap to be attached at both ends of the zipper.) Include the plastic irrigation bottle (peri bottle) you received in the hospital. When you no longer need it for your-self, you can fill it with water and use it for diaper changes. (After your baby is toilet-trained, you can use it for watering plants.) In addition, pack cotton balls, disposable diapers, gallon-size plastic bags (save the ones you get with vegetables at the supermarket and use these for disposing of diapers and/ or as a waterproof sheet under the baby's rear for changing diapers), ointment, tissues (for wiping your sticky fingers after a diaper change), a light blanket, rattles, change of clothing, and two cloth diapers (for burping). Non-nursing mothers should carry bottles of prepared formula (that come complete with the nipple attached) which require no refrigera-tion. Keep a checklist on a card in the bag of all the items you include. When you return home from a short trip, check the contents of the bag against your list and replace used items immediately. This way you're ready to leave at a moment's notice and don't have to reassemble things each time you want to go out with the baby.

INFANT SEAT. The plastic kind that young babies are placed in for eating solids can also be useful for traveling. This is great to take with you to the supermarket so you can put the baby into the shopping cart. First, place large items into the cart to form a platform so the baby will not see the world through a row of bars. Be sure this platform is not dangerously high and is level so the seat will not topple over. Also, if your infant is at the arm-waving or reaching-for-items stage, make sure there's nothing breakable within his or her reach or that can be knocked over or opened. In some areas of the country, supermarkets have a seat section for children who can sit up unsupported. Some infant seats fit crosswise in this section. Some infant seats can also be placed in a mesh umbrella stroller if your pediatrician believes your child is too young to sit against the soft back. (There are also infant seats with rockers. Some babies love to be rocked in an upright position.)

UMBRELLA STROLLER. An umbrella stroller can fold into an umbrella-like parcel and be hung over the arm. Styles vary. Some have firm backs that have one upright position. Other firm-back models also have a reclining position. There are also lightweight umbrella strollers that have seats made of mesh or canvas. Ask your pediatrician when you can begin to use a mesh or canvas stroller. Doctors have different beliefs about the necessity for firm-back support at young ages. If you live in a suburban area, consider keeping the stroller in the trunk of your car so it's easily available when you might need it. This saves you the job of carrying it to the car.

CARRIAGE. There are many different types of carriages available. If you have a car, we suggest that any carriage you purchase (and they are by no means a necessity) be one that comes apart and has a frame that can be folded or collapsed somewhat so that it can fit into the trunk and/or back seat. Never use the body of a carriage as a car bed! Car beds are not safe in an accident. We have found the rain shield, handle-bar bag and package racks to be valuable accessories. Be careful not to put heavy items in a handle-bar bag because that can cause the carriage to tip over.

PORTABLE BEDS. Styles vary from collapsible, soft-sided lightweight "carriers" to actual portable cribs (port-a-cribs) made of wood or aluminum with mesh sides. There is even one type of portable bed that folds up to form a diaper bag complete with carrying strap—unfold it and it's a bed. We see little use for these for short visits to a friend or relative (a blanket on the floor serves as a great temporary bed) and prefer the type of port-a-crib that converts to a playpen. There are several available that have two mattress levels—chest-high and thigh-high, with legs that can be raised or lowered. This serves not only as a portable crib for overnight visits, but as a playpen in your home when the baby is older.

The best time to leave the house for any trip is right after the baby has been fed and diapered. This will maximize the amount of time you have before feeding and changing again become necessary.

Check what facilities are available at the stores and other public places you plan to visit, especially those that have more than one level. Not all such places have elevators, and getting stuck with a baby carriage on the first floor when you need to go to the third can be a frustrating experience. (If it happens, ask if you can use the freight elevator.) Some stores and public places do not allow carriages at all, and many do not allow strollers—even umbrella strollers. Call, ask and guide yourself accordingly.

Knowing in advance what the restroom facilities are like is also helpful. A table, counter, or couch for diapering and an armchair for feeding make life a lot easier, but if not available, you'll have to improvise. A cubicle in the restroom or the try-on room will give you privacy while changing and feeding the baby. Put a folded blanket on the floor with a plastic bag on top, just under the baby's bottom and you've got an instant diapering area. Taking the things you need out of the diaper bag before you begin changing the baby makes the job easier, faster and neater. (While changing a baby boy, it is wise to drop a diaper over his penis while you are cleaning him; this can save you a faceful of liquid aggravation.)

At times, of course, there may be no facilities available whatsoever, and you may find yourself diapering your little one on an unused check-out counter at the supermarket or feeding him in front of an exhibit at the museum. Breastfeeding mothers can easily master the art of unobtrusively nursing in public, with a bit of practice at home. Two-piece outfits work the best. Throw a blanket over your shoulder or turn toward the wall for the few seconds it takes to get nipple and nurseling together. If you lift your blouse or sweater from the bottom, it will frame the baby's head and few people will give you a second glance except to smile at the picture of a contented mother and baby. Babies have been nursed on benches, in ladies' rooms, in the park, on the beach, in cars, in restaurants. Most comments heard are usually positive and often come from women who had breastfed their own children and therefore realized what was going on. Because it can be unobtrusive, most people are not even aware that you are feeding your baby and usually pay absolutely no attention.

En Route to Your Destination

If at all possible, choose the fastest available method of getting where you're going, especially when planning longer trips. The less hassle you have getting there, the more enjoyable you'll find your trip.

Whatever mode of travel you finally select, if you are making a trip of several days, carry one day's supply of disposable diapers (and formula if you are bottlefeeding) with *you—not in your luggage*! This will save you the trouble of searching for supplies or being without supplies if your luggage is lost.

In a plane, bus or train, a breastfeeding mother will have more privacy if she sits next to the window.

Airplane

Airline personnel can be very helpful to parents traveling with children. However, facilities vary, so it's wise to call all airlines which fly to your destination and ask what facilities they have available for you and your family. Be sure to ask if there are nonstop direct flights to your destination. A "direct" flight means that you will not have to change planes, but the plane you are on may make one or more stops; each stop means more time spent traveling. A "nonstop direct" flight removes this problem. When you make your reservations, be sure to tell the booking agent that you're traveling with a baby and that you'd like to reserve the bulkhead seats near a window. These are the seats at the very front of each compartment and they have more leg room than other seats—therefore more room to stow your diaper bag during the flight. (For take-off and landing, all carry-on baggage must be under the seat or in special storage compartments.) Note: the first row of the middle section of each compartment in a wide-bodied plane may also be referred to as a bulkhead, but it is less convenient because there is less privacy and if a movie is shown, the light flickering in the baby's face can keep him or her awake. Be sure to request your seats near a window. Request a bassinet, if available, so the baby will be able to lie down for at least part of the flight. During take-off and landing, regulations state that you must hold your child. The cabin personnel will show you the required position.

When you check in at the airport, remind the staff of your seating needs and that you requested a bassinet. If, for some reason, reservations got mixed up, they can be corrected while you're on the ground. Do not wait until you're on the plane to discover someone else sitting where you wanted to sit. As you are being seated, tell the cabin personnel you'd like the bassinet (another way of ensuring it's really there while the plane is still on the ground). When you reconfirm your return reservations, be sure to request the bulkhead seats near a window and the bassinet once again.

Anyone who has flown has experienced the ear-popping sensation caused by the change in cabin pressure as the airplane takes off and lands. Chewing gum or swallowing hard can alleviate this uncomfortable feeling, but this does not help your baby. Ask the person next to you to give the baby a bottle while you hold the infant (take-off and landing regulations require that you hold him or her with both hands). This forces the baby to swallow and relieves some of the discomfort. Ideally, breastfeeding mothers should be allowed to nurse their infants at these times. During a very gradual descent on a flight into Chicago's O'Hare airport, one of the authors of this book observed a stewardess offering plastic cups stuffed with hot towels to be placed over the ears of children who were experiencing ear pain. She requested it for her own children, and found that it worked! This may be worth a try if your baby is having difficulty. Also, it's important to know that ear pain during a flight may indicate that the baby has an ear infection. It might be wise to have a doctor check the baby at your destination. Colds can also contribute to difficulty during a flight. If your baby has a cold and you will be traveling by air, check with your pediatrician. He or she may suggest a decongestant to be administered just before the flight.

If there are no facilities for diapering your child, you can do so across your mate's lap or on your seat. (Spread the blanket and the plastic bag. The toilet compartment is generally too small.)

If you will be traveling abroad, try to anticipate what baby supplies you will need while out of the country and check that they're not only available but reasonably priced. Disposable diapers can be very costly in other parts of the world. If bottlefeeding, check on the availability of prepared formula, and ask your pediatrician's advice on whether the local water supply can be trusted or whether to use bottled water for the baby. He or she may also suggest sterilizing bottles and nipples, etc., depending on where you are going. It's probably wise to give some thought to how this will be managed.

Bus/Train

A baby carrier is invaluable for short bus and train rides. It frees your arms for fare paying, package carrying, or just holding on. It also positions the baby close to your body and ensures that he or she won't fall if you don't. If you're on a train or bus that is lurching every few moments, starting and stopping frequently, try to avoid diapering your baby, no matter how many of your fellow passengers wrinkle their noses in your direction, or point out a growing dark stain. You may feel that the whole world thinks you're neglecting your child, but it's hard to manipulate diaper changing supplies on a moving vehicle while ensuring that the baby doesn't go flying. Wait until you reach your destination.

For longer trips, check what facilities are available. Will you have to hold your child for the entire trip? (For a newborn who sleeps most of the time, that might not be a disadvantage, depending on the length of the trip.) What provisions if any, are made for mothers to breastfeed? Diaper their babies? If you plan an overnight trip, where will you sleep? How will you eat while holding the child? As on a plane, if there are no diaper-changing facilities, use your mate's lap or a seat. (Spread a blanket and the plastic bag.)

Car

It is unwise to diaper or breastfeed a child in a moving car because this necessitates taking the child out of the restraint. It is wiser to pull off the road for the time involved. Also, by law in some states, infants must be strapped in.

Some pediatricians object to keeping a young infant in a restraint for any extended period of time, so check with your doctor before planning any lengthy car trips.

Tying rattles across the car seat or along the side (depending on the style of the seat) for the baby to play with will help keep your child amused. For additional distraction, someone other than the driver can wave some brightly colored objects for the baby to reach for—making sure that they are not in the driver's line of sight, blocking the view of the road. Also, your car radio tuned to a music station—some babies prefer classical, others rock—can do wonders to help keep your baby happy.

Final Notes

We believe it's important to book hotel/motel reservations in advance, for as much of your trip as possible. You will have enough to think about when you arrive in town without having to find a place to stay every night. Before you make reservations, find out what facilities are available (sound familiar?). Some hotels provide cribs at no extra charge. Some, especially in resort areas, have babysitters on staff. There are even some resort facilities that offer nurseries. Parents can spend as much or as little time with their infants during the day as they choose.

If you are planning a visit to a friend or relative who has no babies or young children, inquire into the possibility of renting or borrowing a crib. If none are available and your child is small enough, line a laundry basket with blankets, or, if a firm couch or armchair is available, place a rubber sheet over the cushions, cover this with a regular sheet, turn it so the seat part is against the wall, and pretend it's a crib.

Wherever you're going, if you plan ahead, you can relax and enjoy.

FINANCES

Whether or not there is a decrease in the family income after your baby is born, a baby and the paraphernalia that goes with him or her are expensive. Money problems produce tension in any marriage and ideally the postpartum period should be as free of outside pressures as possible. You'll have enough to worry about with the addition of a new baby! The following are ways you can minimize general household and baby-related expenses.

Medical

●If you have no medical insurance, ask your obstetrician or nurse midwife and pediatrician if, barring any medical contraindications, you and the baby can leave the hospital a day earlier than usual.

●Many hospitals have a pediatric clinic available for the baby's monthly check-ups and immunizations, if you prefer this to a private doctor's services. You also may be able to locate a local health clinic that provides free or moderately priced well-baby check-ups.

●Perhaps you can arrange an exchange of services with a local pediatrician. It's possible, for example, that you or your mate have abilities in carpentry or decorating and a local doctor wants to remodel his or her office. Keep in mind, however, that you may incur tax obligations as part of your swap.

•If a circumcision performed by a physician would be covered under your medical insurance but you are Jewish and will have a mohel circumcise your son, check whether the insurance plan will cover the mohel's fee. Frequently it will.

Food

•Breastfeeding your baby can minimize expenses.

•To cut costs, when the baby is older you can make your own baby food instead of purchasing prepared foods. If you have a blender, a baby food grinder is not necessary, although it is convenient. Blend the food with a bit of water, gravy or juice, depending on what you're preparing, until it is the proper consistency. To store, freeze the baby food in ice cube trays and, once frozen, transfer the cubes to a plastic bag and defrost as needed.

•If you do purchase baby foods, cereals and juices, read the labels. Is there a difference between "baby apple juice," for example, and regular apple juice you might purchase for your family anyway, which is usually substantially less expensive? Always ask yourself if there is an "adult" equivalent for the "baby food" that might save you money.

•Learn to read the labels of all packaged foods you purchase. The ingredients are listed in the order of the amounts contained in the product—the ingredient making up the highest percentage of the product is listed first, the rest in decreasing order. If two brands of salad dressing, for example, cost the same and one lists water as the first ingredient, while the other lists oil, you're getting more value if you buy the second.

•When you compare the prices of items in different size containers, do so on the basis of price per unit. For example, in comparing the cost of a 16-ounce and 12-ounce package, divide the number of ounces into the cost to figure out the cost per ounce of each. Larger sizes are not necessarily less expensive. Some supermarkets list "unit price" information on labels attached to the shelf directly under the products they sell. Be aware of what you are comparing. One label might list the price per quart, the next the price per pound of similar items.

●Locate thrift bakeries selling day-old baked goods and/or see if these items are reduced at your supermarket. Also, some supermarkets that are closed on Sundays lower the cost of all produce and baked goods an hour or two before closing on Saturday night.

●Supermarkets and produce stores will often reduce the price of bruised fruit and vegetables that are otherwise fresh. Check for a display of reduced merchandise.

●Learn to use beans. They are an excellent, inexpensive source of protein and can be prepared in many different ways by themselves or in combination with other foods.

●Clip cents-off coupons from newspapers and magazines for items you use. Save these in a box or jar until you need the items.

●If storage space permits, stock up on frequently used staples when they're on sale. (Using your cents-off coupons to purchase sale items adds to your savings!)

●Check government regulations to see if you qualify for food stamps.

●Form a food-buying co-op that can purchase in bulk from wholesalers. For information on starting a food co-op, write to the Superintendant of Documents, U.S. Government Printing Office, Washington, D.C. 20402.

Shelter/Furniture

●Conserve energy and thereby lower your gas, electric and oil costs. Cover windows with plastic. If you own your own washing machine, don't wash clothing until you have a full load. Hang clothes to dry instead of using the dryer. Turn off lights that are not in use. Bake several things at once, etc.

●Locate used baby furniture that you can refinish. (Be sure that crib slats are 2⅜" apart, to conform to federal standards, and that the paint does not contain lead. Be aware of product recalls. One type of Bassett brand cribs, for example, was taken off the market because of the design of the headboard, which had decorative spaces between a center raised portion and a spindle at each end that babies could catch their heads in. Go to garage sales, or ask your obstetrician, nurse midwife, pediatrician, childbirth educator or La Leche League leader if they know of anyone who wants to sell used baby items. You can frequently locate cribs, carriages, rockers, playpens, highchairs, etc. at very low prices or at no charge. Also, check bazaars, thrift shops and newspaper ads for these items. The U.S. Consumer Product Safety Commission can provide information on current safety standards for cribs, toys and other accessories (1-800-638-2772).

●Have a yard or garage sale to raise money by selling goods you rarely use.

●It is not necessary to buy a bathinette. You can use a simple plastic tub or even the kitchen sink lined with a towel to bathe the baby.

●It is not necessary to buy a beautiful, expensive, coach-type carriage. All you need is a sturdy stroller that allows the baby to recline or a carriage with a body that lifts off its frame and can be placed in the back of the car without the baby, while the frame collapses to an easy-to-handle size for the trunk. Never drive the car with the baby in the carriage-bed. The baby can be thrown in an accident.

●You don't need a bassinette or cradle for the early weeks. Young infants can sleep very well in laundry baskets or even unused dresser drawers (lined with blankets) pulled out and placed on the floor.

Clothing

●Consider investing in a sewing machine if you do not have access to one. You can make baby clothes from remnants, or even recycle some of your old clothing. Also, you can learn to remodel your clothes to conform to changes in styles and maybe even learn to make inexpensive gifts for others.

●Locate sources of secondhand baby clothing. Some people are very willing to give away clothes that are no longer needed. Ask your obstetrician, nurse midwife, pediatrician, childbirth educator, and La Leche League leader if they know of any sources. Also, there are secondhand clothing shops (sometimes called "consignment" shops) in some communities. Make a clothing swapping arrangement with other young families or check newspaper ads.

●Try to locate factory outlet stores in your area.

●When shopping for baby clothes, always purchase things the baby can grow into. For example, if your child can fit into a 6-month size now, buy a 9-month size or even a 12-month size. If too long, sleeves and pants legs can be rolled up to extend the use of garments. Stretch suits can be worn slightly large. Infants grow very quickly and most often outgrow rather than wear out their garments. Be aware that there is no standardization of sizing for infant clothes, and therefore one manufacture's 12-month size may equal another's 9-month size. Make sure you can return or exchange any garment you purchase.

●After your baby outgrows the newborn size of disposable diapers, consider using cloth diapers with plastic pants. The initial investment will be large, but if you have your own washing machine, the money you can save by not using disposables will more than compensate for the soap, hot water and electricity you will have to pay for.

●Take advantage of "end of season" clothing sales.

Baby Toys

●Make your own baby toys. (One good book on how to turn common household items into baby toys is called *Smart-Toys*, co-authored by Kent Burtt and Karen Kalkstein.)

●Be aware that many toys on the market appeal to parents more than babies. Do some reading on early infant development and consider the developmental value of any toy.

●Arrange to swap toys with a friend or relative who has a baby about the same age as yours. You can trade back in a few weeks when your baby will be interested in the "new toy."

Transportation

●If feasible, walk instead of driving or taking public transportation.

●Carpool to the supermarket, office, shopping center, etc.

Entertainment

●Locate sources of free entertainment—outdoor concerts, programs at the library, schools, museums, art shows, etc.

●Locate inexpensive movie theaters, half-price live theater shows, pre-theater reduced-rate restaurants, etc.

●Consider joining a local YM/YWCA or YM/YWHA, or a community center if it has programs that appeal to you. For a flat fee per year you will have access to many different types of activities.

●Explore places of historical interest in your community. These are often free or inexpensive.

●When you entertain and serve mixed drinks, it is not necessary to use the most expensive brands of liquor. Save your better brands for people who prefer non-mixed drinks. Also, consider serving punch made with fruit juices and vodka. (Also be aware that in some states, hosts are legally accountable if one of their guests leaves the party having had too much to drink, drives and is involved in an automobile accident.)

●Consider hosting a covered-plate supper where each couple contributes a part of the dinner.

●It is often less expensive to attend the movies or go out to dinner (even to fast-food places) in the middle of the week instead of on weekends. (Bringing your own snacks to the movies cuts costs even further.)

●To eliminate the cost of babysitters, form a co-op.

●While the initial investment is large, purchasing a video cassette recorder and recording or renting films you'd like to see may be less expensive in the long run than going to the movies. Also, if you have a VCR and can afford a video camera, it may be less expensive for you to make video tapes than movie films of the baby's early years.

VENDORS AND SOLICITORS

As new parents you will probably find yourselves deluged with calls and letters from merchants who want to congratulate you by selling you something. One new mother counted twenty-six phone calls from the same insurance company within a three-week period. Calls came as early as 9 A.M. and as late as 10 P.M.

One very effective way to get off the phone quickly, if you don't want to talk to the individual, is to tell the caller that you or your mate is a photographer, insurance agent, florist, or whatever is appropriate, depending on who is calling, and hang up. If you receive multiple calls from the same company, call or write to the president of the company (if you write, send a copy to the public relations department). Explain you feel you're being harassed and if possible include the name or names of any of the people who have called. (This helps a large company trace the calls to a particular division.)

Beware of merchants who send you letters inviting you to film showings or demonstrations of their products. Some employ scare tactics to induce you to buy merchandise you may not need or want by presenting you with information (possibly in the form of a film) to lead you to believe your child will be in grave danger if you use any brand of crib, highchair, car seat, etc., other than the one they are selling. Use a source such as *Consumer Reports* to check on the comparative safety of items you consider purchasing. Discount coupons and free gifts are other lures sales people will use to get you to visit their stores. No matter how attractive an offer may seem, do some comparison shopping before you purchase any item.

Beware of photographers who offer "free" pictures of your child. If you agree to it, the photographer will come to your home to photograph the baby. When the proofs are ready, you will have the choice of one "free" picture and then the "option" of selecting package deals including enlargements of other poses. If you elect to take just the free one, you suddenly may find there's a "service charge" involved and/or a nasty attitude or remark from the photographer. Besides, any pictures of your newborn may seem irresistible at any price, no matter how outrageous, and you may find you eventually purchase far more than you can afford. Sometimes the caller says that someone you know signed you up for the free photo, or that you won a drawing and are entitled to the free photograph. Usually, if pressed for information as to who supplied your name, the individual will admit that he or she does not have or cannot give you that information. In general, we have found that the best value in terms of quality, quantity, and lack of pressure to purchase comes from photographic packages offered at local department stores. You can often spot special offers for these services being advertised in local newspapers.

HOW TO HANDLE ADVICE

New parenthood often brings with it a certain vulnerability to advice and criticism. People who wouldn't consider commenting on your way of dress think nothing of telling you what they think about the way you are dressing your baby. Everyone—including strangers, friends who have no children, and relatives who haven't spoken to you in years—somehow seem compelled to share their knowledge and expertise, or lack thereof.

The problem is that all this advice comes at a time when most new parents are unsure of themselves and how to handle their babies. Therefore some view advice as a declaration that they are not totally succeeding at parenthood. Because for many parents having a baby represents the final step into adulthood, they especially resent any statements or actions they feel are indications that their parents or other relatives still view them as children. "If they don't accept that I'm an adult now that I'm a mother, when will they believe it?" is a common question new parents ask.

Understand that the postpartum period is a time for learning. Through trial and error and using common sense you learn how to care for your child. Of course, reading, interacting with other new parents, and listening to—although not always accepting—the advice of people you respect can give you insights into how to handle a situation, but in any new area, mistakes are made and should be expected. Advice does not necessarily mean that you have made a mistake, however; it only means that you are doing things differently from the advice giver.

Although you may not feel secure in the knowledge of your baby's habits and even your own needs during the first few weeks, this assurance will develop as you make the adjustments to new parenthood, as your baby becomes more predictable and as you see yourself handling the child successfully. You are at least as intelligent and have at least as much common sense as all the people giving you advice, and while they may have more experience handling children, they have no knowledge of your particular child or your views and needs.

Your friends and relatives raised their children the way they chose to and you have the right to do the same. The fact that a particular cradle, for example, has rocked several generations in your family, does not obligate you to use it, nor are you obliged to dress your baby the way your mate's mother dressed him or feed your baby the way your mother fed you. You have the right to determine what is and is not appropriate for your child, and this includes returning or not using gifts that you feel are not to your taste.

You are the baby's parent—not the woman behind the counter in the drugstore, not your aunt down the block, not your mother or mother-in-law. All decisions you make regarding your baby's welfare are based on what you and your mate feel is best for him or her and you need not justify your decisions to anyone.

We don't mean to imply that new parenthood is a time for breaking off relationships or of curtly informing people that their advice is unappreciated. Much good advice can be handed down from generation to generation and from peers who have been where you are now—all based on good old experience and trial and error. Be open and willing to hear it; consider it, learn from it—and that means learn what *will* be helpful for you and your baby and what *will not* necessarily be helpful or to your taste. You may be surprised at the gems of advice you can benefit from and be ever thankful for! However, all advice cannot possibly be taken and the advice givers must be made to understand this.

If you are confronted with people who persist in giving unsolicited advice, there are several strategies you can use to deal with it.

Perhaps the simplest thing to do is listen politely and ignore any advice that is not agreeable to you. This is the easiest way to handle strangers, acquaintances, and people who need never know you don't agree with them. You can even thank them for their concern and tell them you appreciate their help —this will make them feel good and you haven't lost a thing in the process. If you argue with such an individual, the result will be an exchange of bad feelings. You will rarely, if ever, see that person again, so why invite a confrontation?

If someone asks a question that you do not want to answer or you feel implies criticism ("How can you take the baby out on a terrible day like this!" or, "You're out *without* the baby? Where is he?"), reply in a polite yet firm manner that lets the individual know you are not intimidated. ("My pediatrician says taking the baby out during a snow storm is a great idea —it helps build stamina!" or "The baby is home taking care of his father. Isn't it wonderful to have helpful children?") Another strategy is to stare back wordlessly for several moments —implying you are shocked that someone could even think to ask that particular question in the first place.

Handling close friends and relatives requires a bit more tact. They are often in a position to know their advice is being ignored and may comment on that fact in addition to their original complaints. An effective way to phrase your response is "I know *you* believe that babies should be eating solid foods by three weeks, but I believe it's better to wait." Said firmly, this carries a lot of weight because it breaks down the objection/advice to a question of beliefs that are open to varying interpretation, not a dispute over facts. It is also an assertion of you, the individual, the adult, the parent—with beliefs of your own. You can also "blame" things on your baby nurse or pediatrician, if you choose to: "This is the way my doctor told me to do it." (You might even suggest they call your pediatrician and speak with him or her if they really give you a hard time. An understanding pediatrician will most probably be only too happy to assist!) You can also attribute your decisions to articles you've read (very few relatives will question your source). You can even imply that they are out of touch with current trends in baby care. "But that's the latest theory! You mean you didn't know?!"

If a situation develops where you absolutely must tell close relatives or friends that you don't want their advice, control, gifts, whatever, politely remind them that they had the freedom to choose their own path through new parenthood and you'd appreciate the same courtesy. Tell them that you appreciate their concern and understand that it comes out of love for you and your baby, but you are the baby's parent and the decisions are yours to make. If all else fails, you can simply resort to being straight, open, direct: "Thank you. But I'm going to do it my way."

HEALTH AND SAFETY HAZARDS

●Baby powder should not be freely showered on or near your baby's face. It is dangerous if inhaled and poses a threat to the eyes.

●All paints used where children will be present must be lead-free. Brain damage may result if babies and older children suck and chew on lead-painted surfaces.

●Crib slats which are more than 2⅜" apart have caused fatal injuries to babies. Also, be aware of product recalls when buying used baby furniture. When purchasing or borrowing any item for your baby, be sure that used car seats, etc. conform to *current* safety standards. Call the U.S. Consumer Product Safety Commission at 1-800-638-2772 for information on safety standards for cribs, toys and other accessories. The National Highway Traffic Safety Administration (1-800-424-9393) will provide the same information about car seats.

●If you are bottlefeeding, be sure the formula is refrigerated after the can is opened. After feeding the baby, discard any formula left in the bottle because bacteria may have begun to form in it. Never prop a bottle and leave your baby unattended during a feeding.

●Never leave your baby alone in the house.

●Never leave your baby unattended in a carriage or stroller outside a store or out of your sight.

●Never leave your baby unattended in the car—especially in the summer with the windows closed.

●Never leave your baby unattended on the changing table or on a bed or couch. If you must turn your head for a moment, place one hand on the baby's abdomen so you will feel the baby shift position or begin to roll.

●Never use plastic bags (such as those used by dry cleaning stores) for the baby to sleep on or near. He or she can pull it over the face and suffocate.

●Do not purchase dangerous pacifiers—those that are made of more than one piece and are pliable and small enough to become lodged in a baby's throat. A safe pacifier is one which is one piece and has a firm, round or oblong shield large enough that it cannot go beyond the baby's lips.

●After a feeding, burp the baby before placing him or her in the crib. Place the baby on his or her belly or side (propped against the bumper) so that if any milk is later burped up, it can drain out of the mouth. Lying face up, the baby is in danger of choking on whatever comes up.

●Do not place a pillow in the crib or carriage.

●Never feed your baby honey until he or she is over one year of age. It may contain botulism spores your infant's digestive system can't handle, resulting in serious illness.

●Do not rinse your baby under running water in the sink. Water pressure and temperature can change suddenly, or you can accidentally turn the faucet to hot.

●Never give your baby an alcohol rub. Inhaling alcohol fumes can be dangerous to the baby.

POSTPARTUM ADJUSTMENT RELATED TO HOSPITAL POLICIES

For the majority of mothers today, the postpartum period begins in the hospital. Your experience with that institution—the attitudes and policies of its medical and nursing staff—can influence the kind of postpartum period you will have. If your feelings weren't considered, if you are treated as just another bed in Room 211, if a nurse argues that the baby she is offering you to feed "*is* yours!" but you know it is not and she refuses to look at the ID anklet band to prove it, if you're told to stop crying because "you're not a baby and you should be happy you have a healthy child," if you are told by a nurse that "your poor baby must be starving, so stop breastfeeding and give him a bottle," such behavior can be traumatic and difficult to handle during the very shaky postpartum period.

If you have a good hospital experience (for example, if the nurses were supportive, understanding, gentle and kind; if hospital policies were "humanized"), be sure to write a letter to the hospital's administrator and the director of obstetrics telling them how pleased you were. If you were not pleased, also write a letter stating what bothered you and what you would like to see changed by the next time you have a baby.

Since it means so much for the postpartum parent to have a good start from the very beginning, look into the benefits offered by other hospitals. Join local groups working toward getting more family-centered maternity care policies adopted. Join with us, with childbirth educators, parents and health care professionals who are calling for the hospital policies listed below, which are being adopted in more and more hospitals across the country as they become responsive to consumer needs.

•Prenatal tour of labor and delivery rooms and nursery.

●Childbirth preparation classes available in hospital or at other certified classes—to prepare for vaginal or cesarean delivery, hospital procedures, the newborn and postpartum.

●Father or any other support person the woman chooses present in labor and delivery rooms.

●Availability of birthing room.

●Wrists unrestrained on the delivery table if the mother is awake.

●Baby examined within the mother's view in delivery room (or birthing room).

●Eye treatment to baby delayed until attempts at mother/infant and father/infant eye contact are made.

●Breastfeeding and/or holding and getting to know the baby in delivery room or recovery room.

●Rooming-in available.

●Sibling visitation permitted.

●All-day father visitation.

●Postpartum class or support group.

●Infant care classes.

●Supportive of breastfeeding.

Because yours may be an unexpected cesarean delivery, you may want to know that the hospital you will be using is sensitive to the needs of cesarean mothers. The following is a list of hospital policies recommended by cesarean support groups such as C/SEC.

●Tour of cesarean delivery room and nursery.

●Adequate preparation for cesarean childbirth in standard childbirth preparation classes (including indications, anesthetics, procedures before, during and after surgery).

●Special classes to prepare parents who *expect* cesarean delivery.

●Father or other support person present in cesarean delivery room.

●After delivery and if not in immediate danger, baby placed in father's or mother's arms or on mother's shoulder for contact and bonding.

●One or both arms free from restraint after delivery so that mother can touch newborn or hold him or her at her shoulder.

●Baby not routinely placed under observation for eight to twenty-four hours in a special care unit, but each baby's need for such care judged on his or her own condition at birth.

●Baby examined within the mother's view in delivery room.

●If father is not present for delivery, he is kept informed.

●Breastfeeding and/or holding and getting to know baby in delivery room or recovery room if mother feels up to it.

●Cesarean mother given a room with other cesarean mothers if at all possible.

●Cesarean mother given a room as close to the nursery as possible, minimizing extent of walking.

●Cesarean mother given an electronically operated bed, if at all possible, for greater self-mobility.

●Cesarean mother is given help with care of the infant at her bedside.

●Sibling visitation (cesarean mother usually remains in the hospital away from her other children for five to ten days).

●Ready availability of wheelchair for cesarean mother to visit her baby in intensive care unit if on another floor.

●All-day father visitation.

●Hospital stay shortened if desired and if medically permissible.

●Cesarean couples to be referred to local cesarean support groups.

4. Having a Second Child

PREPARING FOR POSTPARTUM

"Deciding to have a second child was much more difficult than deciding to have a first. I guess it's because this time I knew what I was getting into—the sleepless nights, the spit up. I wasn't sure I wanted that again."

"I felt excited about the new baby coming and the new dimension about to be added to our lives, but I was scared too. I feel such an intense love for our son and I know that things will change once the baby is here. I'm not sure how, though, and that's the scary part."

"I wonder if my children will be close friends growing up. I hope our decision about how far apart to space our children was the right one."

Parents decide to add a second (or subsequent) child to the family for many reasons. Some find that parenthood has added such a wonderful dimension to their lives and that raising children is so interesting and rewarding that they can't conceive of life without more. For others, the decision is motivated by doing what's "right" for the first child. These parents believe that being an only child is not advantageous and they want to avoid problems for their first by providing him or her with a sibling. Sometimes there is great family pressure to have a certain number of children and also, some religious beliefs preclude the use of contraception, which can result in larger families. Whatever the reason for deciding to increase the family size, many parents awaiting the birth of a second or subsequent child express feelings of apprehension about how the baby will change their lives, especially their relationship with their older children. Some wonder if perhaps they are making a mistake and fear that by having another child who will demand their attention, they will be taking something away from the firstborn. The implication in this concern is that this loss of attention will be harmful to their older child, that he or she will have great difficulty in making the adjustment or that he or she will be so angry with them that at best things will be difficult to deal with, at worst it would irreparably damage the parent/child relationship. Perhaps these parents also fear that they will not have enough love for two or more children. While some children do have a difficult time adjusting to the birth of a sibling because they are not particularly adaptable and/or because they are in a particularly dependent developmental stage, most adjust well, if handled with understanding and patience. And despite their fears, most parents find that they are so captivated by the new life they have created that the love flows to all of their children.

The issue of the age difference between the two children is one of concern to some—frequently based on desires to recreate the experience the parents had as children, or to make up for an experience that they desired but did not have. Some parents assume that because closely spaced children will have more experiences in common they will feel a greater sense of "kinship" and that this is desirable. While in many cases this is true, in others the relationship is not a close one and many siblings who are not close in age do feel close in spirit.

"My sister and brother are only two years apart. I'm six years younger than my brother. I feel they had an exclusive relationship that I missed out on."

"When my brother was born I was seven years old. I was involved in Little League and piano lessons. Yes, I was interested in his early years and enjoyed playing with him. I even got a kick out of sharing the results of my experiences with him and giving him my advice as an 'older' person. Now that he's finished college and getting married I find that we're getting even closer."

"My sister and I are a year apart but we're such different people and lead such different lives that I can't describe us as close. Yes, I love her, but she can't understand me and will never really be a friend."

Some parents have the opposite concern. They worry that children who are closely spaced will feel more competitive—initially for parental attention and time, ultimately for friends and position in school.

"My sister and I are two years apart. While we were best friends while we were growing up, we tended to have the same teachers in school. Susan was an excellent student—a fact my teachers never let me forget. I am determined not to force that experience on my children."

"My mother was always too busy with my younger sister that she never seemed to have time for me. I want to enjoy both my children and let them both enjoy me. We decided to space ours at least three years apart so one will be more independent when the other comes along."

The long-term effect of the spacing you choose probably depends more on the atmosphere in the family and the emphasis the parents place on family togetherness and unity than on whether the children are one or six years apart, although, undoubtedly, children who are very far apart in age do have less in common with their siblings. Also, it's important to remember that the personalities of the children themselves will play a vital role in determining what their relationship will be as they get older.

Another concern to some parents expecting a second child is the issue of time. This is especially true when both parents work outside the home. "Having one child takes up an incredible amount of time. How will I manage with two?"

"We constantly juggle our one child and two careers. It's going to get a lot harder when our second is born."

"My friends say that having a second child is not twice as much work, it's four times as much work."

Concerns about the health of the unborn child are also common.

"My first is so healthy—I almost feel I'm tempting fate by having another."

"My first child was so severely malformed, he died soon after birth. While the doctors assure me it's not likely to happen again—I worry."

Worries about the birth experience, especially if things did not go as planned the first time around, are also common.

"I will be trying for a vaginal delivery this time. When my daughter was born, the cord was wrapped around her neck and I had to have an emergency cesarean. I hope things are less complicated this time."

"I switched doctors because I really didn't like the way my first doctor dealt with me while I was in labor. I only hope that I am happy with my new doctor."

"I really wasn't much of a labor coach when Sharon gave birth to Steve. I found the whole experience difficult to deal with and wasn't as supportive as I should have been. I want to be with her and not let her down this time."

Many women express concern about whether the actual physical experience of labor and delivery will be different and about how well they will be able to cope if it is more difficult this time.

"I had such a rough time when my first was born. While I know that most second labors are shorter, several of my friends had harder deliveries with their second babies. I'm scared it might happen to me."

"I had an easy time giving birth to Keith. I almost feel I deserve to labor longer this time to make up for last."

How the older child will cope with Mommy's absence during labor and delivery and any hospital stay is also a frequent concern, as is meeting the needs of the older child during the exhausting weeks of new parenthood.

Facing up to these concerns and any others you may experience, discussing them and beginning to formulate strategies for dealing with them and any problems you can anticipate is the first step in preparing for postpartum the "second time around." In addition, there are several practical things you can do during pregnancy to help make life easier after the baby is born.

•*Get organized.* Reread the first section of "Preparing for Postpartum." The hints in that section are even more important when a second child is being added to the family.

•Plan in advance to spend a small part of each day—even if only ten minutes—with your other children, who will need your undivided attention at some time. If you do not make this resolution in advance, you may find it difficult to do it at the time.

•Plan to *rest* whenever the baby sleeps. If you have other children, it is not always feasible to nap when the baby does —especially if your toddler may dismantle your living room while you are sleeping! Perhaps you can rest in bed while playing quiet games, putting puzzles together or reading aloud with your other child or children. This serves two purposes at the same time: you get your rest while your children have your undivided attention. Another strategy is to ask whomever is helping with the household tasks—perhaps the children's grandparents—to play with the other child so you can rest.

•If your older child needs constant supervision, many parents find it helpful to have a supply of "new" toys and playthings on hand. (These can sometimes be obtained by dividing the child's toys into two groups and putting aside half the toys until the baby is born. If your child is under eighteen months old, he or she will probably think they're new when they "reappear.") Have these handy when you are feeding the baby, have no help in the house and need to entice the older child to stay in the room with you. (Garage sales and friends are a good source of inexpensive "extra" toys.) Stockpiling favorite toys in sections of the house where you are likely to feed the baby can also be helpful.

•If anyone asks what you would like as a baby gift, consider asking them to prepare dinner, do the shopping or laundry, or care for your older child for an afternoon or evening to enable you to get some sleep or spend some time with your mate.

•If you have a video cassette recorder, taping several episodes of your child's favorite programs and obtaining tapes of children's movies to keep your child occupied on tough days can help. (Note: We do *not* advocate the use of television as a constant babysitter for young children and intend this suggestion only as a "What do I do in a pinch?" type of idea.) Showing old tapes of your child as a baby is also frequently appealing to young children.

•Arranging for your older child to participate in a toddler playgroup or enrolling him or her in daycamp or nursery school *in advance of the baby's birth* will also result in more time for you to rest. Caution: Consider how your older child will get to and from the preschool, etc. before you make arrangements. The program that might optimally meet your youngster's social, intellectual and emotional needs might not be the most conveniently located. Perhaps arrangements can be made for someone else to transport your child—possibly a friend who asks what he or she can give you as a baby gift, or a parent whose child is in the same program. You can offer to reciprocate when the baby is several months old. Many parents are concerned that, if they put their older child in a playgroup, that child will feel left out of what is happening at home and feel he or she is no longer wanted around the house because the baby is there. While there will undoubtedly be a certain amount of curiosity about what is going on at home while they are away (sometimes manifested as a refusal to go to school when the baby is several weeks old), most children who are comfortably settled into a nurturing group environment before the birth of a sibling look forward to their time in preschool because there they are in their "own space" and the attention of the group and the adults responsible for their care is on him or her and not on the younger sibling. While the optimal arrangement is to begin the group situation several weeks or months in advance of the baby's birth, this is not always possible. (Many babies *are* born in September!) A child who is not particularly adaptable may need some extra help to adjust if this is the case. (Many children have little or no difficulty at all.)

PREPARING YOUR OLDER CHILD FOR THE BIRTH

Many parents wonder how soon to tell the older child that a sibling is expected. Our belief is that this depends to a great extent on the child's age. Remember, young children have difficulty understanding time concepts. For children who have not yet mastered what an hour, a day, or tomorrow means, the idea that a brother or sister will be born in six months can cause anxiety because they're not quite sure what a brother or sister is and because they're not quite sure *when* this unknown quantity will be arriving in their household. As the pregnancy progresses, the child will undoubtedly ask questions about why Mommy looks so different. Many parents find it helpful to use their child's questions as a guide and only provide the amount of information asked for in the question. If the child requires more information, or if you've answered the wrong question, he or she will probably continue to ask until satisfied. Be aware that many children also express an interest in how the baby got in Mommy's uterus in the first place. It's a good idea to think about how you will answer any questions about conception that may come up. And remember, think about your child's question before answering it. There's an old joke about a child who comes home and asks, "Daddy, where did I come from?" Daddy, who was a well-prepared, responsive individual (probably from reading this book) told his offspring in great detail all about eggs and sperm and how they get together. Wiping the perspiration off his brow and preparing to pat himself on the back for dealing with a difficult situation, he heard his child sigh and say, "That's strange. Mitchell said he came from Cleveland!"

Think about what your child really needs to know about having a brother or sister and how much he or she can understand. At some point you will have to discuss what will happen when you go to the hospital or birthing center, who will take care of him or her, how soon he or she will be able to visit you and how long you will be away. It can be helpful to take your child for a visit to the birth site so he or she will have a visual image of where the baby will be born. If the hospital or center does not allow siblings to visit, bring them to see the outside of the building. If your child is old enough, perhaps he or she can participate in the decision about who will care for him or her. Have these discussions no earlier than several weeks before the birth unless your child raises these issues sooner. In the case of a young child, you might incorporate into your play with the child this information about what will happen when Mommy goes into labor. You might say, "Let's pretend Mommy is going to the hospital . . ." and go through the motions of whatever will accompany the event, such as taking a favorite toy and pretending to get in the car to go to Grandma's.

Be prepared for a certain amount of anxiety in your child as the event grows nearer. Think about how hard it is for adults to understand and prepare for the birth of a baby and how much more difficult this must be for a small child. If your child is old enough to understand, it might be helpful to reassure him or her that, yes, things will change, but that you will all work together to help each other deal with whatever changes occur. Adding a baby to the family may diminish the time you will have to spend with him or her but will never take away the love you have. In time, as he or she adjusts to the reality of the baby, this anxiety will fade.

Some parents ask if it is appropriate to buy a special gift for the older child, a "big brother or sister" present or a gift from the baby. Most older children realize that babies don't buy gifts—if not at the outset, then when Mommy and baby arrive at home and they realize how limited in abilities their new siblings actually are. If the parents enjoy shopping for and giving the child a present, that is, of course, fine, but it probably will not make the adjustment to having a sibling any easier for the child involved.

In the final analysis, a warm, nurturing atmosphere in the home—helping your child to feel valued and important as a unique individual, listening to your child's questions and doing your best to identify and meet his or her needs at each stage of development—is the best way to prepare a child for the birth of a sibling.

FEELINGS AFTER THE BIRTH

(Note: We suggest you reread Part II, "After the Birth" for information about physiological changes, procedures involving the mother, etc.)

Most second-time parents feel confident about their ability to handle a baby. Through the experience of caring for and dealing with their first child, they learned that babies do not "break" and they established their own methods of dealing with the day-to-day problems of childcare. Consequently, if this is your second time around, you are probably less worried about the effects of every decision you make, what to do when the baby cries, whether or not to take the baby out in inclement weather, whether or not to give him or her a rattle that dropped on the floor without sterilizing it first, etc. You know that children eventually do recover from colds and you are probably not as concerned about the color, frequency, and texture of each bowel movement as you may have been with your first child. You are more relaxed about everyday childcare matters. But while the practical aspects of childraising may be easier, other things are more difficult.

The second-time mothers who shared their feelings with us

almost unanimously expressed feelings of being torn apart in several directions and of having little or no time for their own needs. You may find you have more difficulty juggling priorities after your second than you experienced after your first child was born. You may be troubled by having to decide who should come first—the new baby, the older child, your mate, yourself. You'll probably find your relationship with your older child changes somewhat after the birth of your second —that the same quality of closeness no longer exists between mother and child. Some mothers even express the feeling that they have lost a little friend. You may find yourself feeling guilty that you don't have as much time to spend with the second as you had with the first, and/or that you are now neglecting the first because the second demands so much time. Some women experience "down" feelings to a greater degree after their second baby is born than they experienced after the birth of their first. This can be attributed in part to additional fatigue and isolation, but women who plan no additional children also mention a sense of loss—a feeling that their child-bearing years are over and another chapter in their lives has closed. You may find you worry about whether or not you'll have enough love for both children. It may seem hard to believe during pregnancy or in the early postpartum weeks, but the overwhelming majority of mothers find that they do.

Fatigue is especially common in mothers whose children are spaced close together. Caring for an infant and a toddler can be difficult and time-consuming. It's hard to sit quietly and feed a newborn when you know your toddler is emptying your spice rack, for example, and keeping track of the diaper needs of two children certainly isn't easy. While parents said that the first year after the second child was born was rough, they pointed to the fact that their closely spaced children grew up as playmates and entertained each other in the years that followed.

Parents who spaced their children several years apart often said they appreciated being able to watch their first child grow as an individual before the second came along. Also, due to the age difference, childcare was easier because the older child was more independent. But some—especially those with children spaced more than three years apart—expressed the sentiment that, after growing out of the routine baby-care stage involving spending more time in the house, it was difficult to get used to being "tied down" again. They had grown used to uninterrupted nights of sleep and now had to adjust to feeding a baby in the middle of the night again. They had grown used to easily understanding their older child and anticipating his or her needs and now had to adapt to learning to "read" a baby's cries again. They had rediscovered quiet hours together after their child had gone to sleep and now had to readjust to the temporary chaos an infant brings. This was not easy and was sometimes accompanied by resentment. After all, they'd been through it before; they'd "paid their dues." Somehow going through it again seemed unfair to these parents. Perhaps they'd forgotten how time-consuming a newborn actually is, and experiencing it all again came as a shock.

After a second child is born, family dynamics change once again. Parents have to adjust to considering the needs of two children at very different stages of development. At the same time, they have to adjust to having even less time together. It suddenly becomes more difficult to find the time and place to be alone. You can't exactly make love in the living room on a Saturday morning while the baby is asleep in your room, because, chances are, your oldest will be on the couch watching *Sesame Street*. Most second-time fathers complain that their mates are busier, more tired, and less available, even for simple conversations, after the birth of the second child. Many fathers describe a new closeness developing between them and the older child. Very often, the father spends more time with the older child after the second is born—playing together after work or going on evening or day-long excursions. Men who couldn't relate to their children as infants suddenly seem to "rediscover" them at this time, perhaps because they see how much the older child has grown in comparison to the baby. Maybe they appreciate this more communicative stage. While many parents are struck by how much older their first child seems after their second is born, there is a danger in assuming that he or she is more grown-up than you might otherwise expect. It's important to remember how old he or she actually is and to base your expectations of his or her behavior accordingly.

Many second-time parents are surprised at how different their children are. While the first may have been a calm, passive baby who adapted to new situations quite easily and slept most of the time, it's quite possible the second is highly reactive, constantly in motion—the exact opposite of the older sibling. If your first slept through the night at six weeks, you might expect the second will do the same and be sorely disappointed if he or she does not. It's important to realize that each child is an individual with a distinct set of behavioral characteristics and pattern of development. Comparing their rates of growth and expounding on who rolled over, crawled, etc., at what age, can only serve to intensify any feelings of rivalry or competition that already exist in the older child.

Because of these differences it's entirely possible that you may feel closer to one child than the other. Perhaps you find that one child's characteristic response pattern is more compatible with your own, perhaps he or she resembles a relative you were especially fond of, or perhaps the child is going through a growth stage you find particularly cute and appealing. It is possible that this preference will shift back and forth from one to the other as both grow and develop. Understand that you are only human and that while you may try to treat both your children equally, this is rarely achieved to perfection.

HELPING YOUR OLDER CHILD ADJUST

The adjustment to having a second child in the house is greatly complicated by the fact that not only do you have your own reactions as parents to deal with, but also you have to consider the feelings and reactions of your older child as well. You may find that on the surface he or she seems to accept the new baby and even express a good deal of outward affection for the new sibling. He or she may be anxious to help you with baby-care tasks and may seem not to miss being the center of your attention. He or she may express jealousy and/or resentment subtly—by squeezing the baby a "little too hard" or by knocking into the baby's bassinet "accidentally." Diapers, bottles, etc. may mysteriously "disappear" or "spill over." The older child may suddenly get into more mischief than you ever believed possible—playing with items he or she knows are forbidden, emptying cabinets he or she has long ago learned are off-limits, even talking back when reprimanded—but insisting all the while that he or she loves the new baby. Other children are more obvious about their feelings—hitting the baby and/or the mother and saying, "I hate him" or "I hate you," throwing tantrums, etc. One young lady even directly informed her parents very politely that she'd had enough of her new brother. "It's time to take him back to the hospital now." The reactions may not begin immediately and may start as long as a few weeks or several months after the baby is born. You may find they are strongest when the older child watches you feed the baby and sees the look of love on your face as you cuddle the infant close to you.

It's important for both parents to help the child realize that he or she is entitled to feelings of anger, hostility, resentment, etc. and to show him or her appropriate ways to express these strong, uncomfortable feelings. After all, the older child *has* been displaced to some degree. You don't have as much time to spend with him or her exclusively as you both had been used to. But while it is all right to have these feelings, the older child must learn that you will *not* permit him or her to take them out physically on you or the baby by hitting, biting, misbehaving, etc. Depending on his or her age and level of comprehension, let the child know you understand how he or she feels and let it be known that you too miss the time you formerly spent alone with him or her. Indicate that hurtful actions are unacceptable, not angry feelings. Try to get the older child to verbalize these feelings if at all possible, and if he or she does say, "I hate the baby" or "I hate you," try not to respond with "Oh now, I'm sure you don't hate him. You're a good brother" or "I know you really love me." Chances are that, inside, the child is feeling guilt for his or her negative feelings or actions. Your negating what he or she tells you only reinforces the idea that the child is bad for having these feelings. Acknowledge that you understand how he or she is feeling. Respond, "I see you are feeling unhappy because we can't spend as much time together as we used to." Or "You're so angry with the baby you hate him." Let the child know that you accept him or her as is, that negative feelings are allowed, and that he or she can feel free to express them to you without fear of belittlement or punishment. Acknowledge that strong negative feelings may require physical expression and suggest that your child punch his or her pillow, beat up a punching bag or go into his or her room, close the door and scream until he or she feels better. This can go a long way toward preventing or stopping any inappropriate physical expression of hostility.

Some parents find it helpful to present their older child with a set of small dolls or stick figures that can represent "Mommy," "Daddy," "baby," "big sister," etc. Get the child to play with the dolls and say, "Here's the baby doll crying again just when the big sister and the mommy were going to read a book [or whatever scenario you choose to present]. How do you think that big sister feels now? What do you think she'd like to do to that baby? Let's help her deal with her feelings better." Children will often talk about their own feelings and reactions and can be helped to resolve difficulties through the medium of play.

If at all possible, offer a solution to problems that your older child presents. For example, tell the child that if he or she helps you fold the laundry, make the beds, clear the table, etc., you'll have a little more free time to spend with him or her. Then follow through and spend the time you saved together! Or forget about the housework entirely—tell the child that being together is more important to you than the laundry and that you will put it aside for a few moments sometimes and play together.

Realize also that a lot of what may appear to be mischief may in reality be only testing behavior. When something new occurs, children have a tendency to test what this change will mean in terms of what they will be permitted to do. For example: "I have a new sister. What has changed? Can I now write on the walls with crayons? What will happen if I do? Will Daddy still say 'No' and take my crayons away, or will there be different consequences?" It is important and reassuring to enforce the same limits you had established before the baby's birth. Many parents of older children find it helpful to tell their children in the appropriate context that the rules of the household have not changed, that they will not be allowed to destroy property, to hurt themselves, or others, etc., and that if they have trouble remembering the rules or keeping themselves safe, you will have to help them behave by restricting their activities.

Realize that your older child may temporarily regress to an

earlier stage of development when your baby is born. If toilet-trained, he or she may begin to have "accidents." If drinking exclusively from a cup, he or she may demand breast or bottle. Try to handle this with the understanding that it is not "misbehavior" but merely an expression of the child's desire to be a baby again in order to have your total attention (or perhaps testing behavior to see what will happen if he or she insists on bottle- or breastfeeding).

When you feed the baby, try to have books or puzzles nearby so you can cuddle the older one and read or play with him or her while you care for your infant. If he or she also wants breast or bottle, you'll have to decide how to handle the situation based on what you feel comfortable with. You might tell the older child he or she is so grown-up now because he or she can drink from a cup. (If you ask the older child, "What do you want to be, a baby?" you just might get the answer, "Yes!") Tell the child that you used to feed him or her this way too and that when the baby gets older he or she will also drink from a cup. Some breastfeeding experts feel that if the older child wants to nurse and you let him or her try once or twice, the child will quickly lose interest because it will no longer have a "forbidden" quality. This might be worth trying. However, if your child is at an age where you feel that this might be inappropriate, some mothers find it helpful to express some breastmilk into a glass for the older child to taste and thereby satisfy his or her curiosity. Stress the advantages of being older. Point out the activities the child can perform because he or she is no longer a baby, the privileges which the tiny sibling does not have, the things an older child does with you and enjoys that the baby cannot share. Acknowledge that at times we all feel a need to be "babied" and tell your child that if he or she feels that way, let you know and you will give him or her some extra cuddling.

In addition, arrange to spend some time with your older child alone. This may be no more than fifteen minutes, or an hour or two per day in the early weeks. Tell him or her that you are going to have this time together and let him or her select the activity you'll share—reading, coloring, playing with clay, singing, etc. Let the child know *approximately* when this time will be so that he or she can look forward to it and see a progression of events that leads to time with you. For example, say that your time together will begin when the baby falls asleep after lunch and will last as long as the baby naps, or whatever. You can remind him or her of this as the day goes on and say how much you are looking forward to it. Don't specify a particular time of day, because something may come up at that particular moment to postpone your time together. Even if you've hired a sitter to take care of the baby while you spend time with your older child, tell him or her you'll spend time together "after Mrs. Smith arrives," not stating a specific hour.

As the baby get older, try to arrange for an afternoon away from the house once a week with the older child alone (and, also, an afternoon or evening by yourself!). Make it a "trip" day—take him or her to places he or she would find interesting—a fire house, a bakery, the zoo, behind the scenes at the post office, etc. You can do this together with your mate or each of you can take the child on excursions individually. You might even include lunch out at a fast-food place, or take a picnic lunch with you! One father told us of a trip to the airport to "touch a plane." The airline representative actually took the child onboard and into the cockpit while the father had to wait behind security lines. His child was thrilled!

Try to make the older child responsible for one aspect of the baby's care, if he or she accepts it and doesn't consider it an imposition. Even eighteen-month-olds can make wonderful diaper monitors. Put the diapers on a shelf he or she can reach and tell the child that, whenever the baby needs to be changed, it's his or her job to fetch a diaper (or petroleum jelly, or whatever). Make sure he or she hears you telling other people—on the phone or in person—how lucky you are that he or she is around to help you with the baby. When people call or visit, try to tell them about *his* or *her* latest achievements before going into a discussion of what the baby is doing.

Some second-time parents try to have a supply of small wrapped gifts on hand so that if a guest arrives with a present for the baby, the older child has something to unwrap as well. While this can be embarrassing to the guest, these parents feel that their child isn't old enough to understand why he or she isn't getting gifts too and that the consideration of his or her feelings should come first. Other parents prefer that their children learn from the beginning that there are occasions when he or she will get gifts and times the baby will get gifts. We feel the decision should be made based on your child's age, your preference, and his or her level of understanding. In either case, tell visitors in advance that you'd appreciate it if they would spend some time with the older child first before running in to see the baby. In other words, try to include the older child and make him or her feel important whenever possible. Realize that your older child has been used to being the center of attention and it's unfair to ask him or her to relinquish this position suddenly and entirely. On the other hand, don't spend so much time catering to the older child for fear that you'll hurt his or her feelings that you neglect the baby! Your older child must realize that the baby is important and loved, that the baby is an *addition* to the family, not a *replacement* for him or her.

While the adjustment to having a second child in the house is complicated by the need to identify and take into consideration the feelings and needs of the older child in addition to the needs and feelings of the parents, it is made easier by the knowledge that children grow up very quickly. Parents of second children realize that in time the new-baby period will end. All too soon their infant will be a toddler, then a preschooler. While the postpartum period marks the end of being a single-child family, it also marks the beginning of a new and rewarding way of life. Most parents who've made the decision to add a child to their already existing family are glad they did.

RESOURCE ORGANIZATIONS

For Parent and Expectant Parent Information

ASPO/Lamaze (American Society for Psychoprophylaxis in Obstetrics, Inc.) 1840 Wilson Blvd., Suite 204, Arlington, Va. 22201 (800-368-4404)

ICEA (International Childbirth Education Association), P.O. Box 20852, Milwaukee, Wis. 53220

Maternity Center Association, 48 E. 92 St., N.Y., N.Y. 10028

National Organization of Mothers of Twins Clubs, 5402 Amberwood Lane, Rockville, Md. 20853

C/SEC (Cesarean/Support-Education-Concern), 22 Forest Road, Framingham, Mass. 01701 (617-877-8266)

La Leche League International, 9616 Minneapolis Ave., Franklin Park, Ill. 60131 (312-455-7730)

Parents Anonymous, 250 W. 57 Street, N.Y., N.Y. 10019 (800-462-6406)

Children's Bureau, U.S. Department of Health, Education, and Welfare (free literature), Washington, D.C. 20201

Institute for Childbirth and Family Research, 2522 Dana St., Suite 201, Berkeley, Calif. 94702

Postpartum Education for Parents (PEP), c/o Jane Honikman, 927 N. Kellogg, Santa Barbara, Calif. 93111

Sex Information and Education Council of the U.S. (SEICUS) (Information Service), 1715 Broadway, N.Y., N.Y. 10003 (212-673-3850)

Planned Parenthood, 810 7th Avenue, N.Y., N.Y. 10019

Zero Population Growth, Los Altos, Calif. 94022

Association for Voluntary Sterilization (AVS), 122 E. 42 Street, N.Y., N.Y. 10168 (212-573-8350)

National Cesarean Prevention Movement, P.O. Box 152, University Station, Syracuse, N.Y. 13210 (315-424-1942)

National Institutes of Health (NIH), 9000 Rockville Pike, Bethesda, Md. 20205

American College of Obstetricians and Gynecologists (ACOG), 600 Market Ave., S.W., Washington, D.C. 20024-2588

American College of Nurse Midwives, 1522 K St., N.W., Suite 1120, Washington, D.C. 20005

HELP (Support for Herpes Victims), P.O. Box 100, Palo Alto, Calif. 94302

NAPSAC (National Association of Parents and Professionals for Safe Alternatives in Childbirth), P.O. Box 267, Marble Hill, Mo. 63764

Parents Without Partners, 7910 Woodmont Ave., Bethesda, Md. 20814 (301-654-8850)

TWYCH (Traveling With Young Children), 80 8th Ave., N.Y., N.Y. 10011

Special Delivery/Special Handling, 147-32 15 Drive, White-stone, N.Y. 11357

International Association of Infant Massage Instructors, National Stress and Health Center, N.T. Enloe Memorial Hospital, W. 5th Ave., Esplanade, Chico, Calif. 95926

Family Resource Coalition, 320 N. Michigan Ave., Chicago, Ill. 60601

For Bereaved Parents

Compassionate Friends, P.O. Box 1347, Oakbrook, Ill. 60521 (312-323-5010)

SHARE (miscarriage & neonatal deaths), St. John's Hospital, 800 E. Carpenter, Springfield, Ill. 62769 (217-544-6464)

Aiding a Mother Expecting Neo-Natal Death (AMEND)— also known as The Life Seekers—c/o Mrs. Maureen Connelly, 4324 Berrywick Terrace, St. Louis, Mo. 63128

For Infant and Child Health Information

American Academy of Pediatrics, P.O. Box 72103, Chicago, Ill. 60678

The National Foundation–March of Dimes, 1275 Mamaroneck Ave., White Plains, N.Y. 10605 (914-428-7100)

United Cerebral Palsy Association, 66 E. 34 St., N.Y., N.Y. 10016 (212-481-6300)

Mental Retardation Institute of New York Medical College, West Medical Center, Valhalla, N.Y. 10595

Association for Help of Retarded Children, 200 Park Ave. So., N.Y., N.Y. 10003 (212-254-8203)

National Council on Family Relations, 1219 University Ave., S.E., Minneapolis, Minn. 55414

American National Red Cross, 17th & D Streets, Washington, D.C. 20006

Society for Protection of Unborn Through Nutrition (SPUN), 17 North Wabash, Suite 603, Chicago, Ill. 60602

American Foundation for the Blind, 15 W. 16 St., N.Y., N.Y. 10011 (212-620-2000)

Children in Hospitals, 31 Wilshire Park, Needham, Maine 02192

Down's Syndrome Congress, 16470 Ronnies Drive, Mishawaka, Ind. 41544

National Association for Down's Syndrome, 682 Ashland, River Forest, Ill. 60305

Sickle Cell Disease Foundation, 209 W. 125 Street, N.Y., N.Y. 10027 (212-865-1201)

Action for Child Transportation Safety (ACTS), 400 Central Park West, Apt. 15P, N.Y., N.Y. 10025

Jewish Board of Family & Children's Services, 120 W. 57 St., N.Y., N.Y. 10019 (212-582-9100)

National Institute for Mental Health, 5600 Fishers Lane, Rockville, Md. 20857

Family Service Association of America, 44 E. 23 St., N.Y., N.Y. 10010 (212-674-6100)

National SIDS [Sudden Infant Death Syndrome] Foundation, Two Metro Plaza, Suite 205, 8240 Professional Pl., Landover, Md. 20785 (800-221-SIDS), or in Maryland: 301-459-3388 (for parent support)

National Center for Prevention of SIDS (referral & information service), 330 N. Charles St., Baltimore, Md. 21201 (301-547-0300)

Spina Bifida Association of America, 343 South Dearborn St., Chicago, Ill. 60604 (800-621-3141), or in Illinois: 312-663-1562

Epilepsy Institute (information & referrals), 67 Irving Place, N.Y., N.Y. 10003 (212-677-8550)

National Multiple Sclerosis, 205 East 42 St., N.Y., N.Y. 10017 (212-986-3240)

Arthritis Foundation, 1314 Spring Street, N.W., Atlanta, Ga. 30309 (404-872-7100)

National Center on Child Abuse & Neglect, P.O. Box 1182, Washington, D.C., 20013 (202-245-2840)

Consumer Product Safety Commission (CPSC), Washington, D.C. 20207 (800-638-2772)

National Committee for Prevention of Child Abuse (NCPCA), 332 South Michigan Ave., Suite 950, Chicago, Ill. 60604 (312-663-3520)

BIBLIOGRAPHY

Books

American Red Cross. *Preparation for Parenthood: Instructor's Guide*. The American Red Cross: 1976.

Annas, George J. *The Rights of Hospital Patients*. New York: Avon, 1975.

Apgar, Virginia, and Joan Beck. *Is My Baby All Right? A Guide to Birth Defects*. New York: Trident, 1973.

Arnstein, Helene S. *The Roots of Love: Helping Your Child Learn to Love in the First Three Years of Life*. New York: Bantam, 1977.

Ashdown-Sharp, Patricia. *A Guide to Pregnancy and Parenthood for Women on Their Own*. New York: Vintage Books, 1977.

Benson, Barbara, and Ben Bova. *Survival Guide for the Suddenly Single*. New York: St. Martin's, 1974.

Biller, Henry, and Dennis Meredith. *Father Power*. New York: McKay, 1974.

Bing, Elisabeth. *Moving Through Pregnancy*. New York: Bantam, 1975.

____, and Libby Colman. *Making Love During Pregnancy*. New York: Bantam, 1977.

Boston Women's Health Collective. *Our Bodies, Ourselves*. New York: Random House, 1978.

Brazelton, T. Berry. *Infants and Mothers: Differences in Development*. New York: Delacorte Press, 1969.

Brewster, Dorothy P. *You Can Breastfeed Your Baby in Special Situations*. Emmaus, Pa.: Rodale Press, 1979.

Burtt, Kent G., and Karen Kalkstein. *SmartToys for Babies from Birth to Age Two*. New York: Harper & Row, 1981.

Caplan, Frank, ed. *The First Twelve Months of Life*. New York: Grossett & Dunlap, 1973.

Cahill, Mary Ann. *The Heart Has Its Own Reasons, Mothering Wisdom for the 1980s*. Franklin Park, Ill.: La Leche League International, 1983.

Chess, Stella, et al. *Your Child is a Person*. New York: Viking, 1975.

Dodson, Fitzhugh. *How to Parent*. New York: Signet, 1970.

Donovan, Bonnie. *The Cesarean Birth Experience: A Comprehensive Reassuring and Practical Guide for Parents and Professionals*. Boston: Beacon Press, 1977.

Eiger, Marvin, M.D., and Sally Olds. *The Complete Book of Breastfeeding*. New York: Bantam, 1973.

Fitzpatrick, Elise, et al. *Maternity Nursing* (12th ed.). Philadelphia: Lippincott, 1971.

Galinsky, Ellen. *Between Generations: The Six Stages of Parenthood*. New York: Times Books, 1981.

Gerard, Alice. *Please Breast-Feed Your Baby*. New York: Hawthorne, 1970.

Guttmacher, Alan. *Pregnancy, Birth and Family Planning*. New York: Signet, 1973.

Hellman, Louis M., and Jack A. Pritchard. *Williams Obstetrics* (14th ed.). New York: Appleton-Century-Crofts, 1971.

Heslin, Jo-Ann, and Anne Natow. *No Nonsense Nutrition for Your Baby's First Year*. New York: Simon & Schuster, 1978.

Kenda, Margaret Elizabeth, and Phyllis S. Williams. *The Natural Baby Food Cookbook*. New York: Avon Books, 1972.

Kippley, Sheila. *Breast-feeding and Natural Child Spacing. The Ecology of Natural Mothering*. New York: Harper & Row, 1974.

Klaus, Marshall H., and J.N. Kennell. *Maternal-Infant Bonding*. St. Louis: C.V. Mosby Co., 1976.

Leboyer, Frederick. *Birth Without Violence*. New York: Knopf, 1975.

La Leche League International. *The Womanly Art of Breastfeeding*. Franklin Park, Ill.: La Leche League International, 1963, 1980.

Levine, James A. *Who Will Raise the Children? New Options for Fathers (and Mothers)*. New York: Bantam, 1977.

McBride, Angela Barron. *The Growth and Development of Mothers*. New York: Harper & Row, 1973.

McCauley, Carole Spearin. *Pregnancy After 35*. New York: E.P. Dutton, 1976.

McDonald, Linda. *The Joy of Breastfeeding*. South Pasadena: Oaklawn Press, 1978.

Masters, W.H. and Virginia Johnson. *Human Sexual Response*. Boston: Little, Brown & Co., 1966.

Montagu, Ashley. *Touching: The Human Significance of the Skin*. New York: Columbia University Press, 1971.

Noble, Elizabeth. *Essential Exercises for the Childbearing Year*. Boston: Houghton Mifflin, 1976.

Peck, Ellen. *The Baby Trap*. New York: Bernard Geis Associates, 1971.

Pryor, Karen. *Nursing Your Baby*. New York: Pocket Books, 1975.

Ribble, Margaret A. *The Rights of Infants*. New York: Signet, 1965.

Rozdilsky, Mary Lou, and Barbara Banet. *What Now?* New York: Charles Scribner's Sons, 1975.

Salk, Lee. *Preparing for Parenthood*. New York: McKay, 1974.

____, and Rita Kramer. *How to Raise a Human Being*. New York: Random House, 1979.

Schiff, Harriet Sarnoff. *The Bereaved Parent*. New York: Crown, 1977.

Schneider, Vimala. *Infant Massage: A Handbook for Loving Parents*. New York: Bantam, 1982.

Spock, Benjamin. *Baby and Child Care*. New York: Pocket Books, 1976.

Thevenin, Tine. *The Family Bed: An Age-Old Concept in Child Rearing*. Minneapolis: Tine Thevenin, 1976.

Thompson, Judi. *Healthy Pregnancy the Yoga Way*. New York: Dolphin Books, 1977.

Tucker, Tarvez. *Birth Control*. New Canaan, Conn.: Tobey Publishing, 1975.

Urbanowski, Ferris, and Balaram. *Yoga for New Parents*. New York: Harper's Magazine Press, 1975.

Walton, Vickie E. *Have it Your Way*. Seattle: Henry Philips Publishing Co., 1977.

White, Burton. *The First Three Years of Life*. Englewood Cliffs: Prentice-Hall, 1975.

Worth, Cecilia. *Breastfeeding Basics*. New York: McGraw-Hill, 1983.

Articles and Pamphlets

Admire, Gay, R.N., A.C.C.E., and Sherry Guyton, A.C.C.E. "Tips for Working Mothers Who Are Breastfeeding." *Genesis*. Oct./Nov. 1984.

American College of Obstetricians and Gynecologists. "Vaginal Birth After Cesarean Is Focus of New Guidelines." *Newsletter*: Practice Perspectives. XXIX (February 1985): 2.

———. "Guidelines for Vaginal Delivery After Previous Cesarean Birth." *Newsletter*: Practice Perspectives. XXIX (February 1985): 2.

———. "Benefits, Risks and Effectiveness of Contraception."

American Health Consultants, Inc. *Contraceptive Technology Update*. Atlanta, Ga., January 1985.

Arieti, Silvano, and Eugene B. Brody, eds. "The Post Partum Period." *American Handbook of Psychiatry*, 2nd ed., I. New York: Basic Books, Inc., 1974, 583.

ASPO/Lamaze. "Working Parents." *Genesis, Special Issue* (Oct./Nov. 1984): 5.

Auerback, Stevanne. "All About Day Care—How to Find High Quality Day Care to Suit Your Resources and Satisfy Child's Needs." *Parents Magazine*, LII (April 1977): 40, 46.

Bernstein, Anne C., Ph.D. "How to Fight Fair," *Parents* (February 1985): 54–55.

Cane, Aleta Feinsod. "Frankly Speaking—A Pamphlet for Cesarean Couples." Framingham, Mass.: C/SEC, 1976.

"Car Safety Restraints for Children." *Consumer Reports*, 42 (June 1977): 314–316.

Chan, Janet. "Help for Bereaved Parents." *McCall's*, CV (October 1977): 114.

Child Study Association of America, Wel/Met Incorporated. *Family Life and Child Development: A Selective, Annotated Bibliography*. Child Study Press, 1976.

Citizens' Committee on Infant Nutrition. *White Paper on Infant Feeding Practices*. Washington, D.C.: Center for Science in the Public Interest, 1974.

Cohen, Nancy Wainer. "Minimizing Emotional Sequellae of Cesarean Childbirth." *Birth and the Family Journal* 4 (Fall 1977): 114–119.

Conner, Beth Shearer. "Teach About Cesarean Birth in Traditional Childbirth Class." *Birth and the Family Journal* 4 (Fall 1977): 107–113.

Countryman, Betty Ann, R.N., M.N. "Breastfeeding and Jaundice." *Information Sheet No. 10*, La Leche League International, June 1978.

Coyle, Thomas F. "You're Pregnant? Had a Baby? Exercise, M'Lady!" *Mothers' Manual* 13 (May/June 1977): 40.

Dunne, Kathy. "Sexuality During Pregnancy, Post Partum." *Northern Illinois Chapter A.S.P.O. Newsletter*, July/August 1977.

Edwards, Margot. "The Crisis of the Fourth Trimester." *Birth and The Family Journal*, 1 (Winter 1973–74): 19–22.

Enkin, Murray. "Having a Section is Having a Baby." *Birth and the Family Journal*, 4 (Fall 1977): 99–102.

Fein, Robert A. "The First Weeks of Fathering: The Importance of Choices and Supports for New Parents." *Birth and the Family Journal*, 3 (Summer 1976): 53–58.

Flaste, Richard. "Exploring Those Disturbing After Baby Blues." *New York Times*, December 10, 1976, B12.

Fosburgh, Lacey. "Study of New Parents' Looks at the Impact of Baby's Arrival on the Marriage." *New York Times*, January 7, 1978, p. 10.

Franz, Kittie B., R.N., C.P.C.P. "Managing Nipple Problems." *Reprint No. 11*, La Leche League International, March 1982.

Froehlich, Edwina. "Thoughts About Weaning." *Information Sheet 125*, La Leche League International, revised 1973.

____. "Baby's First Solid Food." *Information Sheet 105*, La Leche League International, revised 1975.

Gilbert, Ralph. "Intensive Care Nurseries." *American Baby*, August 1977.

Gilbert Rose. "Decorating and Equipping Your Nursery." *Daily News*, September 25, 1979.

Gochros, Jean S. "Why Fathers Get Jealous." *American Baby*, January 1978.

Gordon, James S., and Celso-Ramon Garcia. "The I.U.D. in Conception Control," *The Female Patient* 3 (April 1978): 43.

Health, Education and Welfare Office of Child Development. "Guide for Working Mothers." *Mothers' Manual*, 13 (September/October 1977): 30–32, 42.

Hechinger, Fred M. "Looking at Quality of Child Care for Its

Own Sake." *New York Times*, February 26, 1985, C11.

Hickernell, Barbara K., ed. *Cesarean Childbirth—A Handbook for Parents*. Westchester: A.S.P.O., 1977.

Hillard, Paula Adams, M.D. "Circumcision." *Parents' Magazine*, April 1984, p. 132.

Hyans, Holly. "A Dozen Ways to Solve Your Day-Care Problems." *McCall's* CV (October 1977): 112–113.

Jewett, Jean. "What Every Parent Should Know About Auto Safety." *American Baby*, September 1976.

Jimenez, Sherry L.M., R.N. "Beating the Baby Blues." *American Baby*, September 1981.

Kunz, Kathleen, "The Day Care Search," *Mothers Today* (March/April 1985): 21–24.

La Leche League International. "Sore Breast: What, Why and What to Do." *Information Sheet 12*, March 1975, Sept. 1977.

———. "P.C.B.s and Mother's Milk." *Information Sheet 78c*, February 1977.

———. "P.B.B.s and Mother's Milk." *Information Sheet 78d*, February 1977.

———. "Environmental Contaminants in Mother's Milk." *Information Sheet 78a*, January 1977.

McCall, Robert B., Ph.D. "Coping With Colic." *Parents' Magazine*, April 1984, p. 138.

———. "Coping With Crying." *Parents' Magazine*. November 1982, p. 114.

MacDonald, Charlotte. "Job Sharing: Part-Time Work with Full-Time Potential." *Woman's Day*, June 28, 1977.

Newton, Michael. "On the Importance of Closeness." *Family Health/Today's Health* 10 (January 1978): 10–12.

Planned Parenthood of New York City, Inc. *Birth Control: What Will Work Best for You?* 1983.

Reed, Constance. "Rapid Post-natal Figure Recovery." Raritan, N.J.: Ortho Pharmaceutical Corp., 1974.

Shearer, Lloyd. "Free Handbook on Child Support." *Parade Magazine*, February 24, 1985, p. 18.

Stanwood, Les. "Problems of a Nursing Father." *Mothers' Manual*, 13 (November/December 1977): 37, 54.

Stewart, David. "Father to Father on Breastfeeding." *Information Sheet 128*, La Leche League International, 1974.

Walker, Greta. "When Parents Disagree About Child-rearing." *Parents*, February 1985, pp. 51–56.

Whittlestone, W.G. "The Biological Specificity of Milk: Cow's Milk for Cows, Human Milk for Humans." *Information Sheet 4*, La Leche League International, 1976.

Winick, Myron, M.D. "Advantages of Breastfeeding for the Infant." *Nutrition and Health*, Institute of Human Nutrition, Columbia University College of Physicians and Surgeons, III, 2, 1981: 1–6.

Wilson, Christine Coleman, and Wendy Roe Hovey. *Cesarean Childbirth: A Handbook for Parents*. 1977.

Wunderlich, Cerry. "Fathers: Attachment and Adjustment to Parenthood." *I.C.E.A. News*, 16 (1977).

Yao, Alice C., and John Lind. "Cord Clamping Time—Influence on the Newborn." *Birth and the Family Journal*, 4 (Fall 1977): 91–98.

ABOUT THE AUTHORS

ELLY RAKOWITZ was a pioneer in the childbirth education movement in 1958 when she worked to introduce and gain acceptance of Lamaze preparation as a viable choice for expectant mothers and fathers. She is a co-founder and former New York City Chapter President of the American Society for Psychoprophylaxis in Obstetrics (ASPO/Lamaze) and member of the International Childbirth Education Association (ICEA). An ASPO-certified childbirth educator, she has instituted and/or taught Lamaze classes in several New York hospitals, works with a group of obstetricians instructing their patients in Lamaze childbirth preparation and has a private practice in New York City.

A public speaker and writer, she has expertise in all issues relating to pregnancy, childbirth and early parenting. Her articles have been published in various childbirth and parenting publications. She has appeared on numerous radio and television programs. She lives in New York City and is the mother of two children.

GLORIA S. RUBIN speaks frequently on parenting issues and support program development to groups of parents and professionals. She offers parenting workshops under various auspices in the New York/New Jersey area and consults on issues of patient/physician communications and program development. Her work with a pediatric practice in Queens, New York to design, impliment and coordinate a comprehensive parents' support and education program has received national attention.

A freelance writer whose articles have appeared in *Baby Talk, Mothers' Manual* (now *Mothers' Today*), *American Baby, A.S.P.O./Genesis, A.S.P.O./Lamaze Parents' Magazine* and *Family Resources Coalition Report,* she has been interviewed on radio and television on the subject of new parenthood. Her writing workshops have been presented in the Oakland, New Jersey public school system as well as several libraries. She lives in northwestern New Jersey with her husband and two children.

INDEX